ART FUNDAMENTALS

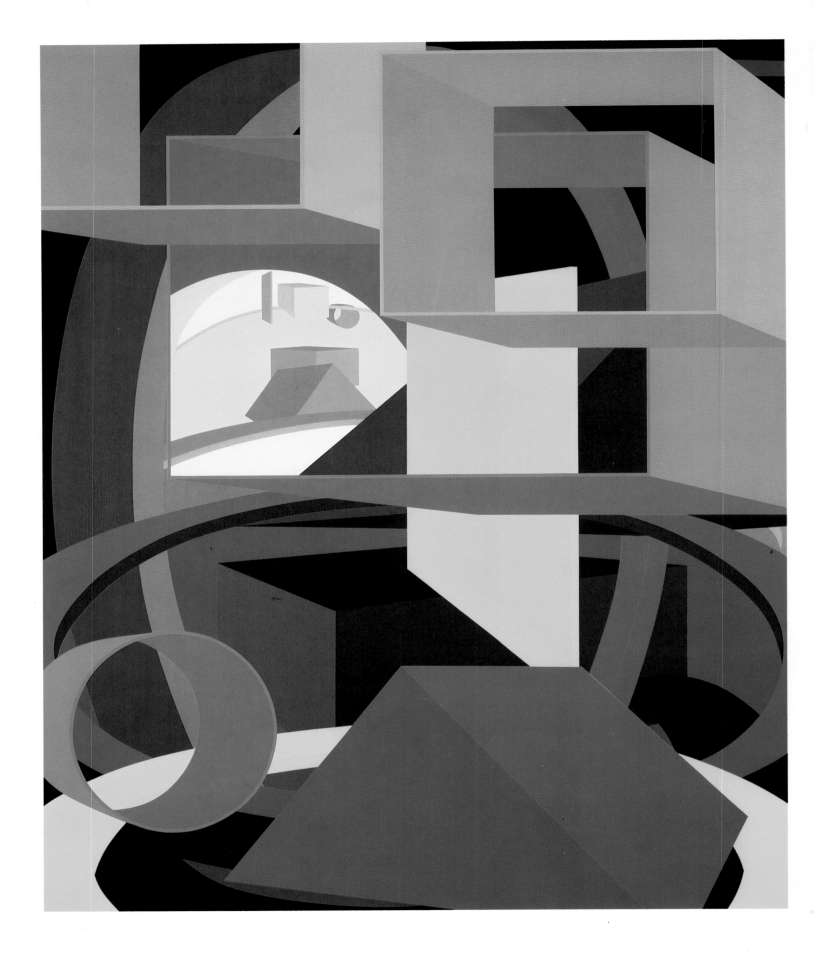

SEVENTH EDITION

ART FUNDAMENTALS

THEORY & PRACTICE

Otto G. Ocvirk ■ Robert E. Stinson ■ Philip R. Wigg
Robert O. Bone ■ David L. Cayton

SCHOOL OF ART/BOWLING GREEN STATE UNIVERSITY

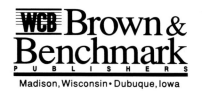

WCB Brown &
Benchmark
PUBLISHERS

Madison, Wisconsin • Dubuque, Iowa

This book is dedicated to the memory of
Robert O. Bone, co-author, teacher, colleague, and friend.

Book Team

Associate Publisher *Rosemary Bradley*
Developmental Editor *Deborah Daniel Reinbold*
Visuals/Design Developmental Consultant *Marilyn A. Phelps*
Visuals/Design Freelance Specialist *Mary L. Christianson*
Publishing Services Specialist *Sherry Padden*
Marketing Manager *Elizabeth J. Haefele*
Advertising Manager *Nancy Milling*

 Brown & Benchmark
A Division of Wm. C. Brown Communications, Inc.

Executive Vice President/General Manager *Thomas E. Doran*
Vice President/Editor in Chief *Edgar J. Laube*
Vice President/Sales and Marketing *Eric Ziegler*
Director of Production *Vickie Putman Caughron*
Director of Custom and Electronic Publishing *Chris Rogers*

WCB **Wm. C. Brown Communications, Inc.**

President and Chief Executive Officer *G. Franklin Lewis*
Corporate Senior Vice President and Chief Financial Officer *Robert Chesterman*
Corporate Senior Vice President and President of Manufacturing *Roger Meyer*

A Times Mirror Company

Library of Congress Catalog Card Number: 93–72768

ISBN 0–697–12545–9

This book was designed and produced by
CALMANN & KING LTD
71 Great Russell Street, London WC1B 3BN

Designer *Barbara Mercer*
Picture Researcher *Susan Bolsom-Morris*

Typeset by Fakenham Photosetting Ltd., Fakenham, UK
Printed in Singapore by Toppan Ltd.

10 9 8 7 6 5 4 3 2 1

Front cover: Helen Frankenthaler, *Storm Center*, 1989. Acrylic on canvas, 7 ft 9¼ in × 7 ft 4¼ in (2.37 × 2.24 m). Kukje Gallery, Seoul, Korea. © Helen Frankenthaler 1993. (Photograph by Steven Sloman, New York.)

Frontispiece: Al Held, *Quattro Centric XIII*, 1990. Acrylic on canvas, 5 × 6 ft (1.52 × 1.83 m). Courtesy of the André Emmerich Gallery, New York. © Al Held/DACS, London/VAGA, New York 1994.

Back cover: Pablo Picasso, *Glass of Absinthe*, spring 1914. Painted bronze with absinthe spoon, 8½ × 6½ × 3⅜ in (21.6 × 16.4 × 8.5 cm); diameter at base, 2½ in (6.4 cm). The Museum of Modern Art, New York. Gift of Mrs. Bertram Smith. © DACS 1994.

Contents

Preface

A great deal of art has "gone over the dam" since our first edition was released on an unsuspecting public. The great tributaries to the art currents of that time, symbolized by giants such as Picasso, Braque, Miró, and others, have faded away and those major currents have been diffused into brooks, streams, creeks, and hidden backwaters. We have attempted to deal with these diversions from the main streams of art by identifying contemporary currents of significance – a difficult task!

Despite the proliferation of stylistic vagaries we believe that the conceptual base of our book is still valid. Art is still a matter of selection and judicious assembly. Art is similar to architecture in that the foundations and supporting members should follow a structural logic. The architecture of art must, of course, be motivated by, and result in, intense feelings that the assemblage assists in communicating. Some of this communication has been made difficult; sometimes artworks depict objects or images solely from the artist's experiences, the significance of which can be lost to observers not privy to those experiences. Most artworks bear a personal stamp and some a veneer, at least, of a geographical style, but, despite personality and provincialism, some can still exude a universal "meaning." This universality of meaning is, however, often absent or not readily apparent.

Your authors have the abiding conviction that, though styles advance and recede like the tides, the principles advocated by this book are the preservative that can afford greater communication and permanence in the works of those who respect them. Like other beliefs this one is, has been, and will probably continue to be challenged as artists continue to look for unique ways of doing things. The success of the book thus far suggests that we still have many adherents. In order to advance our beliefs we have, in this seventh edition, continued our search for greater clarity of expression supported by enlightening illustrations. And, once again, we solicit your reactions.

Acknowledgments

Most of our gratitude for this edition of *Art Fundamentals* must be directed to the members of a "troika" – our readers, our publisher, and our reviewers. Though largely working in isolation from each other they have made significant contributions to the improvement of the book. After seven editions the changes are considerable, but even modest alterations nudge the book closer to the ideal we seek. In this, the Acknowledgments section, we must confess that perfection is still not on the horizon but, with each printing, we feel more comfortable with the product.

A postscript: It may be a bit inappropriate – but still imperative – that we applaud the unsparing efforts of our new co-author, David Cayton, to earn his spurs. This he has done, in noble fashion, meriting the privilege (?) of becoming a permanent member of the "team."

Reviewers

Fred H. Hentchel
Illinois Central College

Mickey S. McCarter
University of North Texas

Paul Nuchims
West Virginia State

Edward Roark
University of Rio Grande

CHAPTER ONE

Introduction

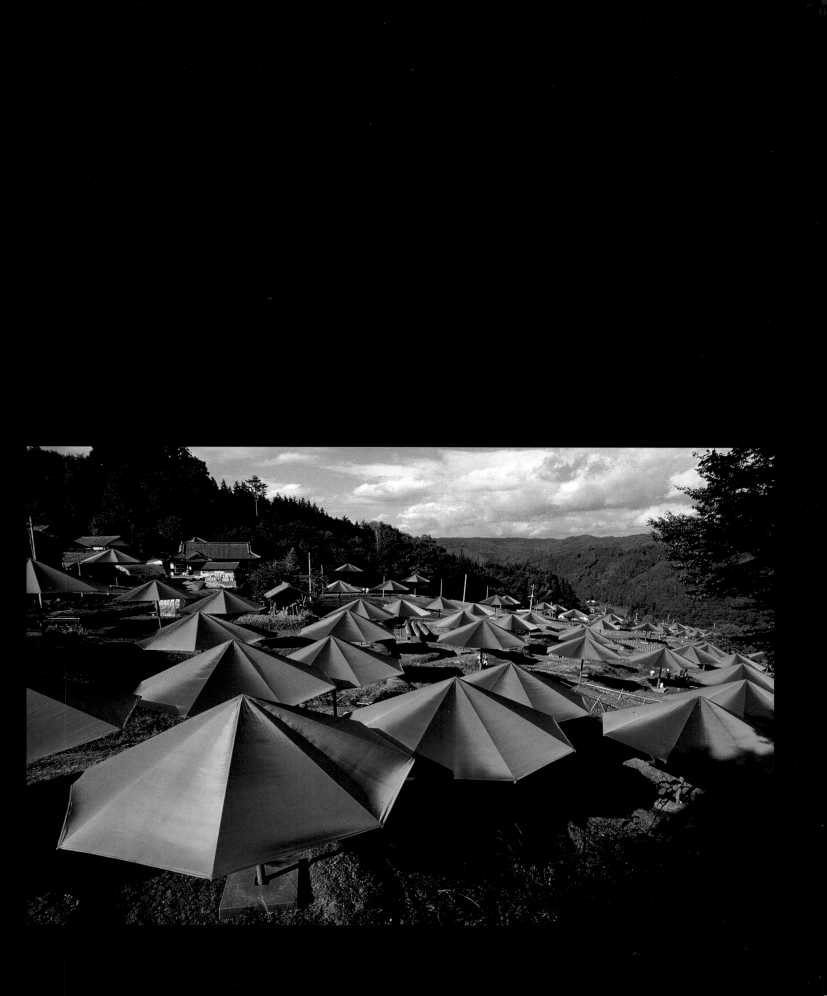

THE VOCABULARY OF INTRODUCTORY TERMS

Art The formal expression of a conceived image or imagined conception in terms of a given medium. (Sheldon Cheney)

abstract, abstraction
A term given to the visual effects that derive their appearance from natural objects but which have been simplified and/or rearranged to satisfy artists' needs for organization or expression. Abstraction is a process of varying degrees of change – from near naturalism through semiabstraction to pure abstraction. Sometimes any resemblance of the final product to the original object(s) is difficult to detect (as in pure abstraction, with its nonrecognizable imagery).

aesthetic, aesthetics
The theory of the artistic or the "beautiful" – traditionally a branch of philosophy, but now a compound of the philosophy, psychology, and sociology of art. As such, aesthetics is no longer solely confined to determining what is beautiful in art, but attempts to discover the origins of sensitivity to art forms and the relationships of art to other phases of culture (such as science, industry, morality, philosophy, and religion). Frequently used in this book to mean concern with artistic qualities of form as opposed to descriptive form or the mere recording of facts in visual form. (See **objective**.)

conceptual perception
Creative vision that derives from the imagination.

content
The expression, essential meaning, significance, or aesthetic value of a work of art. Content refers to the sensory, subjective, psychological, or emotional properties we feel in a work of art, as opposed to our perception of its descriptive aspects alone.

craftsmanship
Aptitude, skill, or manual dexterity in the use of tools and materials.

decorative (art)
Ornamenting or enriching but, more importantly in art, emphasizing the two-dimensional nature of an artwork or any of its elements. Decorative art emphasizes the essential flatness of a surface.

descriptive (art)
A type of art that is based upon adherence to actual appearances.

design
A framework or scheme of pictorial construction on which artists base the two-dimensional nature of their total work. In a broader sense, design may be considered synonymous with the term **form**.

expression
1. The manifestation through artistic form of thought, emotion, or quality of meaning. 2. In art, expression is synonymous with the word **content**.

form
1. The arbitrary organization or inventive arrangement of all the visual elements according to the principles that will develop unity in the artwork. 2. The total appearance or organization.

graphic art
1. Two-dimensional art forms such as drawing, painting, making prints, etc. 2. The two-dimensional use of the elements. 3. May also refer to the techniques of printing as used in newspapers, books, magazines, etc.

mass
1. In graphic art, a shape that appears to stand out three-dimensionally from the space surrounding it, or appears to create the illusion of a solid body of material. 2. In the plastic arts, the physical bulk of a solid body of material (see **plastic**).

medium, media (pl.)
The material(s) and tool(s) used by the artist to create the visual elements perceived by the viewer.

naturalism
The approach to art which is essentially a description of things visually experienced. Pure naturalism would contain no personal interpretation introduced by the artist, but is a physical impossibility.

nonobjective, nonrepresentational (art)
A type of art which is entirely imaginative and not derived from anything visually perceived by the artist. The elements, their organization, and their treatment by the artist are entirely personalized and, consequently, not associated by the observer with any previously experienced natural objects.

objective (art)
A type of art that is based, as near as possible, on physical actuality or optical perception. Such art tends to appear natural or real.

optical perception
A way of seeing in which the mind has no other function than the natural one of providing the visual sensation of object recognition.

organic unity
A condition in which the components of art, that is, subject, form, and content, are so vital and interdependent that they may be

likened to a living organism. A work having "organic unity" is not guaranteed to have "greatness" or unusual merit.

plane
1. An area that is essentially two-dimensional, having height and width. 2. A flat or level surface. 3. A two-dimensional surface having a positive extension and spatial direction or position.

plastic (art)
1. The use of the elements to create the illusion of the third dimension on a two-dimensional surface. 2. Three-dimensional art forms such as architecture, sculpture, ceramics, etc.

realism, Realism (art movement)
A style of art that retains the basic impression of visual actuality without going to extremes of detail. In addition, realism attempts to relate and interpret the universal meanings that lie beneath surface appearances. As a movement, it relates to painters like Honoré Daumier in nineteenth-century France and Winslow Homer in the United States in the 1950s.

representation(al) (art)
A type of art in which the subject is presented through the visual art elements so that the observer is reminded of actual objects (see **naturalism** and **realism**).

style
The specific artistic character and dominant trends of form noted during periods of history and art movements. Style may also refer to artists' expressive use of media to give their works individual character.

subject
1. In a descriptive approach to art, subject refers to the persons or things represented, as well as the artists' experiences, that serve as inspiration. 2. In abstract or nonobjective forms of art, subject refers merely to the visual signs employed by the artist. In this case, the subject has little to do with anything experienced in the natural environment.

subjective (art, shapes, color, etc.)
1. That which is derived from the mind and reflects an individual's viewpoint or bias. 2. Art that is subjective tends to be inventive or creative.

technique
The manner and skill with which artists employ their tools and materials to achieve an expressive effect. The ways of using media can have a strong effect on the aesthetic quality of an artist's total concept.

three-dimensional
To possess, or to create the illusion of possessing, the dimension of depth, in addition to having the dimensions of height and width.

two-dimensional
To possess the dimensions of height and width, especially when considering the flat surface, or picture plane.

volume
A measurable area of defined or occupied space.

THE BOOK: ITS COVERAGE AND USE

This book is subtitled "Theory and Practice." It has long been our belief that the two must coexist and reinforce each other. There is considerable support for this opinion. Josef Albers, a noted painter and art educator, has said that practice precedes theory; this suggests that our subtitle should be reversed. Nevertheless, it is not likely that Mr. Albers would argue with the assertion that some basic theory must precede practice. One cannot strike out blindly. Still, the conclusion of practice in any educational setting should be followed by a theoretical review, whether private or collective. Theory either relieves or induces doubt. Art work is investigative and should be subjected to scrutiny.

The bulk of our audience has consisted of college students and their instructors, and our writing has attempted to communicate with that group. We have waged, and are still waging, a constant struggle for clarity of expression, knowing full well that we have been accused of both oversimplification and overcomplication. We want to avoid pedantry and academic jargon, feeling that the creative pursuit should be interesting and exhilarating. However, we wouldn't want to be misunderstood as implying that art can be done blindly or effortlessly, without study or thought. Far from it!

The study of *art* as advocated by this book, especially with regard to its practice, may be accompanied by studio activities or exercises that are made available in a manual provided for instructors. These exercises are intended to emphasize and illustrate the principles enunciated in the book. They may or may not be used – this decision is left to the instructor. We don't want the manual (or the book, for that matter) to be an inflexible imposition of views and procedures. Such an approach might be suitable for a scientific text but not for one dealing with art, a subject that is hardly compatible with scientific method. The manual attempts to reduce the book's material to a convenient general overview and to provide instructional guidance that is consonant with its overall objectives.

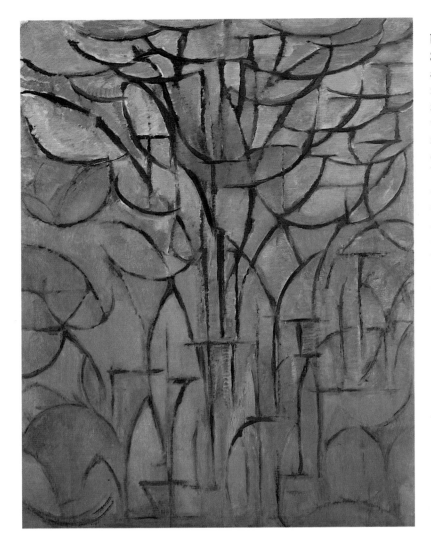

Piet Mondrian, *Tree*, c. 1912. Oil on canvas, 37 × 27½ in (94 × 69.9 cm).
In this work we can see the beginnings of abstraction that marked Mondrian's progress toward the purity of his mature style (see fig. 1.3).
Museum of Art, Carnegie Institute, Pittsburgh, PA, Mondrian Fund. © DACS 1994.

There are a number of features in the book that will make it easier to use. Sometimes certain concepts, artists, their artworks, and perhaps styles or periods are mentioned or listed as examples or illustrations in the text. Some may be unknown to readers. For these, additional information may be found in the last chapter and/or the timeline (p. 316). Any book must determine the limits of its ambitions. Were we to include all the suggestions of our readers we would soon have an encyclopedia of the arts; regrettably we must limit our objectives to work within a practical framework. It is hoped that any interest generated here will be pursued in other sources.

One of the features that we feel is of great importance is the vocabulary that precedes most chapters, in the form of an alphabetized glossary of terms. Discourse on art obviously requires the use of commonly understood terminology; further, the reading of the chapters in this book will be much more meaningful if key words are familiar. Some additional terms not found in the chapter vocabulary lists are included in an overall glossary at the back of the book. Of course we cannot claim omniscience in our definitions, although there is general agreement on them among the authors. We suggest that you put them to the test by redefining them in your own words. Additionally, other persons in the art field may have their own definitions and they may shed more light on the key words and what they represent.

Anyone newly acquainted with art terminology will probably find Chapter 10 ("Content and Style") interesting and enlightening. In that chapter one can find works that exemplify in chronological order the various art styles alluded to in previous chapters. We have limited our review in this chapter to the nineteenth and twentieth centuries – the twentieth because of its immediacy and the nineteenth because it fueled so many comparatively recent artistic ideas. The limitation to two centuries implies no

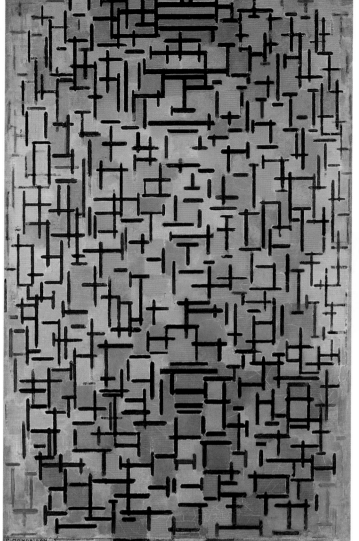

 1 · 2

Piet Mondrian, *Composition, 1916*, 1916. Oil on canvas and wood strip, 47¼ × 29½ in (120 × 74.9 cm).

As a follow-up to figure 1.1, this later work can be seen to be even closer to the severity of Mondrian's final style.

Courtesy of the Solomon R. Guggenheim Museum, New York. © DACS 1994.

▲ 1 · 3

Piet Mondrian, *Composition with Red, Yellow, and Blue*, 1922. Oil on canvas, 16½ × 19 in (41.9 × 48.6 cm).

The primary colors divided by black lines, all in a two-dimensional grid, are typical of Mondrian's later work. This is the style that has generated so much influence through the years.

Toledo Museum of Art, Toledo, OH. Purchased with funds from the Libbey Endowment. Gift of Edward Drummond Libbey, 1978. © DACS 1994.

lack of respect for previous periods of art, as the chronological timeline at the end of the book will attest. This timeline gives us some idea of the vast scope of art history, its outstanding works, and their creators. It will help in finding the proper historical placement of artists whose works are found in the book. Incidentally, for those interested in individuals, artists' names are highlighted in bold type in the general index.

The subjects on which this book centers are the visual arts, specifically those sometimes referred to as the "fine" arts – that is, painting, drawing, sculpture, and printmaking. Our selection of certain arts as "fine" could be dismissed as too narrow by those in design, photography, ceramics, metalwork, and

other disciplines. Admittedly, areas not included in our sanctified group have been important and influential, even transcending our classification. But if these are closely examined one will usually find that their styles were derived from the bedrock arts.

It is not, then, our intention to denigrate the other arts with an elitist distinction; on the other hand, the fine arts have been, throughout history, the fountainhead of significant artistic change and discovery, with great potential for proliferation. One prime example of this can be found in the paintings of Piet Mondrian. The development of his distinctive mature style can easily be traced by an examination of his works (figs. 1.1, 1.2, and 1.3). The final style, the

▶ **1 · 4**

Gerrit Rietveld and Truus Schröder,
Rietveld-Schröder House, **1920–24.**
Rietveld (architect and designer) and Schröder
(client and co-designer) were members, along
with Mondrian, of the de Stijl group in Holland –
a fact that probably accounts for the similarities
in style.

Architectural Association Slide Library, London.

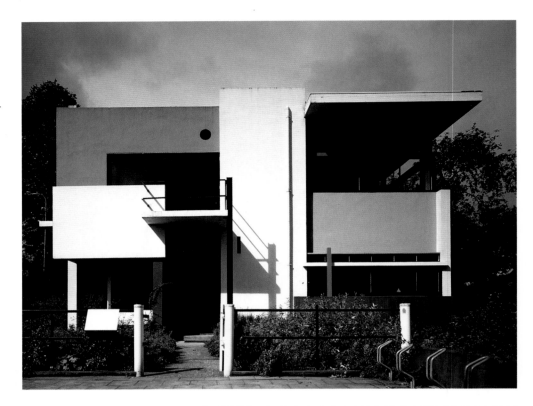

▶ **1 · 5**

Gerrit Rietveld, *Red/Blue Chair*, **designed
1918 (made c. 1950). Pine, ebonized and
painted, 34⅞ × 23⅝ × 29¾ in (88.4 × 60
× 75.5 cm).**
The relationships between horizontals and
verticals and the juxtapositions of color within
an asymmetrical grid are features shared by this
chair and the paintings of Piet Mondrian.

Toledo Museum of Art, Toledo, OH. Purchased with
funds from the Florence Scott Libbey Bequest, in
memory of her father, Maurice A. Scott. © DACS
1994.

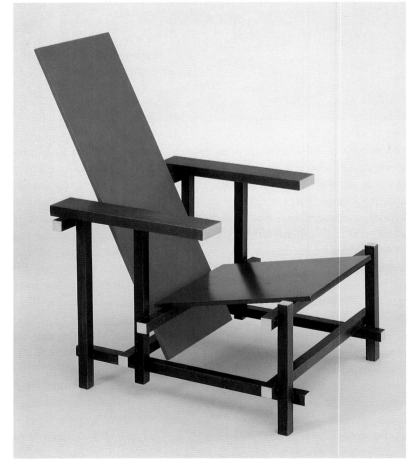

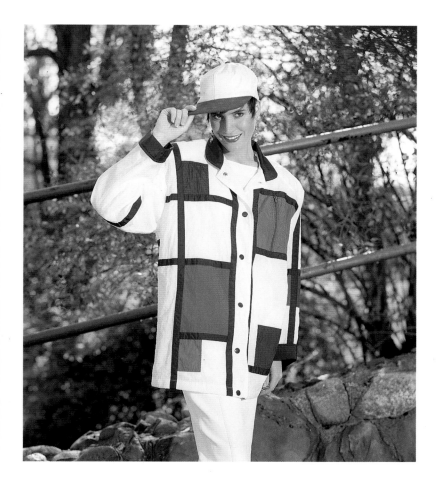

◄ 1 · 6
From Deerskin 1992 catalog, lightweight color block jacket, *item: 2777 F.*
The influence of Mondrian on commercial products is clearly evident in the design of this popular item from the fashion industry.
Courtesy of Deerskin Trading Post, Carlstadt, NJ.

one best known, has been, and is, even today, extremely influential in a very wide variety of applications (figs. 1.4, 1.5, and 1.6). It has, in fact, seeped into the subconscious attitudes of us all – this despite the fact that we may have little taste for the paintings themselves. In similar fashion, other significant artists, those whom we would deem "fine" artists, have subtly and involuntarily altered our vision. Many of those included in this book could be counted among that number.

THE NEED AND SEARCH FOR ART

The study of the past proves that human beings have always had a need for art. From cave paintings to avant-garde works of the twentieth century, a great variety of styles have emerged. Many definitions and interpretations have been applied to these styles, but regardless of the time or place of its creation, art has always been produced because an artist has wanted to say something and chose a particular way of saying it. Over the years, artists have been variously praised, neglected, misunderstood, and criticized. The amount of art being created today is unrivalled by that of the past. In an attempt to give us some insight into the subject, many books have been written. Some have been intended for casual, enjoyable viewing, some for the general artistic enlightenment of the layman, some for passive end-table display, and some for an introduction to the practice of art. Apparently many people want to be actively engaged in art but find that much of what they see is not meaningful to them; this probably adds to the inhibitions of our potential creators.

Some of the inability to understand much of the art being created may be due to the enormous diversity of our world. Sophisticated printing and distribution techniques have made most of the art of the past and present available to us. In addition, television, radio, and air travel have contributed to a great cultural mixing. This is a far cry from the insularity of the periods before our century; in those days, people often had a better understanding and greater acceptance of what they saw because they saw so little.

In order to gain some appreciation for the many forms of art with which we are besieged today, one must understand the basics of art from which they have grown. This book seeks to provide an understanding through illustrated writings. An explanation requires a rationale – a method for providing information. In this book the method is that of a general dissection of the nature and functions of the many factors involved in producing artworks. This is accompanied by an introduction to the principles that normally govern those factors. The authors have tried to avoid the pitfalls of stylistic favoritism by presenting a system for evaluating the structure of art. Analyzing structure may seem a bit cold when applied to a creative field, but structure is necessary to all artistic areas, including music, dance, and literature. Without structure the expression would not come through and the work would lack interest.

THE INGREDIENTS OF ART

Each art field has guiding disciplines for its structure. These disciplines can be applied and interpreted in various ways. In this book, we have chosen certain patterns and procedures of study that are within the discipline of the visual arts. We feel that they can instruct in both the viewing and creation of artworks. In this structure the preliminary emphasis is on the components: subject, form, and content. Following that, we look into the raw materials, the elements: line, shape, value, texture, and color. Furthermore, to stress their importance we will theoretically examine each of these

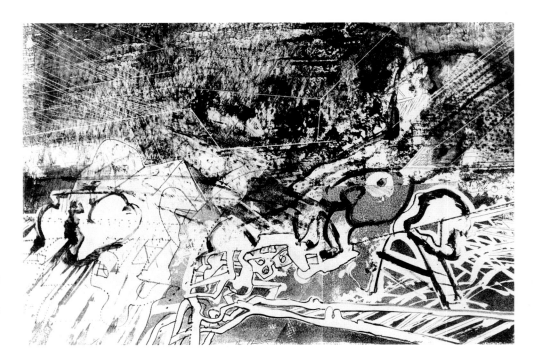

▶ **1 · 7**
Richard Hunt, *Untitled,* **1978. Print (lithograph), 15 × 22¼ in (38.1 × 56.5 cm).**
Without the benefit of an obvious subject, Richard Hunt has expressed an excitement with organic shape, line, and spatial relationships. He does not limit himself to superficial appearances but tries to reveal that which lies deeper.
Collection of Otto Ocvirk.

elements individually in separate chapters. (In reality and practice, the elements and principles cannot be totally divorced from each other; they must be considered collectively as they cooperate to produce the work of art.) This is followed by a review of the principles that organize the elements: harmony, variety, balance, movement, proportion, dominance, and economy. There is rarely any argument about the principles and elements of art, but there have been many ways of ordering and presenting them. In addition, we relate the elements and their ordering principles to two-dimensional and three-dimensional concepts. Our methods, like any others, ultimately depend on the worker's capacity for study, practice, criticism, and self-evaluation.

The components of art

Subject

A *subject* is a person, a thing, or an idea. The person or thing is, as expected, pretty clear to the average person, but the idea may not be. In *abstract* or semi-abstract works, the subject may be somewhat perceivable, but in *nonobjective* works, the subject is the idea behind the form of the work, and it communicates only with those who can read the language of form (fig. 1.7). Whether recognized or not, the subject is important only to the degree that the artist is motivated by it. Thus, subject is just a starting-point; the way it is presented or formed to give it *expression* is the important consideration.

Music, like any area of art, deals with subjects, and it makes an interesting comparison with the visual arts. In the latter, the subject is frequently the particular thing(s) viewed and reproduced by the artist. But at other times art parallels music in presenting a "nonrecognizable" subject; the subject is, of course, an idea rather than a thing. Music sometimes deals with recognizable sounds – thunderstorms and bird songs in Beethoven's *Pastoral Symphony* or taxi

horns in Gershwin's *An American in Paris*. Although rather abstractly treated, these may be the musical equivalents of recognizable subjects in an artwork. By way of contrast, Beethoven's *Fifth Symphony* or Gershwin's *Concerto in F* are strictly collections of musical ideas. In the dance medium, choreography often has no specific subject, but dancing in Copland's ballet *Rodeo* is, to a degree, subject-oriented. All of the arts have subjects that obviously should not be judged alone, but by what is done with them (fig. 1.8).

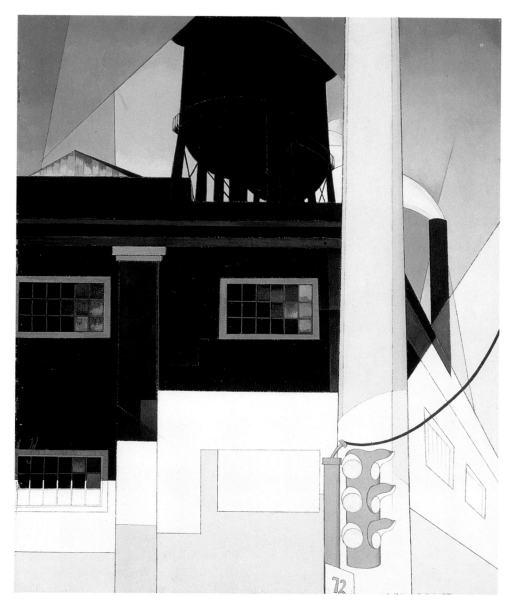

▲ **1 · 8**
Charles Demuth, . . . And the Home of the Brave, 1931. **Oil on composition board, 30 × 23⅝ in (76.2 × 60 cm).**
The subject – manmade structures – is clear enough; however, a work should not be judged by its subject alone, but by how that subject is treated.
Art Institute of Chicago. Gift of Georgia O'Keeffe, 1948.650.

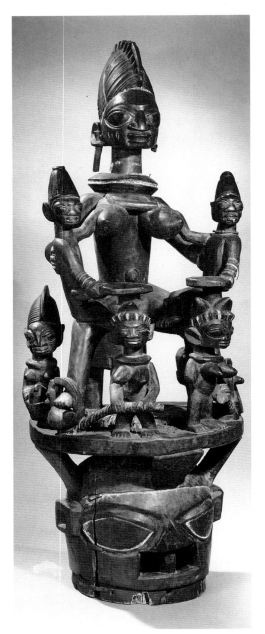

1 · 9
Areogun, Nigerian Mask, Yoruba Tribe, Village of Osi, c. 1900–10. Wood with polychrome painted decoration, 4ft 1½ in (1.26 m) high.
To illustrate the different meanings of the term "form", we can say that the forms in this piece of sculpture are its parts, largely individual figures – or that the form of the work consists of the total assembly of those parts.
Toledo Museum of Art, Toledo, OH. Gift of Edward Drummond Libbey.

Form

The term *form* is used in various ways when referring to art objects. Speaking of a piece of sculpture, one may refer to the individual forms that together make up the piece or one may speak of the sculpture's form, meaning its total appearance (fig. 1.9). As used in this book, form means the latter: the totality of the physical artwork. It involves all of the visual devices available to the artist in the material of his or her choice. Using these devices, artists must make their arrangement and manipulation most effective for what is being expressed. Some artists arrange more intuitively than others, some more logically; but with experience, all of them develop an instinctive feeling for organization.

Form (including the principles of order) is so important to the creation and understanding of art that it is given a special, detailed chapter in this book. The principles of formal order are flexible, with no dogmatic rules; every work is different and has its own unique problems. Nevertheless, despite their flexibility the principles must be observed in order to give the work a meaningful construction.

Content

The emotional or intellectual message of an artwork is its *content*, a statement, expression or mood read into the work by its observer – hopefully synchronized with the artist's intentions. For example, the artist W. Eugene Smith delivers meaning through the subject and associated symbols of death (fig. 1.10). In this work, form provides additional subconscious meaning through the use of blacks and somber grays, a reduced awareness of texture, and the emphasis of low diagonals. For many people content is confined to familiar associations, usually by feelings aroused by known objects or ideas. This is obviously self-limiting – limited to those observers who have had similar experiences. A much broader and,

ultimately, more meaningful content is not utterly reliant on the *image* but reinforced by the form created by the artist. This content is found in abstract and nonobjective as well as more *realistic* works.

Although *all* visual artworks require some degree of abstraction a greater degree is often more difficult to understand and appreciate; sometimes this "appreciation" is, instead, revulsion and confusion! Abstraction is simplification, emphasis, and clarification, but attempts at this are not well received if the observer is conditioned to expect a literal copying of the subject (fig. 1.11). When that expectation is denied the content may be totally misinterpreted. In the case of *non*objective or nonliteral art the *objective* (yes, there is one!) is the content, as in all art. The content in such work is wholly subjective or invented. The ability to respond to art form is an absolute necessity if one is to interpret the true content correctly.

The progress toward content in the development of an artwork generally follows a certain course. The artist is motivated by feelings about a subject (which we shall call the "what"). That subject may or may not be a *representational* likeness. The artist then manipulates the artistic elements (*line*, *shape*, and so on) to create the kind of form (the "how"), that will result in the desired content (the "why"), one that expresses his or her feelings (fig. 1.12). In this process the artist attempts to make all parts of the work mutually interactive and interrelated – as they are in a living organism. If this is achieved we can call it *organic unity*, containing nothing that is unnecessary or distracting, with relationships that seem inevitable.

A television set might be used as an illustration of organic unity because it has a complex of parts intended to function as do the organs in a living body. A television set contains the minimum of parts necessary to function, and these parts work only when properly assembled

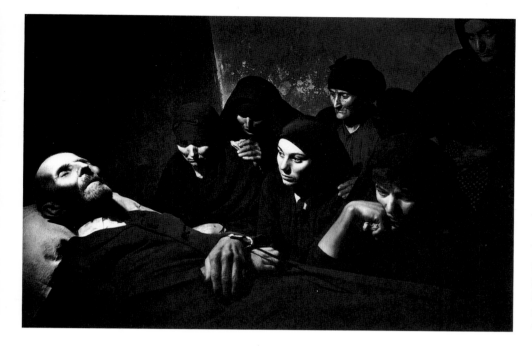

◀ I · 10
**W. Eugene Smith, *Spanish Wake*, 1951.
Photograph.**
The emotional factor in the content of this
photograph is quite evident (and with this
particular subject would probably always be so),
but the artist-photographer has enhanced the
content by his handling of the situation.
W. Eugene Smith, Magnum.

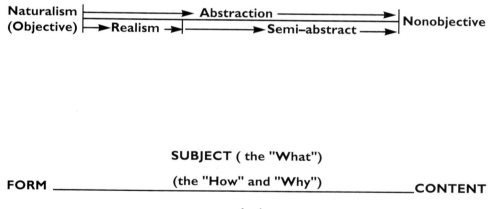

◀ I · 11
When an artist begins with an objective subject,
he or she may choose to duplicate all of the
particulars in a work of art. This artist is a
naturalist. If the artist had decided to make
changes to or edit the natural object, he or she
would be moving toward abstraction. The first
such changes may be termed realism. As the
changes away from the natural object become
more pronounced the works are less
recognizable and approach nonobjective art.

SUBJECT (the "What")

(the "How" and "Why")

FORM _____ CONTENT

producing
ORGANIC UNITY

▲ I · 12
This diagram illustrates how the artist is motivated by his or her feelings about the subject (the
"what"), which may or may not be given a descriptive likeness. He or she manipulates the artistic
elements — line, shape, and so on — to create form (the "how") in the work, which will, in turn,
produce content (the "why") that parallels his or her feelings. In so doing the artist attempts to make
all parts of the work mutually interactive and interrelated as they are in a living organism. This we call
"organic unity"; the work contains nothing which is unnecessary or distracting (the relationships
seem inevitable).

   In some instances the portions of the diagram may be reversed. Although the content results
from form it might, in some instances, be the motivating force. We would then place it foremost, that
is, above the subject. Also, in some cases, the form that develops may mutate into an altogether
different subject or content from that which was originally conceived. Organic unity is always sought,
whatever the progression.

with respect to each other. When all are activated they become organically unified in the same way as the parts of the human body. Surely Dr. Frankenstein would appreciate this analogy! As in the case of sophisticated engineering, this sense of reciprocating "wholeness" is what is sought in art.

This "wholeness" is difficult to detect in the works of some contemporary artists who challenge tradition. In their works the distinctions between subject, form, and content are "muddied" because these components are sometimes treated as identical. This constitutes an obvious break with tradition and requires a shift of gears in our thinking. In *Conceptual art* (a *style* – most art is conceptual, to some degree), the concept is foremost; the product considered negligible; and the concept and subject seem to be one. In Process art (again, a style) the act of producing is the only significant aspect of art, thus reducing form and content to one entity (see "Process and Conceptual art", p. 306). Styles which embrace such goals can be quite puzzling if the aims of the artist are not understood by the viewer.

Even conventional art forms sometimes scramble the roles of the components. Although content results from form, content sometimes functions as the precipitating force, thereby placing it prior to the subject in the scheme of things. Also, in some cases the developing form may mutate into a subject and/or content altogether different from that originally conceived.

Many people expect visual art to be recognizable, representing such familiar items as houses, flowers, people, trees, and so on. When the artist reproduces such things faithfully the vision may be thought of as the "real" world. The artist who works in this manner could be called a "perceptual" artist because he or she records only that which is perceived. But in art the "real" can supersede mere optics; reality in art does often include things seen but, more importantly, includes our reactions to those things (fig. 1.13). Artists who are more concerned with responses than with commonplace perceptions are legitimately called *conceptual* because they are idea-oriented and thus more creative.

Creativity emanates from ideas. Generally speaking an idea is something that takes form in the mind. For the artist it may be an all-encompassing plan, a unique or particularly suitable set of relationships (however broad its scope), an attitude that could be conveyed or a way of conveying an attitude, a solution to a visual problem. In the artist's mind this occurs as mental imagery and may be a "bolt from the blue" (inspiration?) or the end product of much thoughtful searching, some of which may be reflected in numerous notes, sketches, or repeated overhauling of the artwork.

All such creative enterprises are occasionally plagued by idea blocks, but they seem to afflict the fledgling artist most often. For the beginner the idea is conceived at a more pedestrian level, being equated with subject (I don't know what to do!). In such situations a familiar object or experience is the best bet as a starter, supplemented by the brainstorming of anything and everything remotely related. In art, an idea is of value only when converted into visual reality; sometimes this is the more difficult problem, sometimes not, depending on the fertility of one's imagination.

All art is illusory to some extent and some art makes a greater effort to draw us out of our standard existence into a more meaningful state. Artists are aided in this by familiar devices such as frames, stages, exaggerated costumes and gestures, cosmetics, concert halls, and galleries. All of these emphasize the idea that in seeing and hearing the arts we are not in an everyday world but, rather, a hypersensitized world of greater values. By strengthening this illusion art enlarges our awareness.

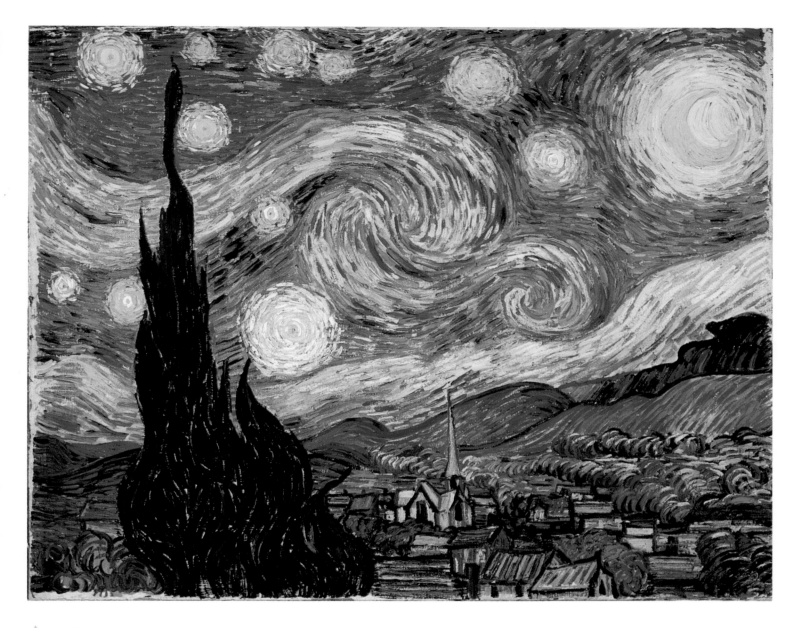

▲ 1 · 13

Vincent van Gogh, *The Starry Night*, 1889.
Oil on canvas, 29 × 36¼ in (73.7 ×
92.1 cm).

Surveying the landscape is a fairly common
experience, but few if any of us see landscapes
with the perception and intensity of van Gogh.

The Museum of Modern Art, New York. Acquired
through the Lillie P. Bliss Bequest.

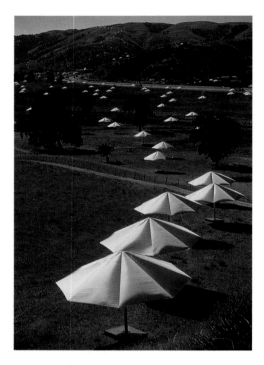

▲ ▼   1 · 14A and B
**Christo, *The Umbrellas, Japan–USA*,
1984–91. Entire (combined) length: 30
miles (48 km). Japan (blue umbrellas);
USA (yellow umbrellas).**
In this self-financed project, using recycled
materials, Christo has displayed two gigantic
environmental installations in two different
countries. The sites, in their different ways,
excite reflections on the availability of the land;
and the umbrellas – houses without walls –
create an inviting inner space within nature.
© Christo, New York, 1991.

Savoring the ingredients

When, in being *subjective*, the artist reaches below surface appearances and uses unfamiliar ways to find unexpected truths, the results can often be distressing for many of us. Such distress frequently follows changes in art styles. The artist is sometimes accused of being incompetent or a charlatan. Much of what we value in art today was once fought for, tooth and nail. General acceptance of the new comes about only when enough time has passed for it to be reevaluated. At this point, the new begins to lose its abrasiveness. Thus there is no need for embarrassment at feeling confused or defiant about an artwork that seems "far-out," but instead a need for continued exposure, thought, and study (figs. 1.14A and B). We all have the capacity to appreciate the beautiful or expressive, as evidenced by the aesthetic choices we make every day. But we must enlarge our sensitivity and taste, making them more inclusive.

One way to extend our responses to art is by attempting to see the uniqueness in things. Gertrude Stein once said that "A rose is a rose is a rose." If we interpret this literally rather than poetically, we realize that every rose has a different character, even with identical breeding and grooming. Every object is ultimately

unique, be it a chair, a tree, or a person. One characteristic that sets the artist apart is the ability to see (and experience) the subtle differences in things. By exposing those differences, the artist can make the ordinary seem distinctive, the humdrum exciting.

Perception is the key. When an artist views an object – a tree branch, say – and is inspired to try to reproduce the original as seen, he or she is using and drawing inspiration from *optical perception*. However, another artist seeing the same branch may find it evokes a crying child or a rearing horse. When the imagination triggers this creative vision and additional images are suggested, the artist is employing *conceptual perception*.

Leonardo da Vinci, writing in his *Treatise on Painting*, recorded an experience with conceptual perception while studying clouds. "On one occasion above Milan, over in the direction of Lake Maggiore, I saw a cloud shaped like a huge mountain made up of banks of fire . . . ." Elsewhere, he recommends staring at stains on walls as a source of inspiration. Following Leonardo, the nineteenth-century French author and painter Victor Hugo found many of his ideas for drawings by studying the blots made by coffee stains on tablecloths.

Another way to enlarge our sensitivity to the visual arts is by ridding ourselves of the expectation that all forms of art should follow the same rules. Photography might serve as an example. We know that many people judge a work of art by how closely it can be made to look like something. It is true that skillful artists can create amazing resemblances, but the camera can win this game! The artist fights a losing battle with the camera if he or she plays by photography's rules. Artists are often proud of their ability to reproduce appearances, but most artists regard this skill as less important. If making lookalikes is the key to art, it is strange that the best photographers are not content simply to point and shoot. Instead, they look for the best view, blur

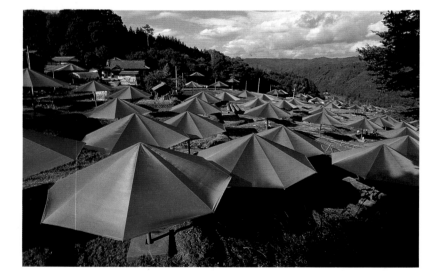

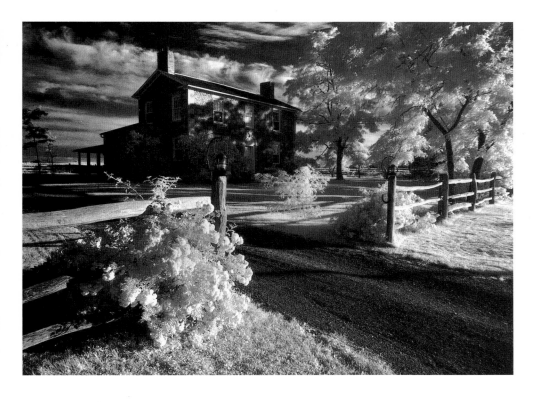

1·15

Minor White, *Cobblestone House, Avon, New York*, 1958. Gelatin silver print.
Photographers may have the edge on other visual artists when it comes to recording objective reality, but photographer-*artists* are not satisfied with obvious appearances and use complex technical strategies to achieve their goals.

The Art Museum, Princeton University, Princeton, NJ. The Minor White Archive. (© 1982 Trustees of Princeton University.)

1·16

Nicolas Poussin, *Mars and Venus*, c. 1633–34. Oil on canvas, 5 ft 2 in × 6 ft 2¾ in (1.57 × 1.90 m).
Poussin has painted a picture story from legend that could have been a mere factual statement; but a study of the work's design reveals that he was strongly influenced by formal considerations.

Toledo Museum of Art, Toledo, OH. Purchased with funds from the Libbey Endowment. Gift of Edward Drummond Libbey.

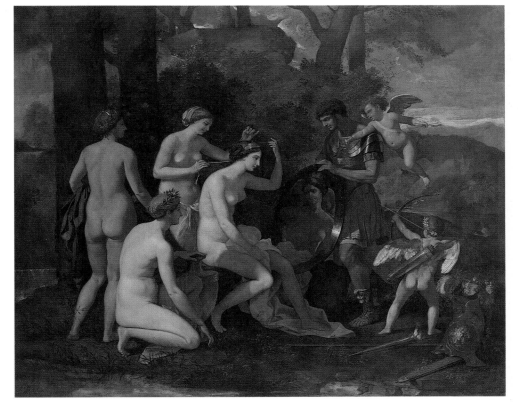

focus, use filters, alter lighting, and make adjustments in developing (fig. 1.15). Photographers become artists when they are not satisfied with obvious appearances. So, too, do *plastic* and *graphic* artists.

People also tend to associate visual art with literature, hoping it will tell a story in a *descriptive* manner. Many fine works have contained elements of story-telling, but artists have no need or obligation to narrate. "Picture-stories" succeed as art only when influenced by formal considerations (fig. 1.16). The visual arts and literature do share certain elements. For the author, objects or things are nouns; for the visual artist, representational subjects are nouns. Nouns are informative, but provide nothing poetic for the author; there is always a need for verbs, adjectives, and so on to establish action, moods, and meanings. Similarly the visual artist's "subject-nouns" rarely inspire except, occasionally, by association. For the visual artist the "verbs" are the combined effect of the elements and their principles; by manipulating these a poetic effect very like that found in literature can be achieved.

In adapting ourselves to the rules peculiar to art, one must also place one's own taste on trial. This means acceptance of the possibility that what is unfamiliar or disliked may not necessarily be badly executed or devoid of meaning. Of course, one should not automatically accept what one is expected to like; instead, open-mindedness is required. Even artists and critics rarely agree unanimously about artists or their works. Fortunately, the authors of this book are generally of the same mind regarding art, but there are some disagreements! Even with training, people's tastes, like Stein's roses, do not turn out to be identical. The quality of art is always arguable and regrettably (?) unprovable. Perhaps the most reliable proof of quality comes only with time and the eventual consensus of sensitive people.

Aside from satisfaction, one of the dividends gained by a better understanding of the visual arts is that it puts us in touch with some remarkably sensitive and perceptive people. We always benefit from contact, however indirect, with the creations of great geniuses. Einstein's perception exposed relationships that have reshaped our view of the universe. Mozart responded to sounds that, in an abstract way, summed up the experiences and feelings of the human race. Though not always of this same magnitude, artists too expand our frames of reference, revealing new ways of seeing and responding to our surroundings. When we view artworks knowledgeably, we are on the same wavelength as the artist's finely tuned emotions.

THE INGREDIENTS ASSEMBLED

In this chapter we have mentioned some of the means by which an artist's emotions are made to surface. You have been introduced to the components, elements, and principles involved in making visual art. You have been given an idea of how all these factors enter into the expression of the artist's feelings. You have been given some counsel on the attitudes to develop in order to share these feelings with the artist. Now, let us consider how these matters fit sequentially in developing a hypothetical work of art.

In any construction project structural elements are needed. Under the supervision of the contractor these are assembled and put together until an edifice of some kind results. The corresponding structural *elements of art* are line, shape, *value*, *texture*, and *color* (some consider *space* an element, but space is produced by these elements). In art the artist is not only the contractor but also the architect; he or she has the vision, which is given shape by the way the elements are brought together. The

contractor is limited by adherence to blueprints, but the artist has the advantage of constant flexibility in the structuring. For example, the raw elements can be manipulated to produce either a *two-dimensional* (circle, triangle, or square) or *three-dimensional* effect (sphere, pyramid, or cube). When two-dimensional, the elements and whatever they produce seem to lie flat on the *picture plane*, but when the elements are three-dimensional, penetration of that *plane* is implied.

There are other terms used in art circles to describe the conditions found in any consideration of dimensionality. *Decorative* is a term that we usually associate with ornamentation, but it is also used to describe the effect produced when the elements of art cling rather closely to the artistic surface. We can say that line (which can decorate in the familiar sense) is decorative if it does not leap toward or away from us dramatically in the format. The same is true of the other art elements. When they are of this nature collectively we can say that the space created by them is decorative, or relatively flat. On the other hand, if the

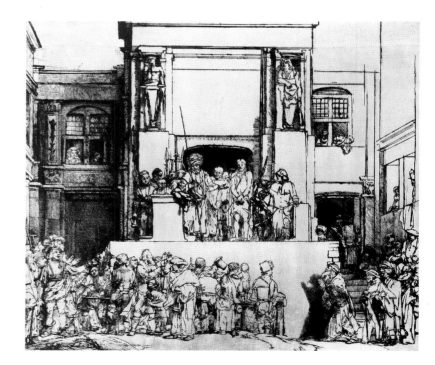

elements make us feel that we could dive into the picture and weave our way around and behind the art elements, the space is plastic.

Thus defined, the term plastic has clear implications for *sculpture*, because we can (we must!) move about the piece. Any *mass* whether actual (as in a statue) or implied (as portrayed in drawing or painting) can be called plastic. Mass is anything that has cohesive, homogeneous bulk, implying a degree of weightiness. *Volume*, on the other hand, is an area of defined containment. An empty living room has volume in its dimensions, but no mass. A brick has mass within its volume. Mass and volume indicate the presence of three-dimensionality in art.

A distinction must be made between plastic and graphic art. The graphic arts include drawing, painting, and photography. These are arts generally existing on a flat surface and which rely on the illusion of the third dimension. By contrast, the plastic arts (sculpture, ceramics, architecture, and so on) are tangible and palpable, occupying and encompassed by their own space. In summary, graphic art may have two-dimensional, decorative effects as defined by art elements of the same description, and plastic art has a three-dimensional plastic aura created by art elements that share these same properties.

An artist must begin with an idea, or germ, that will eventually develop into the concept of the finished artwork. The idea may be the result of aimless doodling, a thought that has suddenly struck the artist, or a notion that has been growing in his or her mind for a long time. If this idea is to become tangible, it must be developed in a *medium* selected by the artist (clay, oil paint, watercolor, and so on). The artist not only controls, but is controlled by, the medium. Through the medium the elements of form emerge, with their intrinsic meanings. These meanings may be allied with a nonobjective or, to different degrees, objective image; in either case, the bulk of the meaning will lie in the form created by the elements.

While developing the artwork, the artist will be concerned with *composition*, or formal structure, as he or she explores the most interesting and communicative presentation of an idea. During this process, *abstraction* will inevitably occur, even if the work is broadly realistic – elements will be simplified, changed, added, eliminated, or generally edited (figs. 1.17A and B). The abstraction happens with an awareness, and within the parameters, of the principles.

As the creative procedure unfolds (not always directly, neatly, or without stress or anguish), the artist fervently hopes that its result will be organic unity. This is an all-inclusive term that refers to the culmination of everything that is being sought in the work. Put simply, it means that every part not only fits, but that each one contributes to the overall content, or meaning. At this point, however arduous or circuitous the artist's route, the work is finished – or is it? Having given the best of themselves, artists are never sure of this! Perhaps the perspective of a few days, months, or even years will give the answer.

And if the work is finished, and it has "organic unity," does it guarantee a "great work of art"? The ingredients assembled – "organic unity" – do not guarantee "greatness" or immortality, but they do assist in giving a vivid oneness.

◀ ▶ **1 · 17A (left) and B (right) Rembrandt Harmenszoon van Rijn, *Christ Presented to the People*, 1606–09, print (etching).**
Rembrandt searched for the most interesting and communicative presentation of his idea. In doing so, he made dramatic deletions and changes, which in this case involved scraping out a portion of the copper plate. Figure 1.17A is the first state of the work, and figure 1.17B is the last.
Metropolitan Museum of Art, New York. Gift of Felix M. Warburg and his family, 1941.

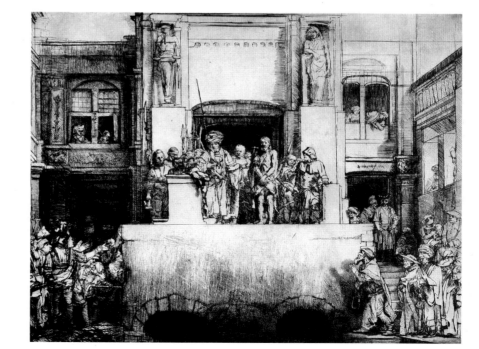

CHAPTER TWO

Form

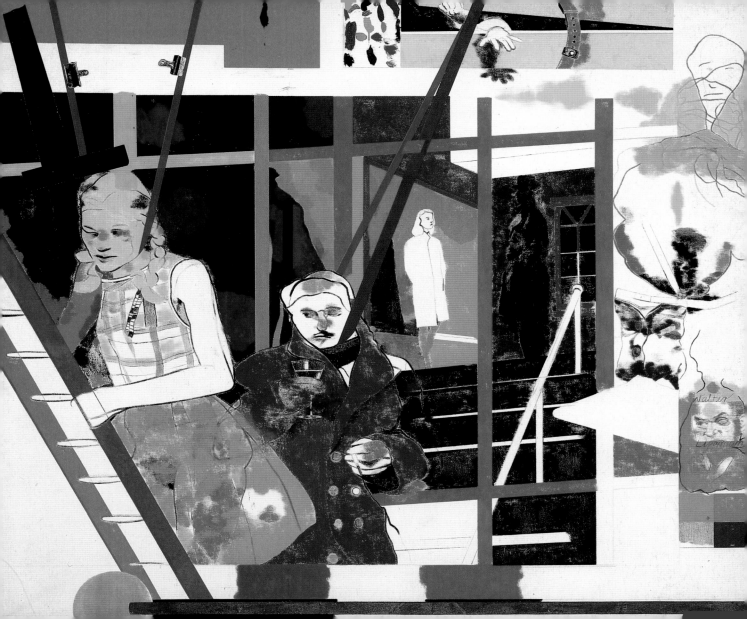

THE VOCABULARY OF FORM

Form 1. The arbitrary organization or inventive arrangement of all the visual elements according to the principles that will develop unity in the artwork. 2. The total appearance or organization.

academic
A term applied to any kind of art that stresses the use of accepted rules for technique and form organization. It represents the exact opposite of the creative approach, which results in a vital, individual style of expression.

allover pattern
Refers to the repetition of designed units in a readily recognizable systematic organization covering the entire surface.

approximate symmetry
The use of similar imagery on either side of a central axis. The visual material on one side may resemble that on the other, but is varied to prevent visual monotony.

asymmetry
Having unlike, or noncorresponding, appearances – "without symmetry." An example: a two-dimensional artwork which, without any necessarily visible or implied axis, displays an uneven distribution of parts throughout.

balance
A sense of equilibrium achieved through implied weight, attention, or attraction, by manipulating the visual elements within an artwork, to accomplish unity.

composition
An arrangement and/or structure of all the elements, as organized by the principles, which achieves a unified whole. Often used interchangeably with the term "design."

dominance
The principle of visual organization in which certain elements assume more importance than others in the same composition or design. Some features are emphasized and others are subordinated.

elements of art
Line, shape, value, texture, and color. These are the basic ingredients that the artist uses separately or in combination to produce artistic imagery. Their use produces the visual language of art.

golden mean/golden section
1. Golden mean – "perfect" harmonious proportions that avoid extremes; the moderation between extremes. 2. Golden section – a traditional proportional system for visual harmony expressed when a line or area is divided into two so that the smaller part is to the larger as the larger is to the whole. The ratio developed is 1:1.6180. . . . or, roughly, 8:13.

harmony
The quality of relating the visual elements of a composition. Harmony is achieved by repetition of characteristics that are the same or similar. These cohesive factors create pleasing interaction.

motif
A designed unit or pattern that is repeated often enough in the total composition to make it a significant or dominant feature. Motif is similar to "theme" or "melody" in a musical composition.

negative area(s)
The unoccupied or empty space left after the positive elements have been created by the artist. However, when these areas have boundaries, they also function as design shapes in the total structure.

pattern
1. Any artistic design (sometimes serving as a model for imitation). 2. Compositions with repeated elements and/or designs which most often are varied, and produce interconnections and obvious directional movements.

picture frame
The outermost limits or boundary of the picture plane.

picture plane
The actual flat surface on which the artist executes a pictorial image. In some cases the picture plane acts merely as a transparent plane of reference to establish the illusion of forms existing in a three-dimensional space.

positive area(s)
The state in the artwork in which the art elements (shape, line, etc.), or their combination, produce the subject – nonrepresentational or recognizable objects. (See **negative area**.)

proportion/scale
The comparison of the art elements one to another in terms of their properties of size, quantity, and degree of emphasis. *Proportion* can be expressed in terms of a definite ratio, such as "twice as big," or be more loosely indicated in such expressions as "darker than," "more neutralized," or "more important than." *Scale* is established when proportional relationships of size are created relative to a gauge or specific unit of measure (for instance, architects normally include models of the human body in their scale drawings).

radial
Describing compositions that have the major images or design parts emanating from a central location.

repetition
The use of the same visual effect a number of times in the same composition. Repetition may produce the dominance of one visual idea, a feeling of harmonious relationship, an obviously planned pattern, or a rhythmic movement.

rhythm
A continuance, a flow, or a sense of movement achieved by repetition of regulated visual units; the use of measured accents.

space
The interval, or measurable distance, between points or images.

symmetry
The exact duplication of appearances in mirrorlike repetition on either side of a (usually imaginary) straight-lined central axis.

unity
The result of bringing the elements of art into the appropriate ratio between harmony and variety to give a sense of oneness.

variety
Differences achieved by opposing, contrasting, changing, elaborating, or diversifying elements in a composition to add individualism and interest; the counterweight of **harmony** in art.

FORM AND VISUAL ORDERING

A completed work of art has three components: subject, form, and content. These components change only in the degree of emphasis put on them. Their interdependence is so great that none should be neglected or given exclusive attention. The whole work of art should be more important than any one of its components. In this chapter we explore the component *form* in order to investigate the structural principles of visual order (fig. 2.1).

When we see images, we take part in visual forming (or ordering). In this act the eye and mind organize visual differences by integrating optical units into a unified whole. The mind instinctively tries to create order out of chaos. This ordering adds *harmony* to human visual experience, which would otherwise be confusing and garbled.

Artists are visual formers with a plan. With their materials they arrange the

▶ **2·1**
Although this is a logical and common order of events in the creation of an artwork, artists often alter the sequence.

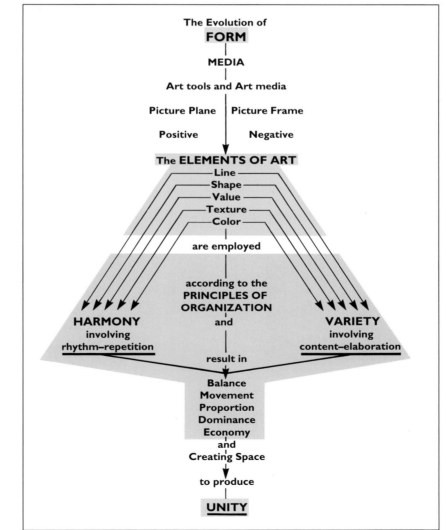

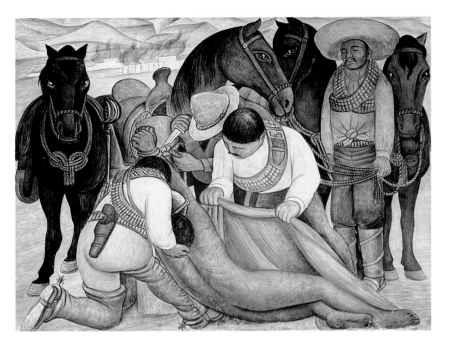

elements – lines, shapes, values, textures, and colors – for their structure. The elements they use need to be controlled and integrated. Artists manage this through the binding qualities of the principles of organization: harmony, *variety*, *balance*, movement, *proportion*, *dominance*, and economy. The sum total of these, assuming the artist's plan is successful, equals *unity*. Unity in this instance means oneness, an organization of parts that fit into the order of a whole and become vital to it.

Form is the complete state of the work. The artist produces this overall condition using the elements of art structure, subject to the principles of organization. The artist's plan is usually a mix of intuition and intellect. Ideally, the plan will effectively communicate the artist's feeling, even though it may change as the work progresses. The plan can be variously termed *composition* or *design* (fig. 2.2.).

Media and techniques

The nineteenth and twentieth centuries have produced numerous advances in scientific technology. These have spun off into many areas, including art. Artistic people have made use of new media and *techniques* as aids to their creative expression. One of the great visual breakthroughs was the development of photography. The camera is not as flexible as the art tool, but photographic innovations have served to broaden our vision. The creative efforts of such photographic artists as Edward Steichen, Alfred Stieglitz, and Ansel Adams (fig. 2.3) are as well known today as the works of many of our important painters and sculptors. From the photographic experiments of such people have come creative film-making, xerography, and the artistic employment of other photographically related media.

Of late, there has been a deluge of new media and techniques. Some are extensions of traditional approaches,

▲ **2 · 2**
Diego Rivera, *The Liberation of the Peon*, 1931. Fresco, 6 ft 2 in × 7 ft 11 in (1.88 × 2.41 m).
Here we see a political artist making use of appropriate and expected subject material. Without the effective use of form, however, the statement would be far less forceful.
Philadelphia Museum of Art, PA. Gift of Mr. and Mrs. Herbert Cameron Morris.

▼ **2 · 3**
Ansel Adams, *Moonrise*, 1944. Photograph (Hernandez, New Mexico).
The invention and development of photography added an important new medium to the repertoire of artists. Now the accomplishments of such photographers as Ansel Adams rank with those of well-known painters, sculptors, and architects.
Photograph by Ansel Adams. (Copyright © 1994 by the Trustees of the Ansel Adams Publishing Rights Trust. All rights reserved.)

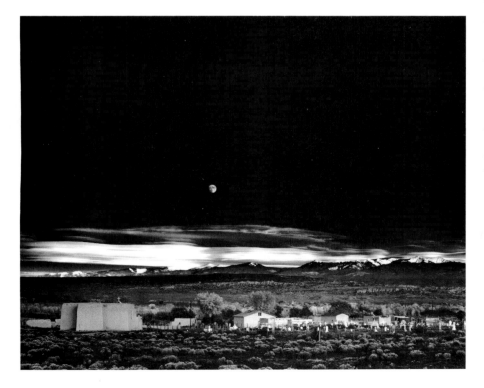

while others are without precedent. All have been absorbed into the artist's armory. Traditional painting media have been expanded by the addition of acrylics, enamels, lacquers, preliquefied watercolors, roplex, and other plastics. Drawing media include new forms of chalk, pastels, crayons, and drawing pens. Sculptors now use welding, plastics, composition board, aluminum, stainless steel, and other materials and techniques. The unique, or nontraditional, media include video, holography, computer-generated imagery, and performances that mix dance, drama, sound, light, even the audience. Very often the traditional and nontraditional are mixed.

Although new and exotic techniques and media have found their way into artists' studios, they generally follow after the artist has already mastered the more traditional art forms. Nontraditional media usually require specialized knowledge (of a somewhat scientific nature) and specialized skill development. The pursuit of this skill and knowledge can become an end in itself unless one has the maturity required to reconcile it with one's artistic aims. For this reason this book is principally concerned with helping to establish a foundation in the more traditional aspects of studio art.

Even the specialized skills required for the mastery of traditional media may take the artist beyond the content of this book. In studio practice the artist must consider the effect of media and tools on imagery, and how surfaces that carry this imagery affect its total form. The natural texture of a paper surface, for instance, may dictate a particular medium and certain tools. A pencil will produce a different effect on smooth-surfaced paper than on rough-surfaced (or "toothed") paper (fig. 2.4). Different grades of graphite in the pencil can become a factor. In ink drawing, a felt-tip pen has a different expressive potential than a crow-quill pen. The softening effect of water in the ink or on the paper can drastically change the meaning of an image.

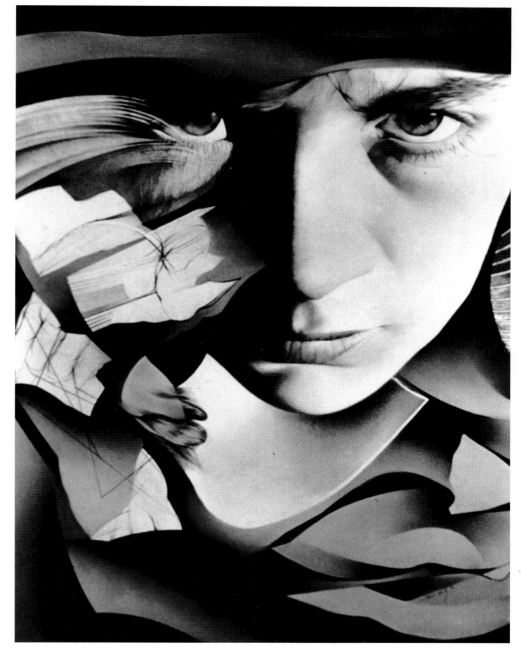

▲ **2·4**

Thomas Hilty, *Margaret*, 1983. Graphite, pastel, and conté on museum board, 33½ × 40 in (85 × 101.6 cm).
This drawing shows the artist's characteristic use of mixed media. He has skillfully blended and rubbed the materials to produce the effect of realistic, polished surfaces. The smooth texture of the museum board (because of its similarity to a photograph) lends a heightened realism to the picture and complements the artist's technique.
Courtesy of the artist.

Picture plane

There are many ways to begin a work of art. It is generally accepted that artists who work with two-dimensional art begin with a flat surface. To artists, the flat surface is the *picture plane* on which they execute their pictorial images. A piece of paper, a canvas, a board, or a plate may be representative of the picture plane. This flat surface may also represent an imaginary plane of reference on which an artist can create spatial illusions. The artist may manipulate forms or elements so that they seem flat on the picture plane, or extend the forms/elements so that they appear to exist in front of or behind the picture plane (fig. 2.5A). In this way the picture plane is used as a basis for judging two- and three-dimensional space.

In three-dimensional art the artist begins with the material – metal, clay, stone, glass, and so on – and works it as a total form against the surrounding space, with no limitation except for the outermost contour (see Chapter 9, "The Art of the Third Dimension.")

Picture frame

A *picture* is limited by the *picture frame* – the outermost limit or boundary of the picture plane (fig. 2.5B). The picture frame should be clearly established at the beginning of a pictorial organization. Once its shape and proportion are defined, all of the art elements and their employment will be influenced by it. The problem for the pictorial artist is to organize the elements of art within the picture frame on the picture plane.

The proportions and shapes of picture frames used by artists are varied. Squares, triangles, circles, and ovals have been used as frame shapes, but the most popular is the rectangular frame, which in its varying proportions offers the artist an interesting variety within two-dimensional space (figs. 2.6, 2.7, 2.8; see fig. 2.24). Many artists select the outside proportions of their pictures on the basis of geometric ratios (see "Proportion", p. 50). These rules suggest dividing surface areas into odd proportions of two-to-three or three-to-five rather than into equal relationships. The results are visually pleasing spatial arrangements. Most artists, however, rely on their instincts rather than on a mechanical formula. After the picture frame has been established, the direction and movement of the *elements of art* should be in harmonious relation to this shape. Otherwise, they will tend to disrupt the objective of pictorial unity.

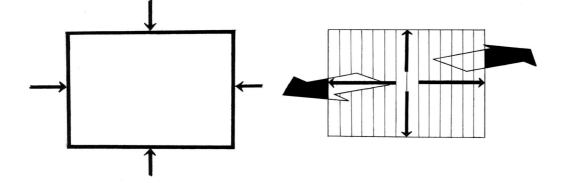

▲ **2·5A**
Picture plane. Movement can take place on a flat surface, as indicated by the vertical and horizontal arrows. The vertical lines represent an imaginary plane through which a picture is seen. The artist can also give the illusion of advancing and receding movement in space, as shown by the two large arrows.

▲ **2·5B**
Picture frame. The picture frame represents the outermost limits, or boundary, of the picture plane. These limits are represented by the edges of the canvas or paper on which the artist works, or by the margin drawn within these edges.

2 · 6

Tom Wesselmann, *Barbara and Baby*, 1979–81. Oil on canvas, 5 ft × 6 ft 4¼ in (1.52 × 1.94 m).
Wesselmann has used an unusual frame shape for a timeless subject. The organic shape evokes a feeling of birth and motherhood.
© Tom Wesselmann/DACS, London/VAGA, New York 1994.

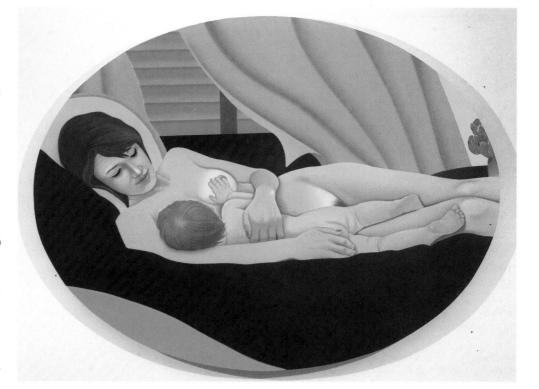

2 · 7

El Greco, *Madonna and Child with Saint Martina and Saint Agnes*, c. 1597–99. Oil on canvas, 6 ft 4⅛ in × 3 ft 4½ in (1.94 × 1.03 m).
The rectangular frame shape, by its proportions, offers the artist a pleasing and interesting spatial arrangement. Here, El Greco has elongated his main shapes to repeat and harmonize with the vertical character of the picture frame.
Widener Collection. (© 1993 National Gallery of Art, Washington, D.C.)

2 · 8

Fra Angelico and Fra Filippo Lippi, *The Adoration of the Magi*, c. 1445. Tempera on wood, diameter 4 ft 6 in (1.37 m).
The artists have used figures and architecture, and the direction and movement of the art elements, in harmonious relation to a circular picture frame.
Samuel H. Kress Collection. (© 1993 National Gallery of Art, Washington, D.C.)

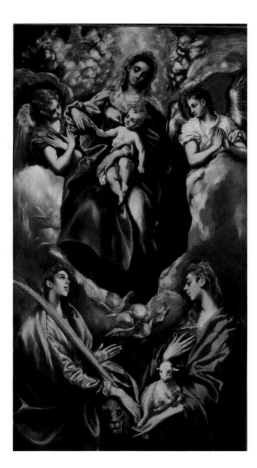

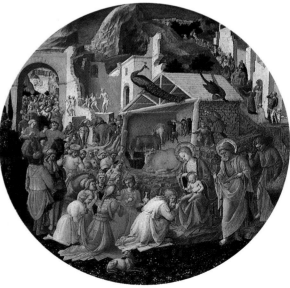

Positive and negative areas

All of the surface areas in a picture should contribute to unity. Those areas that represent the artist's initial selection of element(s) are called *positive areas*. Positive areas may depict recognizable objects or nonrepresentational elements. Unoccupied spaces are termed *negative areas* (figs. 2.9A and B). The negative areas are just as important to total picture unity as the positive areas, which seem tangible and more explicitly laid down. Negative areas might be considered as those portions of the picture plane that continue to show through after the positive areas have been placed in a framed space (fig. 2.10).

Traditionally, figure and/or foreground positions have been considered positive and background areas negative. The term figure probably came from the human form, which was used as a major subject in artworks and implied a spatial relationship with the figure occupying the position in front of the remaining background (fig. 2.11; see figs. 2.9A and B). In recent times abstract and nonobjective painters have adopted the terms field to mean positive and ground to mean negative. They speak of a color field on a white ground or of a field of shapes against a ground of contrasting value.

The concept of positive–negative is important to beginners investigating art organization, since they usually direct their attention to positive forms and neglect the surrounding areas. As a result, pictures often seem overcrowded, busy, and confusing.

When the artist's tool touches the picture plane, leaving a mark, two things happen. First, the mark divides, to some extent, the picture plane. Generally the mark is seen as a positive image, leaving the remainder to be perceived as a negative area. Secondly, the mark seemingly takes a position in front of, or at some distance behind, the picture plane. Each of these results will continue to be important to the artist as the work develops.

▼ **2 · 9A and B**
John Currin, *The Moved Over Lady*, 1991. Oil on canvas, 46 × 38 in (116.8 × 96.5 cm).
The subject in this painting represents a positive shape that has been enhanced by careful consideration of the negative areas, or the surrounding space. In figure 2.9B the dark area indicates the negative shape and the white area the positive shape.
Andrea Rosen Gallery, New York.

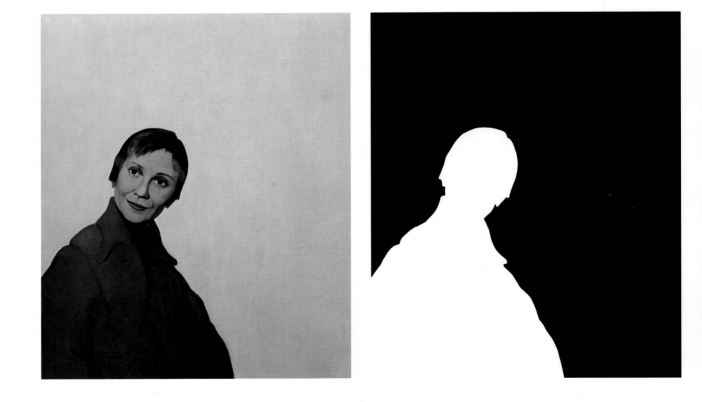

The art elements

The artist employs the media to implement the art elements: line, shape, value, texture, and color. These elements are the fundamental, essential constituents of any artwork. In this textbook the basic elements are thought to be so indispensable to art fundamentals that each will be examined individually in the chapters that follow. The artist's constant concern is with composing the elements. When dealing with objects, the artist reduces the objects to elements. A chair might be seen as a shape or a group of lines, a wall as a value, and a floor as a color.

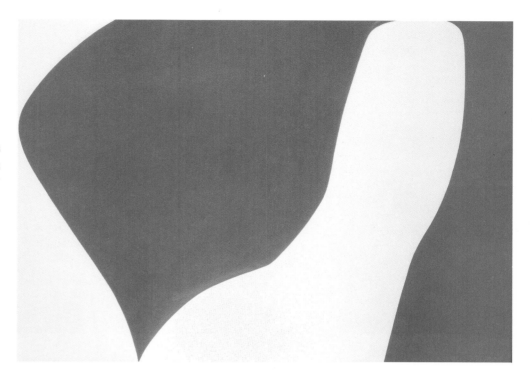

▲ 2·10

Ellsworth Kelly, *Red and White*, 1961. Oil on canvas, 5 ft 2¾ in × 7 ft 1¼ in (1.59 × 2.17 m).

In this nonfigurative (or nonobjective) work, some areas have been painted in, others not. It is very simple, perhaps deceptively so. To the viewer, the darks seem to be the negative shapes, although after some looking, the effect may be reversed.

Hirshhorn Museum and Sculpture Garden, Smithsonian Institution, Washington, D.C. Gift of Joseph H. Hirshhorn, 1972.

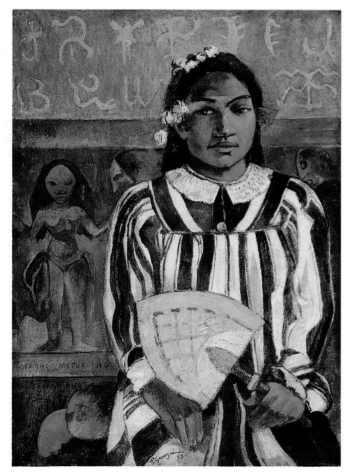

◀ 2·11

Paul Gauguin, *Ancestors of Tehamana*, 1893. Oil on canvas, 30⅛ × 21⅛ in (76.3 × 54.3 cm).

Items in the foreground (generally toward the bottom of the picture plane) are traditionally considered positive areas, whereas unoccupied spaces in the background (upper) are negative areas. This traditional view does not always apply, however, as can be seen by looking at other illustrations in this book.

Art Institute of Chicago. Gift of Mr. and Mrs. Charles Deering McCormick, 1980.613

The principles of organization

As explained earlier, the principles of organization are only guides. They are not laws with only one interpretation or application. These principles are used to help to organize the elements into some kind of action. The principles of organization may help in finding certain solutions for unity, but they are not ends in themselves, and following them will not always guarantee the best results. Artworks are a result of personal interpretation and should be judged as total visual expressions. In other words, the use of the principles is highly subjective or intuitive.

Organization in art consists of developing a unified whole out of diverse units. This is done by relating contrasts through similarities. For example, an artist might use two opposing kinds of lines, vertical and horizontal, in a composition. Since both the horizontal and vertical lines are already straight, this likeness would relate them. Unity and organization in art are dependent on a dualism of contrast and similarity – a balance between harmony and variety (fig. 2.12).

Harmony

Harmony may be thought of as a factor of cohesion – relating various picture parts. This "pulling together" of opposing forces on a picture surface is accomplished by giving them all some common element(s), be it color, texture, value, and so forth. The repetition or continued introduction of the same device or element reconciles that opposition. *Rhythm* is also established when regulated visual units are repeated. Whether created by *repetition* or rhythm, harmony may create the feeling of boredom or monotony when its use is carried to extremes. But, properly introduced, harmony is a necessary ingredient of unity.

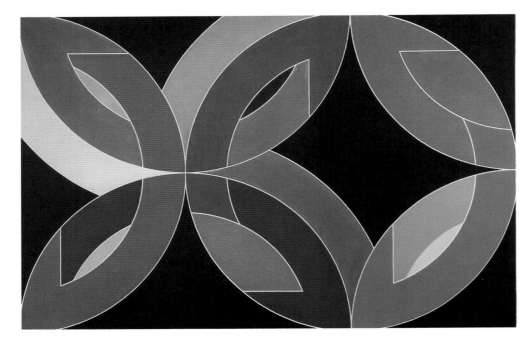

▲ **2 · 12**
Frank Stella, *Lac Laronge IV*, 1969. Acrylic polymer on canvas, 9 ft ⅛ in × 13 ft 6 in (2.75 × 4.11 m).
Stella has harmonized the painting through his insistent use of the curve; he has provided variety by using contrasting colors and shape sizes.
Toledo Museum of Art, Toledo, OH. Purchased with funds from the Libbey Endowment. Gift of Edward Drummond Libbey.

▼ **2 · 13**
Eva Hesse, *Repetition Nineteen III*, 1968. Nineteen tubular fiberglass units, 19–20¼ in × 11–12¾ in (48.3–51.4 cm × 22.9–32.4 cm).
This work, as the title implies, exploits the repetitive dimensions of identical "can forms." These are then given variety by distorting the basic shapes.
The Museum of Modern Art, New York. Gift of Charles and Anita Blatt.

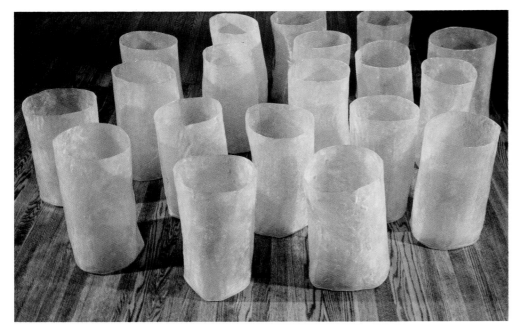

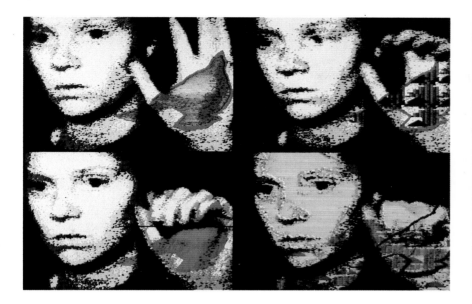

▲ 2 · 14
Copper Giloth, *Bird in Hand*, 1983.
Computer.
Repetition is found in the pattern produced by
the computer as well as in the repeating images.
Nevertheless, the hands change position
periodically, producing some variety.
Courtesy of the artist.

Repetition   Repetition and rhythm
are inseparable; rhythm is the result of
repetition. Repetition reemphasizes visual
units. It connects the parts and binds an
artwork together. Repetition creates
attention or emphasis, and it permits
pause for examination.

Repetition does not always mean exact
duplication, but it does mean similarity or
near likeness. Slight variation of a simple
repetition adds subtle interest to a *pattern*
that might otherwise be tiring (figs. 2.13,
2.14, and 2.15).

Rhythm   Rhythm is a continuance, or
flow, derived from reiterating and
measuring related, similar, or equal parts.
Rhythm is recurrence, a measure such as
meter, tempo, or beat. Walking, running,
dancing, woodchopping, and hammering
are human activities with recurring
measures.

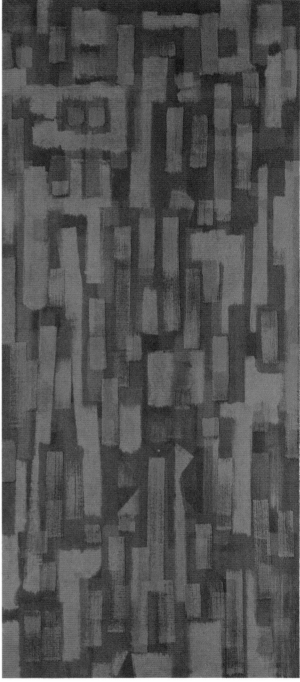

▲ 2 · 15
Ad Reinhardt, *Number 1, 1951*, 1951. Oil
on canvas, 79⅞ × 34 in (202 × 86.4 cm).
The visual units in Reinhardt's painting are
rectangular modules. The repetition of this motif
creates harmony. Variety develops out of subtle
differences in scale and color.
Toledo Museum of Art, Toledo, OH. Museum
Purchase Fund.

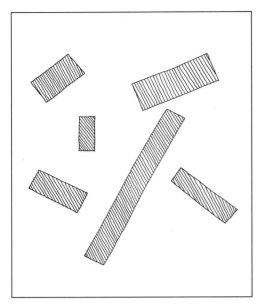

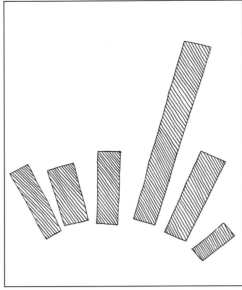

In art, if particular parts are recalled in a rhythmical way, a work is seen as a whole. Rhythm in this instance gives both unity and balance to a work of art (figs. 2.16A and B).

Rhythm exists in many different ways on a picture surface. It may be simple, as when it repeats only one type of measure; it may be a composite of two or more recurring measures that exist simultaneously; or it may be a complex variation that repeats a particular event. Beats, accents, and so on may be made of two parts. One may be thought of as being the positive part – the strike of the beat or the element(s) explicitly laid down. The second part may be considered the negative – the silence between the beats or the space between the elements. José Clemente Orozco charges his pictures with obvious rhythmical order (figs. 2.17A and B). He uses several rhythmical measures simultaneously to create geometric unity. He welds his pictures together by repeating shape directions and edges, value differences, and color modifications.

▲ **2 · 16A**
The rectangles are related to this harmonious arrangement by repeating similar shape configurations. But they are also varied in size and set in opposing directions, which creates tension and interest.

▲ **2 · 16B**
These rectangles are set in a repetitious and rhythmical order. Repetition and rhythm are agents for creating harmony and unity.

▽ **2 · 17A and B**
José Clemente Orozco, *Zapatistas*, 1931. Oil on canvas, 3 ft 9 in × 4 ft 7 in (1.14 × 1.39 m).
A continuous movement is suggested as the zapatistas cross the picture surface from right to left. In passing, these figures form a repetitious beat as their shapes, leaning in the same direction, create a rhythmic order. The diagram in figure 2.17B illustrates the major shapes and their edges arranged in continuous, flowing, and harmonious directions.
The Museum of Modern Art, New York. Given anonymously.

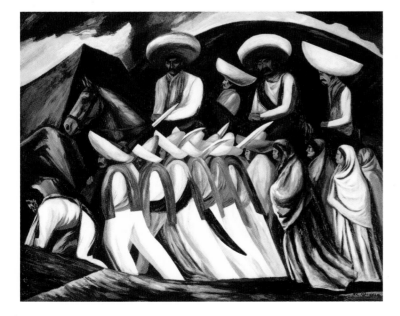

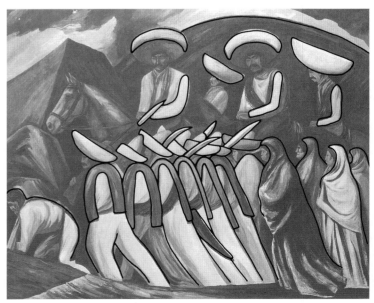

Pattern　Pattern at the most elementary level may be seen as any arrangement or design. At this level pattern may function as the model for imitation or for making things (one or multiples). Examples that might be cited here could be the pattern a dressmaker uses to make a skirt; or the pattern from which a patternmaker or a moldmaker makes a piece of machinery; or that which an artist uses to create artistic designs. On the next level pattern is usually seen as a noticeable formation or set of characteristics that is created when the basic pattern (model) is repeated. The resulting pattern may be made of regular repetitions, as in an "*allover*" *pattern*, or of irregular repetitions. These repetitions may be composed of simple marks, of elements (line, shape, value, texture, or color pattern), or of a series of named complex designs, such as a paisley or a geometric pattern (figs. 2.18A and B).

The generally repetitive nature of such patterns can be used to create harmony and rhythm with pauses and beats that cause flow and connections between parts. They serve to direct eye movement from one part to another. In a more sophisticated sense, pattern may be seen as a series of arranged elements that may be totally invented or suggested by objects – like tree branches and their spaces (fig. 2.19).

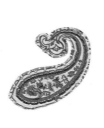 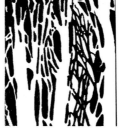

▲　**2 · 18A and B**

In figure 2.18A, the basic pattern is the universally and immediately recognizable paisley shape (see fig. 2.20). Figure 2.18B is a detail (of fig. 2.19), in which the pattern is created by an arrangement of lines and shapes based on an abstraction of trees.

▼　**2 · 19**

Student work, *Patterns: Trees*, c. 1970. Brush, pen, and ink, 18 × 24 in (45.7 × 61 cm).

Although the subject is trees, the distinctive pictorial characteristic of this work is the pattern produced by the tree relationships – a pattern that is developed, though not identically, in all areas of the work, creating unity.

Motif　A motif is a concept closely related to pattern. The difference is that once the basic unit, cell, or original pattern (model) is repeated it is referred to as a *motif*. Once this unit becomes a motif it serves to connect the larger repetitive formation – a conspicuous pattern due to its overall size. This larger pattern may be formed with regularly or irregularly repeated motifs. This new formation (pattern) may be called an allover pattern when the motifs have been repeated in a regular manner over an entire surface. The repeated motifs found in wallpaper designs may be cited as an example. Further, the Pop artist Andy Warhol created "allover pattern" with his soupcan artworks (see fig. 10.83). When an artist doesn't want such a repetitive image, he or she might choose to create an irregular pattern design (fig. 2.20).

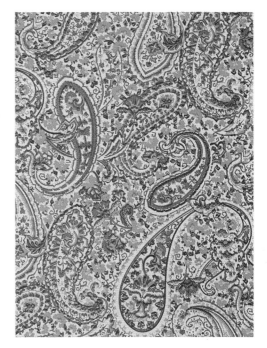

▲　**2 · 20**

Paisley pattern, 1992. Wallcovering.

The paisley is repeated casually to achieve a pattern of more or less irregular design.

Courtesy of Fashion Wallcoverings, Distributors, Cleveland, OH.

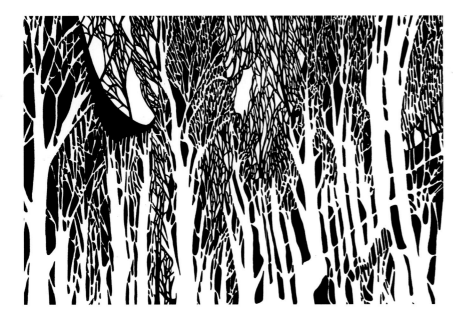

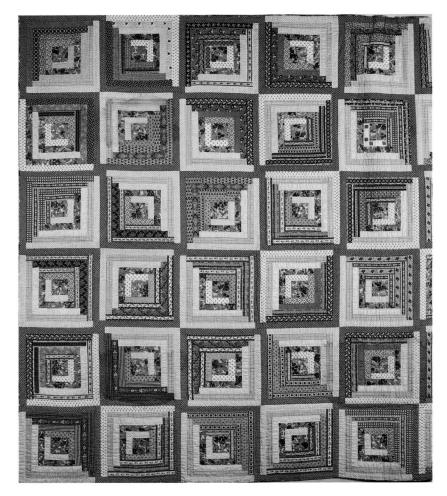

Quiltmakers often rotate their motifs, changing their color, value, texture, and placement. This serves to further accent the change and bring about an entirely new "allover pattern" (fig. 2.21).

Studio artists often find the obvious and continuous repetition of a motif in an "allover pattern" too monotonous. For them, a subtler use of motif would treat it more like a repeated idea, theme, or pattern of notes in music. For example, the "ta-ta-ta-TUM" in Beethoven's *Fifth Symphony* is repeated but constantly changes in terms of tempo, pitch, volume, and the voice of the instrument playing it. Max Ernst, in *The Hat Makes the Man*, uses the idea of a hat in much the same way (fig. 2.22). It is not repeated over and over exactly alike, but rather is introduced as a theme, constantly changing and accented in differing ways.

Sometimes the theme develops for an artist over a long series of work. Consider thirty paintings by an artist, each dealing with a cat in some different attitude or position. In each individual painting the cat would be the subject. But, within a consideration of the total series, the cat may be seen as the artist's repeating theme, idea, or motif. Two examples from a larger series may be seen in the Impressionist artist Claude Monet's *Rouen Cathedral* paintings (see figs. 7.28 and 7.29).

Variety

Variety is the counterweight of harmony. It is the other side of organization essential to unity. While an artist might bring a work together with harmony, it is with variety that the artist achieves individuality and interest. In this instance,

"interest" refers to the ability to arouse curiosity and to hold a viewer's attention. If an artist achieves complete equality of visual forces, the work usually will be balanced, but also static, lifeless, and without feeling. By adding variation to these visual forces, the artist introduces essential ingredients (such as diversion or change) for enduring attention.

Artists use variety to attract attention in different ways. As an example, they may find variety in opposition or contrast, by setting opposing elements and/or their parts in proximity for an intensified effect (fig. 2.23). Other artists may elaborate upon forces that seem formal and acceptable, but lack enduring interest. They will rework areas persistently to express themselves at greater length until an attractive solution is reached. The surfaces are enriched by the extensive

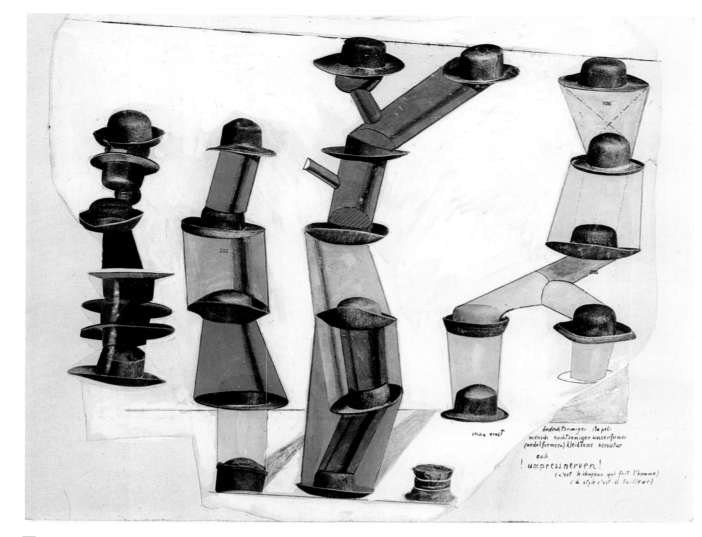

▼ **2 · 23**

George Sugarman, *Inscape*, 1964. Polychromed wood, 24 × 144 × 108 in (61 × 365.8 × 274.3 cm).

The balance between harmony and variety can be tipped to favor either principle of order depending on the artist's intention. George Sugarman is an artist who pushes his balance strongly in the direction of variety. In this three-dimensional work, Sugarman varies the shape contours and colors of his assembled pieces with a personal vigor. He arouses an initial curiosity in his viewer that, after greater reflection, provides enduring vitality.

Robert Miller Gallery, New York. Collection of the artist.

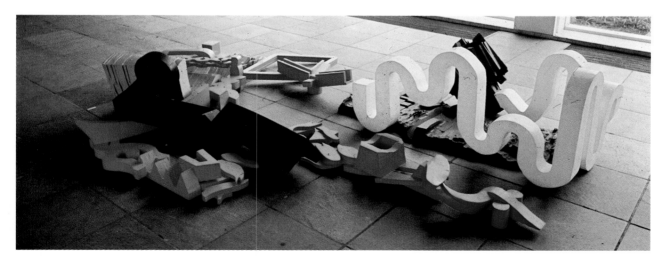

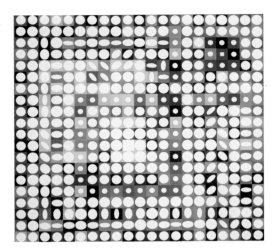

2 · 24

Victor Vasarely, *Orion*, 1956–62. Paper on paper mounted on wood, 6 ft 10½ in × 6 ft 6¾ in (2.09 × 2 m).

While harmony is provided through the recurring use of circles, the artist achieves interest through the variety of the same shapes: some are tipped; some are larger or smaller than the norm; and some are emphasized by contrast with their backgrounds.

Hirshhorn Museum and Sculpture Garden, Smithsonian Institution, Washington, D.C. Gift of Joseph H. Hirshhorn, 1966. (Photograph by Lee Stalsworth). © ADAGP, Paris and DACS, London 1994.

changes, and the artist's concept usually develops dramatic strength and purposeful meaning (see fig. *2.25*).

Drab picture surfaces become more exciting as variations are introduced. In music the higher the pitch the greater the number of vibrations. Similarly, in art, as contrasts are introduced the "pitch" or excitement is increased; reduction in contrast lowers the "vibration" experienced. The frequency of contrasts in a given artwork might also be compared to the key signature in music (a musical key means that certain notes are more important than others); in art it is necessary to give some contrasts greater emphasis than the rest.

One of the most difficult concepts to grasp is that of applying harmony and variety at the same time and to the same element. Consider the use of shape. Victor Vasarely in *Orion* uses circles as a unifying device to create a harmonious

2 · 25

Jean Dubuffet, *Dévidoir Enregistreur*, 1978. Acrylic and paper, collage on canvas, 6 ft 7 in × 9 ft 6 in (2 × 2.90 m).

This work is also compartmentalized (for harmony), but uses different sizes and shapes (for variety). There is consistency in the character of the lines, but enough variation to generate interest.

Albright-Knox Art Gallery, Buffalo, NY. George B. and Jenny R. Mathews Fund, 1979. © ADAGP, Paris and DACS, London 1994.

relationship (fig. *2.24*). However, to avoid monotony, the artist seeks all the different ways that circles can be introduced – changing their size, point of view, and angle. Thus, he has introduced variety by way of the very element (circular shapes) used to create harmony. The same thing could be done with any of the elements. Red, for example, could be used to make a series of shapes relate, providing harmony. But changing the red's value level, intensity or hue could vary the design at the same time. Again, variety and harmony have been developed out of the same basic component.

Harmonious means seem necessary to hold contrasts together. This balance does not have to be of equal proportions; harmony might outweigh variety, or variety might outweigh harmony (fig. *2.25*; see fig. *2.24*).

Balance

We deal with balance daily as we know and/or expect it to function with gravitational forces. Gravity is a universally and an intuitively felt experience. Walking, standing on one leg, or tipping back in a chair reveal our intuitive need for balance. When off balance, there is the anticipation that gravity will resolve our dilemma (that is, we will fall over!). As upright animals we spend our lives resisting gravity's influence. Similarly, in art we deal with the expectation of counteracting gravitational forces. Most artworks are viewed in a vertical orientation – in terms of top, sides, and bottom. Visual compositional balance is achieved by counteracting the downward thrusts and gravitational weights of the components. For example, a ball placed high in the pictorial field produces a sense of *tension*, bringing with it the expectation that gravity will cause that ball to drop (fig. *2.26A*). A ball placed low or on the baseline provides a sense of peace or resolution, gravity having acted on the ball (fig. *2.26B*). Our understanding of the particular image or symbol used has an effect upon its psychological weight and the resulting balance in a composition. For example, if the ball in figure 2.26A becomes a helium-filled balloon, a large negative area under that shape will tend to support or balance it – we may even have the sensation of the balloon lifting up from that area (fig. 2.26C). If the image becomes a lower-positioned bowling ball, its symbolic weight seems to make the composition bottom-heavy – gravity's force seems to be pulling the bowling ball down to a still position on the lane at the picture's bottom (fig. 2.26D). What we know of the weight of actual objects – here a ball, a balloon, and a bowling ball – influences how we judge balance on a picture surface. If we were to replace the objects with nonobjective entities their psychological weight would be created by their shape, value, and/or color, and our view of their balance again would change. Whether objective or nonobjective components are used, the potential creation of psychological weight/balance and its compositional adjustment are endless.

Artists will often offset their pictorial works with a mat – an area between the picture's edge and an actual picture frame (structured of wood, metal, and so on). Even here, psychological factors can affect the visual weight and balance. If a mat with two-inch top, sides, and bottom were used, the bottom would have the illusion of being pinched or smaller than the other sides. The artwork would appear unstable on the wall. Gravity's downward pull creates this illusion. To compensate, the bottom measurements on mats are generally made deeper than the ones at the top, and they seem balanced.

Balance is so fundamental to unity that it is impossible to present the problems of organization without considering it. At the simplest level, balance implies the gravitational equilibrium of a mark on a picture plane. This is clear if one places a single positive unit on a white surface, putting it anywhere but in the center. Balance can

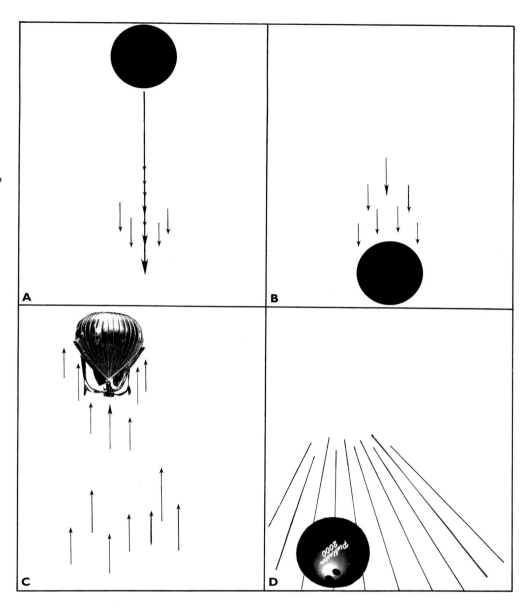

▲ **2 · 26A, B, C, and D**
Balance: gravitational forces and the resulting pictorial tensions.

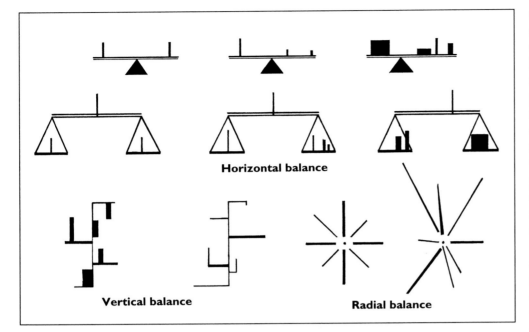

Horizontal balance

Vertical balance

Radial balance

▲ **2 · 27**
Using fairly complex elements, these diagrams illustrate the three main types of balance: horizontal, vertical, and radial.

▼ **2 · 28A and B**
Here, all the chief forms of balance – horizontal, vertical, radial, and diagonal – are combined in two diagrams.

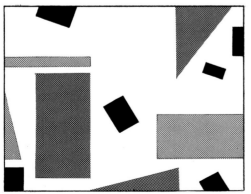

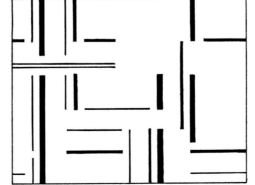

also refer to the gravitational equilibrium of a pair of units symmetrically arranged either side of a central axis. Perhaps the balancing of pairs can best be compared to a weighing scale which has a beam poised on a central pivot (the fulcrum), so as to move freely, and a pan attached to each end of the beam. When we apply this concept to art, balance must be viewed not as an actual physical weighing process but as the visual judgment of an observer, based on his or her past experiences and intuitive knowledge of certain principles of physics.

The illustrations in figure 2.27 provide examples of three basic types of balancing scales. These can be used as preparatory experiences for creating pictorial and/or three-dimensional balance. In the first two rows of scales, the forces are balanced left and right or horizontally, with respect to the supporting balance beam or crossline. The horizontal balance scale shows a line of one physical dimension balancing or counterbalancing a line with the same (or equal) physical characteristics. These examples also point out the balance between lines, shapes, and values that have been modified. A second type of weighing scale, in which forces are balanced vertically, is also illustrated in figure 2.27. The third weighing device shown in the figure points out not only horizontal and vertical balance, but also balance of forces that are distributed around a center point. This is a *radial* weighing scale.

In picture making, balance refers to the "felt" optical equilibrium among all parts of the work. The artist balances forces horizontally, vertically, radially, and diagonally in all directions and positions (figs. 2.28A and B). Several factors, when combined with the elements, contribute to balance in a work of art. These factors or variables are position or placement, size, proportion, character, and direction of the elements. Of these factors, position plays the lead role. If two shapes of equal physical qualities are placed near the left side of a picture frame, the work will appear out of balance with the right side. Such shapes should be positioned to contribute to the total balance of all the picture parts involved. Similarly, the other factors can put a pictorial arrangement in or out of balance according to their use.

As the eye travels over the picture surface, it pauses momentarily at the significant picture parts. These points of interest represent moving and directional forces that counterbalance one another and may be termed *moments of force*. In seeking balance, the artist should recognize that the varied elements create the moments of force, and their discriminating placement will result in controlled tension. In the painting *Handball*, Ben Shahn creates tension between the two figures in the foreground and the number 1 at the top of the wall (fig. 2.29). These forces together support one another. The darker values of the building above the large wall are counterbalanced by those of the left-hand building, and in the figures in the lower portion of the painting.

2 · 29

Ben Shahn, *Handball*, 1939. Tempera on paper over composition board, 22¾ × 31¼ in (57.8 × 79.4 cm).
Collectively, the figures and buildings may be seen as representative forces which the artist sets in a supporting, controlled balance and tension.
The Museum of Modern Art, New York. Abby Aldrich Rockefeller Fund. © Estate of Ben Shahn/DACS, London/ VAGA, New York 1994.

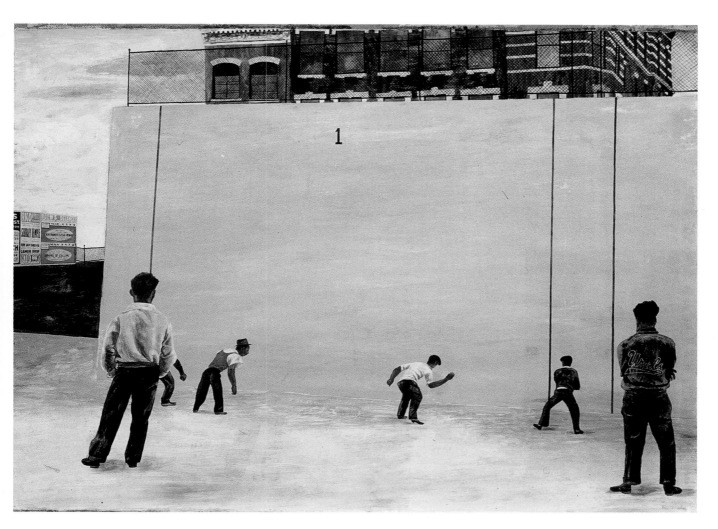

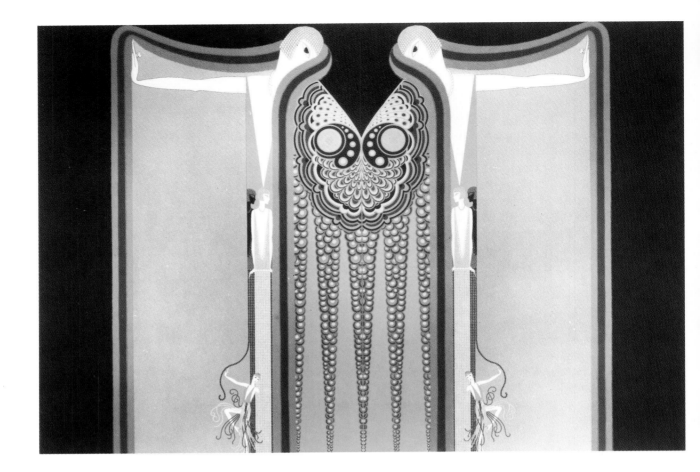

▲ **2·30**

Erté, *Twin Sisters*, 1982. Print (serigraph), 3 ft 4 in × 4 ft 7 in (1.01 × 1.40 m).
The repetitious nature of this symmetrical work is counterbalanced and relieved by the lively details. The composition is divided equally on either side of an imaginary vertical axis.
Circle Fine Art Corporation, Chicago, IL.

Symmetrical balance The beginner will find that symmetry is the simplest and most obvious type of balance. In pure *symmetry* identical optical units (or forces) are equally distributed in mirrorlike repetition on either side of a vertical axis (fig. 2.30). Because of the identical repetition, the effect of pure symmetrical balance is usually dull, tiring, and boring. It is usually too monotonous for prolonged audience attention. However, by its use, unity is easily attained. In spite of these seemingly negative effects, interesting variations can be achieved through the creative use of the elements of art (fig. 2.31).

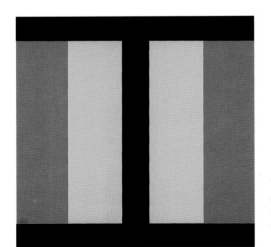

◀ **2·31**

Cary Smith, *Here We Go*, 1992. Oil and wash on canvas, 6 × 6 ft (1.83 × 1.83 m).
A simplified, formal, symmetrical composition that relies on shape, size, value, and color relationships to express spatial relationships. The values and colors black, red, and yellow are used for maximum variety or contrast. Cary Smith painted this in the Neo-Abstract style (see p. 312).
Collection of Lita Hornick, New York. (Photograph courtesy of the Rubin Spangle Gallery, New York.)

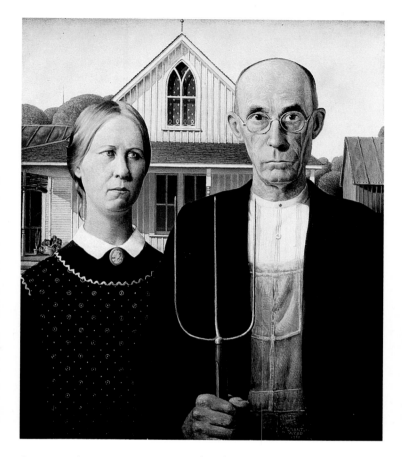

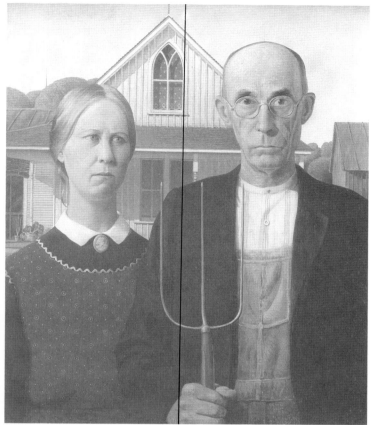

Approximate symmetrical balance The severe monotony of pure symmetry in pictorial arrangements is often relieved by the use of *approximate symmetry* (figs. 2.32A and B). Here, the parts on either side of the axis or axes are varied to hold audience attention, but they are similar enough to make repetitious relationships and their vertical axis optically felt (see also fig. 2.33).

▲ **2 · 32A and B**
Grant Wood, *American Gothic*, 1930. Oil on beaver board, 30 × 25 in (76 × 63.3 cm).
The two figures in this picture create repetitious relationships so that the picture's vertical axis is made to stand out. This is approximate symmetry.

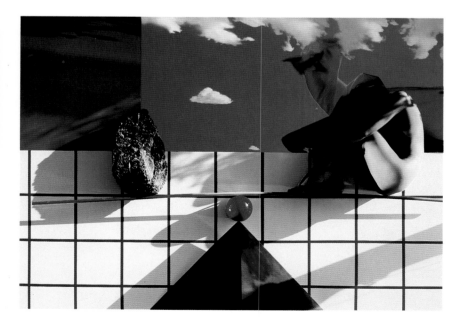

◀ **2 · 33**
Masoud Yasami, *Balancing Act with Stone II*, 1992. Edition of 50, Ilfochrome, 3 ft 4 in × 5 ft (1.02 × 1.52 m).
Approximate symmetry could be said to be the subject as well as the form of this composition.

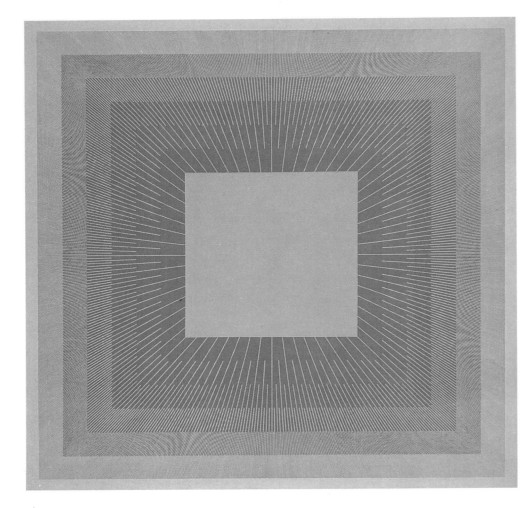

Radial balance Another type of arrangement, called radial balance, can create true or approximate symmetry. In radial balance, forces are distributed around a central point. The rotation of these forces results in a visual circulation, adding a new dimension to what might otherwise be a static, symmetrical balance. Pure radial balance opposes identical forces, but interesting varieties can be achieved by modifying the spaces, numbers, and directions of the forces (figs. 2.34 and 2.35). Although modified, the principle of repetition must still be stressed so that its unifying effect is utilized. Radial balance has been widely used in the applied arts. Jewellers often use radial patterns for stone settings on rings, pins, necklaces, and brooches. Architects have featured this principle in quatrefoils and "rose" windows, in which the petals of flowers are radially arranged. The potter's plates and vessels of all kinds evolve on the wheel in a radial manner and frequently give evidence of this genesis. In two-dimensional work, the visual material producing the radial effect can be either nonobjective or figurative.

▲ **2 · 34**
Richard Anuszkiewicz, *Iridescence*, 1965. Acrylic on canvas, 5 × 5 ft (1.52 × 1.52 m).
In radial balance there is frequently a divergence from some (usually central) source. Note here, though, the different stresses placed on the rays as they move away from the square, creating an almost mystical energy.
Albright-Knox Art Gallery, Buffalo, NY. Gift of Seymour H. Knox, 1966. © Richard Anuszkiewicz/ DACS, London/VAGA, New York 1994.

▶ **2 · 35**
Simon Tookoome, *I Am Always Thinking about Animals*, 1973. Stonecut and stencil, 21½ × 31 in (54.5 × 78.6 cm).
Although opposition of identical forces is usually found in radial balance, this Canadian artist displays imaginative and rich contrasts within the arrangement.
Art Gallery of Ontario, Toronto. Gift of the Klamer family, 1978. (Photograph by Carlo Catenazzi.)

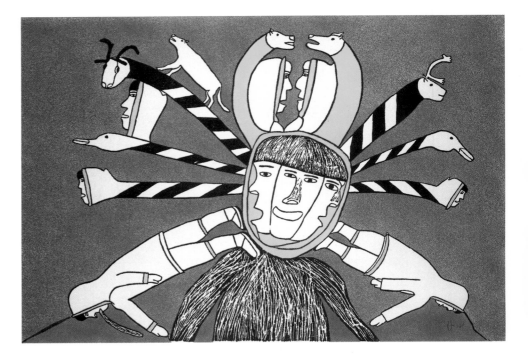

Asymmetrical (occult) balance Asymmetrical balance means visual control of contrasts through felt equilibrium between parts of a picture. For example, felt balance might be achieved between a small area of strong color and a large empty space. Particular parts can be contrasting, provided that they contribute to the allover balance of the total picture. There are no rules for achieving *asymmetrical* balance; there is no center point and no dividing axis. If, however, the artist can feel, judge, or estimate the opposing forces and their tensions so that they balance each other within a total concept, the result will be a vital, dynamic, and expressive organization on the picture plane. A picture balanced by contradictory forces (for instance, black and white, blue and orange, shape and space) compels further investigation of these relationships and thus becomes an interesting visual experience (figs. 2.36 and 2.37).

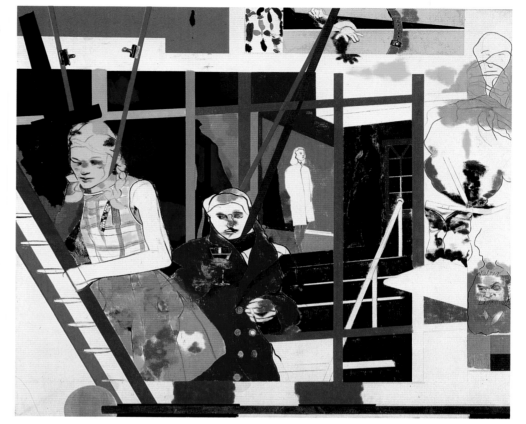

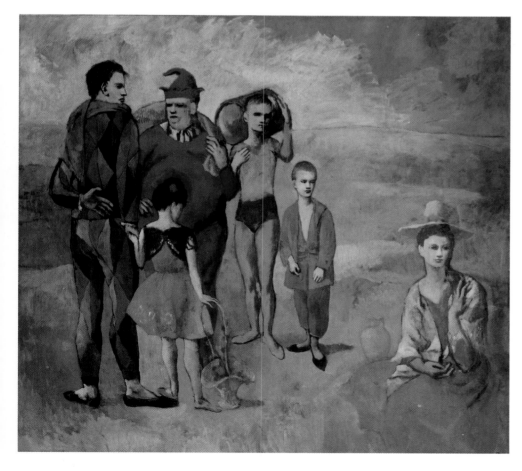

▲ **2 · 36**

Ronald Kitaj, *Walter Lippmann*, 1966. Oil on canvas, 6 × 7 ft (1.83 × 2.13 m).
In concentration of subject matter, this painting is weighted toward the left; but the inverted pyramidal lines produce a degree of equilibrium, and there are eye-catching designs on the right, adding emphasis. The balance is achieved through dissimilar means.

Albright-Knox Art Gallery, Buffalo, NY. Gift of Seymour H. Knox, 1967.

◄ **2 · 37**

Pablo Picasso, *Family of Saltimbanques*, 1905. Oil on canvas, 6 ft 11¾ in × 7 ft 6⅜ in (2.13 × 2.30 m).
An intuitive balance is achieved through the juxtaposition of varying shapes and the continuous distribution of similar values and colors.

Chester Dale Collection. (© 1993 National Gallery of Art, Washington, D.C.) © DACS 1994.

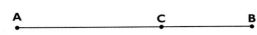

▲ **2·38**

A line is here divided into a geometric relationship known as the mean and extreme ratio – or the Golden Section.

Proportion

Proportion deals with the ratio of individual parts to one another. In works of art the relationships of parts are difficult to compare with any accuracy because proportion often becomes a matter of personal judgment. Proportional parts are considered in relation to the whole and, when related, the parts create harmony and balance.

The term *scale* is used when proportion is related to size and refers to some gauge for relating parts to the whole. Often a "norm" or standard is established as a scale. For example, the human figure is most often considered the "norm" by architects for scaling buildings and often by artists for representations in their artworks.

Artists have been seeking the "ideal" standard for proportional relationships since ancient times. *Classical* Greek philosophy expressed the view that mathematics was the controlling force of the universe and established the *Golden Mean*, sometimes called the *Golden*

Section, to represent the ideal standard for proportion and balance in life and art. The Greek philosopher Euclid held that the Golden Mean was the "moderation of all things," a place between two extremes. The Golden Section, as it applied to works of art, stated that a small part relates to a larger part as the larger part relates to the whole. It may be seen in a geometric relationship in which a line is divided into what is called the mean and extreme ratio (fig. 2.38). When a line AB is sectioned at point C, it does it in such a way that AC is the same ratio to AB as CB is to AC: AC:AB = CB:AC. This extreme and mean ratio has a numerical value of .6180 (see figs. 2.39C–E). Any new unit will be this much smaller or larger than the original unit – making those units in a ratio of 1 to 1.6180. Applying this concept to geometry, the Greeks sought the most beautifully proportioned rectangle that could be created out of a square. They arrived at what is referred to as the Golden Rectangle (figs 2.39A–E and 2.40A–C).

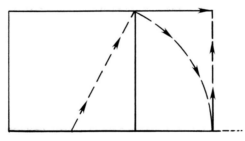

▲ **2·39A**

The Golden Rectangle may be created by starting with a perfect square and extending the baseline in one direction.

▲ **2·39B**

Next, find the center of the bottom of the square. With a compass point fixed on that spot, draw an arc from the upper corner of the square to the extended bottom line. This locates the length of the new rectangle. From this point, a line is drawn perpendicular to the baseline until it reaches a line extended from the top of the square.

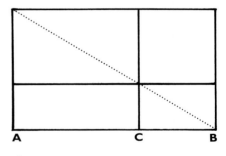

A   C   B

▲ **2·39C**

Once the rectangle is completed, a diagonal line from corner to opposite corner should be added. This diagonal will touch and pass through the side of the square at a point where the Golden Mean should be drawn. Draw it parallel to the baseline of the new Golden Rectangle. An interesting mathematical relationship is revealed by the Golden Rectangle. It may be discovered by comparing the original length of the square (AC) to the length of the new rectangle (AB). This will be in the same ratio as the length of the new addition (CB) is to the original square (AC).

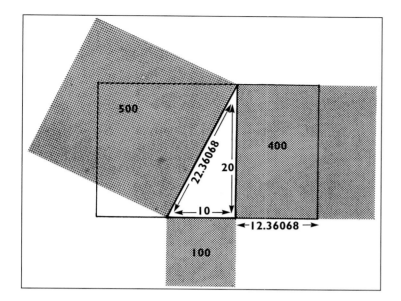

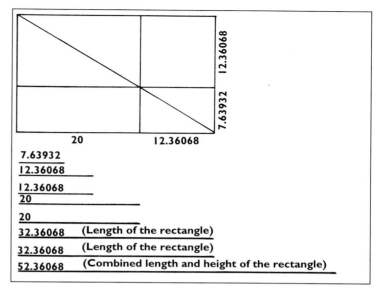

▲ **2·39D**

To see this clearly, find the original triangle established by the hypotenuse, half the baseline, and the side of the square. The Pythagorean theorem from geometry states that the sum of the squared legs of a right triangle equals the square of the third side — the hypotenuse. Apply this to the original triangle and assign lengths. Let the length of the original square be 20; half the base would therefore be 10. Therefore, 20 squared = 400 and 10 squared = 100. 400 + 100 = 500 (which should be equal to the hypotenuse squared). The square root of 500 will equal the length of the hypotenuse, which is 22.36068. This length is also equal to the distance from the bottom center of the square to the end of the new rectangle. If the half-baseline unit of 10 is subtracted from the radius, the result of 12.36068 will be the added length necessary to turn the square into a Golden Rectangle.

▲ **2·39E**

To find how many units of the original square (20) are to be found in the length of the new rectangle (32.36068), simply divide 32.36068 by 20, which equals 1.618034. The mathematical relationship that is revealed is 1:1.618034. Or, to state it another way, the larger shape is .618034 times longer than the smaller shape.

This relationship may also be observed by comparing the length of the new unit necessary to create the Golden Rectangle (12.36068) to the length of the original square (20). Dividing 20 by 12.36068 equals 1.618034, giving us the same ratio. The same relationship may be observed in the units of the smaller rectangle as divided by the Golden Mean (Section). They too are in ratio of 1:1.618034.

Finally, the length of the Golden Rectangle (32.36068), if divided into the combined length and height (52.36068), reveals the same ratio of 1:1.618034.

▼ **2·40A**

Just as the Golden Mean may be achieved by projecting outwardly from a square, it may also be found by projecting into a square. Find the center of the base of the square. With this point making the radius half the baseline, draw a semicircle inside the square.

▼ **2·40B**

Next draw a line from the center point of the baseline to the opposite corner. At the spot where the line intersects the semicircle, establish a radius from the corner. With this new radius, project an arc to points on the top and side of the square.

▼ **2·40C**

Lines drawn from these points, parallel to the sides and top and bottom of the square, will subdivide the square into Golden Rectangles with the mathematical ratio of 1:1.618034. This process may be repeated for the opposite side.

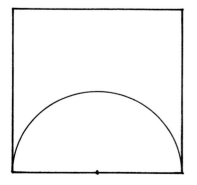

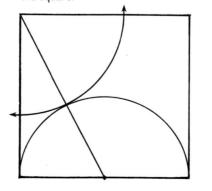

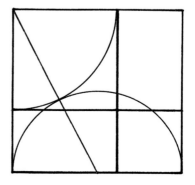

Holding the human figure in highest esteem, the ancient Greeks devised special proportional standards for their figurative works. These standards are found in their sculpture. The scale was based on certain canons or mathematical rules that established ideal relations of human parts. A figure, for example, was determined to be seven and one-half heads tall, and the distance from the top of the head to the chest was said to be one-quarter of the total height. The Greek sculptor Polyclitus is thought to be the first to issue such a canon in the form of a written treatise (which has since been lost). His bronze sculpture of a spear bearer (the original also lost) is sometimes called the canon, because it best demonstrates his standard for figure proportions (fig. 2.41). The idea of affording keenly pleasing proportional relationships extended into all areas of daily Greek life.

Historically these ancient Greek ideals have had continuing effects, influencing generations of artists. Leonardo Fibonacci, a Medieval mathematician of the thirteenth century, discovered a series of related numbers. The sequence was created by adding together the two previous numbers to arrive at each new number: 0, 1, 1, 2, 5, 8, 13, 21, 34, 56, and so on. Published in *Liber Abaci* (Book of the Abacus) in 1202, this sequence is called the *Fibonacci Series* and also demonstrates an increasing ratio of approximately 1:1.618034. Indeed, one may start with any number. Using 10 as an example, one can multiply by 1.6180 to get the number 16. From that point simply adding the previous two numbers will provide the next number (26, 42, 68, etc.) and the growing sequence will have the same ratio as the Golden Section.

Today, scientists recognize this relationship in nature. It is found in the expanding curve of the nautilus shell, the curve of a cat's claw, the spiral growth of a pine cone, the seed patterns in a sunflower's head, or the center of a daisy (fig. 2.42). Botanists study this spiral arrangement (called phyllotaxy) in leaves, scales, and flowers. This spiraling curve may be demonstrated in the continuing projection of the Golden Rectangle into progressively larger and larger units (figs. 2.43A and B).

▷ **2 · 41**

Polyclitus of Argos, *Doryphoros* (Roman copy), 450–440 B.C. Marble, 6 ft 11 in (2.12 m) high.

Polyclitus wrote a theoretical treatise and demonstrated a new system of ideal proportions in a sculpture, which took the form of a young man walking with a spear (the spear is no longer extant). The Greeks called the figure "Doryphoros" (spear carrier). The Polyclitus style was characterized by harmonious and rhythmical composition, and was highly influential on Roman thought.

National Museum, Naples, Italy. (Photograph from Calmann and King Archives, London.)

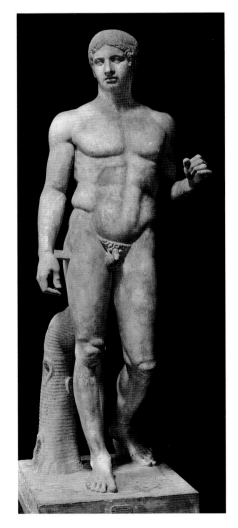

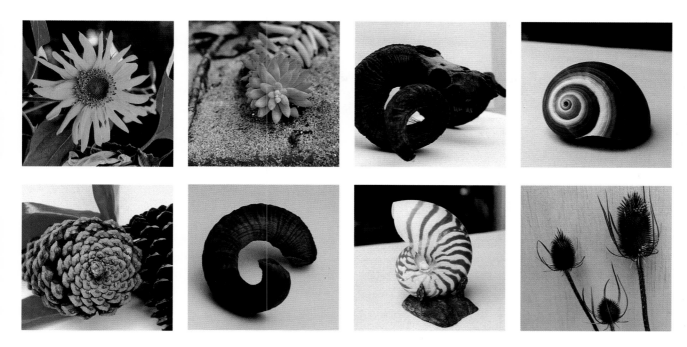

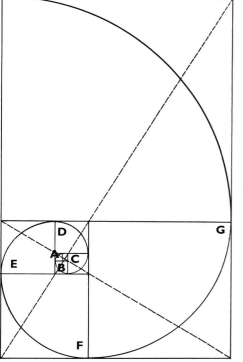

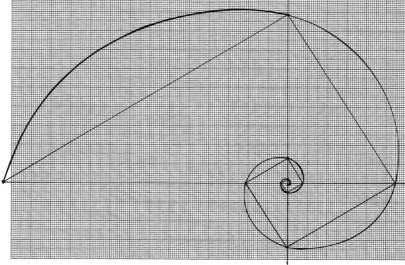

▲ **2 · 42**

Examples of spiraling curves taken from nature.

▼ **2 · 43A**

The spiraling curve is created by the continuing projection of the Golden Section, and may be drawn with the aid of a compass. The inside corner of the square locates the compass point, which scribes an arc from corner to corner. This line is continued into the next square with a new compass point located on the inside center corner of that square. The process continues from square to square until the spiral is completed.

▲ **2 · 43B**

This diagram illustrates the same spiral, created by plotting the numbers from the Fibonacci sequence (1, 1, 2, 3, 5, 8, 13, 21, 34, 55, 89, 144) on a horizontal and vertical axis.

During the Renaissance, artists like Leonardo da Vinci demonstrated renewed interest in mathematically formulated proportional scaling. This can be found, for example, in Leonardo's drawing *Proportions of the Human Figure* (fig. 2.44).

Modern artists also have composed pictures that conform with the standard frame shape of the Golden Rectangle. Georges Seurat, the French painter, was one. He is known for his scientifically measured use of the Impressionistic techniques of Pointillism, light and simultaneously contrasted colors, but he also was intrigued with the mathematical

proportions of the Golden Rectangle. In the painting *Circus Sideshow (La Parade)*, Seurat used subtle variations of Golden Rectangles and squares (figs. 2.45A and B). Notice how he strategically placed the softly rounded figures, the tree, the geometric forms, and the various decorative motifs at Golden Section points.

Most artists seek balance and logical proportions. The dimensions of the images reproduced in this book would reinforce this claim. Some artists choose to disregard the essentials of proportions, that is, harmonious and balanced relationships, in order to emphasize the

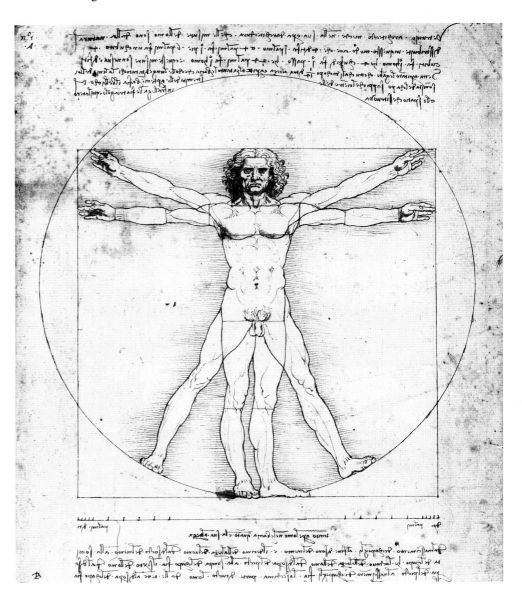

▶ **2 · 44**

Leonardo da Vinci, *Proportions of the Human Figure* (after Vitruvius), c. 1485–90. Pen and ink, 13½ × 9¾ in (34.3 × 24.8 cm).

Here, Leonardo demonstrates his interest in human anatomy. By positioning a male figure within a circle and square, Leonardo was investigating the proportional relationships of the head, body, arms, and legs. Note that the figure's height is equal to its outstretched arms and that the circle's center is located at the point where the legs join.

Accademia, Venice, Italy. (Photograph by Osvaldo Böhm, Venice.)

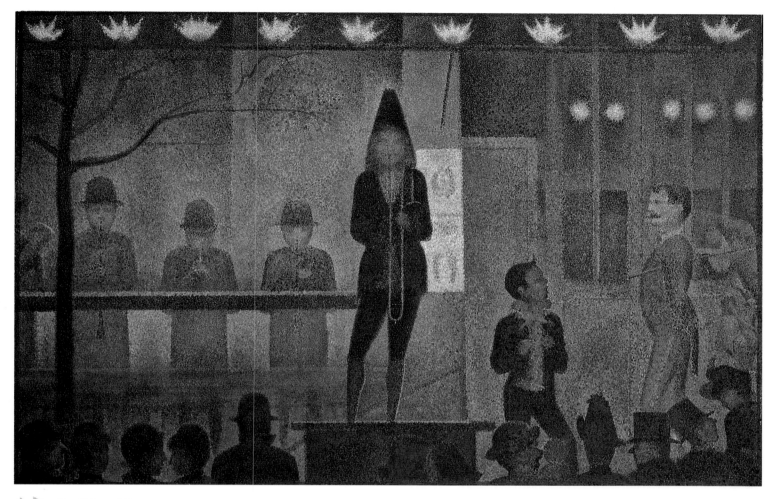

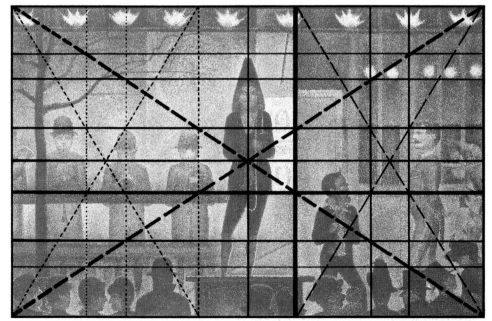

▲ ▶ **2 · 45A and B**

Georges Seurat, *Circus Sideshow (La Parade)*, 1887–88. Oil on canvas, 39¼ × 59 in (99.7 × 149.9 cm).

When this Seurat painting is divided by a diagonal from upper left to lower right (large dashes), it crosses the large square where a Golden Rectangle would be subdivided by a heavy horizontal line. Smaller Golden Rectangles are created in the vertical rectangle on the right. These small rectangles may be further divided by intersecting diagonals. This could continue indefinitely. In addition, when the original square is established on the right side of the picture (small dotted lines) and a diagonal is drawn from lower left to upper right, the left side may be broken down into smaller Golden Rectangles which mirror those on the right side of the diagram. Notice how Seurat has used these lines and their intersections for the strategic placement of figures and imagery.

Metropolitan Museum of Art, New York. Bequest of Stephen C. Clark, 1960. (61.101.17)

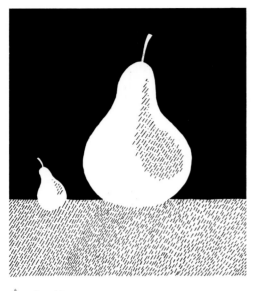

▲ 2 · 46
Because of their juxtaposition, the large pear shouts for attention while the small one dwindles into insignificance. Artists who experiment with extremes of scale and proportion must do so with control if they want to achieve a harmonious result.

extremes of scale. When a very large shape is placed alongside a much smaller one in an artwork, the effect is disproportionate. The two pears in figure 2.46 illustrate the awkwardness of such juxtaposition. The larger pear is much too forceful in its demand for attention, while the smaller one loses significance. Most artists who make judgments in determining proportions will rely on an educated intuition, and will adjust and readjust the sizes of their elements so that they seem to fill the whole work of art.

Still, many artists find a need for enlarging and/or diminishing the sizes of certain elements in order to aid the expression of an idea, or as a means of creating emphasis or dominance. When changes in scale are used for emphasis the artist will find that he or she can harness and sustain the observer's attention. In the Jerome Witkin painting (fig. 2.47), the artist uses enlargement as a means of emphasizing the presence of his figure. The subject, a large, physical man, is presented with a bulky torso in simple,

light values, surrounded by the darker forms of the head, arms, jacket and pants. The artist has positioned the white torso in the center of the composition for primary attention and has sized the figure's image so that it seems to burst the limits of the painting's format. Witkin's exaggerated enlargement and relative scaling came from his perceptions of the actual figure he was to represent. The result is an overpowering portrait.

Another way artists have used inordinate proportion or scaling is to indicate rank, status, or importance of religious, political, military, and social personages. "Hierarchical scaling" is a term used to describe this system whereby figures of greatest importance are made larger in size according to their successive status. In the painting *Madonna of Mercy*, Piero della Francesca doubled the size of his Madonna figure in order to elevate her to a lofty object of reverence (fig. 2.48). The proportions in this painting, and others like it, are subjective in their intent rather than representational.

The physical size of the work in comparison to human scale can also be utilized for expressive purposes. As an example, Jan van Eyck's painting *St. Francis Receiving the Stigmata* seems to acquire an intimate, reverential quality because of its small size – 5 × 5¾ in (12.7 × 14.6 cm) (fig. 2.49). The artist Chuck Close, on the other hand, tends to overwhelm us with paintings of enormous human heads (fig. 2.50). Resulting from their overall size – the portraits range from five to eight feet in height – there is a proportional enlargement of facial details, such as hairs and skin pores. The view of the artist in his studio illustrates the overpowering scale of these enlargements (see fig. 2.50). The heads become heroic, intimidating, and, in some respects, sordid.

To summarize: proportion scaling is used to create emphasis and expressive effects, and to suggest spatial positions, as will be shown in later chapters.

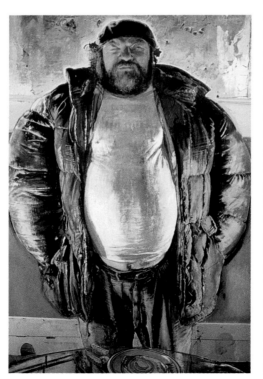

▶ 2 · 47
Jerome Paul Witkin, *Jeff Davies*, 1980. Oil on canvas, 6 × 4 ft (1.83 × 1.22 m).
If there was ever a painting in which one subject dominated the work, this must be it. Most artworks do not need this degree of dominance, but Witkin evidently wanted a forceful presence – and got it.
Palmer Museum of Art, Pennsylvania State University.

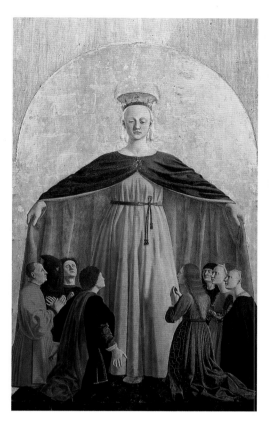

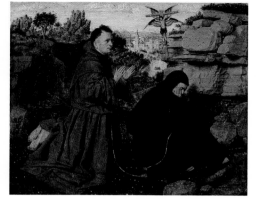

▲ 2 · 49

Attributed to Jan van Eyck, *St. Francis Receiving the Stigmata*, no date. Oil on paper, 5 × 5¾ in (12.7 × 14.6 cm).

As can be seen from the dimensions of this work, van Eyck has created an amazing microcosm. Despite its tiny size, everything is in near-perfect scale. The radical scaling-down creates a subdued, almost precious effect; there is no bombast or superficial heroism.

Philadelphia Museum of Art, PA. John G. Johnson Collection.

▲ 2 · 48

Piero della Francesca, *Madonna of Mercy* (center panel of triptych), 1445–55. Oil and tempera on wood, height about 4 ft 9 in (1.44 m).

The figure of Mary extends her arms to make a shelter of her cape for the smaller figures at her feet. The positioning of the worshipful figures who surround the central columnar form helps to give a sense of depth to the scene. The artist's use of hierarchical scaling also strengthens the maternal and merciful power of the Madonna.

Communal Palace, Borgo San Sepolcro, Italy. (Photograph from Scala, Florence.)

▶ 2 · 50

Chuck Close, *Jud*, 1982. Pulp paper collage on canvas, 8 × 6 ft (2.44 × 1.83 m).

The enlargement of the heads in such paintings involves a scrupulous examination of every textural and "geographical" aspect of the sitter's face.

Courtesy of the Pace Gallery, New York. (Photograph by S. K. Yaeger.)

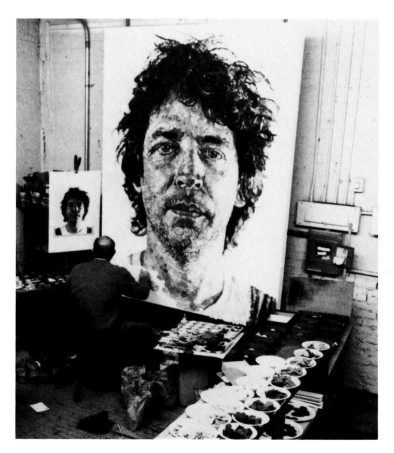

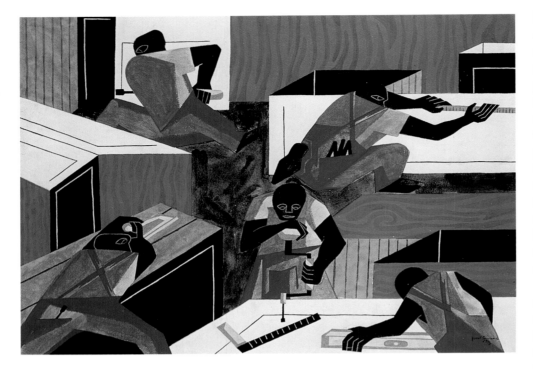

2·51

**Jacob Lawrence, *Cabinet Makers*, 1946.
Gouache with pencil underdrawing on
paper, 21¾ × 30 in (55.2 × 76.2 cm).**
The human figures here become the focal points,
or "optical units" of greatest importance,
because of their size and activity. The dominant
area is where the two central figures merge. The
other figures are lesser players, and the tables
and tools less dominant still.
Hirshhorn Museum and Sculpture Garden, Smithsonian
Institution, Washington, D.C. Gift of Joseph H.
Hirshhorn, 1966. (Photograph by John Tennant.) ©
Jacob Lawrence/DACS, London/VAGA, New York
1994.

▼　**2·52**

**James Ensor, *Fireworks* (detail), 1887. Oil
and encaustic on canvas, 3 ft 4¼ in × 3 ft
8¼ in (1.02 × 1.12 m).**
Centering, color brightness, dynamic movement,
and the semiradial shape make the eruption of
the fireworks the inescapably dominant subject.
Albright-Knox Art Gallery, Buffalo, NY. Albright and
Jenny R. Mathews Fund, 1971. © DACS 1994.

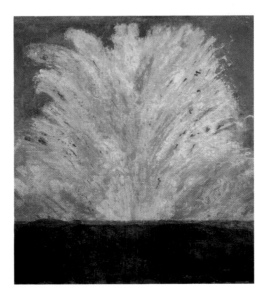

Dominance

Any work of art that strives for interest
must exhibit differences that emphasize
the degrees of importance of its various
parts. These differences result from
medium and compositional
considerations. A musical piece, for
example, can use crescendo; a dramatic
production can use a spotlight. The
means by which differences can be
achieved, in fact, are many. If we
substitute the term contrast for difference,
we can see that emphasis can be produced
by contrasts in scale, in character, and in
the many physical properties of the
elements.

Obviously, the artist intends to use
contrast to call attention to the
significant parts of the work, thereby
making them dominant. Artists who
neglect dominance in their work imply
that everything is of equal importance;
such art not only fails to communicate,
but also creates a confusing visual image
in which the viewer is given no direction.
In one sense, all parts are important,
because even the secondary parts produce
the norm against which the dominant
parts are contrasted.

In dealing with dominance artists have
two problems. First they must see that
each part has the necessary degree of
importance, and second, they must
incorporate these parts, with their varying
degrees of importance, into the rhythmic
movement and balance of the work. In
doing this, artists often find that they
must use different methods to achieve
dominance. One significant area might
derive importance from its change in
value, whereas another might rely on its
busy or exciting shape (figs. 2.51, 2.52, and
2.53; see fig. 5.11).

The basic order created by variations in
dominance (and in hierarchy, more
generally) can be witnessed at every level
of our lives – the star system in the
entertainment field; the hierarchy of
political, ecclesiastical, and civic
organizations; the atomic system; the
solar system – all in very different ways.

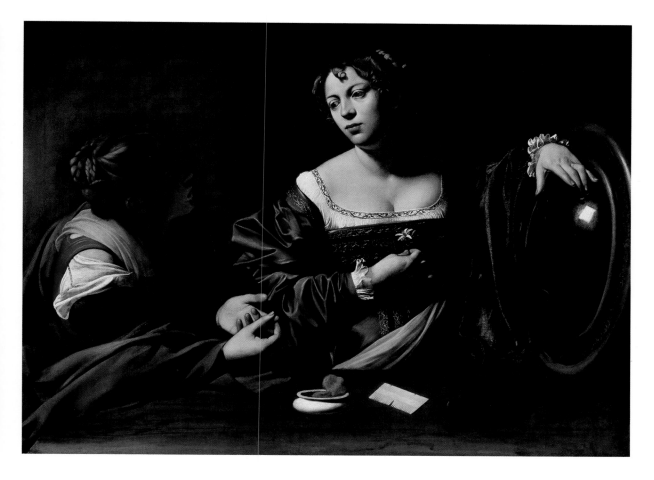

Movement

A picture surface is static; its parts do not move. Any animation in a work must come from an illusion created by the artist through placement and configuration of the picture parts. The written word is read from side to side, but a visual image can be read in a variety of directions. The directions are created by the artist out of a need to bind the various parts together in rhythmic, legible, and logical sequences. The movement should ensure that all areas of the picture plane are exploited – that there are no dead spots. This goal is realized by directing shapes and lines towards each other so that the spectator is subsconsciously swept along major and secondary visual channels. The movement should be self-renewing, constantly drawing attention back into the format (see "Pictorial Representations of Movement in Time," p. 205 and figs. 2.54A and B, 2.55, and 2.56).

Economy

Very often, as a work develops, the artist will find that the solutions to various visual problems result in unnecessary complexity. The problem is frequently characterized by the broad and simple aspects of the work deteriorating into fragmentation. This process seems to be a necessary part of the developmental phase of the work, but the result may be that solutions to problems are outweighed by a lack of unity.

The artist can sometimes restore order by returning to significant essentials, eliminating elaborate details, and relating the particulars to the whole. This is a sacrifice not easily made or accepted because, in looking for solutions, interesting discoveries may have been

▲ 2 · 53

Michelangelo Merisi da Caravaggio, *The Conversion of the Magdalene*, 1597–98. Oil on canvas, 38½ × 52¼ in (97.8 × 132.7 cm).

The contrast of the light value of the head and shoulders with the dark values of the background gives emphasis to the main figure of the Magdalene.

Detroit Institute of Arts, Detroit, MI. Gift of the Kresge Foundation and Mr. and Mrs. Edsel Ford.

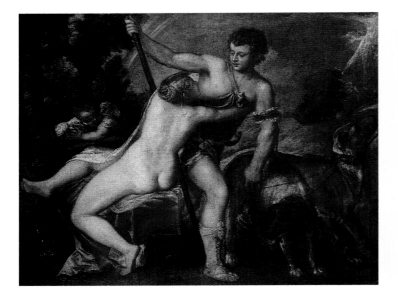
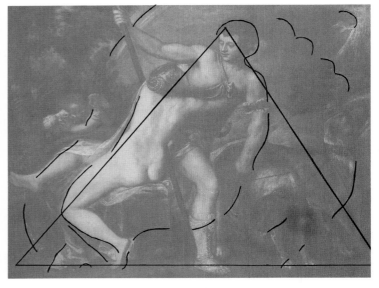

▲   **2 · 54A and B**

Titian, *Venus and Adonis*, c. 1560. Oil on canvas, 3 ft 6 in × 4 ft 5½ in (1.07 × 1.36 m).
The movement in this painting was planned by Titian to carry the spectator's eye along guided visual paths. These were created (as indicated by the accented lines in fig. 2.54B) by emphasizing the figure contours and the light values. The triangular shape made by the main figures serves as a pivotal motif around which secondary movements circulate.

Widener Collection, 1942. (© National Gallery of Art, Washington, D.C.)

▶   **2 · 55**

Gino Severini, *Red Cross Train Passing a Village*, 1915. Oil on canvas, 35 × 45¾ in (88.9 × 116.2 cm).
The Futurists were particularly interested in the dynamism of the modern age. Although somewhat less violent in its movement than many such works, the painting is hardly peaceful, with its great variety of shapes jostling for position on the picture plane.

The Solomon R. Guggenheim Museum, New York. (Photograph by Myles Aronowitz; © The Solomon R. Guggenheim Foundation, New York; 44.944.) © ADAGP, Paris and DACS, London 1994.

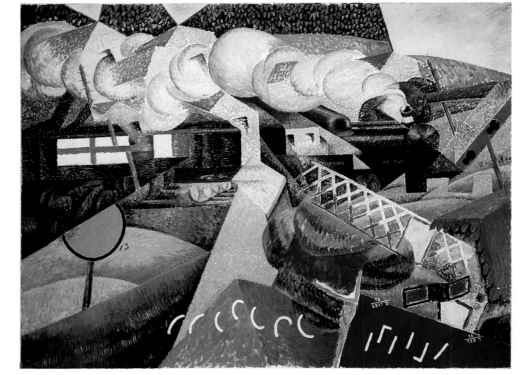

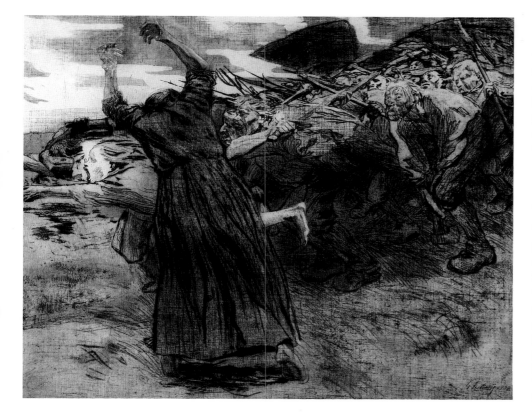

made. But, interesting or not, these effects must often be surrendered for greater legibility and a more direct expression. Economy has no rules, but rather must be an outgrowth of the artist's instincts. If something works with respect to the whole, it is kept; if disruptive, it may be reworked or rejected.

Economy is often associated with the term "abstraction." Abstraction implies an active process of paring things down to the essentials necessary to the artist's style of expression. It strengthens both the conceptual and organizational aspects of the artwork. In a sense, the style dictates the degree of abstraction, though all artists abstract to some extent (fig. 2.57).

Economy is easily detected in many contemporary art styles. The early *modernists* Pablo Picasso and Henri

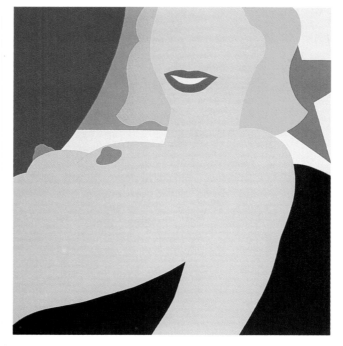

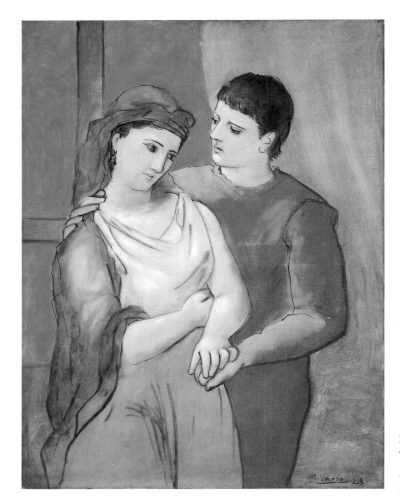

Pablo Picasso, *The Lovers*, 1923. Oil on linen, 51¼ × 38¼ in (130.2 × 97.2 cm). Picasso has simplified the complex qualities of the surface structures of his two figures, reducing them to contour lines and flat color renderings. Through the use of economy, the artist abstracted the two lovers to strengthen the expressive bond between them.

Matisse were among those most influential in the trend toward economical abstraction (fig. 2.58; see fig. 4.7). The "field" paintings of Barnett Newman and Morris Louis, the analogous color canvases of Ad Reinhardt, and the hard-edged works of Ellsworth Kelly all clearly feature economy (see figs. 10.69, 10.70, 2.15, and 2.10). Two sculptors of the Minimalist style (which itself bespeaks economy), Tony Smith and Donald Judd, make use of severely limited geometric forms (see figs. 9.40 and 9.41). They have renounced *illusionism*, preferring instead to create three-dimensional objects in actual space that excludes all excesses. The absence of elaboration results in a very direct statement.

In economizing, one flirts with monotony. Sometimes embellishments must be preserved or added to avoid this pitfall. But if the result is greater clarity, the risk (and the work!) are well worth it.

Space

The artist is always concerned about space as it evolves in artworks. The authors have taken the position that *space* is not an element, but a by-product of the elements as they are put into action and altered by the various principles of organization. Other people regard space as an element in its own right; but however it is classified, the *concept* of space is unquestionably of crucial importance – so much so, in fact, that many chapter sections in the text, and the entire contents of Chapter 8, are devoted to the subject.

If we follow the order in our diagram (see fig. 2.1) we see that a medium is necessary for the creation of an element and that, once an element – a line for example – becomes visible, it automatically assumes a spatial position in contrast with its background.

An artist, when considering space in a work, should look for consistency of relationships. There is nothing that can throw an artwork so "out of kilter" as a jumbled spatial order. If an artist begins with one kind of space, say, a flat two-dimensional representation of a figure, he or she should continue to develop two-dimensional concepts in the succeeding stages of the artwork. Consistency contributes immeasurably to unity.

Our familiarity with space comes, in part, from the exploration of outer space. Of course, we personally become acquainted with space, though on a less exalted level, as we move from point to point in the performance of our normal daily duties. As we do this we are unconsciously aware of the distance between these points and even of the limit of our vision, the horizon. In transferring nature's space to the drawing board or canvas the artist has long been faced with problems – problems which have been dealt with in various ways in different historical periods. The artist must use the art elements to produce the illusion of the spatial phenomena he or she wants represented in the artwork. Quite often the effect sought is one which has the observer viewing the frame as a window into the space, terminating at some point or continuing to infinity. Such space, in an art setting, is called three-dimensional because all of this is condensed into a drawing or painting surface. These surfaces have their natural limits, but, in addition, there is a further measurement, the illusion of depth, giving three-dimensional space.

FORM UNITY: A SUMMARY

Artists select a picture plane framed by certain dimensions. They have their tools and materials and with them begin to create elements on the surface. As they do so, spatial suggestions appear which may conform to their original conception; if not, the process of adjustment begins. The adjustment accelerates and continues as harmony and variety are applied to achieve balance, movement, proportion, dominance, and economy. As the development continues artists depend on their intellect, emotions, and instincts. The ratio varies from artist to artist and from work to work. The result is an artwork that has its own distinctive form. If the work is successful, its form has unity – all parts belong and work together.

A unified artwork develops like symphonic orchestration in music. The musical composer generally begins with a theme that is taken through a number of variations. Notations direct the tempo and dynamics for the performers. The individual instruments, in following these notations, play their parts in contributing to the total musical effect. In addition, the thematic material is woven through the content of the work, harmonizing its sections. A successful musical composition speaks eloquently, with every measure seeming to be irreplaceable.

Every musical element just mentioned has its counterpart in art. In every creative medium, be it music, art, dance, poetry, prose, or theatre, the goal is unity. For the creator, unity results from the selection of appropriate devices peculiar to the medium and the use of certain principles to relate them. In art, an understanding of the principles of form-structure is indispensable. In the first chapters of this book, one can begin to see the vast possibilities in the creative art realm. Through study of the principles of form organization, beginners develop an intellectual understanding that can, through persistent practice, become instinctive.

The art elements – line, shape, value, texture, and color – on which form is based rarely exist by themselves. They join forces in the total work. Their individual contributions can be studied separately, but in the development of a work, the ways in which they relate to each other must always be considered. Because each of the elements makes an individual contribution and has an intrinsic appeal, the elements are discussed separately in the following five chapters. It is necessary to do this for *academic* reasons. But as you study an element, please keep in mind those that preceded it. At the end, all the elements must be considered both individually and collectively. This is a big task, but necessary for that vital ingredient, unity.

CHAPTER THREE

Line

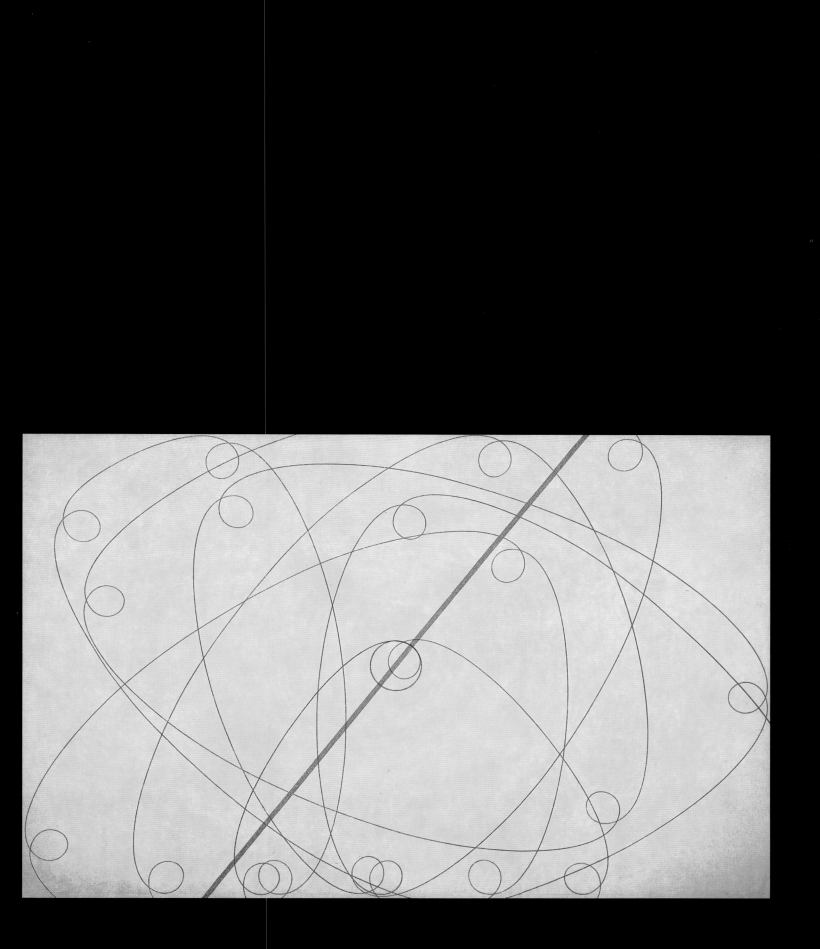

THE VOCABULARY OF LINE

Line The path of a moving point, that is, a mark made by a tool or instrument as it is drawn across a surface. A line is usually made visible by the fact that it contrasts in value with the surface on which it is drawn.

calligraphy
Elegant, decorative writing. Lines used in artworks that possess the qualities found in this kind of writing may be called "calligraphic." They are generally flowing and rhythmical.

contour
In art, the line that defines the outermost limits of an object or a drawn or painted shape. It is sometimes considered to be synonymous with "outline"; as such, it indicates an edge that also may be defined by the extremities of values, textures, or colors.

cross-contour
A line that crosses and defines the surface undulations between, or up to, the outermost edges of shapes or objects.

expression
1. The manifestation through artistic form of a thought, emotion, or quality of meaning. 2. In art, expression is synonymous with the word "content."

hatching
Repeated strokes of an art tool producing clustered lines (usually parallel) that create values. In "cross"-hatching similar lines pass over the hatched lines in a different direction, usually resulting in darker values.

mass
1. In graphic art, a shape that appears to stand out three-dimensionally from the space surrounding it, or appears to create the illusion of a solid body of material. 2. In the plastic arts, the physical bulk of a solid body of material.

nonrepresentational art
A term used to define work encompassing nonrecognizable imagery. This ranges from pure abstraction (nonrecognizable but derived from a recognizable object) to nonobjective art (not a product of the abstraction process, but deriving from the artist's mind).

representation(al) art
A type of art in which the subject is presented through the visual art elements so that the observer is reminded of actual objects.

LINE: THE ELEMENTARY MEANS OF COMMUNICATION

The lineup – "this guy's giving me a line" – the long gray line – "he plays tackle on the line" – the bus line – "the line forms here." These are some of the everyday expressions that share the word *line* with our first element. These common uses of the word imply that something is strung out or stretched a certain distance. You have undoubtedly stood in line for something and found your impatience turn to relief as you reached the front. Your line may have been a single line (narrow) or two abreast (wider). Sometimes lines become straggly – but this had better not be the case in the military, where perfectly straight alignment is enforced. Standing lines often exhibit differences in width due to the different sizes of the people in the line or because people are bunched together.

Art lines and "people lines" have such things in common. Theoretically a line is an extended dot; so, if only one person shows up, a dot is made. But, as other people are added, with their different dimensions and positions, the line's characteristics change. In art, these line variations are called "physical characteristics," and they can be used by the artist to create meanings as well as to reproduce the appearance of the artist's subjects.

It is difficult to imagine line as existing in nature; nature contains only *mass*, which can be described in art by means of *contour*. For the artist, line is a graphic device that can function objectively by describing things or subjectively by suggesting emotional conditions and responses (fig. 3.1). Linear designs in the form of ideograms and alphabets are used by people as a basic means of communication, but the artist uses line in a more broadly communicative manner. Line operates in various ways in the visual arts, describing an edge, as on a piece of

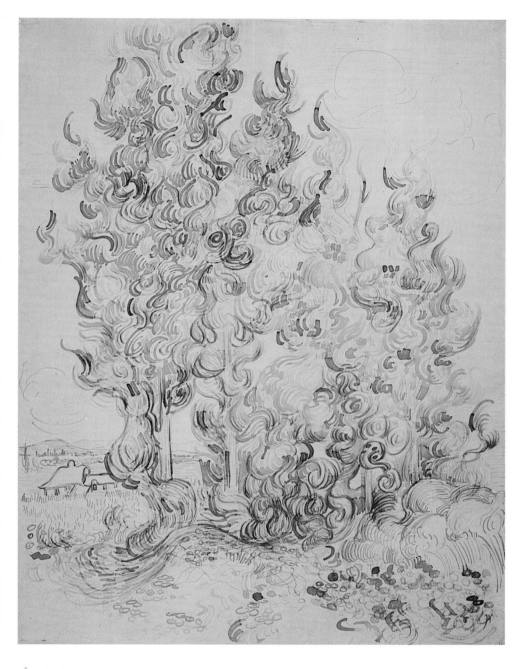

△ **3 · 1**

**Vincent van Gogh, *Grove of Cypresses*,
1889. Reed pen and ink over pencil on
paper, 24½ × 18¼ in (62.5 × 46.4 cm).**
By using broad-stroked lines and arranging them
in a turmoil of flowing movement, van Gogh has
subjectively interpreted his impression of a wind-
blown landscape.

Art Institute of Chicago. Gift of Robert Allerton,
1927.543.

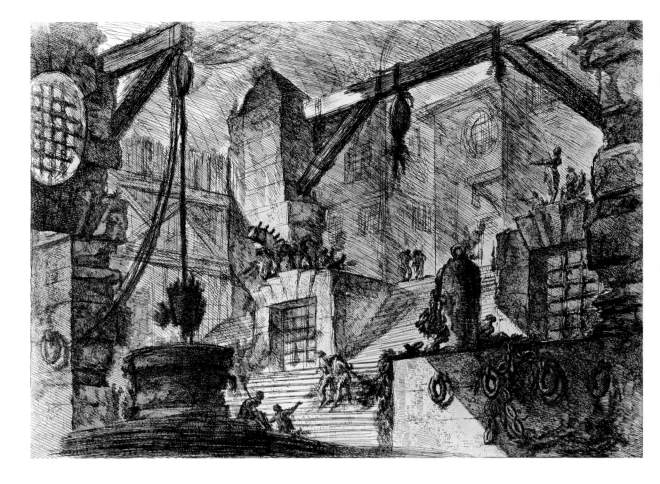

▲ **3 · 2**

Giovanni Battista Piranesi, *The Well*, from *Carceri* (first edition, second issue), 1750–58. Print (etching), 16¼ × 22 in (41.3 × 55.9 cm).

Although this scene is the product of the artist's imagination, the objects are depicted objectively, with line used to define shapes, textures, and shadows.

Rosenwald Collection (© 1993 National Gallery of Art, Washington, D.C.)

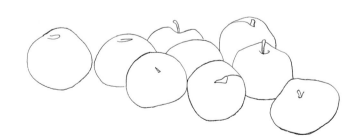

▶ **3 · 3**

Ellsworth Kelly, *Apples*, Paris, 1949. Charcoal pencil, 17 × 22⅛ in (43.4 × 56.4 cm).

Line becomes contour as it encircles an object, giving it a distinctive, and often recognizable, shape.

The Museum of Modern Art, New York. Gift of John S. Newberry (by exchange).

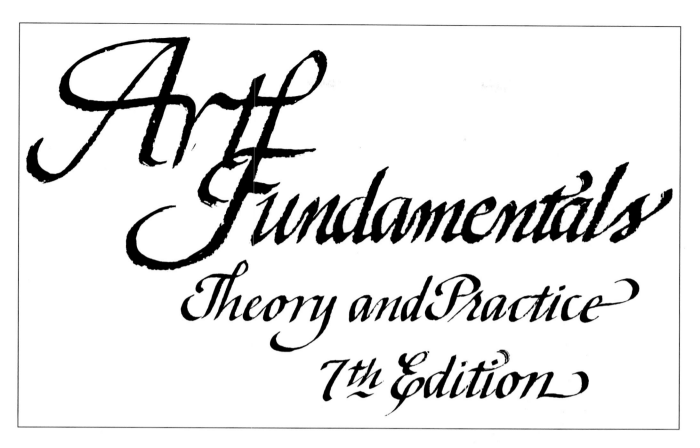

Art Fundamentals
Theory and Practice
7th Edition

sculpture; a meeting of areas where value, textural, or color differences do not blend (fig. 3.2). It also may be a contour, as it defines a drawn shape (fig. 3.3). It may be plastic when suggesting space or calligraphic when embellishing a surface. A calligraphic line is highly personal in nature, similar to the individual qualities found in handwriting; it is flowing and rhythmical, and intriguing to the eye as it enriches an artwork. In comparing the *calligraphy* of figure 3.4 with examples of drawn figures 3.5 and 3.6 one can see the shared qualities of grace and elegance. In addition, line can perform several functions at the same time. Its wide application includes the creation of value and texture, illustrating the impossibility of making a real distinction between the elements of art structure (see figs. 3.17 and 3.19).

When lines are used to reproduce the appearance of subjects in an artwork, this appearance can be reinforced by the

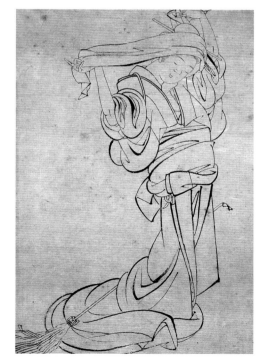

▲ **3 · 4**
Elmer Girten, exercise in calligraphy, 1992. Pen and ink on textured paper, 9 × 12 in (22.9 × 30.5 cm).
This is an example of the handwriting style developed by a professional calligrapher. It demonstrates the technique of flowing lines that has influenced so many graphic artists.
Courtesy of the artist.

◄ **3 · 5**
Katsushika Hokusai, *A Maid Preparing to Dust*, Edo period. Ink on paper, 12½ × 9 in (31.4 × 22.9 cm).
The lines in this drawing exhibit similar qualities to those found in sophisticated calligraphy.
Courtesy of the Freer Gallery of Art, Smithsonian Institution #04.248, Washington, D.C.

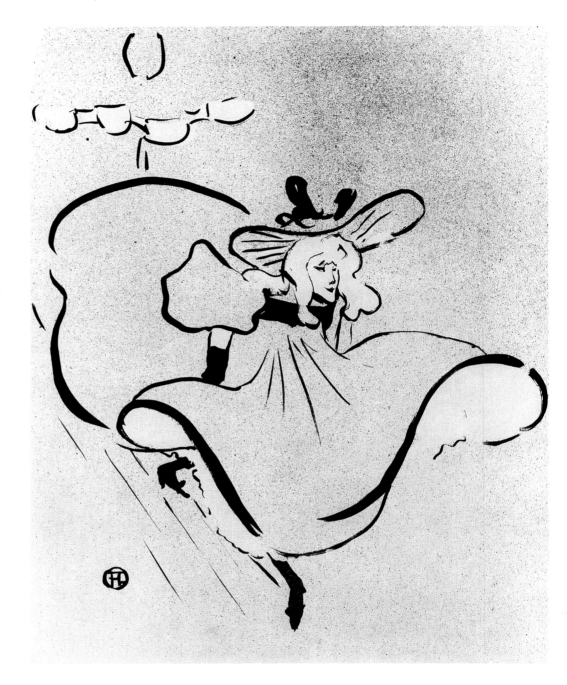

▲ **3 · 6**
Henri de Toulouse-Lautrec, *Jane Avril*,
plate from *Le Café Concert*, 1893.
Lithograph, printed in black, 10½ × 8⁷⁄₁₆ in
(26.7 × 21.4 cm).
The lines in this image seem to have been drawn
with great freedom, communicating the graceful
action of the subject.
The Museum of Modern Art, New York. Purchase
fund.

▶ **3 · 7**
Georges Mathieu, *Montjoie Saint Denis!*
1954. Oil on canvas, 12 ft 3⁵⁄₈ in × 35½ in
(3.74 × .902 m).
Certain intrinsic meanings arise from the
character of the lines – meanings which are the
product of the medium, the tool(s) used, and the
artist's method of application. The meanings of
the lines are further fortified by color.
The Museum of Modern Art, New York. Gift of Mr.
and Mrs. Harold Kaye.

artist's selection of lines that carry certain meanings. In this way the subject may be altered or enhanced, and the work becomes an interpretation of that subject. Line meanings can also be used in conjunction with the other art elements (fig. 3.7).

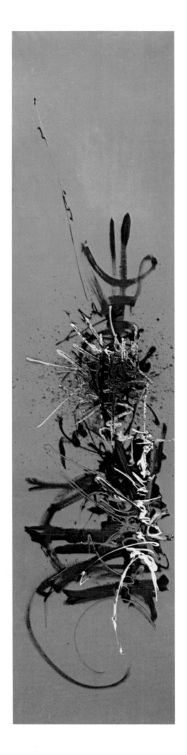

THE PHYSICAL CHARACTERISTICS OF LINE

The physical characteristics of line are many. Lines may be straight or curved, direct or meandering, short or long, thin or thick, zigzag or serpentine. The value of these characteristics to the artist is that they have certain built-in associations. When we say that a person is a "straight arrow" we mean that the person is straightforward and reliable; a "crooked" person, on the other hand, is devious and untrustworthy. Most of us can find adjectives to fit various kinds of lines; those meanings, deriving in part from the associations cited above, make for the possibility of subtle psychological suggestions.

Measure

Measure refers to length and width of line. A line may be of any length and breadth. An infinite number of combinations of long and short, thick and thin lines can, according to their use, divide, balance, or unbalance a pictorial area.

Type

There are many different kinds of line. If the line continues in only one direction, it is straight; if changes of direction gradually occur, it is curved; if those changes are sudden and abrupt, an angular line is created. Taking into consideration the characteristic of type as well as measure, we find that long or short, thick or thin lines can be straight, angular, or curved. The straight line, in its continuity, ultimately becomes repetitious and, depending on its length, either rigid or brittle. The curved line may form an arc, reverse its curve to become wavy, or continue turning within itself to produce a spiral. Alterations of movement become visually entertaining and physically stimulating if they are

▶ **3·8**

Student work, *Cock Fight*.
The abrupt changes of direction in the angular
lines of this drawing create the excitement and
tension of combat.
Bowling Green State University, Bowling Green, OH.

rhythmical. A curved line is inherently
graceful and, to a degree, unstable (see fig.
3.5). The abrupt changes of direction in
an angular line create excitement and/or
confusion (fig. 3.8). Our eyes frequently
have difficulty adapting to an angular
line's unexpected deviations of direction.
Hence, the angular line is full of
challenging interest.

Direction

A further complication of line is its basic
direction, a direction that can exist
irrespective of the component movements
within the line. That is, a line can be a
zigzag type but take a generally curved
direction. Thus, the line type can be
contradicted or flattered by its basic
movement. A generally horizontal
direction could indicate serenity and
perfect stability, whereas a diagonal
direction would probably imply agitation
and motion (fig. 3.9). A vertical line
generally suggests poise and aspiration.
The direction of line is very important
because in large measure it controls the
movements of our eyes while we view a
picture. Our eye movements can facilitate
the continuity of relationships among the
various properties of the element (fig.
3.10).

Location

The control exercised over the measure,
type, or direction of a line can be
enhanced or diminished by its specific
location. According to its placement, a
line can serve to unify or divide, balance
or unbalance a pictorial area. A diagonal
line might be soaring or plunging,
depending upon its high or low position
relative to the frame. The various
attributes of line can act in concert
towards one goal or can serve separate
roles of expression and design. A fully
developed work, therefore, may recognize
and use all physical properties, although it
is also possible that fewer than the total
number can be successfully used. This is

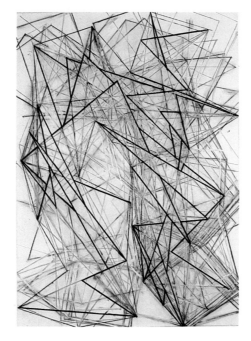

▶ **3·9**

**Mel Bochner, *Vertigo*, 1982. Charcoal,
conté crayon, and pastel on canvas, 9 ft ×
6 ft 2 in (2.74 × 1.88 m).**
Line, the dominant element in this work, is
almost wholly diagonal, imparting a feeling of
intense activity and stress.
Albright-Knox Art Gallery, Buffalo, NY. Charles Clifton
Fund, 1982.

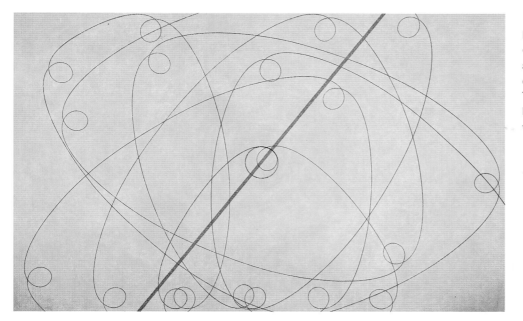

true largely because of the dual role of these properties. For instance, unity in a work might be achieved by repetition of line length, at the same time that variety is being created through difference in the line's width, medium, or other properties.

Character

Along with measure, type, direction, and location, line possesses character, a term largely related to the medium with which the line is created. Different media can be used in the same work to create greater interest. Monotony could result from the consistent use of lines of the same character unless the unity so gained is balanced by the variation of other physical properties. Varied instruments, such as the brush, burin, stick, and fingers, have distinctive characteristics that can be exploited by the artist (fig. 3.11). The artist is the real master of the situation, and it is the artist's ability, experience, intention, and mental and physical condition that determine the effectiveness of line character. Whether the viewer sees lines of uniformity or accent, certainty or indecision, tension or relaxation, are decisions only the artist can make.

3·11
Jonathan Lasker, *The Division of Happiness*, 1991. Oil on linen, 5 ft 3 in × 6 ft 9 in (1.60 × 2.06 m).
The unique character of the line work in this piece is enhanced by the careful choice of color and the shape groupings.
Courtesy of the Sperone Westwater Gallery, New York.

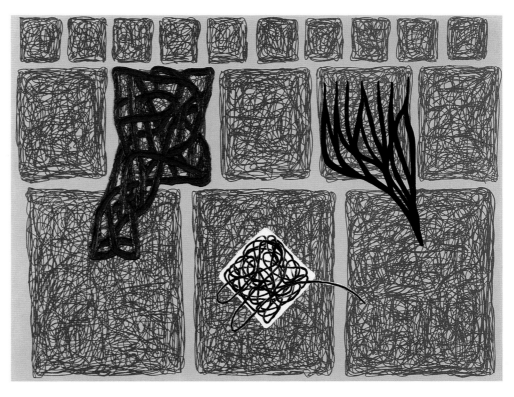

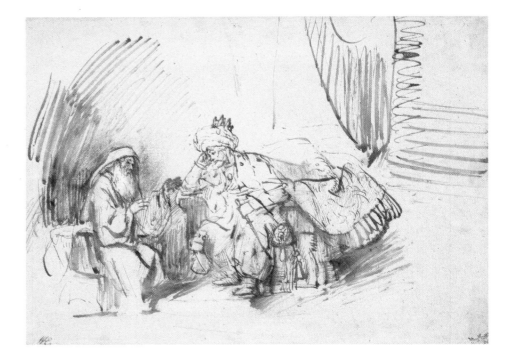

▶ **3 · 12**

Rembrandt Harmenszoon van Rijn,
***Nathan Admonishing David*, no date. Pen**
and brush with bistre, $7\frac{5}{16} \times 9\frac{5}{16}$ in (18.6
× 23.6 cm).
The crisp, biting lines of the pen contrast
effectively with broader, softer lines of the
brush.

Metropolitan Museum of Art, New York. Bequest of
Mrs. H. O. Havemeyer, 1929. The Havemeyer
Collection.

The personality or emotional quality of the line is greatly dependent on the nature of the medium chosen. In Rembrandt's sketch *Nathan Admonishing David*, the expressive qualities created by the soft brush lines of ink, juxtaposed with the precise and firm lines of pen and ink, can be clearly seen (fig. 3.12).

THE EXPRESSIVE PROPERTIES OF LINE

The qualities of line can be described in terms of general states of feeling – somber, tired, energetic, brittle, alive, and the like. However, in a work of art, as in the human mind, such feelings are rarely so clearly defined. An infinite number of conditions of varying subtlety can be communicated by the artist. The spectator's recognition of these qualities is a matter of feeling, which means that the spectator must be receptive and perceptive and have a reservoir of experiences to draw upon.

Through composition and *expression*, individual lines come to life as they play their various roles. Some lines are dominant and some subordinate, but all are of supreme importance in a work of art. Although lines may be admired separately, their real beauty lies in the relationships they help to establish, the form created (fig. 3.13). This form can be representational or nonrepresentational, but recognition and enjoyment of the work on the abstract level is of first importance. Preoccupation with subject identification significantly reduces the appreciation of a work's truly expressive art qualities.

LINE AND THE OTHER ART ELEMENTS

Line has additional physical characteristics that are very closely related to the other art elements. Line can possess color, value, and texture, and it can create shape. Some of these factors are essential to the very creation of line, while others are introduced as needed. These properties might be thought of separately, but nevertheless they cooperate to give line an intrinsic appeal, meaning that line can be admired for its own sake. Artists often exploit this appeal by creating pictures in which the linear effects are dominant, the others subordinate. On the other hand, there are some works that are line-free, depending entirely on other elements.

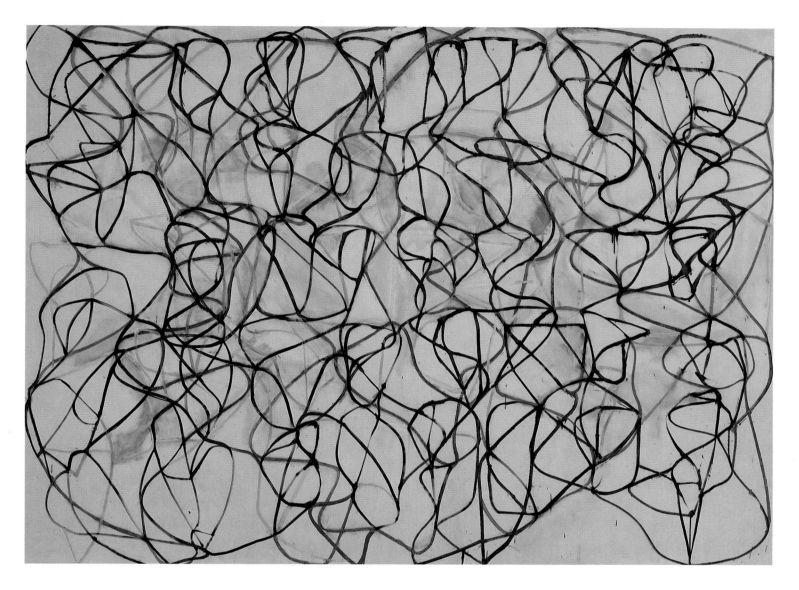

 3 · 13
Brice Marden, *Cold Mountain 3*, 1989–91.
Oil on linen, 9 × 12 ft (2.74 × 3.66 m).
In this painting – from a series he calls *Cold Mountain* (after a Chinese poem) – Brice Marden presents a weblike network of lines that seem to wander in space. This artist, however, works, reworks, and calculates the lines as he engages in spatial exploration. The pale blue lines interact like trails left behind.

© 1994 Brice Marden/ARS, NY.

▶ **3 · 14**

The lines on a topographical map indicate the various elevations of the earth's surface. In a similar way, the artist uses cross-contours to show the configuration of the subject.

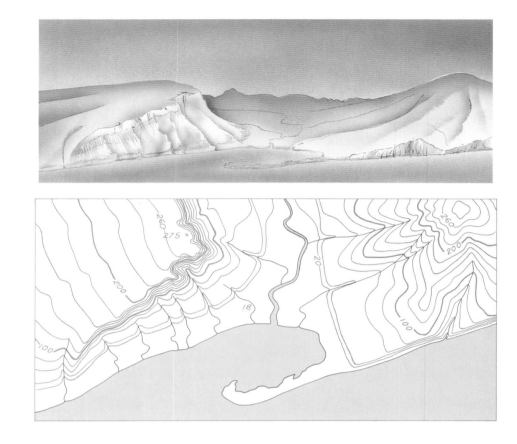

▶ **3 · 15**

Harold Tovish, *Contour Drawing*, 1972. Pencil, 19 × 25 in (48.3 × 63.5 cm).

The cross-contours illustrate the dips and swells of the features. This technique can be used to describe the surface of any subject being interpreted.

Courtesy of Terry Dintenfass Gallery, New York.

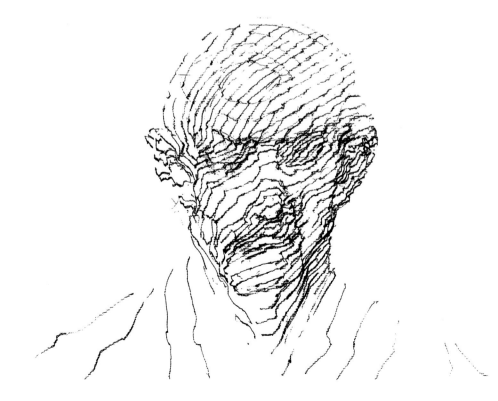

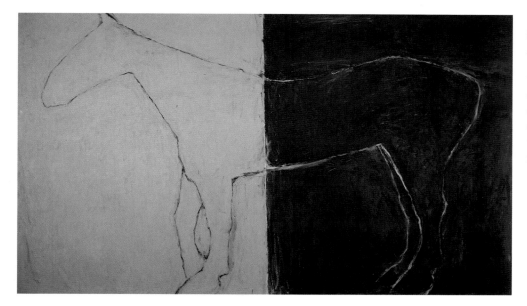

3·16
Susan Rothenberg, *United States,* **1975.**
Acrylic and tempera on canvas, 9 ft 6 in ×
15 ft 9 in (2.90 × 4.80 m).
The line describing the horse in this painting is
called a contour. Susan Rothenberg is a
contemporary artist who is noted for her series
of horses done in a manner that might be
referred to as Minimalist-Abstract.
Saatchi Collection, London.

Line and shape

In creating shape, line serves as a
continuous edge of a figure, object, or
mass. A line that describes an area in this
manner is called a contour. Whereas
contour lines generally describe the
extremities of shapes or masses, *cross-
contours* provide information about the
nature of the surfaces contained within
those edges, somewhat in the manner of a
topographical map (fig. 3.14). If it is
imagined that an ant, saturated with ink,
crawls across one's face, leaving its trail,
one can see that it has described the
features of that face by cross-contour (fig.
3.15). One can use modulated lines, that
is, thick and thin, irregular and curved, to
enhance cross-contours; one can even vary
the pressure when producing the line so
that its darkest portion would seem to
advance and the lightest to recede. Lines,
massed together, can be varied in spacing
from narrow to wide to produce a similar
advancing and/or receding effect. Contour
lines also have the capacity to separate
shapes, values, textures, and colors (fig.
3.16).

A series of closely placed lines creates
textures and toned areas. The
relationships of the ends of these linear
areas establish boundaries that transpose
the areas into shapes (fig. 3.17).

3·17
Group lines produce value. The upper row of
blocks appears to become darker from left to
right because the lines increase in width. In the
second row of blocks, a similar effect is created
as the lines on the right become closer together.

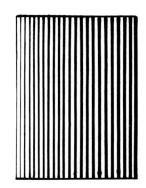
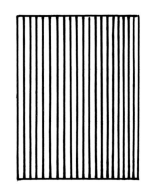
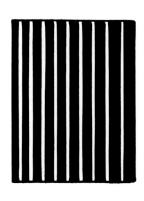
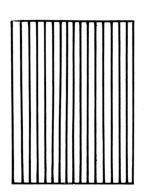
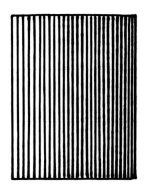

▷ **3 · 18A**

Glenn Felch, *House with Clark Sign*, 1972. India ink and colored felt pens on paper, 17 × 22 in (43.2 × 55.9 cm).

Values can be created by varying the spaces between the lines; the parallel quality of the lines in this sketch also injects a degree of harmony.

Courtesy of the artist.

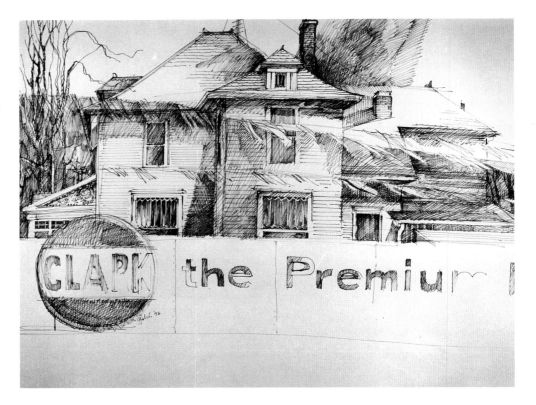

▷ **3 · 18B**

Glenn Felch, *House with Clark Sign* (detail), 1972. India ink and colored felt pens on paper.

This enlargement of a section of figure 3.18A shows the importance of line in creating interesting areas of value difference.

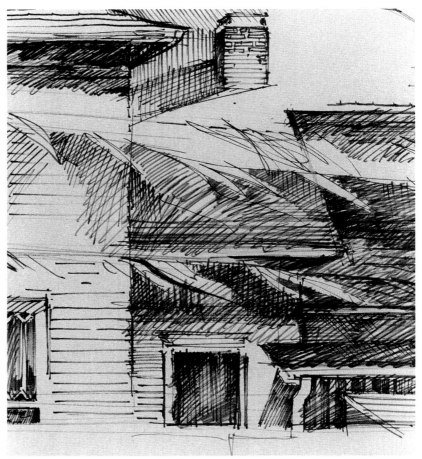

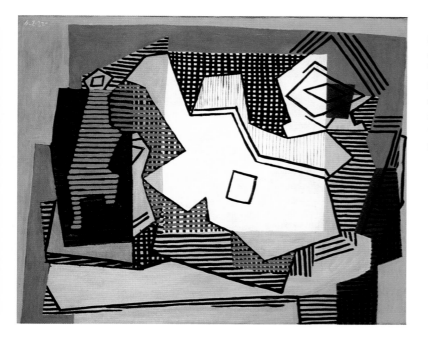

Pablo Picasso, *Still Life*, 1922. Oil on canvas, 32⅛ × 39⅝ in (81.6 × 100.7 cm). The artist often uses groups of lines to achieve the effect of texture. When such groups are combined to produce a flat or two-dimensional effect, pattern results.

The Art Institute of Chicago. Gift of William N. Eisandrath, Jr. 1940.1047.

Line and value

The contrast in light and dark that a line exhibits against its background is called value. Every line must have value to be visible. Groups of lines create areas that can differ in value. Lines can be thick, thin, or any width in between. Wide, heavy lines appear dark in value, while narrow lines appear light in value. Value changes also can be controlled by varying the spaces between the lines. Widely spaced lines appear light, and closely spaced lines appear dark (see fig. 3.17). Value differences also result from mixture of media or amount of pressure exerted. Parallel lines, cross-hatching, and the like are examples of groups of single lines that create areas of differing value (figs. 3.18A and B). Sometimes, when *hatching* is used to produce value, the strokes will be made to define the direction of a surface at any given point.

Line and texture

Groups of lines can combine to produce pattern. If, however, the result stimulates our sensation of touch by suggesting degrees of roughness or smoothness, the effect is called *texture* (fig. 3.19). Texture is

also an inherent characteristic of individual media and tools, and their distinctive qualities can be enhanced or diminished by the manner of handling. Brushes with a hard bristle, for instance, can make either sharp or rough lines, depending on hand pressure, amount of medium carried, and quality of execution. Brushes with soft hairs can produce smooth lines if loaded with thin paint and thick blotted lines if loaded with heavy paint. Other tools and media can produce similar variations of line (fig. 3.20).

Line and color

The introduction of color to a line adds an important expressive potential. Color can accentuate other line properties. A hard line combined with an intense color produces a forceful or even harsh effect. This effect would be considerably muted if the same line were created in a more gentle color. Different colors have come to be identified with different emotional states. Thus, the artist might use red as a *symbol* of passion or anger, yellow to suggest cowardice or warmth, and so forth (see "Color and Emotion," p. 158).

Student artist, *Owls*, c. 1980. Print (woodcut), 12 × 18 in (30 × 45.4 cm). When knives and gouges are used to cut the wood, the lines and textures created are usually somewhat different from those produced by another medium.

Bowling Green State University, Bowling Green, OH.

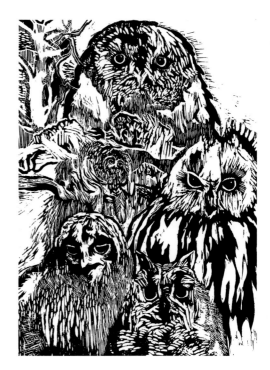

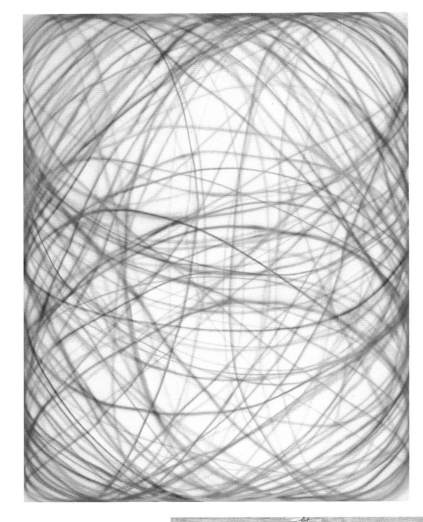

THE SPATIAL CHARACTERISTICS OF LINE

All the physical characteristics of line contain spatial properties that are subject to control by the artist. Mere position within a prescribed area suggests space. Value contrast can cause lines to advance and recede (fig. 3.21). An individual line with varied values throughout its length may appear to writhe and twist in space. Because warm colors generally advance and cool colors generally recede, the spatial properties of colored lines are obvious. Every factor that produces line has something to say about line's location in space. The artist's job is to use these factors to create spatial order (fig. 3.22).

▼ **3 · 22**

Maria da Silva, *The City*, 1951. Oil on canvas, 37¼ × 32¼ in (94.6 × 81.9 cm). The spatial illusion, of such obvious importance in this example, is largely the product of the physical properties of the lines strengthened by contrasting areas of value.

Toledo Museum of Art, Toledo, OH. Gift of Edward Drummond Libbey. © ADAGP, Paris and DACS, London 1994.

▲ **3 · 21**

Daniel Christensen, *GRUS*, 1968. Acrylic on canvas, 11 ft 3 in × 8 ft 3 in (3.12 × 2.51 m). Variations in the continuous curvilinear lines within this painting create illusions of open space. These variations include changes in the physical properties of the measure, direction, location, and character of the lines, as well as changes in value and color.

Hirshhorn Museum and Sculpture Garden, Smithsonian Institution, Washington, D.C. Gift of Joseph H. Hirshhorn. (Photograph by Lee Stalsworth.) © Daniel Christensen/DACS, London/VAGA, New York 1994.

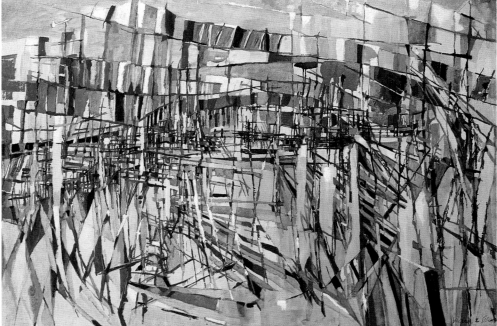

LINE AND REPRESENTATION

Line creates representation on both abstract and realistic levels. In general, we have dealt primarily with abstract definitions, but it is easy to see that the application can be observed equally in a realistic context. For example, we have discussed the advancing–receding qualities of value in a line. If a particular line is drawn to represent the contours of a piece of drapery, the value contrast, as it changes in measure and direction, might describe the relative spatial position of the folds of the drapery (fig. 3.23). An artist drawing a linear portrait of a person might use line properties to suggest a physical presence (fig. 3.24). The artist might also be able to convey – either satirically or sympathetically – much information about the character of the sitter. Thus, line in *representation* has many objective and subjective implications. All are the direct result of the artist's manipulation of the physical properties.

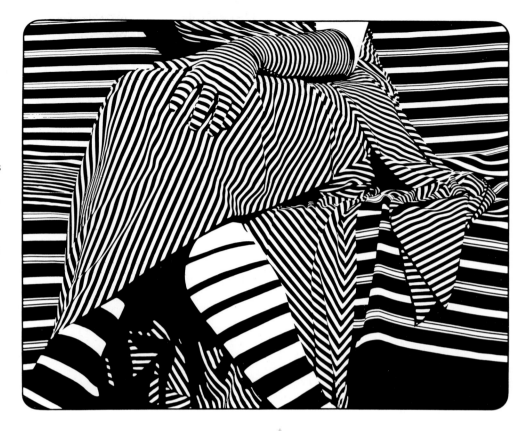

▲ 3 · 23

J. Seeley, *Stripe Song*, 1981. Print (photo silkscreen), 22 × 30 in (81.9 × 76.2 cm).
Seeley is an acknowledged master of the high-contrast image form. Combining the undeniable visual appeal of Op art with the implicit realism of the photographic image, the artist's black-and-white linear abstractions are boldly decorative, highly complex, and a delightful treat for the eye.
Courtesy of the artist. © J. M. Seeley/DACS, London/ VAGA, New York 1994.

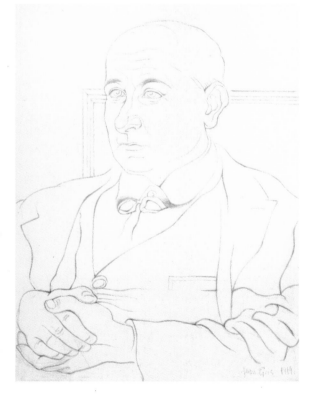

◀ 3 · 24

Juan Gris, *Max Jacob*, 1919. Pencil on paper, 14⅜ × 10½ in (36.5 × 26.7 cm).
This drawing, done entirely in line, provides information on the physical presence as well as the psychological character of the sitter.
The Museum of Modern Art, New York. Gift of James Thrall Soby.

▶ **3 · 25**

Giovanni Battista Tiepolo, Study for *Figure of Falsehood*, no date. Pen and brown ink, 6⅜ × 6 in (16.2 × 15.4 cm).
This gestural drawing clearly illustrates the dramatic action of the activity. Artists often try to sustain this effect beyond the initial stage of a sketch.
The Art Museum, Princeton University, NJ. Bequest of Dan Fellows Platt.

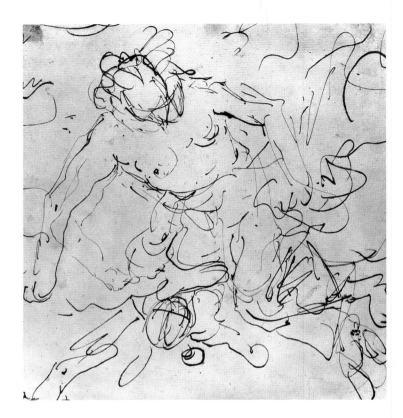

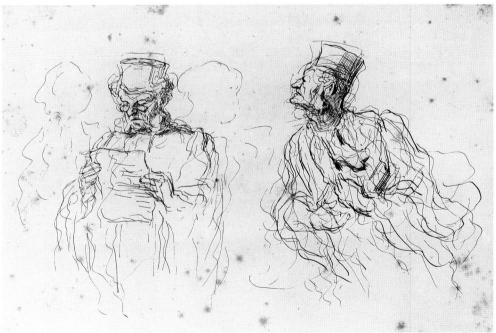

▲ **3 · 26**

Honoré Daumier, *Two Barristers* c. 1866 Pen and ink, 8 × 11⅜ in (20.5 × 29.5 cm).
Gesture relieves the static immobility of a subject, giving it liveliness and excitement.
Victoria and Albert Museum, London.

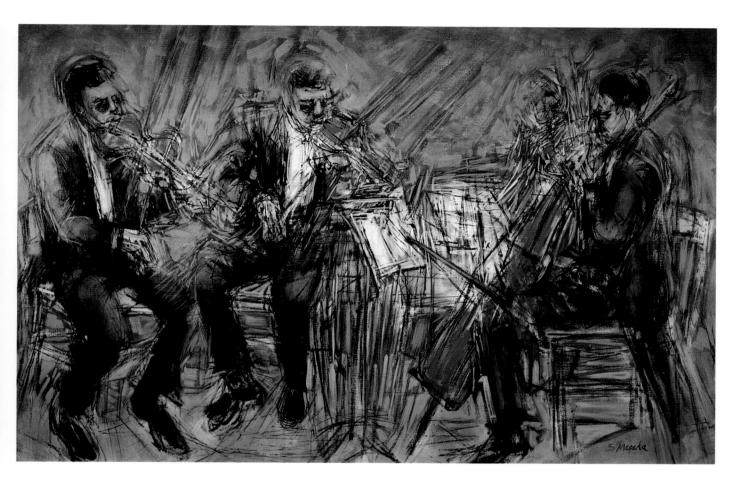

▲ 3 · 27

Steve Magada, *Trio*, c. 1966. Oil on canvas, size and present location unknown.
The gestural lines in this work successfully evoke the movements of the performers.

Photograph courtesy of Virginia Magada.

In its role of signifying ideas and conveying feelings, line moves and lives, pulsating with significant emotions. In visual art, line becomes a means for transcribing the expressive language of ideas and emotions. It describes the edges or contours of shapes, it diagrams silhouettes, it encompasses spaces and areas – all in such a way as to convey meaning.

Line is not used exclusively to express deep emotion and experience in this manner. Often, it depicts facts alone: an architect's plan for a building or an engineer's drawings of a bridge; the lines drawn on maps to represent rivers, roads, or contours; or the lines drawn on paper to represent words. Such use of line is primarily utilitarian, a convenient way of communicating ideas to another person. In addition to its ability to describe facts with precision, line can express action in a "gestural" sense. The gesture in graphic work implies the past, present, and future motion of the drawn subject. Gestural drawing in any medium displays lines that are drawn freely, quickly, and seemingly without inhibition. Many paintings are preceded by and based on the artist's initial gestural response (fig. 3.25). If preserved in the work this response captures the intrinsic spirit and animation seen in the subject. This spirit can pertain to both animate and inanimate subjects – a towel casually thrown over a chair has a unique "gesture" resulting from the way in which it falls, its weight and texture, and the surface it contacts. Obviously this gestural concept applies even more conspicuously to those subjects that are capable of movement (fig. 3.26).

Whichever the emphasis – expression of human emotions, depiction of action, or communication of factual information – line is an important element at the disposal of the artist (fig. 3.27).

CHAPTER FOUR

Shape

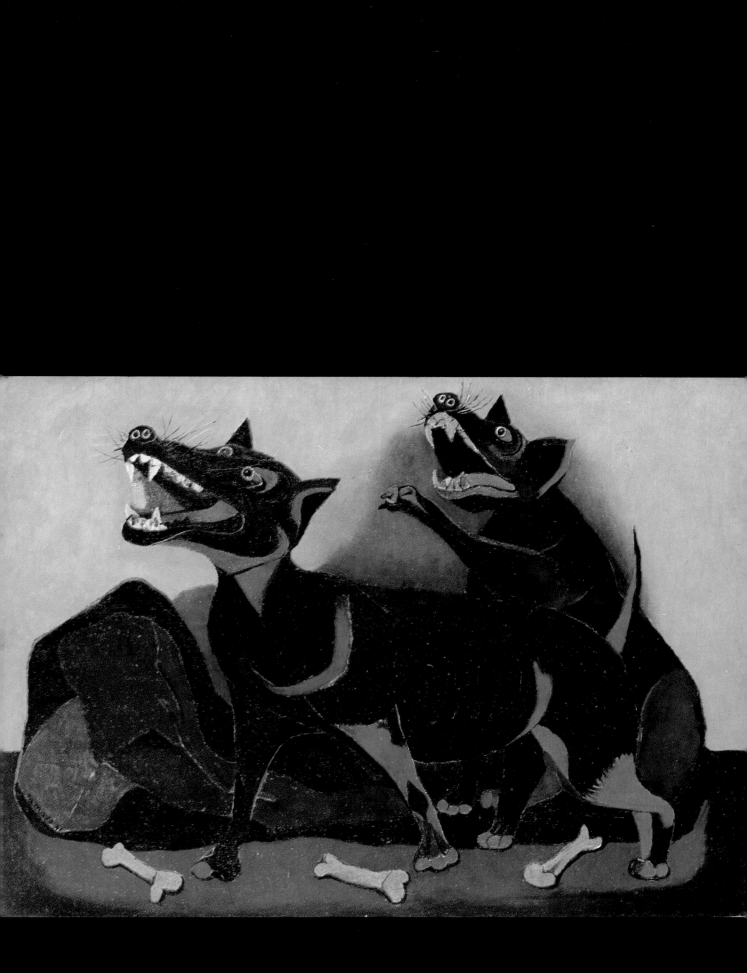

THE VOCABULARY OF SHAPE

Shape An area that stands out from the space next to or around it due to a defined or implied boundary, or because of differences of value, color, or texture.

actual shape
Clearly defined or positive areas (as opposed to an **implied shape**).

amorphous shape
A shape without clarity or definition: formless, indistinct, and of uncertain dimension.

biomorphic shape
Irregular shape that resembles the freely developed curves found in live organisms.

Cubism
The name given to the painting style invented by Pablo Picasso and Georges Braque between 1907 and 1912, which used multiple views of objects to create the effect of their three-dimensionality, while acknowledging the two-dimensional surface of the picture plane. Signalling the beginning of abstract art, it is a semi-abstract style that continued the strong trend away from representational art initiated primarily by Cézanne in the late 1800s.

decorative (shape)
Ornamenting or enriching but, more importantly in art, stressing the two-dimensional nature of an artwork or any of its elements (shape). Decorative art emphasizes the essential flatness of a surface.

geometric shape
A shape that appears related to geometry. Geometric shapes are usually simple, such as triangles, rectangles, and circles.

Gestalt, Gestalt psychology
A German word for "form." Defined as an organized whole in experience. Around 1912 the *Gestalt* psychologists promoted the theory which explains psychological

phenomena by their relationships to total forms, or *Gestalten*, rather than their parts.

implied shape
A shape suggested or created by the psychological connection of dots, lines, areas, or their edges, creating the visual appearance of a shape that does not physically exist. (See **Gestalt**.)

kinetic art
Art that involves an element of random or mechanical movement.

mass
1. In graphic art, a shape that appears to stand out three-dimensionally from the space surrounding it, or appears to create the illusion of a solid body of material.
2. In the plastic arts, the physical bulk of a solid body of material. (See **plastic**, **three-dimensional**, and **volume**.)

objective (shape)
That which is based, as near as possible, on physical actuality or optical perception. Such art tends to appear natural or real.

perspective
Any graphic system used to create the illusion of three-dimensional images and/or spatial relationships on a two-dimensional surface. There are several types of perspective: see atmospheric, linear, and projection systems in Chapter 8.

planar (shape)
Having to do with planes.

plane
1. An area that is essentially two-dimensional, having height and width.
2. A flat or level surface. 3. A two-dimensional surface which extends in a three-dimensional spatial direction.

plastic (shape)
1. The use of the elements (shape) to create the illusion of the third dimension on a two-dimensional surface. 2. Describing three-dimensional art forms such as architecture, sculpture, ceramics, etc. (See **mass**, **three-dimensional**, and **volume**.)

rectilinear shape
A shape whose boundaries usually consist entirely of straight lines.

subjective (shape)
1. That which is derived from the mind and reflects an individual viewpoint or bias. 2. Art that is subjective tends to be inventive or creative.

Surrealism
A style of artistic expression, influenced by Freudian psychology, which emphasizes fantasy and whose subjects are usually experiences revealed by the subconscious mind through the use of automatic techniques (rubbings, doodles, blots, cloud patterns etc.). Originally a literary movement and an outgrowth of Dadaism, Surrealism was established by a literary manifesto written in 1924.

three-dimensional (shape)
To possess or to have the illusion of possessing the dimension of depth as well as the dimensions of height and width.

two-dimensional (shape)
To possess the dimensions of height and width, especially in regard to the flat surface or picture plane.

volume
A measurable area of defined or occupied space. (See **mass**, **plastic**, and **three-dimensional**.)

INTRODUCTION TO SHAPE

Shapes are the building-blocks of art structure. Edifices of brick, stone, and mortar are intended by the architect and mason to have beauty of design, skilled craftsmanship, and structural strength. The artist shares these same goals in creating a picture. Bricks and stones, however, are tangible objects, whereas pictorial shapes exist largely in terms of the illusions they create. The challenge facing the artist is to use the infinitely varied illusions of *shape* to make believable the fantasy inherent in all art. In other words, an artwork is never the real thing, and the shapes producing the image are never real animals, buildings, people – the artist's subjects, if indeed the artist uses subjects at all. The artist might be stimulated by such objects and, in many cases, might reproduce the objects' basic appearances fairly closely. The alterations of surface appearance required to achieve compositional unity may result in a semifantasy (fig. 4.1). On the other hand, the artist may use shapes that are not intended to represent anything at all, or that, even though representational at the outset, may eventually lead to a final work in which copied appearances are almost eliminated. This could be called pure fantasy, because the final image is entirely the product of the artist's imagination. Capable artists, whatever degree of fantasy they employ, are able to convince us that the fantasy is a possible reality. Any successful work of art,

regardless of medium, leads the sensitive observer into a persuasive world of the imagination. In the visual arts, shapes play an important part in achieving this goal.

THE DEFINITION OF SHAPE

We can begin to define shape in art as a line enclosing an area. Such use of line is called outline or contour. However, even when we have only a few elements of form to go by, as illustrated in figure 4.2, our minds adjust to read a visible effect of shape. Apparently, we have an instinctive need for order that enables our minds to fill in the parts that have been left out. This is the principle first put forward by the German *Gestalt* psychologists, during their exploration into human perception in the early twentieth century. They stated that our minds tend to "see" organized wholes, or forms, as a totality (*Gestalt* is the German word for "form"), before they perceive the individual parts. Applied to human visual perception, our minds also tend to insist on creating shapes from approximately related elements such as the four dots perceived as a square. Thus we read the diagrams in figure 4.2 as shapes, even though no contours have been drawn to connect the dots, or around the tips of the lines forming the triangle. The last drawing, in which gaps and dashes are mentally filled in to form a circle, comes closest to illustrating our first definition of a shape as being a line enclosing an area. But the

◁ **4 · 1 (page 85)**
Rufino Tamayo, *Animals*, 1941. Oil on canvas, 30⅛ × 40 in (76.5 × 101.6 cm).
Tamayo has created an air of fantasy by using semiabstract shapes to picture beasts, which are animal-like in general appearance but of no particular species. The stark shapes emphasize the savagery of the environment.
The Museum of Modern Art, New York. Inter-American Fund.

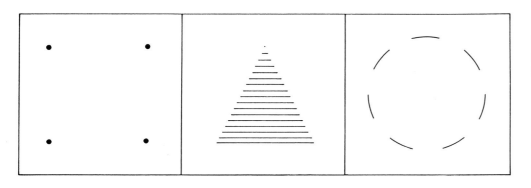

◁ **4 · 2**
The spectator automatically infers fully drawn shapes from those suggested by the dots and lines.

Gestalt theory causes us to question our first definition, since closure is not always an absolutely necessary condition for forming a shape.

There are other definitions of what we call shape which may round out our understanding of this element. Among these are: any visually perceived area of value, texture, color, or line – or any combination of these elements. In pictorial forms of art, shapes are flat, or two-dimensional. In the three-dimensional forms of art (sculpture, architecture, environmental design, and so on), shapes are more often described as solids, or masses. Three-dimensional artists quite often do their initial planning using graphic means; they must therefore be aware that the surface on which they work, the picture plane, is itself a shape. The picture plane conditions the use and characteristics of all shapes and other elements on it, as was already discussed at greater length in Chapter 2.

Shapes in pictorial art sometimes have exact limits, as in the case of geometric shapes, or they may be implied, as illustrated by the preceding diagrams. Or they may be *amorphous* – that is, so vague or delicate that their edges cannot be determined with any degree of exactitude (fig. 4.3). Shapes in the *plastic* arts, however, are more defined, due to the very nature of the materials out of which they are created. Their edges, or outer contours, are the determining factor, no matter what their degree of irregularity or ambiguity (fig. 4.4).

Shapes can vary endlessly, ranging in type from *objective*, *geometric*, and implied to amorphous. They may differ in size, position, balance, color, value, and texture according to the function they need to fulfill in the work of art. Shapes also can be static, stable, active, lively, and seem to contract or expand, depending on how they are used by the artist.

There are different names for categories or families of shape depending on whether they are imaginary (*subjective*) or derived from observable phenomena (objective). The configuration of a shape gives it a character that distinguishes it from others. When the shapes used by an artist imitate those formed by natural forces (stones, puddles, leaves, clouds) they are called by various terms, besides

▼ **4·3**

Claude Monet, *Water Lilies*, 1919–26. Oil on canvas, 6 ft 6¾ in × 13 ft 11¾ in (2 × 4.26 m).

Had he so chosen, Monet could have painted a more distinct version of the lilies in the water, but he was much more interested in the effect of shimmering light on color relationships – hence the misty, amorphous nature of the shapes.

Saint Louis Art Museum, St Louis, MO. Gift of the Steinberg Charitable Fund.

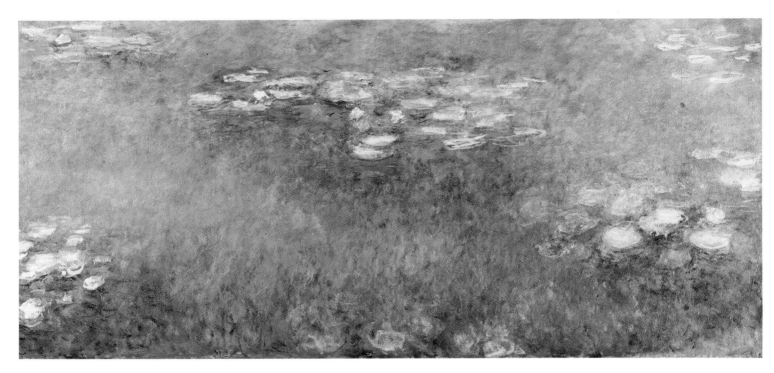

objective, depending on the context of their use. Some of these are naturalistic, representational, and/or realistic. When they seem to have been contrived by the artist, they are also given various names, in addition to abstract. Among these are the terms *nonrepresentational* and *nonobjective*. The distinction between these opposed shape families is not always easily made, because the variations of both are so vast. Hence, several specific terms have been evolved to try and explain these differences.

Natural objects generally seem rounded. We see this in the fundamental organisms encountered in biological studies (such as amoebas, viruses, and cells). Such shapes are normally referred to as organic, but due to the fact that organic shapes are often curved the term *biomorphic* was coined in early twentieth-century art to describe the *curvilinear* shapes in art that suggest life (fig. 4.5; see figs. 10.73 and 10.77).

With the great interest aroused by abstract art (from around 1910 on), the

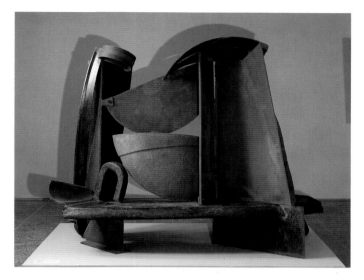

4·4

Anthony Caro, *Odalisque*, 1984. Steel, 6 ft 5 in × 8 ft 1 in × 5 ft 4 in (1.96 × 2.46 × 1.63 m)

Despite the irregularity and complexity of the contours, lighting, and color of these sculptural shapes, the edges of contours read more clearly than is often the case in the graphic arts.

Metropolitan Museum of Art, New York. Gift of GFI/ Knoll International Foundation, 1984. 328a–d.

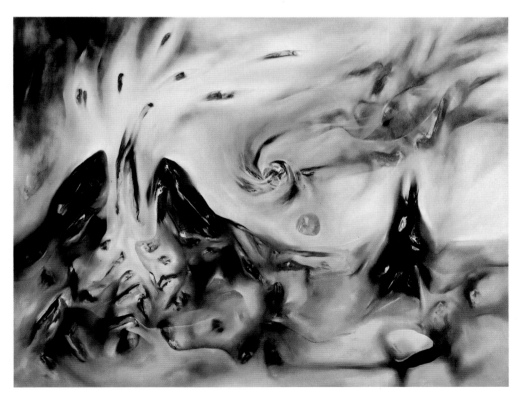

4·5

Roberto Matta, *Listen to Living (Écoutez vivre)*, 1941. Oil on canvas, 29½ × 37⅜ in (74.9 × 94.9 cm).

Within the limits of the human mind's ability to conceive such things, Matta has given us a vision of a completely alien milieu. Though as far as imaginable from everyday reality, this environment seems possible, thanks to the facility of the artist. The blending of shapes gradually makes them indistinct and no longer measurable; their softened, flowing character means that separate components merge and interlock, becoming one.

The Museum of Modern Art, New York. Inter-American Fund. © ADAGP, Paris and DACS, London 1994.

▶ **4 · 6**

Yves Tanguy, *Mama, Papa is Wounded!* 1927. Oil on canvas, 36¼ × 28¾ in (92.1 × 73 cm).

Surrealists such as Yves Tanguy have given considerable symbolic significance to biomorphic shapes. These remind us of basic organic matter or of flowing and changing shapes in dreams.

The Museum of Modern Art, New York. Purchase. © DACS 1994.

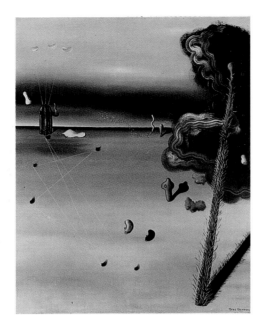

increasing awareness of the microscopic world through science, and the growth of Freudian psychology, the biomorphic shape became a key component in the paintings of *Surrealist* artists. Their interests in the mystic origins of being and in the exploration of subconscious revelations, such as in dreams, attracted them strongly to organic or biomorphic shapes (fig. 4.6). Other artists (Matisse and Braque are examples) abstracted organic forms in a less symbolic and primarily decorative manner (fig. 4.7; see fig. 4.17A).

In contrast to biomorphic shapes are *rectilinear* (straight-lined) shapes, called geometric because they are based on the standardized shapes used in mathematics. The precisionist, machinelike geometric shapes appealed to the *Cubists*, who used them in their analytical dissection and reformulation of the natural world (fig. 4.8).

From these examples, it is clear that, however shapes are classified, each shape or combination of shapes can display a particular personality according to their physical employment and our responses to them.

▽ **4 · 7**

Henri Matisse, *The Blue Window*, 1911. Oil on canvas, 51½ × 35⅝ in (130.8 × 90.5 cm).

Matisse has abstracted organic forms for the purpose of decorative organization.

The Museum of Modern Art, New York. Abby Aldrich Rockefeller Fund. © Succession H. Matisse/DACS 1994.

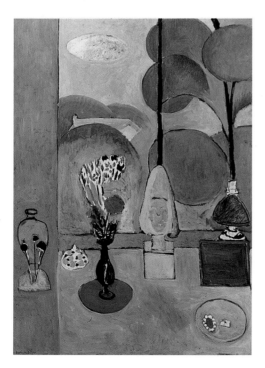

▶ **4 · 8**

Juan Gris, *Breakfast*, 1914. Pasted paper, crayon, and oil on canvas, 31⅞ × 23½ in (81 × 59.7 cm).

Gris, an example of a later Cubist, not only simplified shape into larger, more dominant areas, but gave each shape a characteristic value, producing a carefully conceived light-dark pattern. He also made use of open composition, in which the value moves from one shape into the adjoining shape, as can be seen in this example.

The Museum of Modern Art, New York. Acquired through the Lillie P. Bliss Bequest.

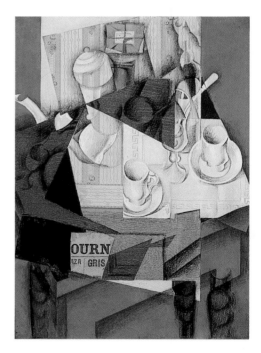

THE USE OF SHAPES

Shapes are used by artists for the two fundamental purposes mentioned in the preceding paragraphs: to suggest a physical form they have seen or imagined, and to give certain visual qualities or content to a work of art.

Shapes in art can be used for some of the following purposes:

1. To achieve order, harmony, and variety – all related to the principles of design discussed in Chapter 3.
2. To create the illusion of mass, volume, and space on the surface of the picture plane.
3. To extend observer attention or interest span.

The last usage listed requires further clarification. Where the arts of music, theater, and dance evolve in time, the visual arts are usually chronologically fixed. This means that the time of an observer's concentration on or mental unity with most works of art is extremely limited. This is particularly true in the pictorial or graphic arts. It is not quite so true with one type of plastic art, *kinetic* forms. *Mobiles*, for example, are a form of sculpture in motion; their constantly changing relationships of shapes usually hold the viewer's attention longer than immobile forms of sculpture or pictorial art.

Shape dimensions

In the preceding parts of this chapter we defined shapes as having either two- or three-dimensional identities. In order to use shape(s) successfully in works of art we must further consider these dimensional aspects. Some people, for example, make a distinction between shape that is *two-dimensional* and shape that is *three-dimensional* (referred to as *mass* and/or *volume*), and consider them to be two separate elements. However, the authors have always considered shape, whether two-dimensional or three-

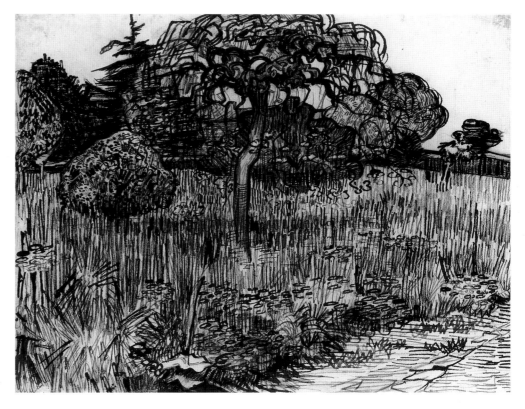

▲ **4·9**

Vincent van Gogh, *Corner of a Park at Arles (Tree in a Meadow)*, 1889. Red and black ink over charcoal, 19⅜ × 24 in (49.3 × 61 cm).

Planar shapes are used to simplify the intricacies of the large centrally located tree. A large oval shape can be superimposed over the outer limits of the foliage, while the inner groups can be seen as smaller organic planes.

Art Institute of Chicago. Gift of Tiffany and Margaret Blake 1945.31. (Photograph courtesy of the Art Institute of Chicago.)

dimensional, to be one element of form. For increased familiarity with the way in which the term "shape" is used in this context, more about shape dimension follows.

The illusions of two-dimensional shapes

Foremost among shapes and probably the most useful is the two-dimensional *plane*. As was noted, in pictorial artworks the flat surface on which artists work is called the picture plane. In addition to being a working surface, a *planar* shape is often used as a device to simplify vastness and intricacies in nature. In sketching trees, for example, an artist will utilize a large, simple planar shape to represent the overall image of the tree. Further, individual clumps of foliage often are shown by a number of smaller varied shapes (fig. 4.9). This use of the plane creates more economical, stable, and readily ordered units, which are useful to the artist not only for preliminary sketches but for finalizing the

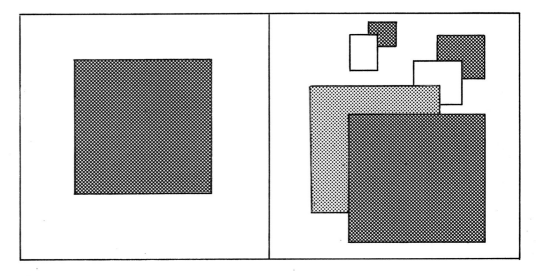

▲ **4 · 10**
Rectilinear planes can suggest the illusion of
depth in a number of ways.

▶ **4 · 1 1 A–D**

The diagrams illustrate how differently shaped
and positioned planes can create illusions of
depth: (A) Curvilinear or circular planes
overlapped to suggest shallow space; (B)
Curvilinear planes placed on edge and tilted to
suggest an effect of greater depth – note how
the circles become elliptical in shape; (C)
Straight-edged or rectilinear planes positioned so
that they float in deep space (see fig. 4.10 for a
shallower effect); (D) Irregular shapes creating a
sense of depth.

   In diagrams B, C, and D, the illusion of depth
is accentuated by thickening the nearest edges of
the planes. Variations of value, size, texture, and
color would further enhance or diminish the
illusion of depth.

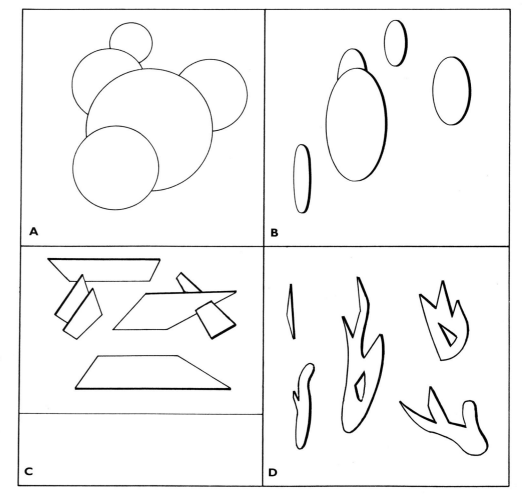

organization of his or her work. Beyond this, planes are extremely useful in creating the illusion of three-dimensionality on the two-dimensional picture plane, whether or not they have the appearance of objects or are abstract.

The use of the plane varies from a flat or *decorative* appearance on a picture plane, to one or more that appear to occupy space. Artists use all kinds of shapes, from geometric to organic, to achieve both these effects. A rectilinear shape – that is, a geometric shape whose boundaries consist of straight lines – might appear flat when lying on the surface of the picture plane, but even a simple overlapping of two or more rectilinear shapes can give them a sense of plasticity or depth. The addition of size, color, value, and texture contrasts to these planes can establish an impression of depth even more definitively (fig. 4.10).

Curvilinear planes, those planar shapes made up of circles, ovals, or irregular organic attributes, can also create shallow effects of space or, through their curving nature, suggest movements into depth. When either curvilinear, rectilinear, or other irregular planes are given a foreshortened appearance by tilting them and making the near end look larger than the distant one, we have a much stronger visual statement of depth than in the decorative use of planes (figs. 4.11A–D).

The illusions of three-dimensional shapes

When the term mass is used to describe three-dimensional shapes in the picture plane, we mean that they have the appearance of solid bodies. If a three-dimensional shape is a void or an area of definable containment it occupies a certain amount of measurable space, and is called a volume. Rocks and mountains are masses, while holes and valleys are volumes; cups are masses, while the areas they contain are volumes (figs. 4.12A and B). When beginning to develop three-dimensional shapes, we should select the kind(s) of shape(s) we wish to portray –

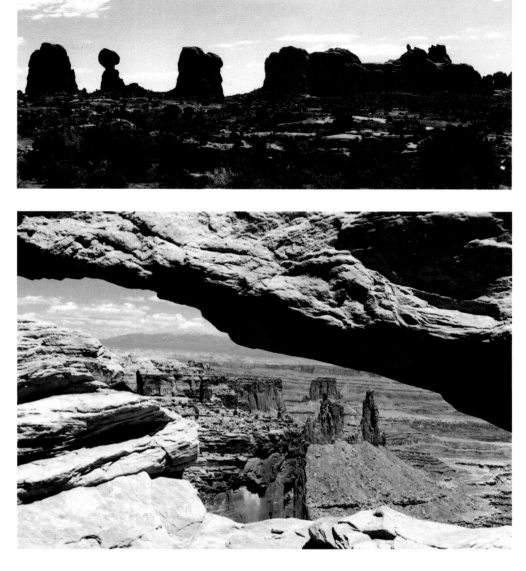

▲　**4 · 12A and B**
Masses and volumes: Arches and Canyonlands National Parks, Utah.

In figure 4.12A, mountainous rock formations and their valleys represent mass and volumes. Figure 4.12B illustrates a close-up view of a gigantic rock formation (mass) with an enormous hole (volume).

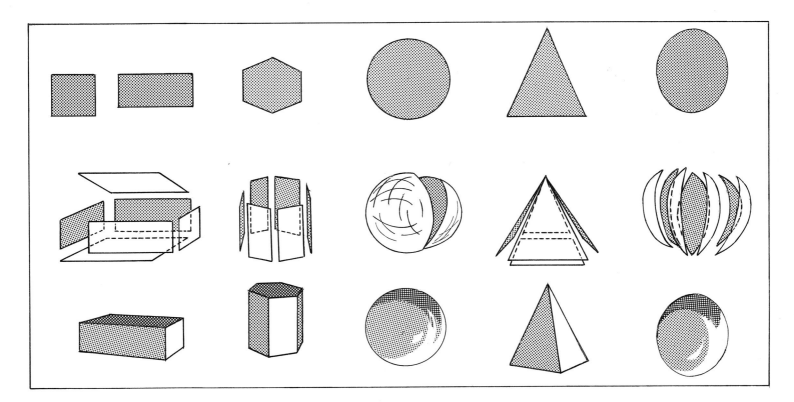

▲ **4·13**

Planes and their three-dimensional equivalents.

geometric, organic, or irregular – just as we did in working with their two-dimensional counterparts. Since geometric shapes, such as the square/rectangle, are the most basic two-dimensional shapes, let us look at the development or transformation into their three-dimensional equivalents – the cube/rectangular solid.

The illusion of rectilinear masses or volumes on the picture plane is produced by arranging two or more planes in relation to one another to give them an appearance of solidity, as shown in figure 4.13. The planes that constitute the sides of these illusionary three-dimensional objects could be detached from the parent mass and tilted back at any angle. In fact, such planes do not have to be closed or joined at the corners in order to afford an appearance of solidity –the *Gestalt* effect again. As we can see in this diagram, there is no limit to the number of shapes than can be shown in three dimensions – the rectangular solid is probably the simplest. Spheres, pyramids, hexagonal and ovoidal solids all have their

counterparts in planar shapes, such as circles, triangles, hexagons, and ovoids.

The illusionary effect of juxtaposing the planes without connecting them makes the arrangement of planes seem less substantial than the mass, but it shows the development of the planes more clearly and is more flexible in the pictorial exploration of volume and space. Presenting the planes in this way highlights the importance of the edges' functions as the planes combine to form the illusion of mass and its depth. In figure 4.14A, the diagram shows planes which have parallel-angled edges. They establish a directional movement (usually away from a central location – an edge/corner). This combination of planes seems to provide solidity, whereas any plane on its own would appear relatively flat.

In the next example of a mass, figure 4.14B, the planes appear to tilt or tip. The planes take on an added feeling of dimension – depth illusion – as they appear to recede away from the spectator. These planes are the converging sides of the mass. When several converging planes are juxtaposed and touching, the spatial illusion of mass and depth is greater than that provided by the use of parallel-edged planes. This is because the illusion of the converging planes receding in depth more closely relates to our optical perception. Under normal conditions one may expect the size of the planes to appear to diminish as they move away from the viewer. However, the use of planes with converging sides is not limited to that concept and interesting qualities of depth occur when the traditional application is reversed as in figure 4.14C. This application of converging edges advancing may appear to exaggerate and distort shape definitions and impart some decorative qualities to the image; however, the individual planes in isolation remain relatively plastic.

Review figures 4.13 to 4.14C and you will find examples of three-dimensional shapes that have planes with parallel, advancing, and receding converging edges. Artists enjoy the freedom of creating imaginative shapes in three dimensions unencumbered by the restrictions of formulae and mechanical processes. Ron Davis in his painting *Parallelepiped Vents #545* employs flat planes, shapes with parallel edges, shapes with converging edges receding, and shapes with converging edges advancing (fig. 4.15). Al Held creatively employs the same types of shape-edge development in his painting *B/WX* (see fig. 8.44).

The creation of three-dimensional shapes and their depth through the use of converging edges (receding and/or advancing) preceded the development of

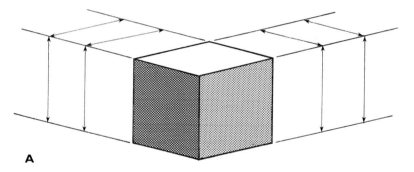

A

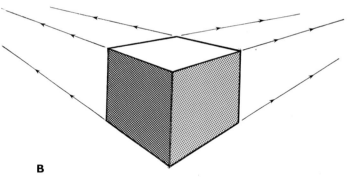

B

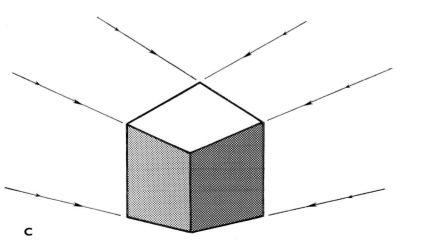

C

4 · 14A

A combination of planes which show parallel edges in depth creates the illusion of mass (shape).

4 · 14B

A combination of planes which show converging edges in depth (moving *away* from the viewer) creates the illusion of mass (shape).

4 · 14C

A combination of planes which show edges converging *toward* the viewer creates the illusion of mass (shape). (This is the reverse effect of the shape in figure 4.14B.)

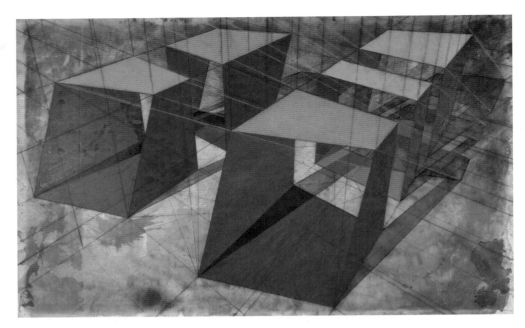

▲ **4·15**
**Ronald Davis, *Parallelepiped Vents #545*,
1977. Acrylic on canvas, 9 ft 6 in × 15 ft
(2.90 × 4.57 m).**
While the strict order of linear perspective is
not observed here, a sense of space is achieved
by other means under the control of the artist's
instincts.
Los Angeles County Museum of Art, CA. Gift of the Eli
and Edythe Broad Fund.

linear perspective but is closely related to
it. Because of linear perspective's
importance to the creation of space it will
be developed in Chapter 8, "Space." The
parallel-edge shape concepts which have
been presented are closely related to the
system of *perspective* used in mechanical
drawings. Within this chapter we are
primarily concerned with the illusions of
shape and depth created by graphic artists.
Other artists employ actual three-
dimensional shapes in their art, but this is
more appropriately discussed in Chapter 9,
"The Art of the Third Dimension."

Shape and principles of design

If artists wish to create order or unity and
increase attention span, they have to
conform to certain principles of order or
design. In observing these principles, they
are often forced to alter shapes from their
natural appearance. It is in this respect
that shapes can be called the building
blocks of art structure. Just as in the case
of line, our first element of artistic form,
shapes have multiple purposes in terms of
visual manipulation and psychological or
emotional effects. These purposes, as
suggested, vary depending on the artist
and the viewer.

The principles determining the
ordering of shapes are common to the
other elements of form. In their search for
significant order and expression, artists
modify the elements until:

1. The desired degree and type of balance
   is achieved.
2. The observer's attention is controlled,
   both in terms of direction and
   duration.
3. The appropriate ratio of harmony and
   variety results.
4. The space concept achieves consistency
   throughout.

While space is a result of the use of the
elements, and harmony and variety have
already been discussed (pp. 36–42), the
concepts of balance, direction, and
duration, as they regard shape, are
important enough to warrant additional
investigation.

Balance

As artists seek compositional balance, they
work with the knowledge that shapes
have different visual weights depending
on how they are used. Although this
principle of form organization was treated
at some length in Chapter 2, it may be
helpful to reexamine balance in particular
regard to shape by reusing the example of
the seesaw, or weighing scale, as depicted
in figure 2.27. We see that placing shapes
of different sizes at varying distances from
the fulcrum can be controlled to create a
sense of balance or imbalance. Since no
actual weight is involved, we assume that
the sensation is intuitive, or felt, as a
result of the various properties composing
the art elements. For example, a dark
value adds weight to a shape, while
substituting a narrow line for a wider line
around it reduces the shape's apparent
weight.

The seesaw is an example of how a few
basic elements can operate along only one
plane of action. Developed artworks, on
the other hand, contain many diverse
elements working in many directions. The
factors that control the amounts of

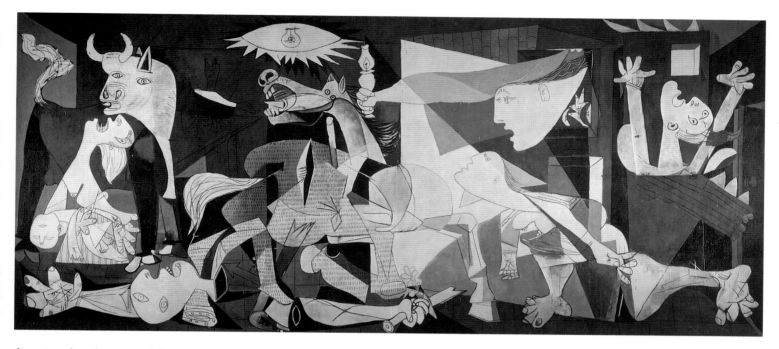

directional and tensional force generated by the various elements are: placement, size, accents or emphasis, and general shape character (including associative equivalents to be discussed under "Duration and Relative Dominance," p. 99). The elements are manipulated by the artist until the energy of their relationships results in dynamic tension.

Control of attention

Direction   Artists can use the elements of form to generate visual forces that will control the movement of our eyes as we view their work. Pathways are devised to provide transition from one pictorial area to another. Artists may help to control the movement of our eyes along these pathways by providing longer shapes pointing in certain directions (shorter shapes have the opposite effect of breaking up visual pathways). Artists may extend the edges so that they link up with the edges of other shapes, or imply by the direction of the edges a related movement in a certain direction (figs. 4.16A and B). A third method is the use of *intuitive space* (see Chapter 8, p. 194) or implied perspective given to shapes, which tip them into the picture plane and direct our

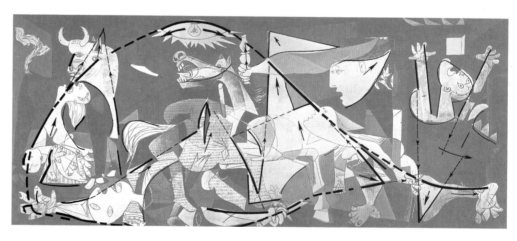

▲   **4 · 16A and B**

Pablo Picasso, *Guernica*, 1937. Oil on canvas, 11 ft 5½ in × 25 ft 5¼ in (3.49 × 7.75 m).
The linear diagram (B) overlaying Picasso's *Guernica* is one of several possible interpretations of the way shape is used as a directional device. The arrows in the middle of shapes indicate their major directional "thrust." The thick solid lines show the edges where a felt direction seems to line up with a corresponding shape edge across a space (indicated by broken lines). These create the major shape directions in the overall composition. Secondary shapes, related in a similar way, are shown by middleweight lines. The lighter lines show curving shape edges counteracting the straighter and more broadly arced edges of the design.
Museo del Prado, Madrid, Spain. © DACS 1994.

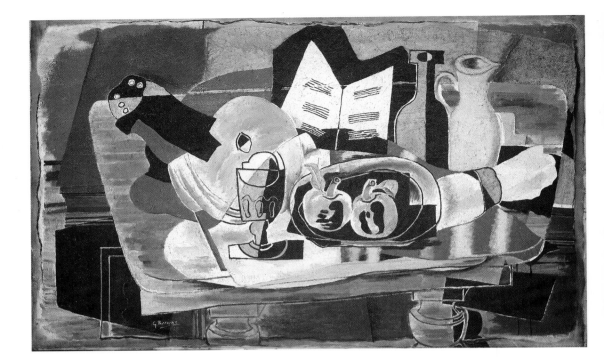

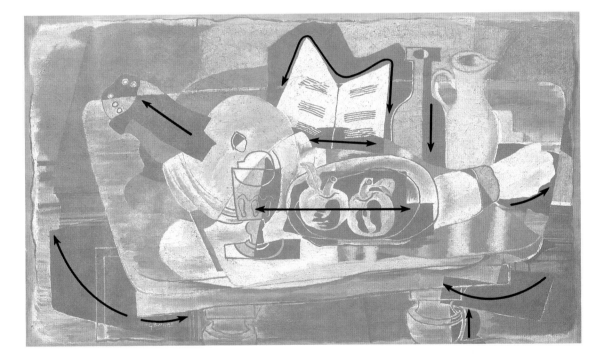

△ **4 · 17A and B**

Georges Braque, *Still Life: The Table*, 1928. Oil on canvas, 32 × 51½ in (81.3 × 130.8 cm). This painting by the French Cubist Georges Braque has many elements that contain direction of force. The simplified grouping of darks in figure 4.17A illustrates the controlled tension resulting from the placement, size, accent, and general character of the shapes used by the artist. In figure 4.17B the black arrows show the natural eye paths by which the artist intended to create visual transition and rhythmic movement.

eyes along their three-dimensional spatial pathways. The latter can be observed in figures 4.11 B, C, and D. The artist usually tries to make the movements along these eye paths rhythmic, thereby providing both pleasurable viewing and a strong unifying factor for the work. The character of rhythmic viewing depends upon the nature of the artist's expressive intentions – jerky, sinuous, swift, or slow (figs. 4.17A and B).

Duration and relative dominance The unifying and rhythmic effects provided by eye paths are also modified by the number and length of the pauses in the eye journey. A viewing experience is relatively more monotonous if the planned pauses are of equal duration. The artist, therefore, attempts to organize pauses so that their lengths are related to the importance of the sights to be seen on the eye journey (fig. 4.18). The duration of a pause is determined by the pictorial importance of the area. A number of factors can control duration. In a work depicting the Crucifixion, for example, we would expect an artist to make the figure of Christ

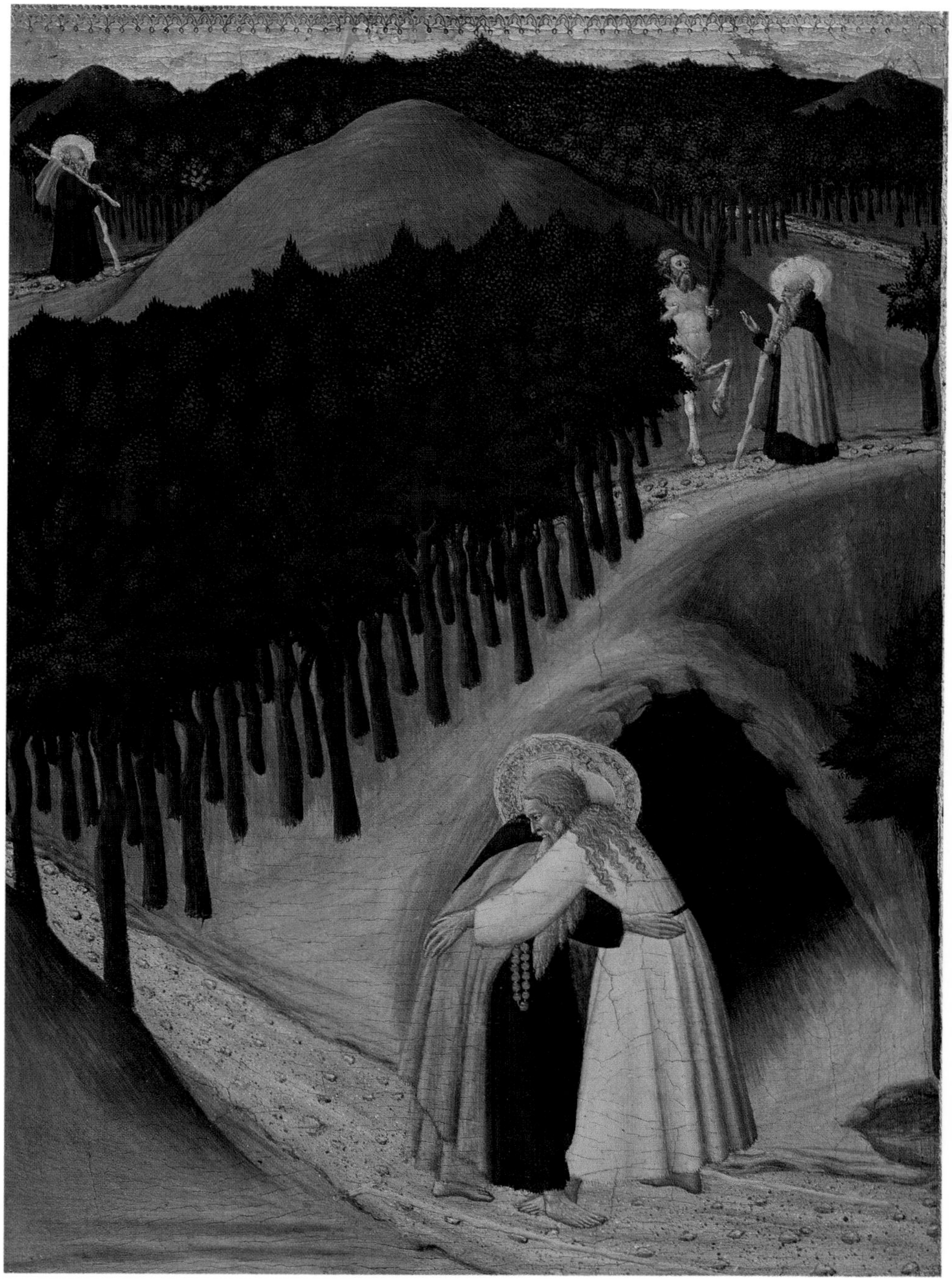

▶ **4·18**

Sassetta, workshop of, *The Meeting of Saint Anthony and Saint Paul*, c. 1440. Tempera on panel, 18¾ × 13⅝ in (47.6 × 34.6 cm).

In this painting by the Italian artist Sassetta, "station stops" of varied duration are indicated by contrasts of value. In addition, eye paths are provided by the edges of the natural forms that lead from figure to figure. This painting also illustrates how late-Gothic artists used shallow space in compositions prior to the full development of perspective.

Samuel H. Kress Collection. (© 1993 National Gallery of Art, Washington, D.C.)

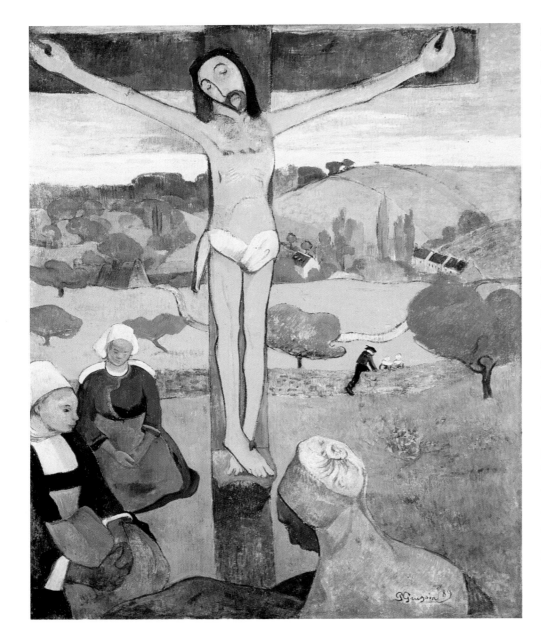

▲ 4·19

Paul Gauguin, *The Yellow Christ*, 1889. Oil on canvas, 36¼ × 28⅞ in (92.1 × 73.3 cm). Gauguin has made the figure of Christ paramount through size, location, shape, and color differences.

Albright-Knox Art Gallery, Buffalo, NY. General purchase funds, 1946.

dominant (fig. 4.19). Artists can control dominance through contrast, size, value, shape, location, color, or any combinations of these. Modification of the physical properties of any of the elements invariably affects spectator attention. Artists develop dominance in a work on the basis of their feelings and they reconcile the various demands of the design principles with those of relative dominance. The degree of dominance is usually in direct proportion to the amount of visual contrast. Relative dominance acts the same way in both

representational and abstract works (see figs. 4.19 and 4.20). The factor of size, for example, makes the body of Christ the dominant feature of figure 4.19, and is also the key factor in making the purple-eyed sphere dominant in figure 4.20. There is, however, another aspect – association, or similarity – that tends to qualify the attention given to shapes or other elements. The oval tree shapes in Gauguin's *The Yellow Christ*, for instance, afford a contrast to Christ's Y-shape that is more dominant than size (see fig. 4.19). In an abstract work of art, an oval shape may well receive more attention if for some reason it reminds us of a head. Although artists may try to avoid such chance interpretations, they cannot always be foreseen. At other times artists can use the innate appeal of associative factors to advantage, weighing them in the balance of relative dominance and forcing them to operate for the benefit of the total organization.

SHAPE AND CONTENT

Whereas the physical effects created by artists are relatively easily defined, the qualities of expression, or character, provided by shapes in a work of art are so varied (due to individual responses) that only a few of the possibilities can be suggested. In some cases, our responses to shapes are quite commonplace; in others, our reactions are much more complex since our own personality traits can show the shapes' character: shyness, aggressiveness, awkwardness, poise, and so forth. These are just some of the meanings or content we can find in shapes. Artists, naturally, make use of such shape qualities in developing their works of art, although much of it is instinctive.

It is hardly conceivable that an architect would use shapes in buildings to suggest natural forms. It has been done during art history, but very rarely. On the other hand, sculptors and pictorial artists have almost always used natural forms in their respective media. Yet the evidence indicates that they were not always interested in using shapes to represent known objects. Artists more often tend to present what they conceive or imagine to be real, rather than what they perceive, or see objectively, to be real. This has been particularly evident in the twentieth century, when whole movements have been based on the nonrepresentational use of shapes – from the abstract movement of the early 1900s to the conceptual movement of the seventies and eighties.

Thus, conception and imagination have always been parts of artistic expression. It is usually a matter of degree as to how much artists use their imagination, and how much their perceptual vision; in trying to say something through their use of subject and form, artists find that their points cannot be made without editing the elements (or "grammar") of form/ expression. So while the work of those artists who are more devoted to representing actual appearances might seem to be quite natural, comparison with the original subject in nature may still show considerable disparities (figs. 4.21 and 4.22). Artists, therefore, go beyond literal copying and transform object

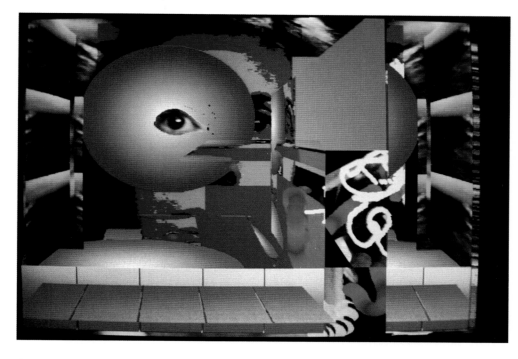

4 · 20
Ronald Coleman, *Supervisory Wife II*, 1992. Computer-aided art.
The principle of relative dominance is generated in this computer print by the large size, contrasting purple color, and the mysterious eye that peers out of the sphere. Further attention is drawn to this spherical shape by the converging front lines and side shapes that are directed to it.
Courtesy of the artist.

4 · 22
Conrad Marca-Relli, *The Picador*, 1956. Oil and fabric collage on canvas, 3 ft 11¼ in × 4 ft 5 in (1.20 × 1.35 m).
Artists differ in their responses to subject matter. It is often a matter of degree as to how much artists use their imaginations and how much their visual perceptions vary. Such differences of response, and the concepts that result, are apparent if one contrasts the similar subjects of figures 4.21 and 4.22.
Hirshhorn Museum and Sculpture Garden, Smithsonian Institution, Washington, D.C. Gift of Joseph H. Hirshhorn, 1966. (Photograph by Lee Stalsworth.)

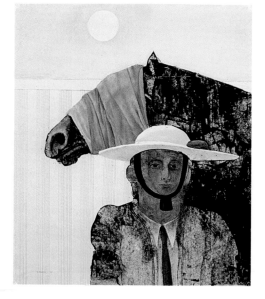

4 · 21
Morris Broderson, *Picador with Horse*, 1967. Mixed media, 33 × 26 in (83.8 × 66 cm).
While it is a straightforward exercise to recognize the subjects in this painting, this should only be a starting-point for getting to grips with the meaning of this ambiguous, symbolic work.
Courtesy of the Anterum Gallery, Los Angeles, CA.

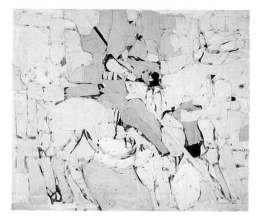

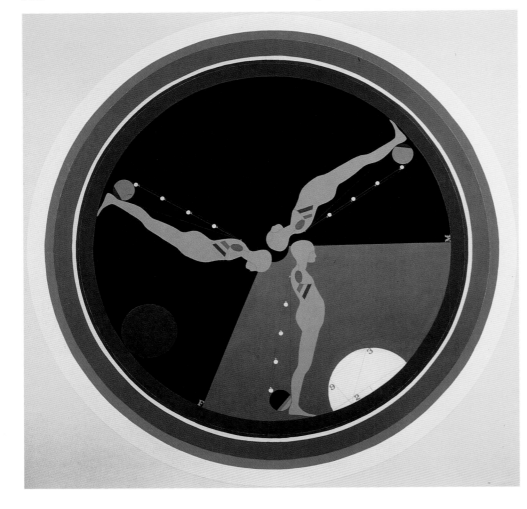

shapes into their personal style or language of form (figs. 4.23, 4.24, and 4.25; see fig. 4.5).

Just as the configuration of a shape gives it the character that distinguishes it from other shapes, so configuration also changes a shape's content or expressive meaning. The abstract artists of the present century seem to have been influenced by the stylization of machinery, for example, to create pristine, clear-cut shape relationships (fig. 4.26). Our reactions to these, or the meanings we find in them, vary with our own psychological conditioning. While many people accept Charles Sheeler's artworks because of their recognizability, some

◀ **4 · 23**
Ernest Trova, *Three Men in a Circle*, 1968. Oil on canvas, 5 ft 8 in × 5 ft 8 in (1.72 × 1.72 m).
The circular elements generate subconscious and generally indefinable reactions, which are in contrast to the cool rectilinear style.
Courtesy of the Owens-Corning Collection. Owens-Corning Fiberglas Corporation, Toledo, OH.

▶ **4 · 24**
Charles Burchfield, *The East Wind*, 1918. Watercolor, 17½ × 21⅝ in (44.4 × 54.9 cm).
The shapes used by Burchfield in this painting are partly psychological and partly symbolic. The approaching storm seems to evoke human qualities, such as the onset of depression or anger.
Albright-Knox Art Gallery, Buffalo, NY. Bequest of A. Conger Goodyear, 1966.

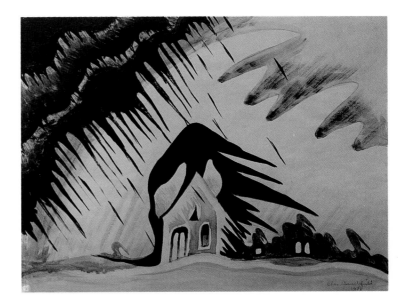

4 · 25

Josef Albers, *Homage to the Square: Star Blue*, 1957. Oil on board, $29\frac{7}{8} \times 29\frac{7}{8}$ in (75.9 × 75.9 cm).

The meaning of the squares in this picture lies not in their resemblance to a real object, but in their relationship to one another.

Contemporary Collection of the Cleveland Museum of Art, 65.1, Cleveland, OH. © DACS 1994.

4 · 26

Charles Sheeler, *Architectural Cadences*, 1954. Oil on canvas, 25 × 35 in (63.5 × 88.9 cm).

The slightly abstract shape relationships of Sheeler's cityscape still have a strong resemblance to the "real world" and evoke the streamlined workings of machines. A more purely abstract approach, such as that of Josef Albers (see fig. 4.25), requires a more intuitive understanding and psychological self-awareness.

Collection of the Whitney Museum of American Art, New York. Purchase 54.35.

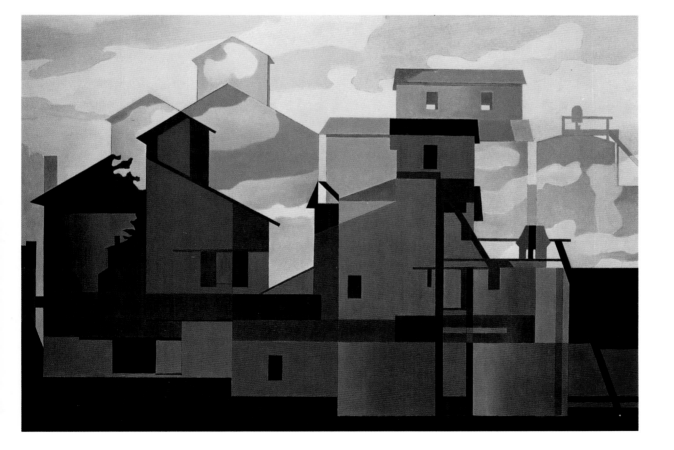

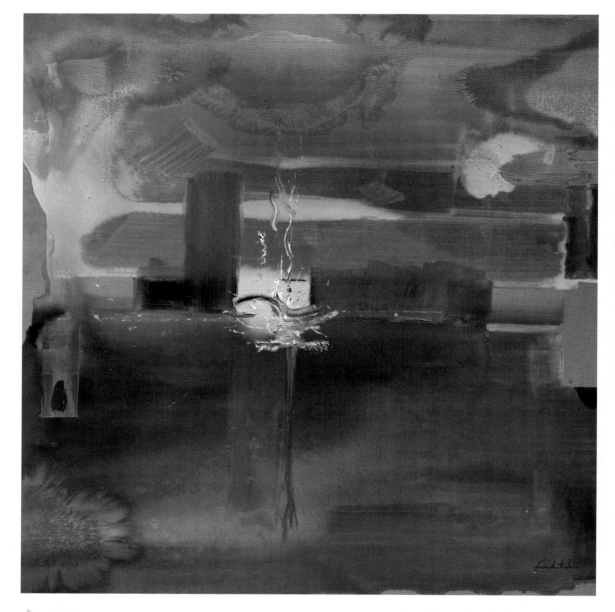

▲ **4 · 27**

**Helen Frankenthaler, *Storm Center*, 1989.
Acrylic on canvas, 7 ft 9$\frac{1}{4}$ in × 7 ft 4$\frac{1}{4}$ in
(2.37 × 2.24 m).**
Many shapes are not meant to represent or even
symbolize. Here, for example, the shape
extremities, the softly changing values of the
larger shapes, and the red ground act against the
explicit verticality of the white and red lines. The
artist provokes a momentary feeling of
excitement within an otherwise quiet mood.
Kukje Gallery, Seoul, Korea. © Helen Frankenthaler
1993. (Photograph by Steven Sloman, New York.)

react adversely to simple abstract shapes
like those in Albers' paintings (see fig.
4.25). While both artists use similar
shapes, visual differences in their
relationships change the shapes'
meanings. There are differences in color
and treatment of value – one flat and the
other blended. In other examples shape
extremities become important, hence the
use of the terms "soft edge" and "hard
edge" (figs. 4.27, 4.28, and 4.29). In
addition, colors, values, textures, and the
application of particular media can affect
whatever feeling or lack of it we intuit in
such works of art. The student only has

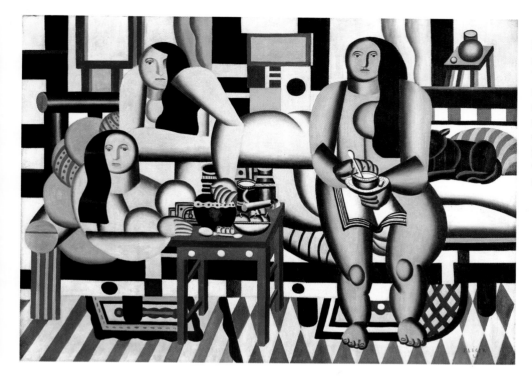

4 · 28

Fernand Léger, *Three Women*, 1921. Oil on canvas, 6 ft ¼ in × 8 ft 3 in (1.84 × 2.51 m).
The Cubist painter Léger commonly used varied combinations of geometric shapes in very complex patterns. Here, due to his sensitive design, he not only overcomes a dominant, hard-edged feel, but imbues the painting with an air of femininity.

The Museum of Modern Art, New York. Mrs. Simon Guggenheim Fund. © DACS 1994.

to glance around a class in which all members are working on a similar exercise to see the variety of personal ways in which the work is carried out, and thus, the differences in style and content that result. How much more can be expected, in terms of endless expressive potential, in the case of trained artists?

All the principles involved in ordering shapes are of little value until one becomes aware of the various meanings that can be revealed through relationships made possible by the language of art. Much of this awareness, of course, comes through practice, as in learning any language.

Artists usually select their shapes to express an idea, but they may initially be motivated by the psychological associations of shape, as in the Matta and Burchfield paintings (see figs. 4.5 and 4.24). Shapes suggest certain meanings, some readily recognizable, others more complex and less clear. Some common meanings ascribable to squares, for instance, are: perfection, stability, stolidity, symmetry, self-reliance, and monotony. Although squares may have

different meanings for different people, many common sensations are shared when viewing them (see fig. 4.25). Similarly, circles, ovals, rectangles, and a vast array of other shapes, possess distinctive meanings; their meaningfulness depends on their complexity, their application, and the sensitivity of those who observe them (see figs. 4.27 and 4.28). How different are our reactions to the biomorphic shapes favored by the Surrealists compared with those to the hard-edged shapes of the geometric abstractionists (see figs. 4.5 and 4.29). That we are sensitive to shape meaning is witnessed in the psychologist's use of the familiar Rorschach (inkblot) test, which is designed to aid in evaluating emotional stability. The evidence from these tests indicates that shapes can provoke emotional responses on different levels. Thus the artist might use either abstract or representational shapes to create desired responses. By using the knowledge that some shapes are inevitably associated with certain objects and situations, the artist can set the stage for a pictorial or sculptural drama.

4 · 29

Harvey Quaytman, *Full Day, Pompeii*, 1991. Acrylic and rust on canvas, 28 × 28 in (71.1 × 71.1 cm).
Harvey Quaytman is representative of the new Postmodern artists who are reviving the hard-edged geometric abstraction of the fifties. Based on a seemingly simple scheme, on closer examination this piece reveals a labyrinth of interlocking rectilinear shapes.

Courtesy of the McKee Gallery, New York. (Photograph by Sarah Wells.)

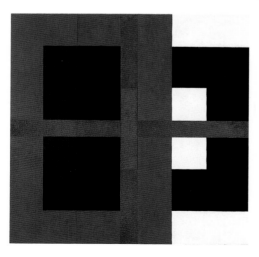

CHAPTER FIVE

Value

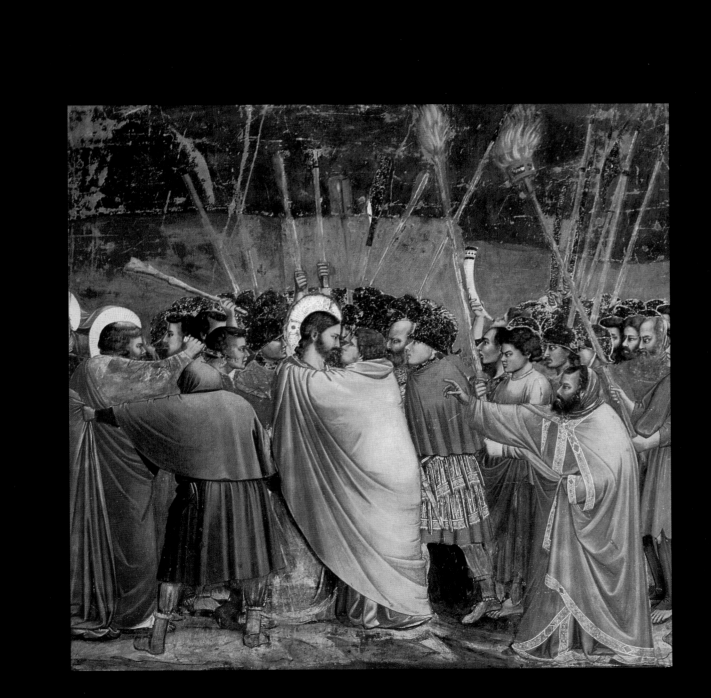

THE VOCABULARY OF VALUE

Value 1. The relative degree of light or dark. 2. The characteristic of color determined by relative light or dark, or the quantity of light reflected by the color.

achromatic (value)
Relating to differences of light and dark; the absence of color.

cast shadow
The dark area that occurs on a surface as a result of something being placed between that surface and a light source.

chiaroscuro
1. Distribution of light and dark in a picture. 2. A technique of representation that blends light and shade gradually to create the illusion of three-dimensional objects in space or atmosphere.

chromatic value
The value (relative degree of lightness or darkness) demonstrated by a given color.

closed-value composition
Values are limited by the edges or boundaries of shapes.

decorative (value)
Ornamenting or enriching but, more importantly in art, stressing the two-dimensional nature of an artwork or any of its elements. Decorative art emphasizes the essential flatness of a surface.

highlight
The portion of an object that, from the observer's position, receives the greatest amount of direct light.

local value
The relative light and dark of a surface, seen in the objective world, that is independent of any effect created by the degree of light falling on it.

open-value composition
Values cross over shape boundaries into adjoining areas.

plastic (value)
1. The use of the elements to create the illusion of the third dimension on a two-dimensional surface. 2. Three-dimensional art forms such as architecture, sculpture, ceramics, etc.

shadow, shade, shading
The darker value on the surface of an object, which gives the illusion that a portion of it is turned away from or obscured by the source of light.

shallow space
The illusion of limited depth. In the case of shallow space, the imagery moves only a slight distance back from the picture plane.

tenebrism
A style of painting that exaggerates or emphasizes the effects of chiaroscuro. Larger amounts of dark value are placed close to smaller areas of highly contrasting lights – which change suddenly – in order to concentrate attention on important features.

value pattern
The organization and total effect of the relationships of light and dark; with the resulting control of the spectator's eye movement there is a unifying effect throughout the composition (the term can be applied to decorative or plastic space).

INTRODUCTION TO VALUE RELATIONSHIPS

The best definition of *value* for the purpose of this book is found in the dictionary, which states that value in art is the relationship of one part or detail to another with respect to light or dark. Artistic vision is concerned with both *chromatic* experiences (reds, greens, yellows, and other hues) and *achromatic* experiences (white, black and the limitless shades of gray). Value is an integral part of both these experiences. Value is also called *tone*, brightness, *shade*, or even color, but these terms have only limited convenience and accuracy in an art context.

Anyone who studies art must consider the relationships of value to the other elements of art form: line, color, texture, and shape. All these elements must exhibit some value contrast in order to remain visible.

The particular value of a line could be the result of the medium used or the pressure exerted on the medium by the artist. For example, the degree of value of a pencil line would be determined by the hardness of the graphite or the force with which it is used. Value can be created by placing lines of the same or different qualities alongside or across each other to produce generalized areas of value; this is sometimes called hatching or cross-hatching (fig. 5.1). Shapes are also created and distinguished by the use of value. In reproducing textures, the shadows and *highlights* peculiar to particular surfaces are copied. The values in abstract textures depart to some degree from the values of the objects being represented.

The intoxicating effects of a particular color often blind people to the fact that color's very existence is entirely dependent upon the presence of value. A standard yellow, for example, is of far greater lightness than a standard violet, although both colors may be modified to a point at which they become virtually equal. A common weakness in painting is the unfortunate disregard for the pattern created by the value relationships of the colors. Black-and-white photographs of paintings often reveal this deficiency very clearly.

DESCRIPTIVE USES OF VALUE

One of the most useful applications of value is in describing objects, shapes, and space (fig. 5.2). Descriptive qualities can be broadened to include psychological, emotional, and dramatic expression. For centuries artists have been concerned with the problem of using value to translate the effect of light playing about the earth and its inhabitants. Objects are usually perceived in terms of the characteristic

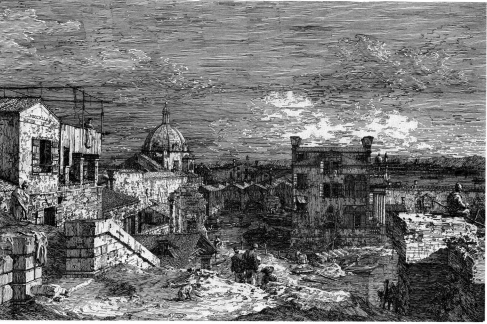

5 · 1

Antonio Canaletto, *Imaginary View of Venice*, 1741. Print (etching), 11¾ × 17¹/₁₆ in (29.8 × 43.3 cm).

A casual glance might make one think that these values were produced with a wash. In fact, they are all composed of hatched and cross-hatched lines scratched through a ground and etched into a metal plate.

Toledo Museum of Art, Toledo, OH. Gift of Edward Drummond Libbey.

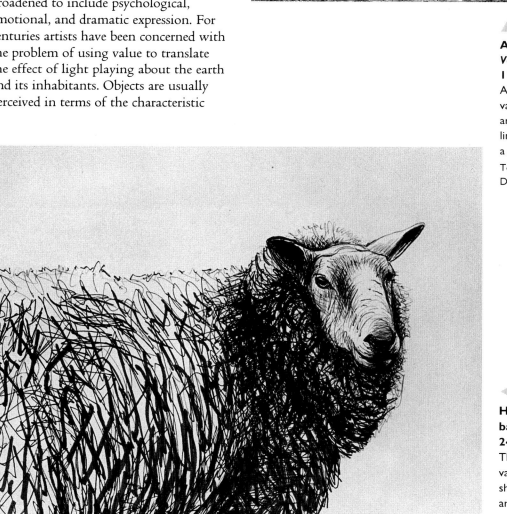

5 · 2

Henry Moore, *Sheep #43*, 1972. Blue-black ballpoint and felt pen, 8 × 9¾ in (20.3 × 24.8 cm).

The degree of line concentration indicates the value of the subject; where tightly bunched shadows are suggested, the forms of the animal are defined.

Courtesy of Mary Moore.

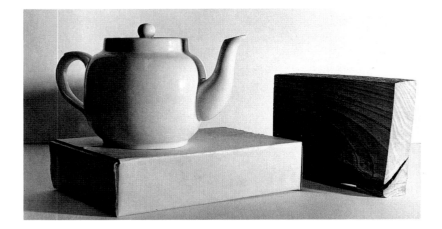

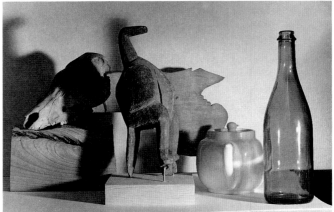

▲ **5·3A**

Russell F. McKnight, *Light and Dark,* 1984. Photograph.

A solid object receives more light on one side than the other because of its proximity to a light source. As the light is blocked out shadows occur. Curved surfaces exhibit a gradual change of value, whereas angular surfaces give sharp changes.

Courtesy of the artist.

▲ **5·3B**

Russell F. McKnight, *Shadows,* 1984. Photograph.

Light can cast overlapping shadows that tend to break up and hide the true character of object forms. When the shapes of shadows are not factored into the composition, results are often disorganized, as in this experiment.

Courtesy of the artist.

 5·4

Philip Pearlstein, *Female Model in Robe, Seated on Platform Rocker,* 1973. Oil on canvas, 6 × 5 ft (1.83 × 1.52 m).

This New Realist painter uses a kind of descriptive lighting derived from photography to represent human figures.

Courtesy of the San Antonio Museum Association, San Antonio, TX.

patterns that occur when those objects are exposed to light rays. Objects, at least normally, cannot receive light from all directions at once. A solid object gets more light from one side than another, because that side is closer to the light source and thus intercepts the light and casts shadows on the other side (fig. 5.3A).

Light patterns vary according to the surface of the object receiving the light. A spherical surface demonstrates an even flow from light to dark; an angular surface shows sudden contrasts of light and dark values. Each basic form has a basic highlight and shadow pattern. Evenly flowing tone gradation invokes a sense of a gently curved surface. An abrupt change of tone indicates a sharp or angular surface (see fig. 5.3A).

Cast shadows are the dark areas that occur on an object or a surface when a shape is placed between it and the light source. The nature of the shadow created depends upon the size and location of the light source, the size and shape of the interposed body, and the character of the surfaces on which the shadows fall. Although cast shadows offer very definite clues to the circumstances of a given situation, they only occasionally give an ideal indication of the true nature of the forms (fig. 5.3B). The artist normally uses, reuses, or creates shadows that aid in descriptive character, enhance the effectiveness of the design pattern, and/or contribute to the mood or expression.

Although contemporary artists have generally rejected the use of value to describe form in a traditional chiaroscuro or descriptive sense, a few of them, particularly the New Realists, do use value in this manner. When value is used to describe volume and space, it can be called *plastic value*. Philip Pearlstein and Richard Estes, for example, are obviously influenced by photography and the cinema (fig. 5.4; see fig. 10.97). Note that neither discipline remains in the disrepute in which some early twentieth-century artists held them as part of their rejection of all descriptive reality.

EXPRESSIVE USES OF VALUE

The type of expression sought by the artist ordinarily determines the balance between light and dark in a work of art. A preponderance of dark areas creates an atmosphere of gloom, mystery, drama, or menace, whereas a composition that is basically light will produce quite the opposite effect. Artists other than naturalists tend to avoid exact duplication of cause and effect in light and shadow, because this practice may create a series of forms that are monotonously light or dark on the same side. The shapes of highlights and shadows are often revised to produce desired degrees of unity and contrast with adjacent areas in the composition. In summary, lights and shadows exist in nature as the by-products of strictly physical laws. Artists must adjust and take liberties with lights and shadows to create their own visual language (fig. 5.5).

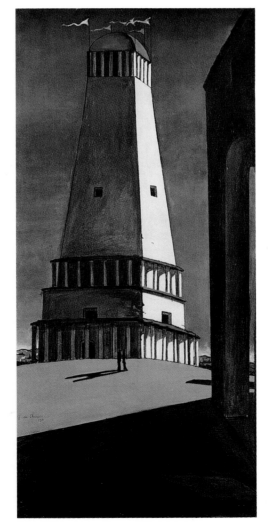

◀ **5·5**
Giorgio de Chirico, *The Nostalgia of the Infinite*, 1913–14? (date on painting is 1911). Oil on canvas, 53¼ × 25½ in (135.3 × 64.8 cm).
Giorgio de Chirico often used shadow effects, strong contrasts of value, and stark shapes to enhance the lonely, timeless nostalgia that is so much a part of his poetic expression.

▶ **5 · 6**

Giotto, *The Kiss of Judas*, Scrovegni Chapel, Padua, 1304–06. Fresco, 7 ft 7 in × 6 ft 7½ in (2.31 × 2.02 m).

Although line and shape predominate in Giotto's works, some early attemps at modeling with chiaroscuro value can be seen.

(Photograph by Edizioni Giorgio Deganello, Padua.)

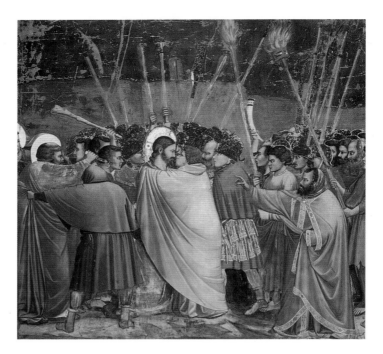

▶ **5 · 7**

Leonardo da Vinci, *Virgin of the Rocks*, c. 1485. Oil on panel, 6 ft 3 in × 3 ft 6 in (1.9 × 1.09 m).

Leonardo extended the range of values set by previous artists; he also developed a technique known as *sfumato*, which featured extremely subtle transitions from light to dark or dark to light.

The Louvre, Paris, France. (Photograph: RMN, Paris.)

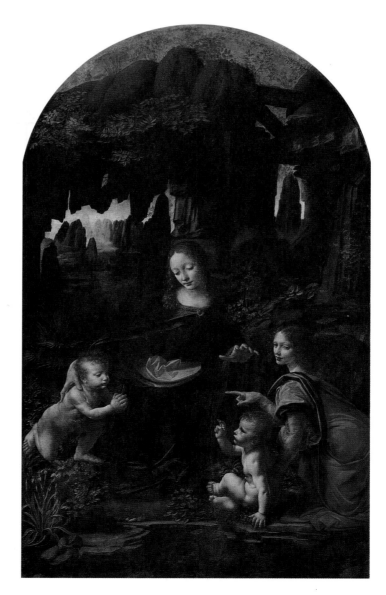

Chiaroscuro

Chiaroscuro refers to the technique of representation that makes forceful use of contrasting lights and darks. The term also alludes to the way in which artists handle those atmospheric effects to create the illusion that the objects are surrounded on all sides by space. *Chiaroscuro* developed mainly in painting, beginning with Giotto (1266–1337), who used darks and lights for *modeling* but expressed shape and space in terms of line (fig. 5.6). The early Florentine masters Masaccio, Fra Angelico, and Fra Filippo Lippi carried chiaroscuro a step further by expressing structure and volume in space with an even, graded tonality (see figs. 2.8 and 8.17A). Leonardo da Vinci employed a much bolder series of contrasts in light and dark but always with soft value transitions (fig. 5.7). The great Venetian painters, such as Giorgione and Titian, completely subordinated line and suggested compositional unity through an enveloping atmosphere of dominant tonality (figs. 5.8 and 5.9).

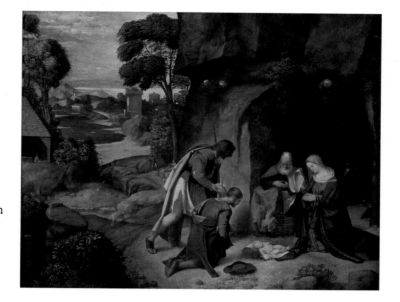

▲ **5 · 8**

Giorgione, *The Adoration of the Shepherds*, c. 1505–10. Oil on wood, 35¾ × 43½ in (90.8 × 110.5 cm).

In Giorgione's work, line was largely disregarded in favor of atmospheric definition.

Samuel H. Kress Collection. (© 1993 National Gallery of Art, Washington, D.C.)

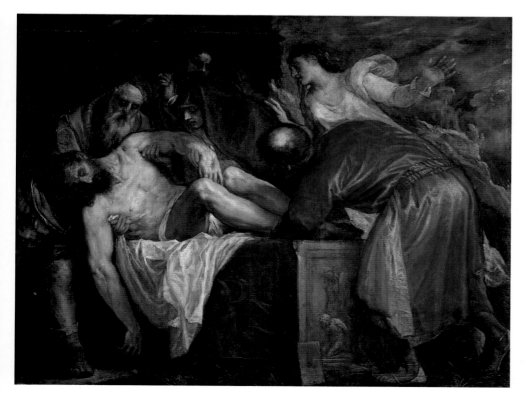

◀ **5 · 9**

Titian, *The Entombment of Christ*, 1559. Oil on canvas, 4 ft 6 in × 5 ft 8⅞ in (1.37 × 1.75 m).

The Venetian master Titian subordinated line (contrasting edges with value) and enveloped his figures in a total atmosphere that approaches tenebrism.

Museo del Prado, Madrid, Spain.

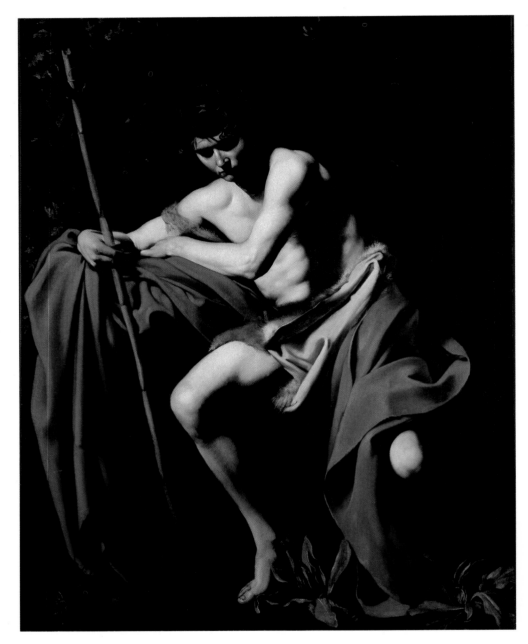

Tenebrism

Painters who use violent chiaroscuro are called *tenebrists*. The first tenebrists were an international group of painters who, early in the seventeenth century, were inspired by the work of Michelangelo da Caravaggio (fig. 5.10). Caravaggio based his chiaroscuro on Correggio's work and instituted the so-called "dark manner" of painting in Western Europe. Rembrandt became the technical adapter and perfecter of this dark manner, which he learned from migratory artists of Germany and southern Holland (fig. 5.11). The dark manner made value an instrument in the characteristic exaggeration of Baroque painting. The strong contrasts lent themselves well to highly dramatic, even theatrical, work of this type.

Later, the dark manner evolved into the pallid, muddy monotone that pervaded some nineteenth-century Western painting. The tenebrists and their followers were very much interested in peculiarities of lighting, particularly the way in which lighting affected mood or emotional expression. They deviated from standard light conditions by placing the implied light sources in unexpected locations, creating unusual visual and spatial effects. In the hands of such superior artists as Rembrandt, these effects were creative tools; in lesser hands, they became captivating tricks or visual sleight-of-hand.

▲ **5 · 10**
Michelangelo Merisi da Caravaggio, *St. John the Baptist*, c. 1604. Oil on canvas, 5 ft 8 × 4 ft 4 in (1.73 × 1.32 m).
Caravaggio was essentially the leader in establishing the dark manner of painting in the sixteenth and seventeenth centuries. Several of the earlier north Italian painters, however, such as Correggio, Titian, and Tintoretto, show a strong tendency toward compositions using darker values.
Nelson-Atkins Museum of Art, Kansas City, MO. (Nelson Fund.) 52–25.

▶ **5 · 11**
Rembrandt Harmenszoon van Rijn, *After, Descent from the Cross*, c. 1655 (altered at a later date). Oil on canvas, 4 ft 8¼ in × 3 ft 7¾ in (1.43 × 1.11 m).
Rembrandt often used inventive, hidden light sources that deviated from standard conditions to enhance the mood or emotional expression.
Widener Collection. (© 1993 National Gallery of Art, Washington, D.C.)

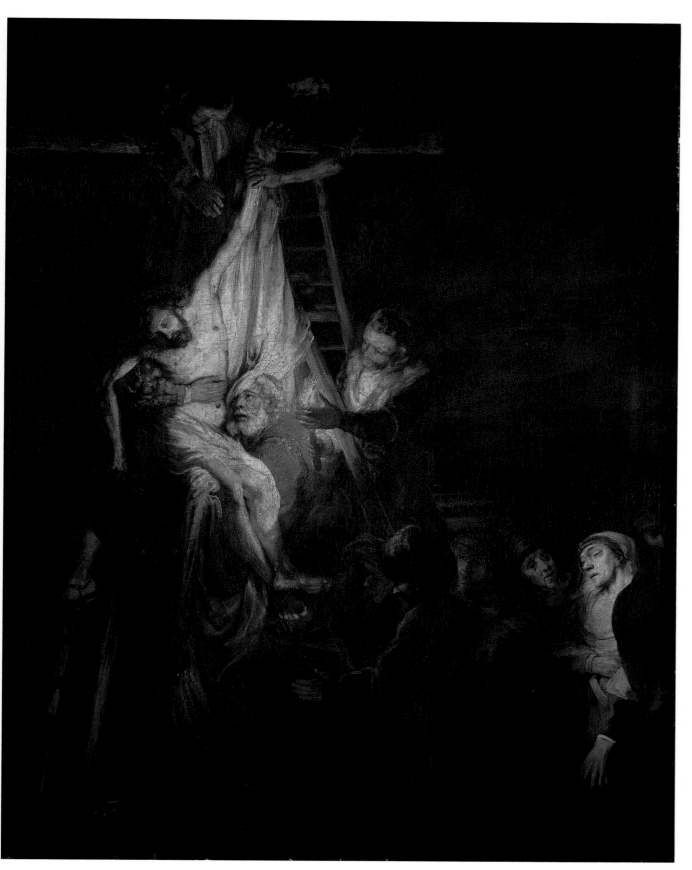

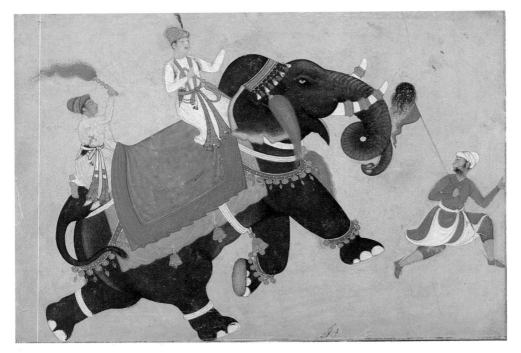

DECORATIVE VALUE PATTERNS

Art styles that stress *decorative* effects usually ignore conventional light sources or neglect representation of light altogether. If light effects appear, they are often a selection of appearances based on their contribution to the total form of the work. This admixture is characteristic of the artworks of children and of primitive and prehistoric tribes, traditional East Asians, and certain periods of Western art, notably the Middle Ages. Many contemporary artworks are completely free of illusionistic lighting. An artwork that thus divorces itself from natural law is obviously based on pictorial invention, imagination, and formal considerations. Emotional impact is not necessarily

▲ **5 · 12**

Signed: Work of Khemkaran, *Prince Riding an Elephant*, Mughal, period of Akbar, 1556–1605. Leaf from an album, gouache on paper.

Historically, south Asian artists have often disregarded the use of light (illumination) in favor of decorative value compositions.

Metropolitan Museum of Art, New York. Rogers Fund, 1925.

▼ **5 · 13A and B**

Russell F. McKnight, *Effect of Light on Objects*, 1984. Photograph.

Figure 5.13A demonstrates how light from one source emphasizes the three-dimensional qualities of an object and gives an indication of depth. The cast shadows also give definite clues to the descriptive and plastic qualities of the various objects. The photograph in figure 5.13B shows the group of objects under illumination from several light sources. This form of lighting tends to flatten object surfaces and produces a more decorative effect.

Courtesy of the artist.

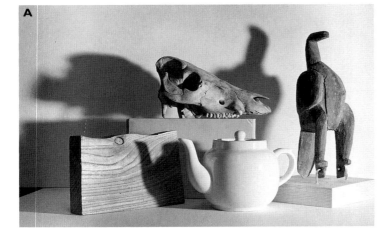

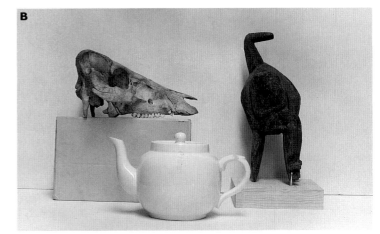

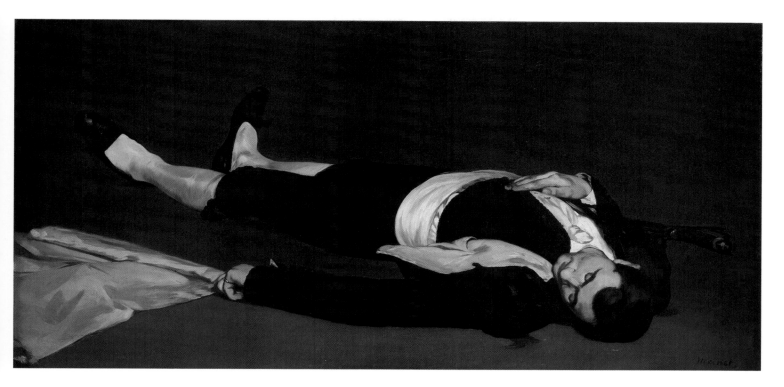

sacrificed (as witness Medieval art), but the emotion speaks primarily through the forms and is consequently less extroverted.

The trend away from illumination values gained strength in the nineteenth century, partly because of growing interest in Middle Eastern and east Asian art forms (fig. 5.12). It was given a scientific, Western interpretation when the Impressionist Edouard Manet observed that a multiplicity of light sources tended to flatten object surfaces. He found that this light condition neutralized the plastic qualities of objects, thereby minimizing gradations of value (figs. 5.13A and B). As a result, he laid his colors on canvas in flat areas, beginning with bright, light colors and generally neglecting shadow (fig. 5.14). Some critics have claimed this to be the basic technical advance of the nineteenth century, because it paved the way for nonrepresentational uses of value and helped revive interest in the *shallow-space* concept.

▲ **5 · 14**

Edouard Manet, *The Dead Toreador*, c. 1864. Oil on canvas, 29⅞ × 60⅜ in (75.9 × 153.4 cm).

Manet, a nineteenth-century naturalist, was one of the first artists to break with traditional chiaroscuro, making use, instead, of flat areas of value. These flat areas meet abruptly, unlike the blended edges used by artists previous to Manet. This was one of the great technical developments of nineteenth-century art.

Widener Collection (© 1993 National Gallery of Art, Washington, D.C.)

COMPOSITIONAL FUNCTIONS OF VALUE

The idea of carefully controlled shallow space is well illustrated in the works of the early Cubists and their followers. In those paintings, space is given its order by the arrangement of flat planes abstracted from the subject matter. In the initial stages of this trend, the planes were shaded individually and semi-illusionistically, although giving no indication of any one light source. Later, each plane took on a characteristic value and, in combination with others, produced a carefully conceived two-dimensional light-dark pattern. Eventually, the shallow spatial effect was developed in terms of three-dimensional pattern (or balance), through attention to the advancing and receding characteristics of value (see fig. 4.8). The explorations of these early twentieth-century artists helped focus attention on the intrinsic significance of each and every element. Value was no longer forced to serve primarily as a tool of superficial transcription, although it continued to be of descriptive usefulness. Most creative artists should think of value as a vital and lively participant in pictorial organization. An artist can strengthen underlying compositional structure by controlling contrast of value; it is instrumental in creating relative dominance and two-dimensional pattern, establishing mood, and producing spatial unity (fig. 5.15).

Artists have long explored possible variations for a composition's value pattern – its underlying movement and ground system – by making small studies of the value structure called thumbnail sketches. These *value patterns* may be thought of as the compositional skeleton which supports the image. When properly integrated into the final work, the movement, tension, and structure of the value pattern explored in the sketches reinforces the subject. It does not distract from the image nor separate itself as an overpowering entity, an isolated component. The advantage of small-scale preliminary value studies is that they allow an artist to quickly explore compositional variations before selecting a final solution. In figures 5.16, 5.17, and 5.18, for example, Nicolas Poussin and Barry Schactman develop large rhythmical dark shapes across the bottom, while intermingling smaller receding toned shapes in the middle areas.

Often it is difficult to relate such small studies to the final work because of scale. Small drawings may look exciting because of the way the areas of value are drawn – with rapid sketchy strokes. When enlarged

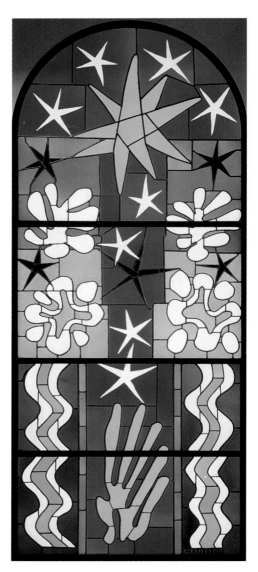

▶ **5 · 15**

Henri Matisse, *Nuit de Noël* **(stained-glass window commissioned by** *Life* **magazine), 1952. Metal framework, 11¾ × 54¾ × ⅝ in (29.8 × 139.1 × 1.6 cm), executed in workshop of Paul and Adeline Bony (Paris) under artist's supervision.**

Matisse chose to use a two-dimensional value pattern enhanced by stained glass.

The Museum of Modern Art, New York. Gift of Time, Inc. © Succession H. Matisse/DACS 1994.

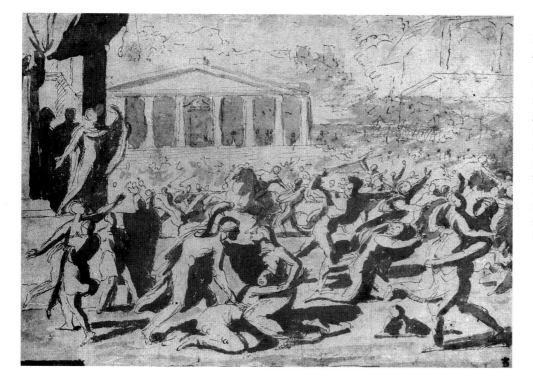

◀ **5 · 16**

Nicolas Poussin, study for *Rape of the Sabines*, c. 1633. Pen and ink with wash, 6½ × 8⅞ in (16.4 × 22.5 cm).

Preparatory or "thumbnail" sketches give the artist the opportunity to explore movement, ground systems, value structure and compositional variations. In the Poussin sketch it seems likely that the artist was striving for rhythmical movement within the horizontal thrust of the composition.

Devonshire Collection, Chatsworth, England. Reproduced by permission of the Trustees of the Chatsworth Settlement. (Photograph from Courtauld Institute of Art, London.)

▼ **5 · 17**

Barry Schactman, *Study after Poussin*, 1959. Brush and ink with wash, 10 × 7⅞ in (2.6 × 19.8 cm).

By using thumbnail sketches artists can quickly position subjects in several locations before arriving at the final composition.

Collection of Yale University, New Haven, CT.

▼ **5 · 18**

Barry Schactman, *Study after Poussin*, 1959. Brush and ink with wash, 10 × 7⅞ in (2.6 × 19.8 cm).

Loose, rapid sketches can also be used to explore value patterns, color structure, and movement.

Yale University Art Gallery, New Haven, CT. Transfer from Yale Art School.

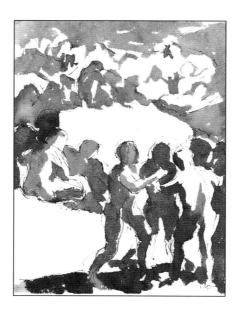

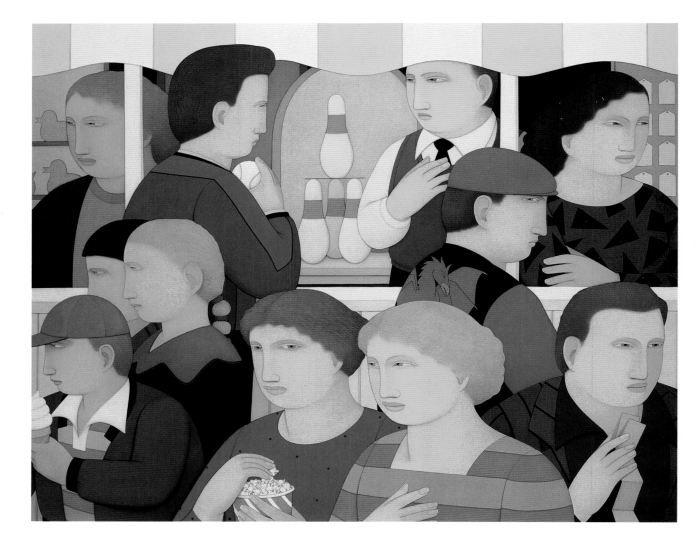

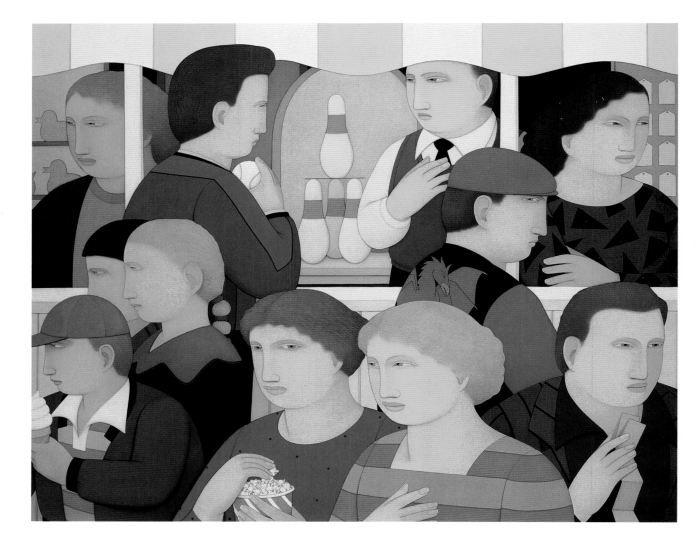

5 · 19

Andrew Stepovich, *Carnival*, 1992. Oil on linen, 4 × 5 ft (1.22 × 1.52 m).

In the Stepovich painting, a closed composition, the color values lie between prescribed and precise limits, usually object edges or contours.

Adelson Galleries, New York.

many times, small strokes become large enough to be seen as bold flat shapes which no longer have the same visual appeal. The new, enlarged shapes of value often require a refinement of detail before the proper relationship of value and mood can be established.

Open and closed compositions

While integrating the value structure and the image, the artist should be aware of two approaches for developing the value pattern – closed or open compositions. In *closed-value* compositions, values are limited by the edges or boundaries of shapes (fig. 5.19). This serves to clearly identify and, at times, even isolate the

shapes (see fig. 5.15). In *open-value* compositions, values can cross over shape boundaries into adjoining areas. This helps to integrate the shapes and unify the composition (fig. 5.20; see fig. 4.8). With both open- and closed-value compositions, the emotive possibilities of value schemes are easy to see. The artist may employ closely related values for hazy, foglike effects (see fig. 4.5). Sharply crystallized shapes may be created by dramatically contrasting values (see figs. 4.21 and 5.5). Thus, value can run the gamut from decoration to violent expression. It is a multipurpose tool, and the success of the total work of art is in large measure based on the effectiveness with which the artist has made value serve these many functions.

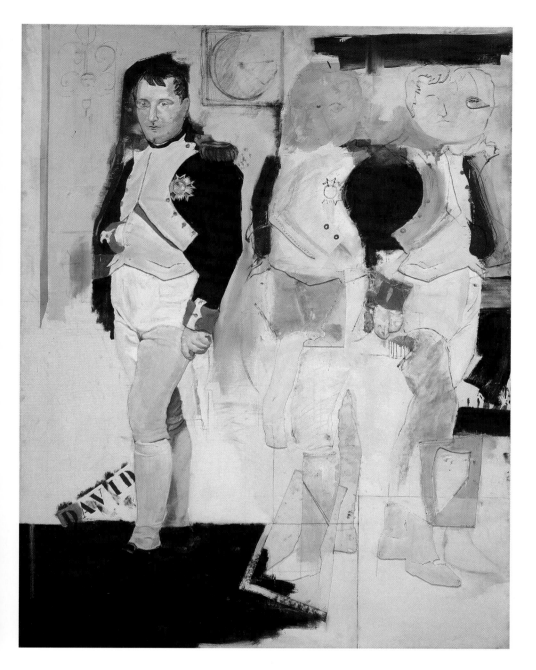

▲ **5·20**
**Larry Rivers, *The Greatest Homosexual*,
1964. Oil, collage, pencil, and colored
pencil on canvas, 6 ft 8 in × 5 ft 1 in (2.03
× 1.55 m).**
In this work values pass freely through and
beyond the contour lines that normally serve as
boundaries of color separation. This is an
example of open composition.

Hirshhorn Museum and Sculpture Garden, Smithsonian
Institution. Gift of Joseph H. Hirshhorn, 1966.
(Photograph by John Tennant.) © Larry Rivers/DACS,
London/VAGA, New York 1994.

CHAPTER SIX

Texture

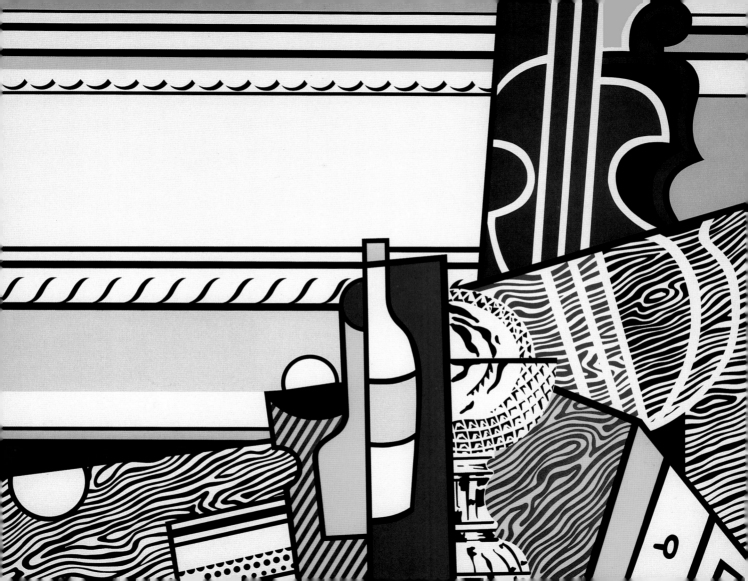

THE VOCABULARY OF TEXTURE

Texture The surface character of a material which can be experienced through touch or the illusion of touch. Texture is produced by natural forces or through an artist's manipulation of the art elements.

abstract texture
A texture derived from the appearance of an actual surface but altered by the artist to satisfy the demands of the artwork.

actual texture
A surface that can be experienced through the sense of touch (as opposed to a surface visually simulated by the artist).

artificial texture
A texture made by humans, as opposed to one produced by nature.

assemblage
A technique which brings together individual items of rather bulky three-dimensional nature that are displayed *in situ* in their original position rather than being limited to a wall.

atmospheric (aerial) perspective
The illusion of deep space produced in graphic works by lightening values, softening details and textures, reducing value contrasts, and neutralizing colors in objects as they recede.

collage
A pictorial technique in which the artist creates the image, or a portion of it, by adhering real materials that possess actual textures to the picture plane surface, often combining them with painted or drawn passages.

genre
Subject matter that concerns everyday life, domestic scenes, family relationships, etc.

illusionism
The imitation of visual reality created on the flat surface of the picture plane by the use of perspective, light-and-dark shading, etc.

invented texture
A created texture whose only source is in the imagination of the artist. It generally produces a decorative pattern and should not be confused with an **abstract texture**.

natural texture
Textures that are created as the result of nature's processes.

paint quality
The use of paint to enrich a surface through textural interest. Interest is created by the ingenuity in handling paint for its intrinsic character.

papier collé
A visual and tactile technique in which scraps of paper having various textures are pasted to the picture surface to enrich or embellish areas. In addition to the actual texture of the paper, the printing on adhered tickets, newspapers, etc. functions as visual richness or decorative pattern similar to an artist's invented texture.

pattern (texture)
1. Any artistic design (sometimes serving as a model for imitation). 2. Compositions with repeated elements and/or designs which most often are varied, and produce interconnections and obvious directional movements.

simulated texture
The copying, or imitation, of object surfaces.

tactile
A quality that refers to the sense of touch.

trompe l'oeil
Literally, a "trick of the eye"; a technique that copies nature with such exactitude that the subject depicted can be mistaken for natural forms.

INTRODUCTION TO TEXTURE

Texture is an experience that is always with us. Whenever we touch something, we feel its texture. By concentrating on your hands and fingers holding this book you will realize that you are experiencing *texture*. If your fingers are against the open side, they will feel the ridged effect of the stacked pages; if on the surface of a page, its smoothness. By looking around the room in which you sit, you will find many textures. In fact everything has a texture, from the hard glossiness of glass through the partial roughness of a lampshade to the soft fluffiness of a carpet. If your room happens to contain a painting or art reproduction, the work most likely illustrates textures that can be seen, not felt – but that are made to look as if they could be felt.

TEXTURE AND THE VISUAL ARTS

Texture is unique among the art elements because it activates two sensory processes. It is more intimately and dramatically known through the sense of touch, but we also can see texture and thus, indirectly, predict its feel. In viewing a picture, we may recognize objects through the artist's use of characteristic shapes, colors, and value patterns. But we may also react to the artist's rendering of the surface character of those objects. In such a case we have both visual and *tactile* experiences (fig. 6.1).

Whether the artist is working in the two-dimensional or three-dimensional field, our tactile response to the work is always a concern (fig. 6.2). Sculptors become involved with the problem of texture by their choice of material and the type and degree of finish they use. If they wish, sculptors can re-create the textures that are characteristic of the subject being interpreted. By cutting into the surface of the material, they can suggest the exterior qualities of hair, cloth, skin, and other textures (fig. 6.3).

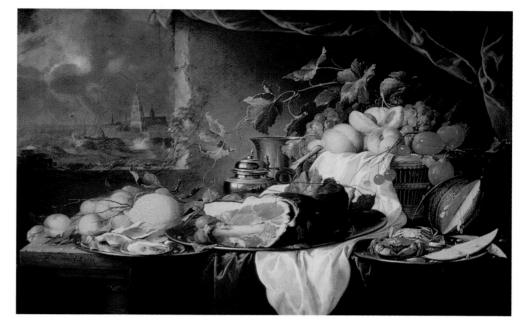

 6 · 1
Jan Davidszoon de Heem, *Still Life with View of the Sea*, **1646. Oil on canvas, 23⅜ × 36½ in (59.4 × 92.7 cm).**
The amazing naturalism of Dutch and Flemish still-life paintings is largely due to the artists' careful simulation of surfaces.
Toledo Museum of Art, Toledo, OH. Gift of Edward Drummond Libbey.

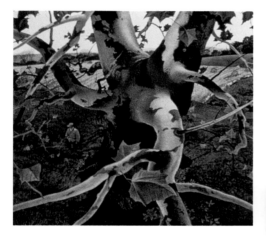

6 · 2
Andrew Newell Wyeth, *The Hunter*, **1943. Tempera on masonite, 33 × 33⅞ in (83.8 × 86 cm).**
Skillful manipulation of the medium can effectively simulate actual textures.
Toledo Museum of Art, Toledo, OH. Elizabeth C. Mau Bequest Fund.

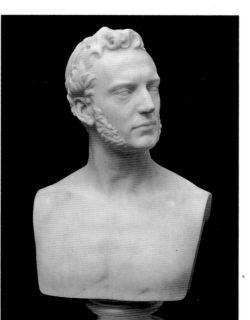

6 · 3
Hiram Powers, *Horatio Greenough*, **1838. Marble, 26½ × 14 × 9¼ in (67.3 × 35.5 × 23.5 cm).**
This sculptor has polished portions of the bust in order to bring out the natural textural qualities of the marble. In addition, he has created actual and visual textures to simulate his subject's characteristics.
Bequest of Charlotte Gore Greenough Hetrosches du Quillou. Courtesy of the Museum of Fine Arts, Boston, MA.

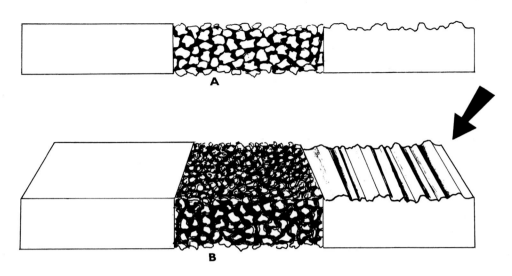

▲ **6 · 4A and B**

(A) A cross section of three materials. On the left is a hard, smooth substance; in the middle is cinderblock; and on the right is weathered wood. The texture of the three upper surfaces can be clearly seen and could be felt if stroked. (B) The same cross section showing its upper plane. The arrow indicates the light source. The texture is defined by the highlights and shadows formed by this illumination. The material to the left, being smooth, produces no shadows (if glossy, it would show reflections). In the cinderblock shadows are cast among the small stones. The undulations in the weathered wood have shadows on the left side and highlights on the right. The nature of the texture in materials is defined by light and shadow patterns.

THE NATURE OF TEXTURE

The sense of touch helps to inform us about our immediate surroundings. Our language, through such words as "smooth," "rough," "soft," and "hard," demonstrates that touch can tell us about the nature of objects. Texture is really surface, and the feel of that surface depends on the degree to which it is broken up by its composition. This determines how we see it and feel it. Rough surfaces intercept light rays, producing lights and darks. Glossy surfaces reflect the light more evenly, giving a less broken appearance (figs. 6.4A and B).

TYPES OF TEXTURE

The artist can use four basic types of texture: actual, simulated, abstract, and invented.

Actual texture

Actual texture is the "real thing"; it is the way the surface of an object looks and feels. Generally, the emphasis is on the way it feels to the touch, but we can get a preliminary idea of the feel by viewing the object (fig. 6.5). Historically, *actual texture* has been a natural part of three-dimensional art, but it has rarely been present in the graphic arts. An exception might be the buildup of paint on, say, a van Gogh canvas, in which the paint has been applied in projecting mounds or furrows (fig. 6.6; see fig. 1.13). The usual artistic application of actual texture involves fixing a textured object to the working surface. When this is done, the texture simply represents itself, although a texture may sometimes be used out of context by displacing an expected texture. The adhering of textures in two-dimensional art probably began with Picasso and Braque in the early twentieth century. In 1908 Picasso pasted a piece of paper to a drawing. This is the first

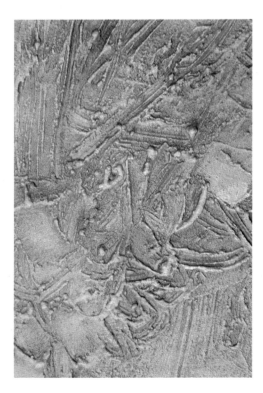

▶ **6 · 5**

Robert Mazur, *Floral* (detail), 1990. Polymer acrylic medium and silica sand, 3 ft 6 in × 4 ft 4 in (1.07 × 1.32 m).

The aggregate, which is mixed into the paint, is supported by a careful selection of color to create a total effect similar to the surfaces found in nature.

Collection of Mr. and Mrs. John Martin.

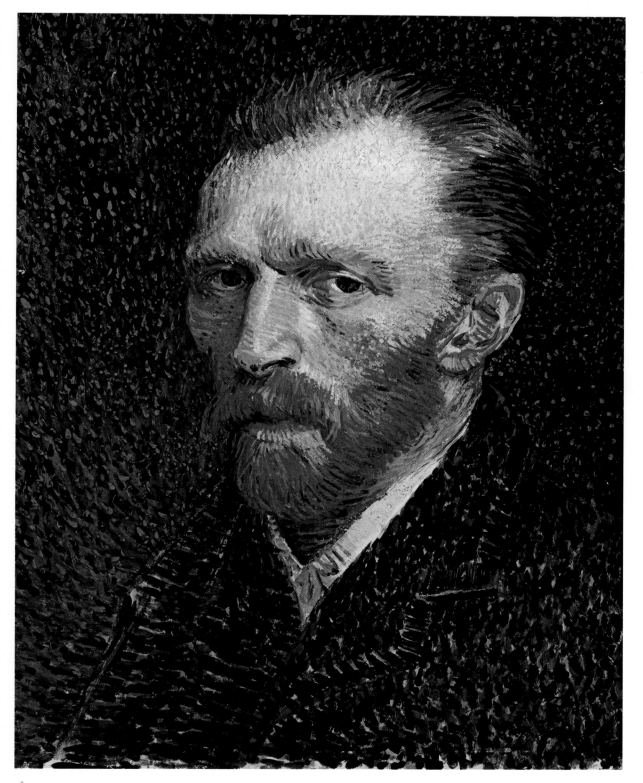

▲ 6 · 6

Vincent van Gogh, *Self-Portrait*, c. 1886–87. Oil on artist's board mounted on cradled panel, 16⅛ × 12¾ in (41 × 32.5 cm).

The massing of paint on van Gogh's canvases creates actual textures. Paint was often applied directly from the tube or built up and scraped clean with the palette knife. The ribbons of paint in van Gogh's work follow or create the rhythm sensed in nature, and frequently simulate natural forms.

Art Institute of Chicago. Joseph Winterbotham Collection, 1954.326.

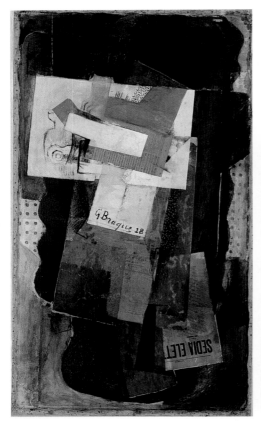

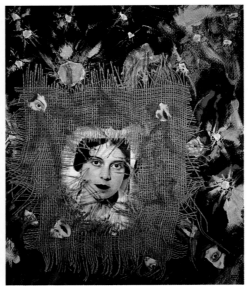

◀ **6·8**

Ilse Bing, *My World*, 1985. Mixed media, 14 × 17 × 3¾ in (35.6 × 43.2 × 9.5 cm).
The inspiration behind the use of burlap in this artwork stems ultimately from the first collages of Picasso and Braque – then a revolutionary, and now a fairly commonplace technique.
Courtesy of the Simon Lowinsky Gallery, New York. (© Ilse Bing.)

▲ **6·7**

Georges Braque, *Still Life*, c. 1917. Pasted newspaper, paper, gouache, oil, and charcoal on canvas, 51¼ × 29 in (130.2 × 73.7 cm).
This Cubist painter helped to pioneer the papier collé and collage forms – art created by fastening actual materials with textural interest to a flat working surface. These art forms may be used to simulate natural textures but are usually created for decorative purposes.
Philadelphia Museum of Art, PA. Louise and Walter Arensberg Collection. © ADAGP, Paris and DACS, London 1994.

▶ **6·9**

Max Weber, *Chinese Restaurant*, 1915. Oil on canvas, 3 ft 4 in × 4 ft (1.02 × 1.22 m).
This painting shows the concern for surface enrichment that grew out of the use of actual textures. In this example of rococo Cubism, many areas are given a decorative pattern that in most cases does not seem to derive from anything but the artist's need for decoration.
Collection of the Whitney Museum of American Art. Gift of Gertrude Vanderbilt Whitney, 31.382.

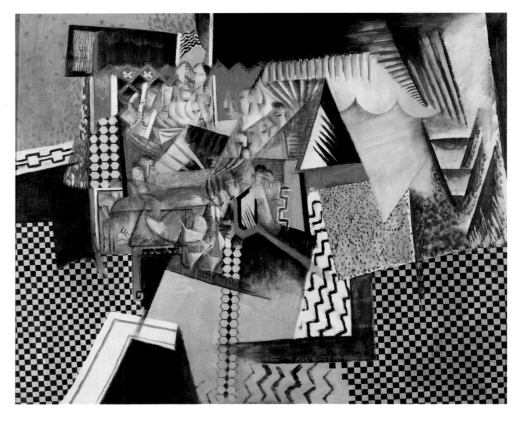

▶ **6·10**

Robert Rauschenberg, *Fossil for Bob Morris, New York*, 1965. Paper, metal, plastic, rubber, and fabric on canvas, 7 ft ⅞ in × 5 ft ⅝ in (2.16 × 1.54 m).
Perhaps the dividing line between collage and assemblage, as illustrated by this example, lies in the greater bulk and variety of the objects found in assemblages.
Hirshhorn Museum and Sculpture Garden, Smithsonian Institution, Washington, D.C. Gift of Joseph H. Hirshhorn, 1972. (Photograph by John Tennant.) © Robert Rauschenberg/DACS, London/VAGA, New York 1994.

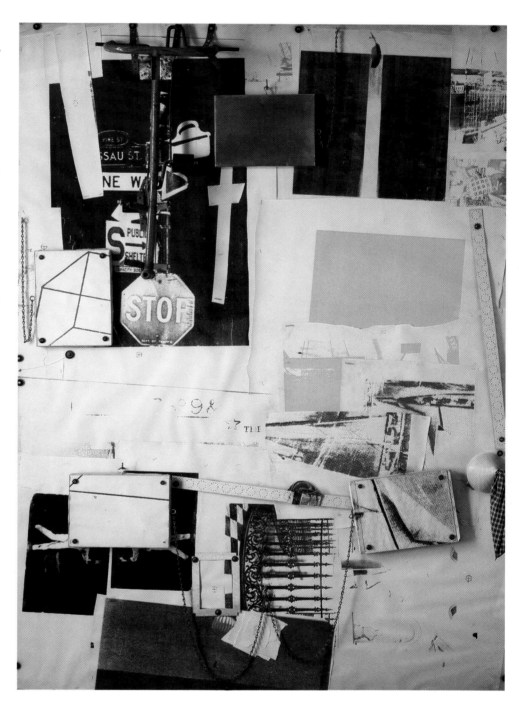

known example of *papier collé*. This practice was later expanded to include the use of tickets, portions of newspapers, menus, and the like.

Papier collé soon led to *collage*, an art form in which actual textures, in the form of rope, chair caning, and other articles of greater substance than paper, were employed. Sometimes these were used in combination with simulated textures (fig. 6.7). The use of papier collé and collage is not always accepted easily; it leads to an uncertainty that can be perplexing. The problem created by mixing objects and painting is: What is real – the objects or the artistic elements, or both? Do the painted objects have the same reality as the genuine objects? Whatever the answers, the early explorations of the Cubists (the style of Picasso and Braque, about 1907–12) stimulated other artists to explore new attitudes toward art and made them much more conscious of surface (fig. 6.8). A concern for *pattern*, arising out of interest in texture, eventually flowered in the works of many artists (fig. 6.9). In the art of today, we find many forms of surface applications. Aside from the more familiar texture of manipulated paint we may find aggregate (sand, gravel, and so on) mixed into the paint to make the surface smoother or rougher, for whatever reason.

Actual textures contribute to a fairly recent development called *assemblage*. If there is any distinction to be made between collage and assemblage it would be that assemblages usually bring together rather bulky individual items which are displayed in different positions rather than on a wall. These objects, of course, possess actual texture in their own right (fig. 6.10; see figs. 10.82 and 10.88).

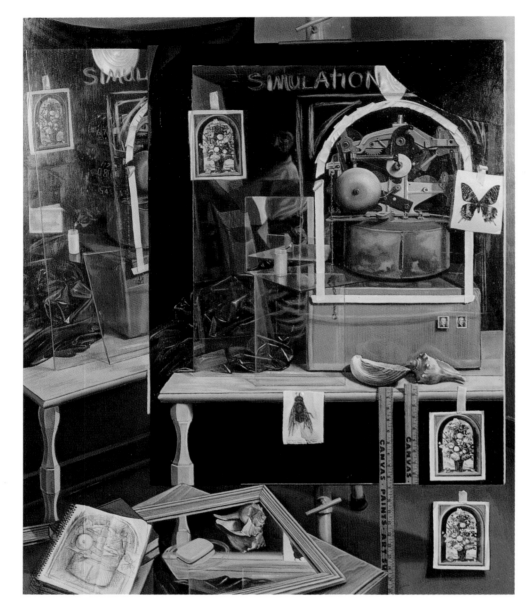

<figure>▲ 6·11

Gary Schumer, *Simulation*, 1979. Oil on canvas, 3 ft 6½ in × 4 ft 4½ in (1.08 × 1.33 m).

As the title implies, the artist is concerned with the simulation of natural textures.

Courtesy of the Owens-Corning Collection, Owens-Corning Fiberglas Corporation, Toledo, OH.

Simulated texture

A surface character that looks real but, in fact, is not, is said to be *simulated*. Every surface has characteristic light and dark features as well as reflections. When these are skillfully reproduced in the artist's medium (as in the case of the seventeenth-century Dutch painters), they can often be mistaken for the surfaces of "real" objects. Simulation is a copying technique, a skill that can be quite impressive in its own right; but it is far from being the sum total of art. Simulated textures are useful for making things identifiable; moreover, we experience a rich tactile enjoyment when viewing them. The Dutch and Flemish artists produced amazing naturalistic effects in still-life and *genre* paintings. Their work shows the evident relish with which they moved from one textural detail to another. Simulated textures are often associated with *trompe l'oeil* paintings, which attempt to "fool the eye" (fig. 6.11).

Simulated texture can serve to illustrate the dual character of texture. Imagine an artist painting a picture that includes a barn door. The door is so weathered and eroded that its wood grain stands out prominently; it would feel rough if stroked. The roughness results from the ridges and valleys, formed by exposure to the elements. These ridges and valleys can be felt but are visible only because they are defined by light and shadow. In rendering (or simulating) the door's texture the artist copies the highlights and shadows from a photograph (fig. 6.12) and, if performed with skill, it works like a feat of magic. The copied door appears to be rough, but is, in fact, smooth, as can be confirmed by stroking the surface of the work.

Abstract texture

Very often artists may be interested in using texture, but instead of simulating textures, they *abstract* them. Abstract textures usually display some hint of the original texture but have been modified to suit the artist's particular needs. The result is often a simplified version of the original, emphasizing pattern. Abstract textures normally appear in works where the degree of abstraction is consistent throughout. In these works they function in a decorative way; obviously there is no attempt to "fool the eye" but they serve the role of enrichment in the same way that simulated textures do. Besides helping the artist to simplify his or her material, abstract textures can be used to *accent* or diminish areas (relative dominance) and to control movement. They can be a potent compositional tool (fig. 6.13).

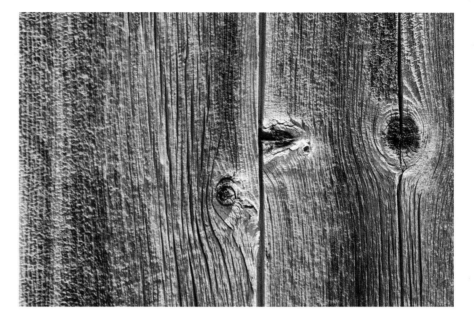

▲ **6 · 12**

A closeup of a wooden barn door shows a detailed view of its grain. The wood has been so eroded by the weather that the grain and knots stand out. If you were to touch the actual surface of the door it would feel rough, but if you stroke the surface of the photographic reproduction on this page it feels perfectly smooth. The picture is, in fact, a simulation of the textured barn door.

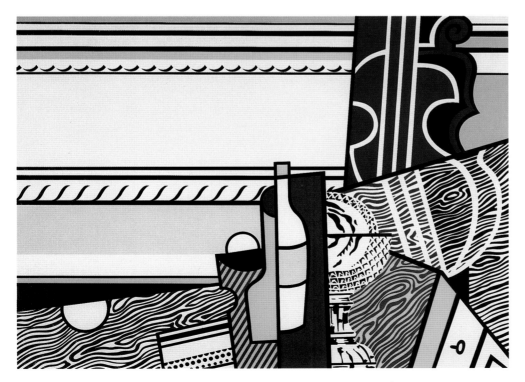

◄ **6 · 13**

Roy Lichtenstein, *Still Life with Crystal Bowl*, 1976. Screenprint/lithograph (edition of forty-five), 32 × 43$\frac{1}{2}$ in (81.3 × 110.5 cm).

The wood grain in this work is not abstracted beyond recognition; it is clearly derived from wood, though simplified and stylized.

Golden Gallery, Boston, MA. © Roy Lichtenstein/ DACS 1994.

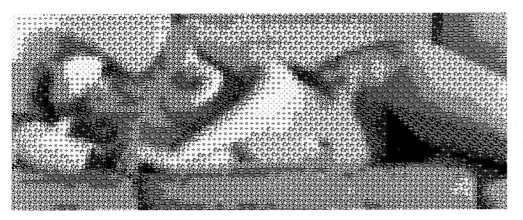

Invented texture

Invented textures are textures without precedent; they neither simulate nor are they abstracted from reality; they are purely the creation of the artist's imagination. In some settings they may suggest that they function as another type of texture but such references are not generally intended by the artist. *Invented textures* usually appear in abstract works, as they are entirely nonobjective. It is sometimes difficult to distinguish abstracted from invented textures, because an artist with the same level of skill as the simulator (but probably with more imagination) can invent a texture and make it appear to have a precedent where none exists (fig. 6.14). In such a case it is difficult to know how, if necessary, to classify the texture; although the texture is created, and not re-created, it still seems to be derived from some source. When used in a realistic or semirealistic work it is probable that the invention would have some resemblance to a subject's texture. By contrast, there are invented textures in which such references to the objective world are not intended. These textures would most likely show up in abstract works in which one might not know whether they were invented or abstracted. Usually the uses of invented textures are much the same as those cited for abstract textures. And, in the hands of a Surrealistic artist, it is possible that they could be inserted in an unlikely context for a surprise or shock effect.

▲ **6 · 14**

Kenneth Knowlton and Leon Harmon, *Computerized Nude*, 1971. Computer-generated image.

This reproduction of a photograph by a specially programmed computer has not only a range of dark and light values, but also a variety of interesting textures. It illustrates the concept that invented textures can in themselves contribute an important aesthetic dimension to an ordinary subject.

Printed with permission of AT&T Bell Laboratories, Murray Hill, NJ.

TEXTURE AND PATTERN

Because texture is interpreted by lights and darks, there is a very fine line between texture and pattern (which is created in a similar way). Ordinarily pattern does not have texture; according to the dictionary, it is essentially a design. This implies that it is not concerned with surface feel but with appearance. Pattern serves the artist mainly as ornament, independent from

▶ **6 · 15A, B, and C**

This figure illustrates the differences and similarities between pattern and texture. (A) Piece of material with a light-and-dark allover pattern. (B) Cross section of material A, assuming it to be a piece of wallpaper. The dark spots are ink; the ink sits on the surface and penetrates the material. (C) Cross section of material A, assuming it to be a piece of carpet. The pattern comes from color changes and tufted areas (texture). Thus we have both pattern and texture in example C.

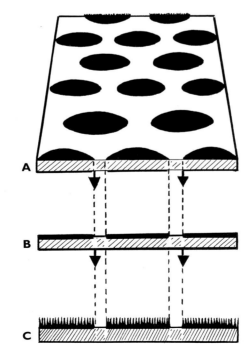

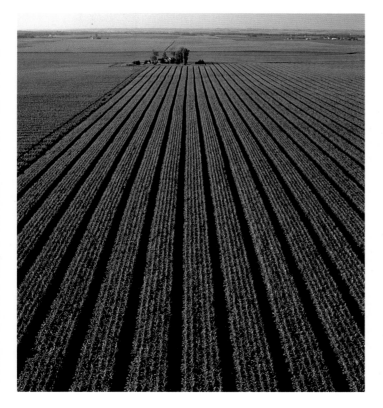

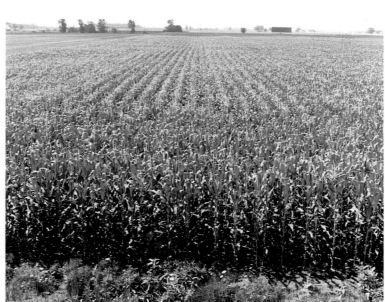

▲ **6 · 16**

In this photograph of a corn field we have examples of both pattern and texture. The rows of corn and the gaps between them create a striped pattern, while the massed stalks produce a texture.

Art Directors Photo Library, London. (Photograph by Craig Aurness.)

any tactile possibilities. But there is an overlap, because texture can create pattern (figs. 6.15A–C).

Pattern usually suggests a repetition, sometimes rather random, sometimes more controlled. A planter sows corn seeds at regular intervals in a field. As the corn grows, the stalks can produce the effect of both pattern and texture. An aerial view of the field would show the pattern primarily, but when closer, the texture would become more visible (figs. 6.16 and 6.17). Unless it is smooth, like glass or steel, texture is normally identified with a three-dimensional disruption of a surface.

Pattern, by contrast, is generally thought of in two-dimensional (or flat) terms.

In most cases the distinction between texture and pattern is clearly defined, but in others it is not so apparent. In addition, the basis of the distinction is itself problematic and debatable. Some people argue that scale makes the difference – that pattern units are generally larger than textural units. By contrast some people assert that the difference lies in distance, in other words that generally the closer one gets to a surface the more it takes on the qualities of a texture. Your authors have debated both these points of view without coming to a firm conclusion, but we incline toward the latter position. In any event, there is little doubt that texture is the product of the nature of a surface. Consider the contrast between a pane of glass and a shag carpet; the smoothness of glass might be regarded as a texture of sorts, but there is no doubt as to the carpet's texture.

▲ **6 · 17**

The individual corn stalks with their leaves and husks can be clearly seen in this low-altitude view of a field. In the foreground the corn, taken as a whole, appears as a huge three-dimensional texture. In the distant view over the top of the field the corn forms patterned rows.

TEXTURE AND COMPOSITION

Relative dominance and movement

The sense of touch aside, texture is seen as variations of light and dark. These variations, apart from their ability to stimulate our sense of touch, are often exciting and attractive. In drawing our attention, these textural areas may create a problem because they are competing with other parts of the artwork. If the texture area is too strong in its hold on the spectator, other areas, possibly more important ones, may not get the attention they deserve; the texture must then be diminished. On the other hand, if an area is "dead," or not attractive, a texture can be added or emphasized to make it come to life.

Our attention is constantly being maneuvered about the surface of an artwork by (among other things) the degree of emphasis given to the various areas of that surface. The movement of our eyes is directed from one attractive area to another, passing over, or through, the "rests" (or deemphasized areas). The control of textures obviously can be a part of the directional thrusts that move through the work; it shares this role with the other art elements. The abstract textures in Picasso's *Dog and Cock*, for example, draw our eyes to the more significant parts of the painting (fig. 6.18).

Psychological factors

Textures can provoke psychological or emotional responses in us that may be either pleasant or unpleasant. In doing this, the textures are usually associated with environments, experiences, objects, or persons from our experience. Textures have symbolic or associative meanings. When we say a person is "slippery as a snake" or "a roughneck," tactile sensations are being linked to personality traits. Similarly, textures can be used as supplementary psychological devices in art. The artist can also use textures to stimulate our curiosity, shock us, or make us reevaluate our perceptions (fig. 6.19).

TEXTURE AND SPACE

Texture can also help to define space. The character of the texture of leaves, for example, differs with distance. When textures appear blurred and lack strong contrasts, they make objects seem distant, but if they are sharp and have strong contrasts, they make them move forward. This is one of the principles of *atmospheric perspective*, a commonly used technique in academic painting. A less academic artist might use textures from far to near and produce controlled variations or surprising contradictions (fig. 6.20).

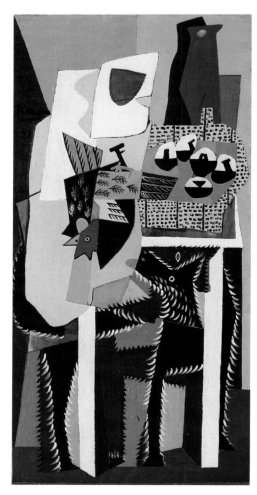

▶ **6 · 18**

Pablo Picasso, *Dog and Cock*, 1929. Oil on canvas, 60⅞ × 30⅛ in (154.6 × 76.5 cm). Abstract texture can be a compositional tool that is important for capturing and directing attention. Clearly the abstracted white fur of the dog attracts us and creates movement.

Yale University Art Gallery, New Haven, CT. Gift of Stephen Carlton Clark, B.A. 1903. © DACS 1994.

TEXTURE AND ART MEDIA

Most of this discussion has dealt with the graphic arts, but textural possibilities are also considered in making other kinds of artworks. The architect balances the smoothness of steel and glass with the roughness of stone, concrete, and brick (see figs. 9.9 and 9.10). The ceramist works with glazes, aggregates in the clay, and various incised and impressed textures (see fig. 9.12). Jewelers, using different techniques, show concern for texture when making pins, rings, necklaces, brooches and bracelets (see fig. 9.11). Printmakers use textures that are transferred on to paper after being etched into the printing plate (see fig. 5.1). Sculptors manipulate the textures of clay, wood, metal, and other natural and artificial materials (see fig. 9.4). From this we can see that texture is involved in all art forms, as it is in many life experiences – however unconscious of it we may be.

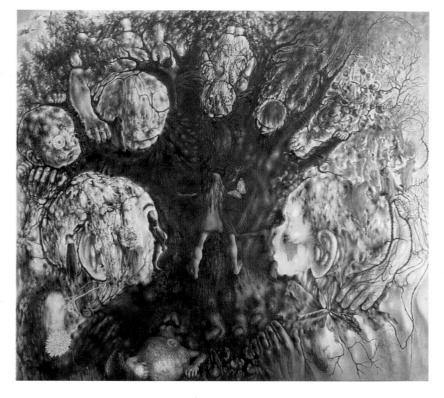

▲ 6·19

Pavel Tchelitchew, *Hide-and-Seek*, 1940–42. Oil on canvas, 6 ft 6½ in × 7 ft ¾ in (1.99 × 2.15 m).

A personal textural style is greatly responsible for much of the emotional quality in this painting. Here, instead of obvious invented patterns, we find a subtle textural treatment of organic matter that evokes a feeling of biological mystery.

The Museum of Modern Art, New York. Mrs. Simon Guggenheim Fund.

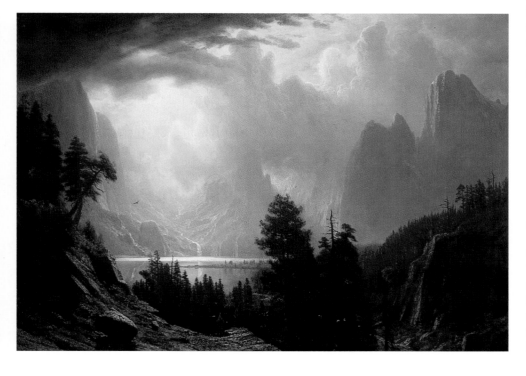

◄ 6·20

Albert Bierstadt, *Untitled Landscape*, c. 1868. Oil on canvas, 27¾ × 38½ in (70.5 × 97.8 cm).

The foreground areas move forward because of their greater contrasts and clarity, while other areas are thrust into space by grayness and only the faint suggestion of details.

Columbus Museum of Art, Columbus, OH. Bequest of Rutherford H. Platt.

CHAPTER SEVEN

Color

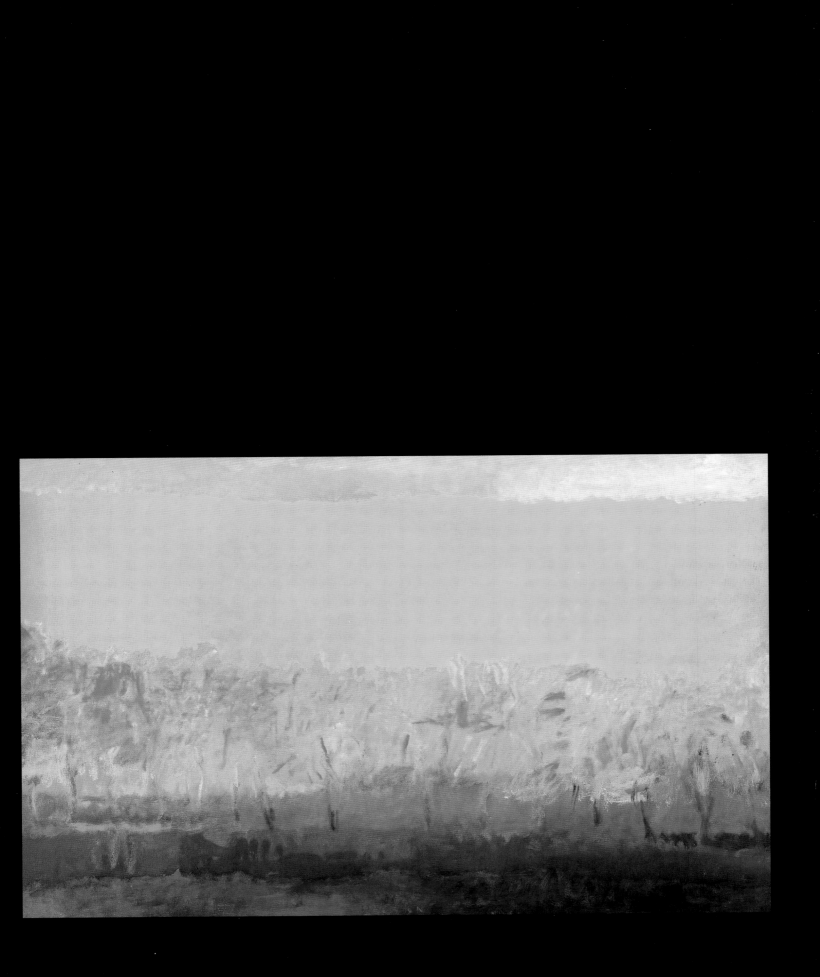

THE VOCABULARY OF COLOR

Color   The visual response to the wavelengths of light identified as red, green, blue, etc.

additive color
Color created by superimposing light rays. Adding together (or superimposing) the three physical primaries (lights) – red, blue, and green – will produce white. The secondaries are magenta, yellow, and cyan.

analogous colors
Colors that are closely related in hue(s). They are usually adjacent to each other on the color wheel.

chroma
1. The purity of color or its freedom from white, black, or gray. 2. The intensity of hue.

chromatic
Pertaining to the presence of color.

chromatic value
The value (relative degree of lightness or darkness) demonstrated by a given color.

color tetrad
Four colors, equally spaced on the color wheel, containing a primary and its complement and a complementary pair of intermediates. This has also come to mean any organization of color on the wheel forming a rectangle which could include a double split-complement.

color triad
Three colors spaced an equal distance apart on the color wheel forming an equilateral triangle. The twelve-color wheel is made up of a primary triad, a secondary triad, and two intermediate triads.

complementary colors
Two colors directly opposite each other on the color wheel. A primary color is complementary to a

secondary color, which is a mixture of the two remaining primaries.

high-key color
Any color which has a value level of middle gray or lighter.

hue
Designates the common name of a color and indicates its position in the spectrum or on the color wheel. Hue is determined by the specific wavelength of the color in a ray of light.

intensity
The saturation, strength, or purity of a color. A vivid color is of high intensity; a dull color, of low intensity.

intermediate color
A color produced by a mixture of a primary color and a secondary color.

local (objective) color
The color as seen in the objective world (green grass, blue sky, red barn, etc.).

low-key color
Any color which has a value level of middle gray or darker.

monochromatic
Having only one color; the complete range of value of one color from white to black.

neutralized color
A color that has been grayed or reduced in intensity by being mixed with any of the neutrals or with a complementary color.

neutrals
1. The inclusion of all color wavelengths will produce white, and the absence of any wavelengths will be perceived as black. With neutrals, no single color is noticed – only a sense of light and dark or the range from

white through gray to black. 2. A color altered by the addition of its complement so that the original sensation of hue is lost or grayed.

pigments
Color substances which give their color property to another material by being mixed with it or covering it. Pigments, usually insoluble, are added to liquid vehicles to produce paint or ink. Colored substances dissolved in liquids, which give their coloring effects by being absorbed or staining, are referred to as dyes.

primary color
A preliminary color that cannot be separated into any other colors. When primaries are mixed, they can produce all of the remaining colors. Red, blue, and green are the additive primaries; red, blue, and yellow, the subtractive.

secondary color
A color produced by a mixture of two primary colors.

simultaneous contrast
When two different color tones come into direct contact, the contrast intensifies the difference between them.

spectrum
The band of individual colors that results when a beam of white light is broken into its component wavelengths, identifiable as hues.

split-complement(s)
A color and the two colors on either side of its complement.

subjective (color)
1. That which is derived from the mind and reflects an individual's viewpoint or bias. 2. Art (color) that is subjective tends to be inventive or creative.

THE NATURE OF COLOR

Color is the element of form that arouses universal appreciation and the one to which we are most sensitive. *Color* appeals instantly to children as well as adults; even infants are more attracted to brightly colored objects. The average layperson, although frequently puzzled by what he or she calls "modern" art, usually finds its color exciting and attractive. This person may question the use of distorted shapes, but seldom objects to the use of color, provided that it is harmonious in character. In fact, a work of art can frequently be appreciated for its color style alone.

Color is one of the most expressive elements because its quality affects our emotions directly. When we view a work of art, we do not have to rationalize what we are supposed to feel about its color; we have an immediate emotional reaction to it. Pleasing rhythms and harmonies of color satisfy our aesthetic desires. We like certain combinations of color and reject others. In representational art, color identifies objects and creates the effect of illusionistic space. The study of color is based on scientific facts that are exact and easily systematized. We will examine these basic characteristics of color relationships to see how they help to give form and meaning to the subject of an artist's work.

Light: the source of color

Color begins with and is derived from light, either natural or artificial. Where there is little light, there is little color; where the light is strong, color is likely to be particularly intense. When the light is weak, such as at dusk or dawn, it is difficult to distinguish one color from another. Under bright, strong sunlight, such as in tropical climates, colors seem to take on additional intensity.

Every ray of light coming from the sun is composed of waves that vibrate at different speeds. The sensation of color is aroused in the human mind by the way our sense of vision responds to the different wavelengths. This can be experimentally proven by observing a beam of white light which passes through a triangle-shaped piece of glass (a prism) and then reflects from a sheet of white paper. The rays of light bend, or refract, as they pass through the glass at different angles (according to their wavelength) and then reflect off the white paper as different colors. Our sense of vision interprets these colors as individual stripes in a narrow band called the *spectrum*. The major colors easily distinguishable in this band are red, orange, yellow, green, blue, blue-violet, and violet (scientists use the term "indigo" for the color artists call "blue-violet"). These colors, however, blend gradually so that we can see several intermediate colors between them (figs. 7.1 and 7.2).

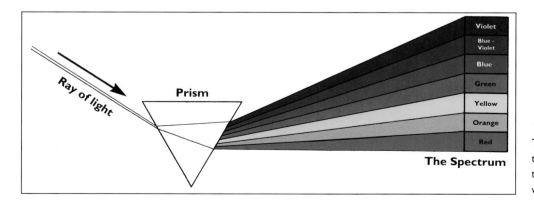

Violet

Blue - Violet

Blue

Green

Yellow

Orange

Red

Ray of light

Prism

The Spectrum

7·1

The rays of red have the longest wavelength and those of violet the shortest. The angle at which the rays are bent, or refracted, is greatest at the violet end and least at the red.

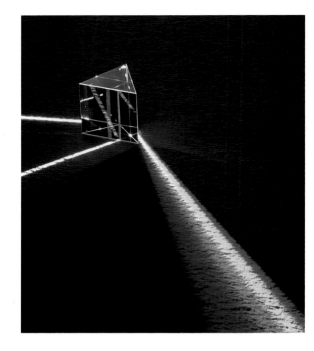

▲ **7 · 2**

A beam of light passes through a triangular-shaped piece of glass (prism). The rays of light are bent, or refracted, as they pass through the glass at different angles (according to their wavelengths), producing a rainbow array of hues called the spectrum.

Science Photo Library, London. (Photograph by David Parker.)

Additive color

The colors of the spectrum are pure, and they represent the greatest intensity (brightness) possible. If we could collect all these spectrum colors and mix them in a reverse process from the one described in the previous paragraph, we would again have white light. When artists or physicists work with rays of colored light they are using *additive color*. Some interesting things happen when rays of red, blue, and green (the additive primaries) are overlapped. Where red and blue light overlap, magenta is produced; where red and green light overlap, yellow is produced; where green and blue light overlap, cyan is produced. Where red, blue and green light rays overlap, white light is produced – proving that white light may be created by the presence of all color wavelengths (fig. 7.3).

The television industry uses this additive color mixing process. The modern color monitor is made up of small triplet phospor units of red, blue, and green. Seen in 525 horizontal lines, they are illuminated singly or in various combinations to produce the sensation of every color possible. Each image is made up of two scans of alternate lines – odd-numbered lines then even. This takes place at a rate of 60 scans per second. At viewing distance the lines and stripes of glowing colored phospors cannot be distinguished as the eye merges them all together into a sharp image in full color. It is important for an artist to be familiar with the additive color system because it is used in video production, computer graphics, the neon sign industry, for slide and multimedia presentations, laser light shows, and landscape and stage lighting. In each case, artists and technicians work with light and create color by mixing the light primaries – red, blue, and green.

▶ **7 · 3**

The projected additive primary colors – red, blue, and green – create the secondary colors of cyan, yellow, and magenta when two are overlapped. When all three primaries are combined, white light is produced.

Reprinted courtesy of the Eastman Kodak Company.

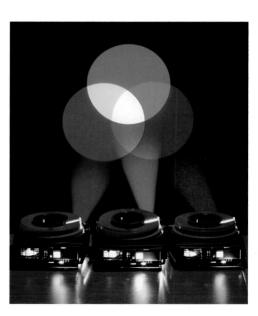

Subtractive color

Since all the colors are present in a beam of light, how are we able to distinguish a single color as it is reflected from a natural object? Any colored object has certain physical properties called color quality or pigmentation that enable it to absorb some color waves and reflect others. A green leaf appears green to the eye because the leaf reflects the green waves in the ray of light while absorbing all the other colors. An artist's *pigment* has this property, and when applied to the surface of an object, gives it the same characteristic. The artist may also alter the surface pigmentation of an object through the use of dyes, stains, and chemical washes or gases (as applied to sculpture).

Regardless of how the surface pigmentation is applied or altered, the sensation of color is created when the surface absorbs all the wavelengths except those of the color experienced. In this case, the artist is working with reflected light known as *subtractive color* rather than actual light rays or additive color (fig. 7.4). For example, when a piece of pure white paper is viewed, all of the light wavelengths of color are reflected back to the viewer – none is subtracted or absorbed by the paper. When red pigment covers the surface, only the red wavelengths are reflected back to the viewer – all others are subtracted or absorbed by the pigment. As a result, red is experienced. The total energy subtracted by the surface (the wavelengths not reflected) would equal green – the reflected color's opposite or complement. The opposite would be true if a green pigment was applied to the paper. Green, a mixture of the remaining two primaries – blue and yellow – would only reflect the green wavelengths while absorbing or subtracting all others, equalling red (see fig. 7.33).

When all the pigment primaries – blue, yellow, and red – are mixed together a color is created which is capable of absorbing or subtracting all the wavelengths in a ray of white light. The color should not reflect any light and should appear as black – the absence of any wavelengths. (This is the opposite of additive color mixing, which produces white by mixing all the light primaries.) However, because of adulterants and imperfections in artist's pigment, any surface may not perfectly absorb all the wavelengths except for those being reflected. In addition, the pigment may reflect more than just one dominant color and/or a certain amount of white. For these reasons, a mixture of pigment complements – containing all the

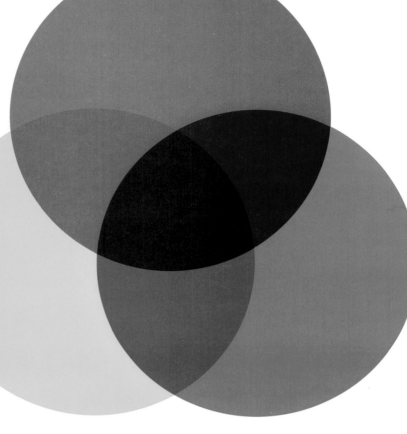

▲ **7·4**

The primary colors of the subtractive color system include yellow, cyan, and magenta. Where they are mixed they produce red, blue, and green. When all three are combined, they produce black. Notice that the subtractive color primaries are the additive secondary colors and that the subtractive secondary colors are the additive primary colors.

primaries – will not produce black but a dark gray.

Regardless of whether pure or mixed, subtractive color refers to color created when an image reflects only the wavelengths of the color seen, while absorbing all others. For the remainder of this chapter when we discuss color, we will be concerned with the artist's pigment made visible by reflected light rather than the sensation of mixed colored light or additive color.

Pigment color mixing

As previously mentioned, the spectrum contains red, orange, yellow, green, blue, blue-violet, and violet, with hundreds of subtle color variations at their greatest intensity. This range of color is available in pigment as well. Children or beginners working with color are likely to use only a few simple, pure colors. They do not realize that simple colors can be varied. Many colors can be created by mixing two other colors.

Three colors, however, cannot be created from mixtures; these are the hues red, yellow, and blue, known as the *primary colors* (fig. 7.5). When the three primaries are mixed in pairs, in equal or unequal amounts, they can produce all of the possible colors. Mixing any two primaries produces a *secondary color*: orange results from mixing red and yellow; and green results from mixing yellow and blue (fig. 7.6). Moreover, certain *intermediate colors* are created by mixing a primary color with a neighboring secondary color. The number of intermediate colors is unlimited, because a change of proportion in the amount of primary or secondary colors used will change the resultant hue. In other words, not just one yellow-green is possible from mixing green and yellow. If more yellow is used, a different yellow-green results than when more green is used (fig. 7.7). Occasionally artists refer incorrectly to intermediate colors as tertiary colors. *Tertiary colors* result from the mixture of two secondary colors – not a primary and a secondary. They will be discussed in more depth shortly.

If we study the progression of mixed color from yellow to yellow-green to green, and so on, we discover a natural order that may be presented as a color wheel (fig. 7.8). Our ability to differentiate subtle variation allows us to see a new color at each position.

The triadic color system

The three primary colors are equally spaced apart on this wheel, with yellow usually on the top because it is closest to white. These colors form an equilateral triangle, called a *primary triad* (see fig. 7.5). The three secondary colors are placed

▼ **7·5**
Primary triad. When the colors of the primary triad are mixed together, the resulting color is gray.

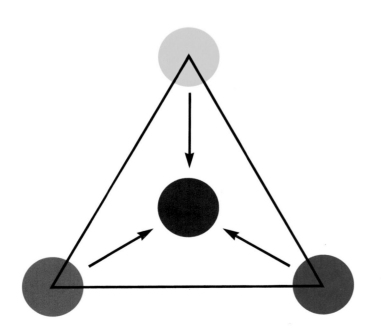

▼ **7·6**
Secondary triad. When the colors of the secondary triad are mixed together, the resulting color is gray.

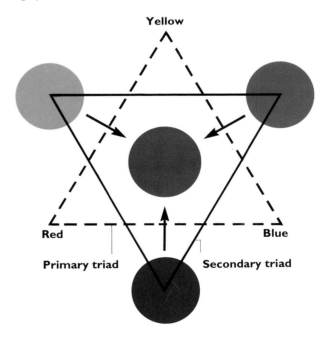

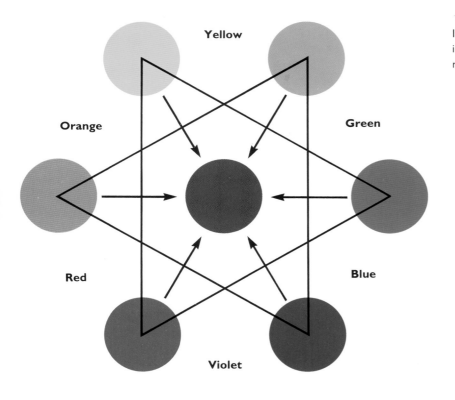

Yellow

Orange

Green

Red

Blue

Violet

◀ **7 · 7**
Intermediate colors. When the colors of the intermediate triads are mixed together, the resulting color is gray.

▼ **7 · 8**
This color wheel includes the primary, secondary, and intermediate hues – the "standard" hues; of course, the number of possible hues is infinite. As one moves from a hue to its opposite on the color wheel, the smaller circles indicate the lessening of intensity due to the mixing of these opposites, or complementaries.

The inner circle is the location of the tertiary hues – those colors resulting from the mixture of two secondary colors. They will have the same character and appearance as those colors on the inner circles which are mixed by adding complements. The features of tertiary colors are a loss of intensity and a neutralization of hue.

between the primaries from which they are mixed; evenly spaced, they create a *secondary triad* composed of orange, green, and violet (see fig. 7.6). Intermediate colors placed between each primary and secondary color create equally spaced units known as *intermediate triads* (see fig. 7.7). The placement of all the colors results in a twelve-color wheel. The colors change as we move around the color wheel because the wavelengths of the light rays that produce these colors change. The closer together colors appear on the color wheel, the closer are their hue relationships; the farther apart, the more contrasting they are in character. The hues directly opposite each other afford the greatest contrast and are known as *complementary colors* (see figs. 7.14 and 7.15).

The complement of any color is based upon the triadic system. For example, the complement of red is green – a mixture of equal parts of the remaining points of the triad, yellow and blue. Thus, the color and its complement are made up of the

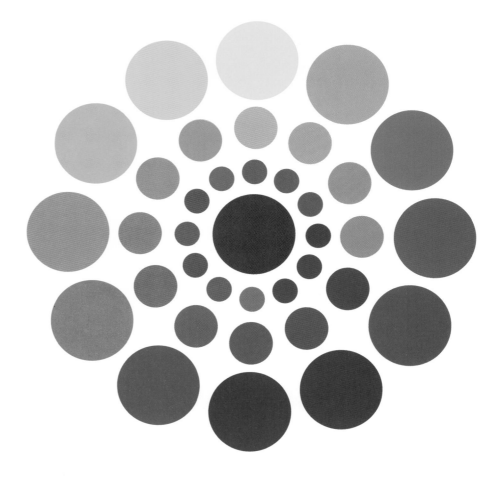

three primary triadic colors; the complement of yellow is created by mixing blue and red, resulting in violet. If the color is a "mixed," secondary hue (orange, say) its complement may be found by knowing what primaries created the color (red and yellow); the remaining member of the triad (blue) will be the mixed color's complement.

Neutrals

Not all objects have the quality of color. Some are black, white, or gray, which do not look like any of the colors of the spectrum. No color quality is found in these examples; they differ merely in the quantity of light they reflect. Because we do not distinguish any one color in black, white, and gray, they are called *neutrals*. These neutrals actually reflect varying amounts of the color wavelengths in a ray of light.

One neutral, white, can be thought of as the presence of all color because it occurs when a surface reflects all of the color wavelengths to an equal degree.

Black, then, is usually called the absence of color because it results when a surface absorbs all of the color rays equally and reflects none of them. Absolute black is rarely experienced except in deep caves, and so forth. Therefore, most blacks will contain some trace of reflected color, however slight.

Any gray is an impure white because it is created by only partial reflection of all the color waves. If the amount of light reflected is great, the gray is light; if the amount reflected is little, the gray is dark. The neutrals are indicated by the quantity of light reflected, whereas color is concerned with the quality of light reflected.

The physical properties of color

Regardless of whether the artist works with paints, dyes, or inks, every color used must be described in terms of three physical properties: *hue, value,* and *intensity* (figs. 7.9 and 7.10).

Hue

Hue is the generic color name – red, blue, green, and so on – given to the visual response for each range of identifiable

wavelengths in visible light (fig. 7.11; see fig. 7.1). Hue designates a color's position in the spectrum or on the color wheel. Every color actually exists in many subtle variations, although they all continue to bear the simple color names. Many reds, for example, differ in character from pure red yet we recognize the redness of the hue in all of them. In addition, a color's hue can be changed by adding it to another color; this actually changes the wavelength of light. There are an unlimited number of steps (variations) that may be created by mixing any two colors – between yellow and green, for example. Yet, for the sake of clarity, artists universally recognize the hues as positioned (identified or named) on the twelve-step color wheel.

Value

A wide range of color tones can be produced by adding black or white to a hue. This indicates that colors have characteristics other than hue. The property of color known as value distinguishes between the lightness and darkness of colors, or the quantity of light a color reflects. Many value steps can exist between the darkest and lightest appearance of any one hue. To change the tone value of a pigment, we must mix it with another pigment that is darker or lighter. The only dark or light pigments available that would not also change the color's hue are black and white.

Each of the colors reflects a different quantity of light as well as a different wavelength. A large amount of light is reflected from yellow, whereas a small amount of light is reflected from violet. Each color at its maximum intensity has a normal value that indicates the amount of light it reflects. It can, however, be made lighter or darker than normal by adding white or black, as previously noted. We should know the normal value of each of the colors in order to use them effectively. This normal value can be most easily seen when the colors of the wheel are placed next to a scale of neutral values

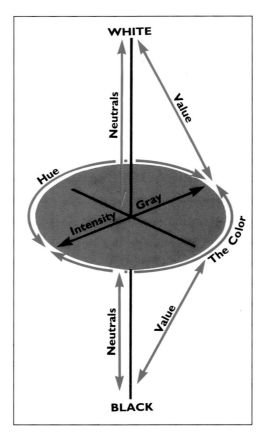

7 · 9
This diagram demonstrates the three physical properties of color. We can see all the color variations as existing on a three-dimensional solid (a double cone). As the colors move around this solid, they change in hue. When these hues move upward or downward on the solid, they change in value. As all of the colors on the outside move toward the center, they become closer to the neutral values, and there is a change in intensity (see also fig. 7.10).

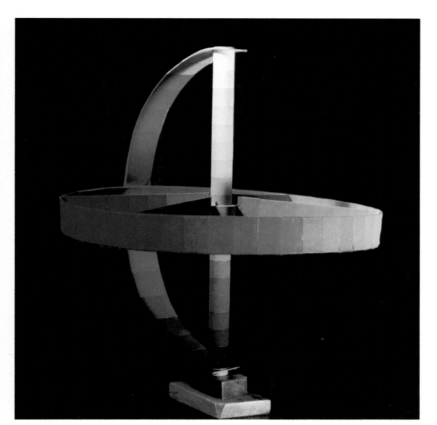

7·10
A three-dimensional model illustrating the three main characteristics of color (see also fig. 7.9).

Photograph courtesy of Ronald Coleman.

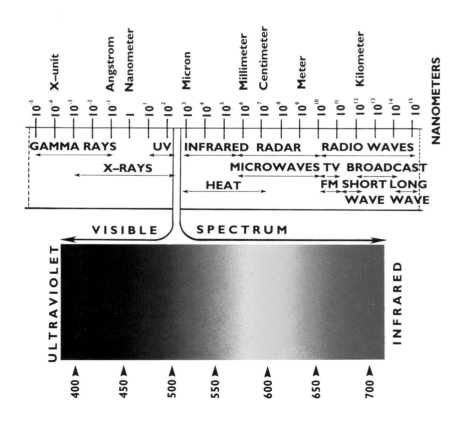

7·11

The electromagnetic spectrum. The sun, being the most efficient source of light, sends radiation to the earth in a series of waves known as electromagnetic energy. This may be likened to throwing a pebble into the middle of a pond. Waves radiate from that point and can be measured from the crest of one ripple to the crest of the next ripple. Similarly, waves from the sun range from mere atmospheric ripples – gamma rays which measure no more than 6 quadrillionths of an inch (.000000000000006) – to the long, rolling radio waves, which stretch $18\frac{1}{2}$ miles from crest to crest.

The wavelengths visible to the human eye are found in only a narrow range within this electromagnetic spectrum; their unit of measure is the "nanometer" (nm), which measures one billionth of a meter from crest to crest. The shortest wavelength visible to mankind measures 400 nm – a light violet. The sensations of yellow, orange, and red are apparent as the waves lengthen to between 600 and 700 nm. Contained in a ray of light but invisible to the human eye are infrareds (below reds) and ultraviolets (above violets): see figure 7.1.

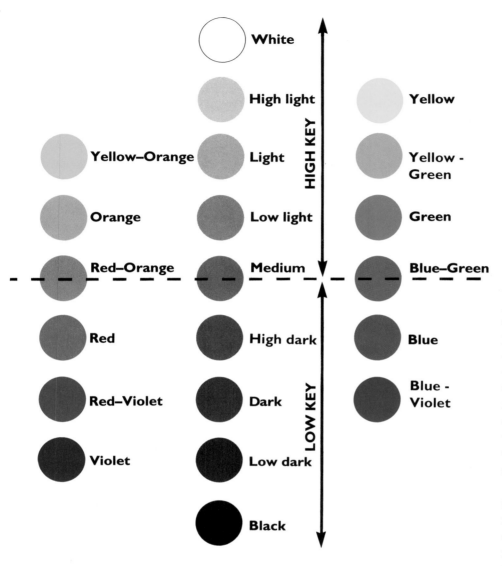

Intensity

The third property of color, intensity (sometimes called saturation or *chroma*), refers to the quality of light in a color. We use the term intensity to distinguish a brighter tone from a duller one of the same hue; that is, to differentiate a color which has a high degree of saturation or strength from one which is grayed or neutralized. The saturation point, or the purest color, is actually found in the spectrum produced by a beam of light passing through a prism. However, the artist's pigment that comes closest to resembling this color is said to be at maximum intensity. The purity of the light waves reflected from the pigment produces the variation in brightness or dullness of the color. For example, a pigment that reflects only the red rays of light is an intense red, but if any of the complementary green rays are also reflected, the red's brightness is dulled or neutralized. If the green and red rays are equally absorbed by the reflecting surface, the resulting tone is a neutral gray. Consequently, as a color loses its intensity, it tends to approach gray.

There are several ways to change the intensity of a color. A common approach is to place one color next to its complement, which will appear to increase the color's intensity. Other methods of changing intensity require the mixing of pigments (fig. 7.13). This will automatically lower the intensity of the color being affected. The illustration shows the alteration of a hue (pigment) by adding a neutral (black, white, or gray). As white is added to any hue, the tone becomes lighter in value, but it also loses its brightness or intensity. In the same way, when black is added to a hue, the intensity diminishes as the value darkens. We cannot change value without changing intensity, although these two properties are not the same. The illustration also shows an intensity change created by mixing the hue (pigment) with a neutral gray of the same value. The resulting mixture is a variation

▲ **7·12**
Color values. This chart indicates the relative normal values of the hues at their maximum intensity (purity or brilliance). The broken line identifies those colors and neutrals at the middle (50 percent) gray position. All neutrals and colors above this line are high key and any below it are low key.

from black to white (fig. 7.12). On this scale (and in the color wheel), all colors that are above middle gray are called *high-key* colors. All colors that are below middle gray are referred to as *low-key* colors. Whether a color remains low or high key is up to the artist. As noted, a low-key violet may be lightened with white. That adjustment may raise violet's value level until it corresponds to the value level of gray for any color along the neutral scale; violet could be made equal in value to yellow-orange by checking the gray scale. Similarly, a high-key color like yellow may be adjusted with enough black until it has become a low-key color.

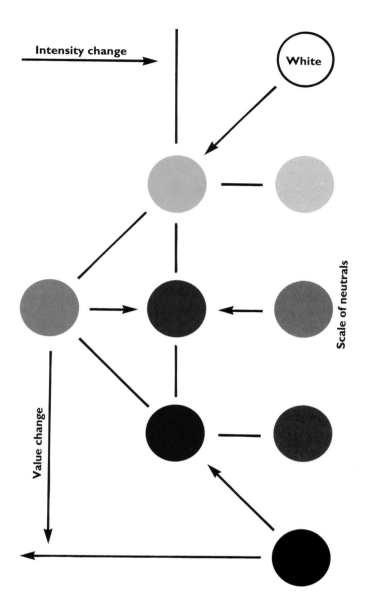

Intensity change →

White

Value change

Scale of neutrals

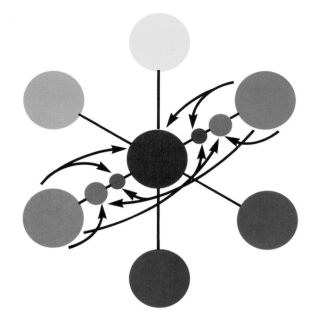

▲ **7·14**

This diagram indicates change of intensity by adding to a color a little of its complement. For instance, by adding a small amount of green to red, a gray red is produced. In the same way, a small amount of red added to green results in a gray green. When the two colors are balanced (not necessarily in equal amounts), the resulting mixture is a neutral gray.

in intensity without a change in value. The color becomes less bright as more gray is added, but it will not become lighter or darker in tone. The most efficient way to change the intensity of any hue is by adding the complementary hue. Mixing two hues that occur exactly opposite each other on the color wheel, such as red and green, blue and orange, or yellow and violet, actually results in an equal balance of all three primaries. This produces a neutral gray, which, because of impurities and an inability to absorb all the reflected wavelengths, may be

▲ **7·13**

This diagram illustrates the way neutrals may be used to change the intensity of color. As white is added to bright red, the value changes, but the resulting color is lowered in intensity. In the same way, the addition of black to bright red creates a dark red closer to the neutral scale because the intensity changes. When a neutral gray is added to the spectrum color, the intensity is lowered, but the value is neither raised nor lowered.

considered as a lightened form of black (see "The Subtractive Color Mixing System" p. 154). When mixed in unequal proportions, it is the dominating hue in the mixture of the two complementary colors that gives the resulting tone its specific character. The lesser complementary color, instead of being pure gray, is a grayed or neutralized form of the color used in the larger amount. When hues are neutralized by mixing complements, the resulting colors have a certain liveliness of character not present when they are neutralized with a gray pigment. This neutralization also occurs when tertiary colors are created by mixing two secondary colors sharing a common color. They will have the same character and appearance as those colors created by the neutralization of a color by its complement. Tertiary colors are located on the inner circle and appear as the browns (neutralized oranges), olives (neutralized greens), and so on. They are characterized by a loss of intensity and a neutralization of hue. They are not to be found on the outer circle as mixtures of a secondary and a primary (see fig. 7.8).

In addition, it must be pointed out that it is difficult to change a color's intensity (by adding a little of its complement) without *also* changing its value level (fig. 7.14). A small amount of green (lighter value) was added to red (darker value), with the result being a loss of intensity and a lightening of value for the red. Conversely, when a small amount of red (darker value) was added to the green (lighter value) the green lost some of its intensity and became darker in value. This dual relationship, affecting the change of intensity and value, is perhaps more easily seen with yellow and violet. However, it occurs with every pair of complements except one – red-orange and blue-green. They are the only pair of complements which may be used to lower each other's intensity *without* changing the value level. This occurs because they begin at the same value level – middle gray.

Developing aesthetic color relationships

When listening to music, we find a single note played for a long period of time rather boring. It is not until the composer begins to combine notes in chords that harmonic relationships of sound are

▼ **7·15**
Complementary colors (extreme contrast).

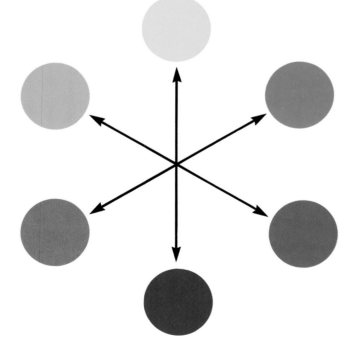

▼ **7·16**
Split-complementary colors. This example shows yellow and its split-complementary colors, red-violet and blue-violet, on either side of yellow's complement, violet.

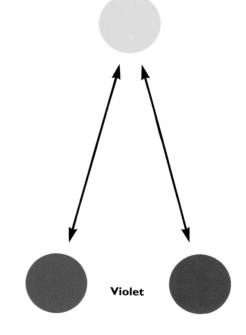

Violet

created. All sounds work together differently – some are better than others at creating unique harmonic effects. The same is true for an artist working with color. No color is important in itself; each is always seen on the picture surface in a dynamic interaction with other colors. Combinations and arrangements of color express content or meaning. Consequently, any arrangement – objective or nonobjective – ought to evoke sensations of pleasure because of its well-ordered harmonious system of tonality (see fig. 7.40). To develop a discerning eye, study the wonderfully harmonious relationships of color found in nature – in the feather pattern of birds, on insects, or on plantlife. It must be said that there are no exact rules for creating pleasing effects in color relationships, only some guiding principles.

The successful use of color depends upon an understanding of some basic color relationships. A single color by itself has a certain character, creates mood, or elicits an emotional response; but that character may be greatly changed when the color is seen with other colors in a harmonic relationship. Just as the musician can vary combined tones to form different harmonies, so too can the artist create different relationships (harmonies) among colors that may be closely allied or contrasting.

Complements and split-complements

Color organizations that rely on the greatest contrast in hue occur when two colors that appear directly opposite each other on the color wheel (complementaries) are used together (fig. 7.15). Here, because of the great contrast, there is agitation. Each color tends to increase the apparent intensity of the other color, and when used in equal amounts, they are difficult to look at for any length of time. This can be overcome by reducing the size of one of the colors or introducing changes in the intensity or value level of one or both colors.

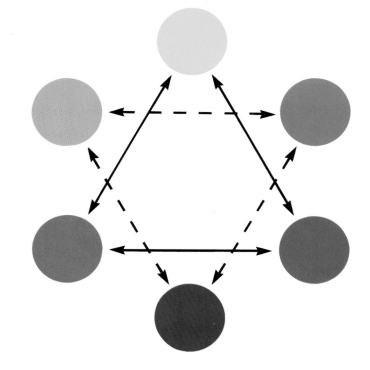

A subtle variation with slightly less contrast would be the *split-complement* system, which incorporates a color and two colors on either side of its complement (fig. 7.16). This color scheme provides more variety than the straight complementary system, because the color is opposed by two colors closely related to the color's complement. Even greater variety or interest may be achieved by using an intensity change or selecting tones from the complete value range of any or all of the colors in this color scheme.

Triads

A triadic color organization is based on an even shorter interval between colors, giving less contrast between the colors. Here, three equally spaced colors form an equilateral triangle on the color wheel: triads are used in many combinations. A primary triad, using only primary colors, creates striking contrasts (fig. 7.17). With the secondary triad, composed of orange, green, and violet, the interval between hues is the same but the contrast is softer.

▲ **7 · 17**
Triadic color interval (medium contrast). Primary intervals are indicated in solid lines, while secondary intervals are shown in broken lines.

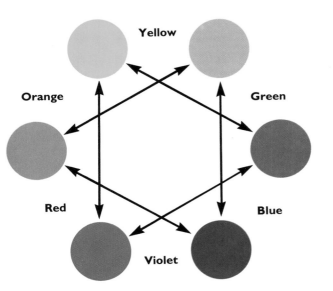

▲ 7 · 18
Intermediate color intervals showing two triadic relationships.

▽ 7 · 19
Color tetrad intervals (squares and rectangles). The color tetrad is composed of four colors equally spaced to form a square. A more casual relationship would have a rectangle formed out of two complements and their split complements. The rectangle or square may be rotated to any position on the color wheel to reveal other tetrad color intervals.

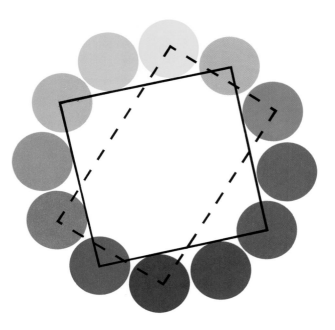

This effect probably occurs because any two hues of the triad share a common color: orange and green both contain yellow; orange and violet both contain red; and green and violet both contain blue. Intermediate color schemes may be organized into two intermediate triads (fig. 7.18). Here, too, as we move further away from the purity of the primaries, the contrast among the two triads is softer.

Tetrads

Another color relationship is based on a square rather than an equilateral triangle. Known as a *tetrad*, this system is formed when four colors are used in the organization. They are equally spaced around the color wheel and contain a primary, its complement, and a complementary pair of intermediates (fig. 7.19). A tetrad has also come to mean, in a less strict sense, any organization of color forming a "rectangular structure" which could include a double split-complement. This system of color harmony is potentially more varied than the triad because of the additional colors present. Try to avoid the temptation of using all the colors in equal volumes and the increased variety will be even more interesting.

Analogous and mono-chromatic colors

Colors that appear next to each other on the color wheel have the shortest interval and therefore the most harmonious relationship. This is because three or four neighboring hues always contain one common color that dominates the group. They are *analogous colors* (fig. 7.20). *Monochromatic color* schemes use only one color, but explore the complete range of value from black to white for that hue. Even with thousands of shades of one color, this scheme is potentially the most monotonous. However, monochromatic

▷ 7 · 20
Analogous colors (close relationships).

studies are encouraged as a test of the artist's understanding of the value range of that hue.

Warm and cool colors

Color "temperature" may be considered as another way to organize color schemes. All of the colors can be classified into one of two groups: "warm" colors or "cool" colors. Red, orange, and yellow are associated with the sun or fire, and thus are considered warm. Any colors containing blue, such as green, violet, or blue-green, are associated with air, sky, and water; these are called cool. This quality of warmth or coolness in a color may be affected or even changed by the hues around or near it. For example, the warmth of red, like its intensity, may be heightened by locating it near a touch of its complement, green.

Simultaneous contrast

While trying to match colors, an artist may mix a color on a palette only to find that it appears entirely different when juxtaposed with other colors on the canvas. Why does a red-violet appear to change color when placed beside a violet? The effect of one tone upon another is

explained by the rule of *simultaneous contrast*. According to this rule, whenever two different color tones come into direct contact, the contrast intensifies the difference between them. This effect is most extreme, of course, when the colors are directly contrasting in hue, but it occurs even if the colors have some degree of relationship. For example, a yellow-green surrounded by green appears more yellow, but if surrounded by yellow, it seems more strongly green. The contrast can be in the characteristics of intensity and value as well as in hue. A grayed blue looks brighter if placed against a gray background; it looks grayer or more neutralized against a bright blue background. The most striking effect occurs when complementary hues are juxtaposed: blue is brightest when seen next to orange, and green is brightest when seen next to red. When a warm tone is seen in simultaneous contrast to a cool tone, the warm tone appears warmer and the cool tone cooler. A color always tends to bring out its complement in a neighboring color. When a neutralized gray made up of two complementary colors is placed next to a strong positive color, it tends to take on a hue that is

opposite to the positive color. When a person wears a certain color of clothing, the complementary color in that person's complexion is emphasized.

All these changes in appearance make us realize that no one color should be used for its character alone, but must be considered in relation to the other colors present. For this reason it is better to develop a color composition all at once rather than trying to finish one area completely before going on to another. To become comfortable with color organization the student is encouraged to develop an ability by studying and analyzing color schemes that appeal to him or her. This study should be followed by experiment and practice with these color schemes.

The evolution of the color wheel

In this book the circular arrangement of the color wheel is based on a subtractive system of artist-pigmented colors using red, yellow, and blue as primaries. This triadic primary system has evolved over many centuries.

The origins of color systems

Sir Isaac Newton first discovered the true nature of color around 1660. Having separated color into the spectrum – red on top and violet on the bottom – he was the first to conceive of it as a color wheel. Ingeniously, he twisted what was a straight-lined spectrum, joined the ends, and inserted purple, a color leaning to red-violet – a color not found in the spectrum. This red-violet he saw as a transition between violet and red. Newton's wheel contained seven colors, which he related to the seven known planets and the seven notes of the diatonic scale in music (the standard major scale without chromatic half-steps), red corresponding to note C, orange to D, yellow to E, green to F, blue to G, indigo to A, and violet to B.

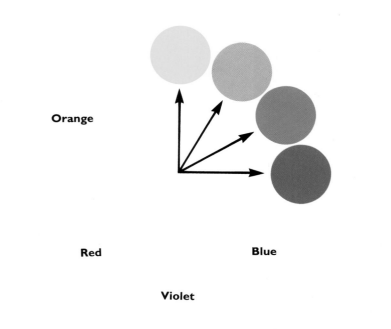

Orange

Red

Blue

Violet

The discovery of pigment primaries

Around 1731, J. C. Le Blon discovered the primary characteristic of the pigments of red, yellow, and blue and their ability to create orange, green and violet. To this day, his discovery remains the basis of much pigment color theory.

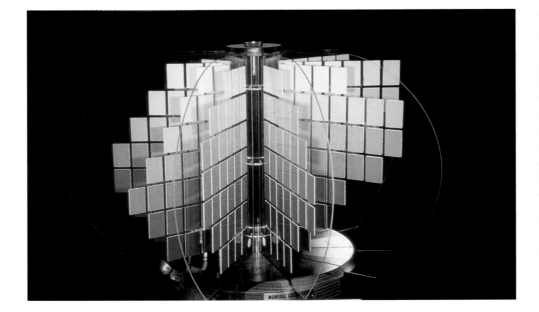

▼ 7·21

Munsell color tree, 1972. Clear plastic chart, 10½ × 12 in (26.7 × 30.5 cm); base size 12 in (30.5 cm) diameter; center pole size 12⅝ in (32.1 cm) high; chip size ¾ × 1⅜ in (1.9 × 3.5 cm).

The Munsell system in three dimensions. The greatest intensity of each hue is found in the color vane farthest from the center trunk. The value of each vane changes as it moves up and down the tree. The center trunk changes only from light to dark. The colors change in hue as they move around the tree.

Courtesy of Macbeth, a division of Kollmorgen Corporation, Baltimore, MD.

The first triadic color wheel

The first wheel in full color and based on the three primary system was published around 1766. It appeared in a book entitled *The Natural System of Colours* by Mr. Morris Harris, an English engraver. In the first decade of the nineteenth century Johann Wolfgang von Goethe began placing the colors, with their triangular arrangements, around a circle. In addition, Philipp Otto Runge created the first color solid (a three-dimensional color organization) by exploring tints, tones, and shades of color.

The discovery of simultaneous contrast

At about the same time, a French chemist, M. E. Chevreul, became interested in color theory. He discovered the principle of simultaneous contrast and the interaction of color. Eugène Delacroix was an early student of these principles and once said, "Give me mud and I will make the skin of a Venus out of it, if you will allow me to surround it as I please." The *Impressionists* and the *Post-Impressionists* were also influenced by Chevreul and often juxtaposed complements – increasing the intensity of each through simultaneous contrast.

American educators

In the United States, many educators advanced the red, yellow, and blue primary color wheels. Most noted among them was Louis Prang, who published *The Theory of Color* in 1876. Modern-day scholars like Johanness Itten and Faber Birren have done much to explore the relationship between color and expression. Their research has also clarified the historical development of the triadic color system.

The Ostwald color system

A distinguished German chemist and physicist, Wilhelm Ostwald, developed a color system around 1916 related to psychological harmony and order. Because the system was created from pigment hues technically available at the time, it uses red, yellow, sea green, and blue, with the secondaries orange, purple, turquoise, and leaf-green. The colors were placed in a circle and expanded by mixing neighboring colors into a 24-hue circle. The organization was capable of further expansion. Complements were placed opposite each other – blue opposite yellow, for example. Ostwald used his color arrangement in accordance with certain strict rules for standardizing colors for industrial application. While developing a three-dimensional model he placed each color on the point of a triangle and black and white on the other two points. The color harmonies were based upon mathematical relationships which doubled the tonal color change at each step from white to black – providing an even progression in the steps. This system concentrated on value changes, with intensity being controlled by and limited to the initial point of the triangle. The system is primarily used today by designers for color matching and was never fully adopted for industrial application.

The Munsell color system

Around 1936, the American artist Albert Munsell formulated a system to show the relationships between different color tints and shades based on hue, value, and intensity. This system was an attempt to give names to the many varieties of hues that result from mixing different colors with each other or with the neutrals. American industry adopted the Munsell system in 1943 as its material standard for naming different colors. The system was also adopted by the United States Bureau of Standards in Washington, D.C.

In the Munsell system the five basic hues are red, yellow, green, blue, and purple (violet). The mixture of any two of these colors that are adjacent on the color wheel is called an intermediate color. For example, the mixture of red and yellow is intermediate color red-yellow. The other intermediate hues are green-yellow, blue-green, purple-blue, and red-purple.

To clarify color relationships, Munsell devised a three-dimensional color system that classifies the different shades or variations of colors according to the qualities of hue, value, and intensity (or chroma). His system is in the form of a tree. The many different color tones are adhered to transparent plastic vanes that extend from a central trunk like tree branches. The column nearest the center trunk shows a scale of neutral tones that begin with black at the bottom and rise through grays to white at the top. The color tone at the outer limit of each branch represents the brightest hue possible at each level of value (fig. 7.21).

The most important part of the Munsell color system is the color notation, which describes a color in terms of a letter and numeral formula. The hue is indicated by the notation found on the inner circle of the color wheel. The value of the colors is indicated by the numbers on the central trunk shown in figure 7.21. The intensity, or chroma, is shown by the numbers on the vanes that radiate from the trunk. These value and intensity relationships are expressed by fractions, with the number on top representing the value and the number beneath indicating the intensity (chroma). For example, $5Y^8_{12}$ is the notation for a bright yellow.

It is interesting to compare the Munsell color wheel with the one used in this book (fig. 7.22; see fig. 7.8). Munsell places blue opposite yellow-red and red opposite blue-green, while we place blue opposite orange and red opposite green.

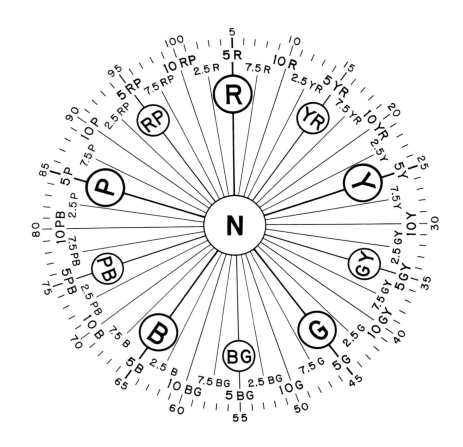

▲ **7 · 22**

Munsell color wheel. This diagram shows the relationships of the hues on the wheel in terms of a specific type of notation (as explained in the text).

Courtesy of Macbeth, a division of Kollmorgen Corporation, Baltimore, MD.

The subtractive color mixing system

Another system, subtractive color theory, mentioned earlier, does not use the artist's pigment primaries of red, yellow, and blue when applied to color mixing. Instead subtractive color mixing primaries are cyan, yellow, and magenta (see fig. 7.4). It is interesting to note that these colors are the additive primary colors' secondary hues (see fig. 7.3).

Great advances in color reproduction have been made by the printing industry using subtractive color mixing applied to the four-color printing process. Several existing techniques have been brought together to make this process possible. Monochrome photography provides images in black, white, and a full tonal range of unbroken grays. Halftoning allows all the shades of gray to be printed by one shade of ink – black on white paper. This is done by translating all the grays into a network of tiny black-and-white dots of differing sizes for different values. Photographing a colored image through various colored filters and adding halftoning provides a printing plate with the proper range of tone for each of the primaries – magenta, yellow, and cyan. This is accomplished by photographing through filters of green, blue, and red – complements of the colors desired. Filters absorb or subtract light wavelengths just as the pigment on a painting does – eliminating all but those that create the color. However, filters, unlike the opaque pigments used by artists, allow the unabsorbed wavelengths to pass through.

When the printing plates of cyan, magenta, and yellow are printed together, all the colors possible are created. Where

▶ 7 · 23

These illustrations show the yellow (A), magenta (B), cyan (C), and black (D) printing plates used in the four-color printing process. When printed together, they produce the full color image (E) o a detail of Modigliani's *Gypsy Woman with Baby* (see fig. 10.25). An enlargement shows the dots printed from each plate and the colors created where the yellow, magenta, cyan, and black inks overlap (F).

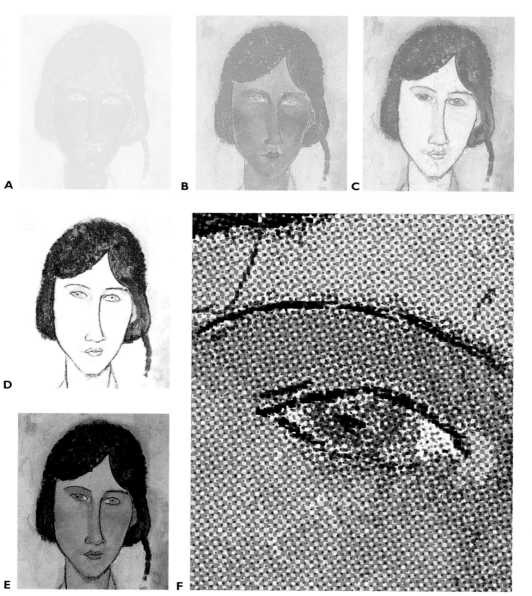

the magenta and yellow overlap, red (a pigment primary for the artist's palette) is created as a secondary color. Where the magenta is decreased and the yellow increased the color swings more toward orange – and so on, depending on the adjustment of the two colors. Similarly, the other subtractive color mixing secondary colors are created by overprinting the remaining primaries: cyan plus magenta produces blue, and cyan plus yellow produces green. Overprinting cyan, magenta, and yellow creates something close to black but that is usually heightened by printing the fourth plate in black to add definition (fig. 7.23).

Color photographers also use magenta, cyan and yellow. Instead of artists' pigment, they often develop color using dyes and gelatin emulsions. Colored film contains three layers of emulsion which respond to blue, red and green light. When exposed to the image a multilayered negative results. Light-sensitive silver halide compounds are converted to metallic compounds by the developer. In the process, they oxidize and combine with "coupler" compounds to produce dyes. Each layer forms one of the three dyes which are the subtractive primaries – yellow, magenta, and cyan. A yellow image is formed on the blue-sensitive layer; a magenta image forms on the green-sensitive layer; and a cyan image is created in the red-sensitive layer. Next, the silver is bleached out of each layer, leaving only the appropriate colored dye on the correct layer. Color negatives, positive color transparencies (slides), and color printers all involve this same basic process (fig. 7.24).

The discovery of light primaries

Paralleling early developments with pigment was the discovery around 1790 of the red, green, and blue light primaries. These concepts were explored by scientists Hermann von Helmholtz of Germany and James Clerk Maxwell of Great

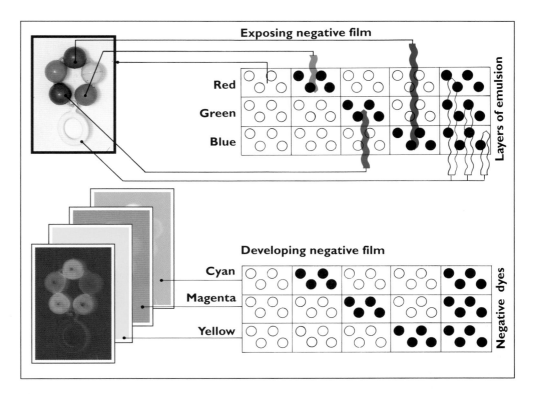

7 · 24

When color negative film is exposed, the blue-, green-, and red-sensitive layers of emulsion (color spots) record latent images (gray dots) that can be developed into black-and-white negatives. Colors that are mixtures of the primaries are recorded on several layers. Blacks do not expose any of the emulsion, while white light is recorded in all layers. Each color thus leaves a corresponding negative black-and-white impression.

When exposed color negative film is developed, a black-and-white negative image is produced in each emulsion layer (black dots). During this development, a colored dye is combined with each black-and-white negative image. The dyes are cyan, magenta, and yellow. Once the silver is bleached out, the three layers (colored dots) show the subject in superimposed negative dye images.

(Photograph by John Riddy, London.)

Britain. Some additive-light primary systems have been represented as circles, but they should not be confused with color systems designed for artists' pigment. Space does not permit discussion of all the color systems that have evolved.

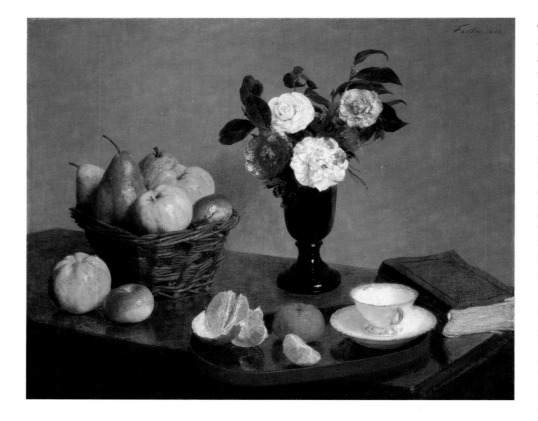

▲ **7 · 25**
Henri Fantin-Latour, *Still Life*, 1866. Oil on linen, 24⅜ × 29½ in (62 × 74.8 cm).
This still life is painted in local color – color that simulates the hues of the objects in nature.
Chester Dale Collection. (© 1993 National Gallery of Art, Washington, D.C.)

USES OF COLOR

Being familiar with the sources of color and its principal properties is of little value unless we understand how the artist uses these facts. Based upon the triadic pigment mixing system, color serves several purposes in artistic composition. These purposes, however, are not always separate and distinct, but instead frequently overlap and interrelate. Color can be used in the following ways:

1. To give spatial quality to the pictorial field.
   a. Color can supplement, or even substitute for, value differences to give plastic quality.
   b. Color can create interest through the counterbalance of backward and forward movement in pictorial space.
2. To create mood and symbolize ideas.
3. To serve as a vehicle for expressing personal emotions and feelings.
4. To attract and direct attention as a means of giving organization to a composition.
5. To accomplish aesthetic appeal by a system of well-ordered color relationships.
6. To identify objects by describing the superficial facts of their appearance.

The last function, that of describing superficial appearances, was considered most important when painting was seen as a purely illustrative art. For a long period in the history of Western art, color was looked upon as something that came from the object being represented. In painting, color that is used to indicate the natural appearance of an object is known as *local color* (fig. 7.25). A more expressive quality is likely to be achieved when the artist is willing to disassociate the color surfaces in the painting from the object to which the color conventionally belongs. An entirely *subjective color* treatment can be substituted for local color. The colors used and their relationships are invented by the artist for purposes other than mere representation (fig. 7.26). This style of treatment may even deny color as an objective reality; that is, we may have purple cows, green faces, or red trees. Most of the functions of color are subjective; they are of particular importance in modern art and should be examined separately.

The plastic quality of color

As used by the present-day artist, color that does not describe the surface of an object may give the essential reality of the object's plastic character. This ability to build a form comes from the advancing and receding characteristics of certain colors. When placed upon a surface, colors actually seem to have a spatial dimension. For example, a spot of red on a flat surface seems to be in front of that surface; a spot of blue, similarly placed, seems to sink back into the surface. In general, warm colors advance, and cool colors recede. The character of such effects, however, can be altered by differences in the value and/or intensity of the color (see fig. 7.40).

▶ **7 · 26**
Marie Laurencin, *Mother and Child*, 1928. Oil on canvas, 32 × 25½ in (81.3 × 64.8 cm).
This French artist used color to construct a personal (or subjective) interpretation that creates the charming mood of the painting.
The Detroit Institute of Arts, Detroit, MI. City of Detroit Purchase. © ADAGP, Paris and DACS, London 1994.

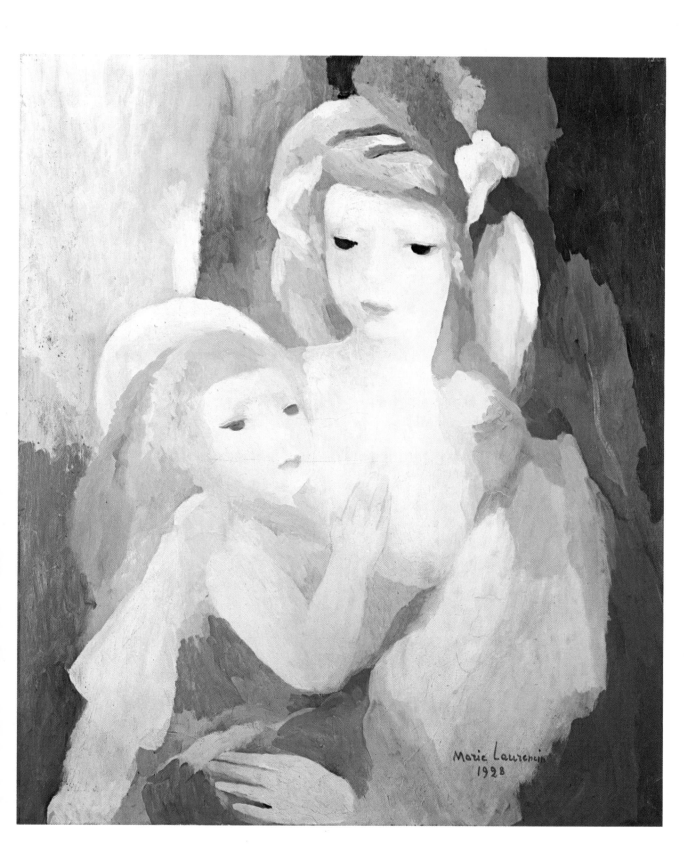

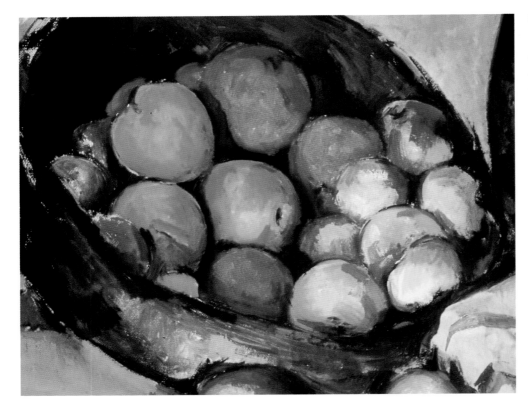

▲ **7 · 27**
Paul Cézanne, *The Basket of Apples*
(detail), c. 1895. Oil on canvas, 25¾ × 32 in
(65.5 × 81.3 cm).
Cézanne used changes of color as a means of
modeling form. The use of warm and cool colors
makes the fruit advance and recede rather than
merely indicating a change in value.
Art Institute of Chicago. Helen Birch Bartlett Memorial
Collection 1926.252.

These spatial characteristics of color
were fully developed by the French artist
Paul Cézanne in the latter part of the
nineteenth century. He admired the
sparkling brilliancy of the Impressionist
artists of the period but thought their
work had lost the solidity of earlier
painting. Consequently, he began to
experiment with expressing the bulk and
weight of forms by modeling with color

tones. Previous to Cézanne's experiments,
the traditional *academic* artist had
modeled form by changing values in
monotone (one color). The artist then
tinted these tones with a thin, dry local
color that was characteristic of the object
being painted. Cézanne discovered that a
change of color on a form could serve the
purpose of a change of value and not lose
the effectiveness of the expression. He felt
that the juicy richness of positive colors
expressed the actual structure of a solid
object. Later, modern artists realized that
Cézanne's advancing and receding colors
could also create those backward and
forward movements in space that give
liveliness and interest to the picture
surface (fig. 7.27). Many abstract artists
have used the relationships of balance and
movement in space to give content
(meaning) to a painting, although no
actual objects are represented (see fig.
10.47). Line, value, shape, and texture are
greatly aided by the ability of color to
create space and content (meaning).

Color and emotion

A second function of color involves its
ability to create mood, symbolize ideas,
and express personal emotions. Color, as
found upon the canvas, can express a
mood or feeling in its own right, even
though it is not descriptive of the objects
represented. Light, bright colors make us
feel joyful and uplifted, while cool, dark,
or somber colors are generally depressing.
The different hues of the spectrum have
different emotional impacts. Psychologists
have found that red is happy and exciting,
whereas blue is dignified, sad, or serene.
Also, different values and intensities of
the hues in a *color tonality* may affect its
feeling tone. A wide value range (strongly
contrasting light or dark hues) gives
vitality and directness to a color scheme;
closely related values and low intensities
suggest subtlety, calmness, and repose
(figs. 7.28 and 7.29). We cannot escape the
emotional effects of color because it
appeals directly to our senses.

Artists may also take advantage of the
power of color to symbolize ideas, thus
making their work stronger in content or
meaning. Such abstract qualities as virtue,
loyalty, honesty, evil, and cowardice are
symbolized by the colors that have come
to be traditionally associated with them.
In many cases we do not know the origin
of these associations but are nevertheless
affected by them. For example, blue is
associated with loyalty and honesty (true
blue), red with danger, yellow with
cowardice (yellow streak), black with
death, green with life or hope, white with
purity or innocence, and purple with
royalty or wealth. Some colors have many
different associations. Thus, red can
connote fire, danger, bravery, sin, passion,
or violent death. The colors in a painting
may enhance the impact of the subject
matter by suggesting meanings associated
with them.

In addition to expressing meanings by
association, color may express an artist's
personal emotions. Most truly creative
artists evolve a personal style of color tone

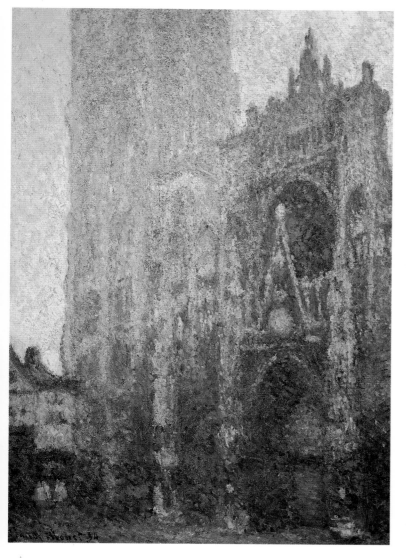

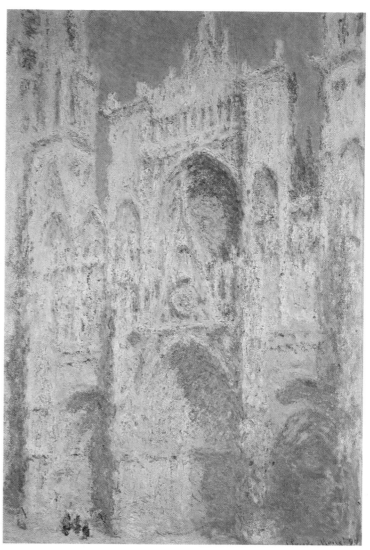

▲ 7 · 28

Claude Monet, *Rouen Cathedral; Morning*, 1894. Oil on canvas, 42 × 29 in (106.7 × 73.5 cm).

The Impressionist Monet took a deep interest in the characteristics of light, and often painted the same subjects at different times of the day. As a result the hues, values, and intensities are markedly affected, as can be seen by comparing this painting with figure 7.29.

Galerie Beyeler, Basel, Switzerland.

▲ 7 · 29

Claude Monet, *Rouen Cathedral, West Façade, Sunlight*, 1894. Oil on linen, 39½ × 26 in (100.2 × 66 cm).

In giving the impression of a passing moment the artist has deliberately sacrificed detailed architectural information for the effect of sunlight, color, and atmosphere playing on that form. This also applies to figure 7.28.

Chester Dale Collection. (© 1993 National Gallery of Art, Washington, D.C.)

that comes primarily not from the subject but from their feelings about the subject. John Marin's color is essentially suggestive in character with little expression of form or solidity (see fig. 8.47). It is frequently delicate and light in tone, in keeping with the medium in which he works (watercolor). The color in the paintings of Vincent van Gogh is usually vivid, hot, intense, and applied in

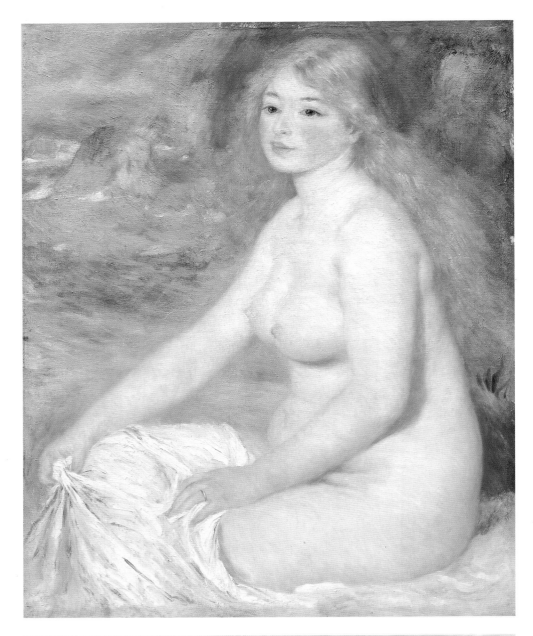

snakelike ribbons of pigment (see fig. 1.13). His use of texture and color expresses the intensely personal style of his work. The French artist Renoir used a luminous, shimmering color when painting human flesh, so that his nudes have a glow that is not actually present in the human figure (fig. 7.30). The emotional approach to color appealed particularly to the Expressionistic painters, who used it to create an entirely subjective treatment having nothing to do with objective reality (see fig. 10.31). Modern-day artists like Wolf Kahn continue to interpret their environment in terms of personal color selection (fig. 7.31).

◀ **7 · 30**
Pierre-Auguste Renoir, *Blonde Bather*, 1881. Oil on canvas, 32¼ × 25⅞ in (81.8 × 65.7 cm).
Renoir was fascinated by the effect of light on surfaces. In this picture, his rapid brushwork adds to the luminosity of this nude, bathed in a shimmering light.
Sterling and Francine Clark Art Institute, Williamstown, MA.

◀ **7 · 31**
Wolf Kahn, *At Green Mountain Orchards*, 1991. Oil on canvas, 3 ft 6 in × 5 ft 6 in (1.07 × 1.68 m).
Wolf Kahn is one contemporary painter who subordinates his subject – landscape – and all the other art elements to color. The hallmark of his later work is a vibrant, even risky use of color, making it instantly recognizable.
Courtesy of the artist. © Wolf Kahn/DACS, London/ VAGA, New York 1994.

The aesthetic appeal of color tonality

The final function of color involves its ability to evoke sensations of pleasure through its well-ordered system of tonality (see fig. 7.40). This appeal refers to the sense of satisfaction we derive from seeing a well-designed rug or drapery material whose color combination is harmonious. The same appeal can be found in a purely nonobjective painting. There are no exact rules for arriving at pleasing effects in color relationships, but there are some guiding principles. The problems are, first, the selection of hues to be used together in a composition and, second, their arrangement in the pictorial field in the proper amounts for color balance. No color is important in itself; each is always seen on the picture surface in a dynamic interaction with other colors. Combinations and arrangements of color express content or meaning; consequently, any arrangement ought to have a definite aesthetic appeal. In talking about pleasing color, we must realize that there can be brutal color combinations as well as refined ones. These brutal combinations are satisfying if they accomplish the artist's purpose of exciting us rather than calming us. Some of the German *Expressionist* painters have proven that these brutal, clashing color schemes can have definite aesthetic values when used purposefully (fig. 7.32).

▼ **7 · 32**

Emil Nolde, *Christ among the Children*, 1910. Oil on canvas, 34⅛ × 41⅞ in (86.8 × 106.4 cm).

The Expressionists usually employed bold, clashing hues to emphasize their emotional identification with a subject. Intense feeling is created by the use of complementary and near-complementary hues.

The Museum of Modern Art, New York. Gift of Dr. W. R. Valentiner.

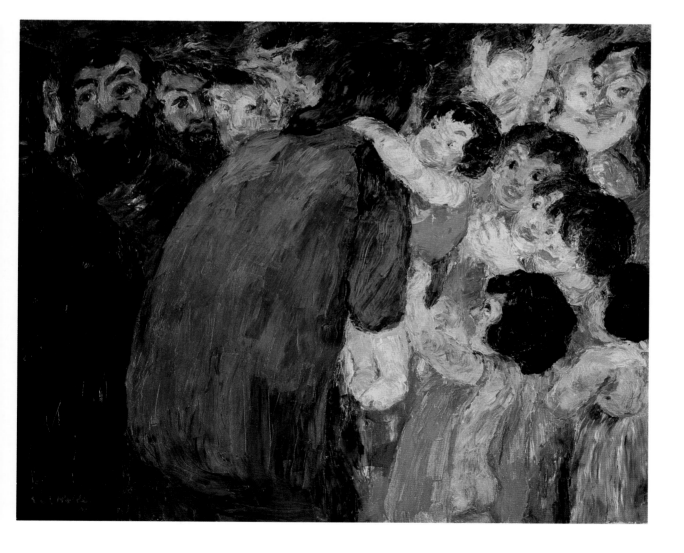

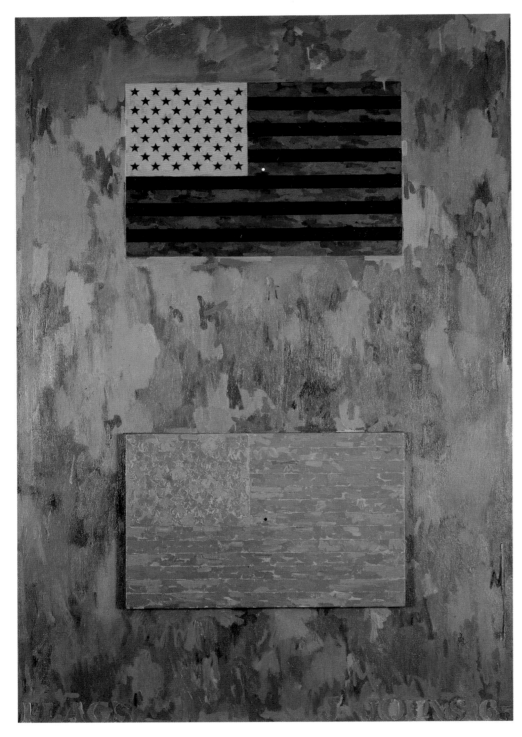

Color balance

All good color combinations have some relationships and some contrasts. Where colors are related in hue, they can exhibit contrast in value and/or intensity. The basic problem is the same one present in all aspects of form organization: variety in unity. There must be relationships between the color tones, but these relationships must be made alive and interesting through variety. A simple way to create unity and balance is by repeating similar color tones in different parts of a composition. An important aspect of color balance is based upon our perception of complementary hues. If we look fixedly at a spot of intense red for a few moments and then shift our eyes to a white area, we see an afterimage of the same spot in green, its complement. The phenomenon can be noted when any pair of complementary colors is used (fig. 7.33). This psychological fact is the basis for our use of a note of complementary color to balance the dominating hue in many color schemes (fig. 7.34).

The pleasing quality of a color pattern frequently depends on the amounts or proportions of color used. In general, equal amounts of different colors are not as interesting as a color arrangement where one color, or one kind of color, predominates (fig. 7.35). We are often confused by color schemes in which all of

◀ **7 · 33**

Jasper Johns, *Flags*, 1965. Oil on canvas with raised canvas, 6 × 4 ft (1.83 × 1.22 m).

With this painting, Johns wanted the viewer to experience an afterimage. This occurs when the retina's receptors are overstimulated and are unable to accept additional signals. They then project the wavelengths of the complementary color. Stare at the white dot on the upper flag for forty seconds. Shift focus to the dark dot on the lower flag, and an afterimage will be seen in red, white, and blue.

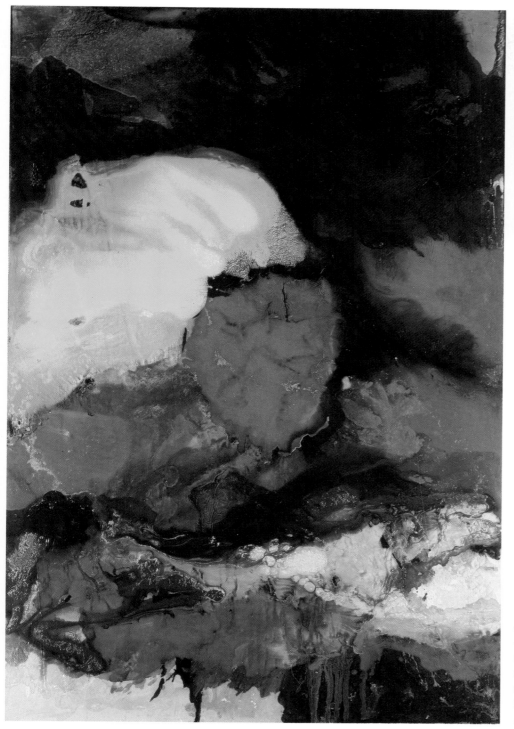

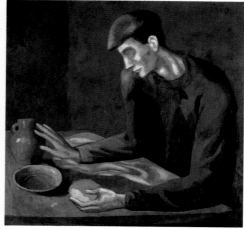

▲ **7 · 35**

Pablo Picasso, *The Blind Man's Meal*, 1903. Oil on canvas, 37½ × 37¼ in (95.2 × 94.6 cm).

Although other colors appear in this painting, it is the predominant blue hue which provides the overall unity.

Metropolitan Museum of Art, New York. Gift of Mr. and Mrs. Ira Haupt, 1950. (50.188.) © DACS 1994.

◄ **7 · 34**

Noriyoshi Ishigooka, *Spring in the Château du Repas*, 1987. Oil on canvas, 6 ft 4¾ in × 4 ft 3¼ in (1.95 × 1.30 m).

Large areas of green and yellow dominate in this use of double complementary colors. Smaller areas of their complements, red and violet, balance the total color pattern.

Collection of the Pierre Gohill Corporation.

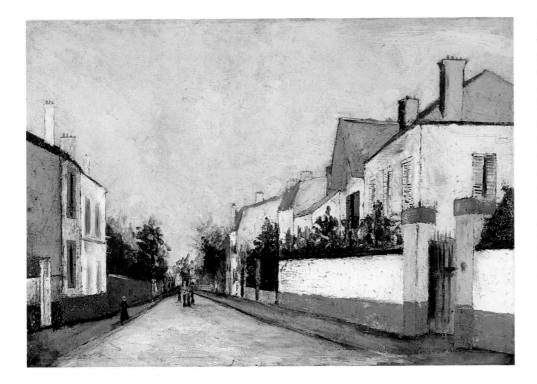

7·36

Maurice Utrillo, *Street in Sannois*, c. 1911. Oil on canvas, 21½ × 29¼ in (54.6 × 74.3 cm).

Blue is a dominant hue in this painting by Utrillo. He achieves a dynamic balance by using smaller areas of complementary orange (adjusted in value and intensity) and neutral white, gray, and black.

Virginia Museum of Fine Arts, Richmond, VA. Collection of Mr. and Mrs. Paul Mellon. © ADAGP/ SPADEM, Paris and DACS, London 1994.

much on how we distribute our tones as on the relationships among the tones themselves. Most combinations, however, can be reduced to two basic types of color organization. In the first, the unity of the hues is dominant (see fig. 10.58); in the second, hue combinations that depend on strong contrast and variety of color are used (see fig. 7.31). In the unified color scheme, enough variety must be introduced to keep the effect from becoming too monotonous; in the contrasting color scheme the basic problem is to unify the contrasts without destroying the general strength and intensity of expression. In the first type of color pattern the hue intervals are closely related, as in analogous colors; in the second type the hue intervals are further apart, the greatest possible interval being that between two complementary colors.

the tones demand equal importance, because we cannot find a dominant area on which to fix our attention. The dominance of any one color in a pattern can be due to its hue, value, or intensity; dominance can also be affected by the character of the surrounding hues (fig. 7.36). A small, dark spot of color, through its lower value, can dominate a large, light area. A spot of intense color, though small, can balance a larger amount of a grayer, more neutralized color. Also, a small amount of warm color usually dominates a larger amount of cool color, although both may be of the same intensity. Complementary colors, which of course vie for our attention through simultaneous contrast, can be made more attractive if one of them is softened or neutralized.

Color combinations

Any attempt to base the aesthetic appeal of color pattern on certain fixed theoretical color harmonies will probably not be successful. The effect depends as

Unified color patterns

Unity is often produced in a color scheme by stressing one hue only. Naturally, variety can only be achieved by using contrasting values or intensities (fig. 7.37). This scheme can be varied by introducing a small amount of a subordinate contrasting hue or even a contrasting neutral such as white or black. Another way to relate colors and achieve unity is by adjusting a number of colors toward one hue, as in figure 7.38. This one hue will be a harmonizing factor if a little of it is mixed with every color used in the combination. The same effect can be created by glazing over a varicolored pattern with a single tone of color, which becomes the unifying color. A third type of unified pattern is found when all warm or all cool colors are used in combination. Again, however, a small amount of a complementary color or a contrasting neutral can add variety to the color pattern (see fig. 7.40). As a rule, where warm and cool colors are balanced against each other in a composition, it is better to allow one temperature to dominate.

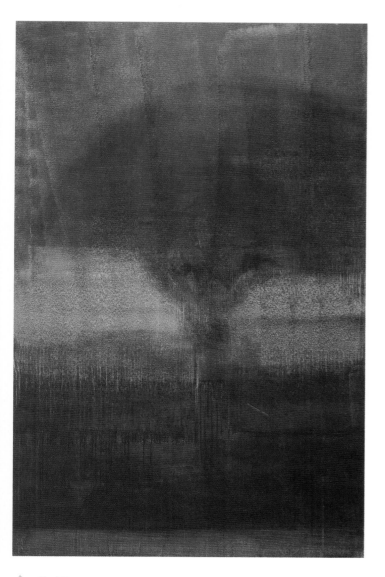

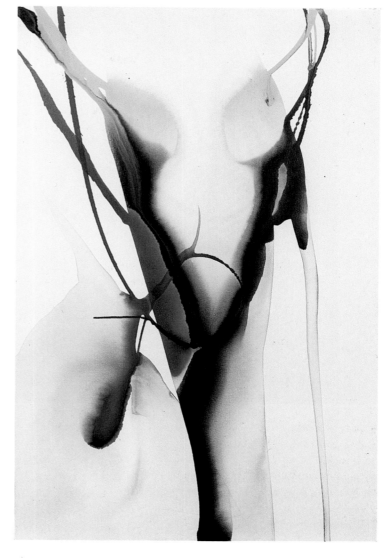

▲ 7 · 37
Ellen Phelan, *Umbrella Pine*, 1991. Oil on canvas, 5 ft 4½ in × 3 ft 5 in (1.64 × 1.04 m).
While concentrating on the orange color family, the artist has changed value and intensity to emphasize developing forms. The image was created using paint rollers to apply the medium in thin layers.
Courtesy of Dorsey Waxter Fine Art, Millbrook, NY.

▲ 7 · 38
Paul Jenkins, *Phenomena Shield and Green*, 1969. Acrylic on canvas, 40 × 26 in (101.6 × 66 cm).
Analogous (related) colors can produce harmony, while touches of a complementary color contribute variety.
Courtesy of the Owens-Corning Collection, Owens-Corning Fiberglas Corporation, Toledo, OH.

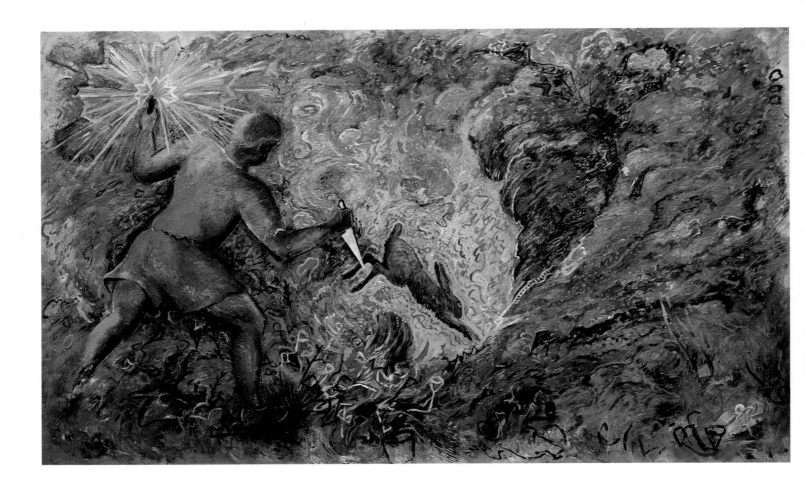

Sandro Chia, *Rabbit for Dinner*, 1981. Oil on canvas, 6 ft 8⅞ in × 11 ft 1½ in (2.05 × 3.39 m).

The Italian Sandro Chia, a Neo-Expressionist, uses contrasting hues to charge his picture with emotion. The hues are neutralized with black to achieve unity without losing liveliness.

Stedelijk Museum, Amsterdam, The Netherlands.

Contrasting color patterns

Color schemes based upon strong contrasts of hue, value, or intensity have great possibilities for expressive effect (fig. 7.39). These contrasts can sometimes be controlled by the amount of opposing color used. Where the basic unity of a color pattern has been established, strong contrasts of color can be used in small accents; their size, then, prevents them from disturbing the basic unity of the color theme (fig. 7.40). Low-key and high-key compositions benefit greatly from such contrasting accents, which add interest to what might otherwise be a monotonous composition (see figs. 10.8 and 4.19). Another commonly used method of controlling contrasts is to separate all or a part of the tones by a neutral line or area. Absolute black or white lines are the most effective neutrals

for this purpose because they are so positive in character themselves. They not only tie together the contrasting hues, but also enhance their color character because of value contrast. The neutral black leading between the brilliant colors of stained-glass windows is an example of this unifying character. Such modern painters as Georges Roualt and Max Beckmann found a black line effective in separating their highly contrasting colors (see figs. 10.26 and 10.31). A similar unifying effect can be brought about by using a large area of neutral gray or a *neutralized color* as a background for clashing contrasts of color (see fig. *2.22*).

Finally, we should remember that artists frequently produce color combinations which defy these guiding principles but which are still satisfying to the eye. Artists use color as they do the other elements of art structure – to give a highly personalized meaning to the subject of their work.

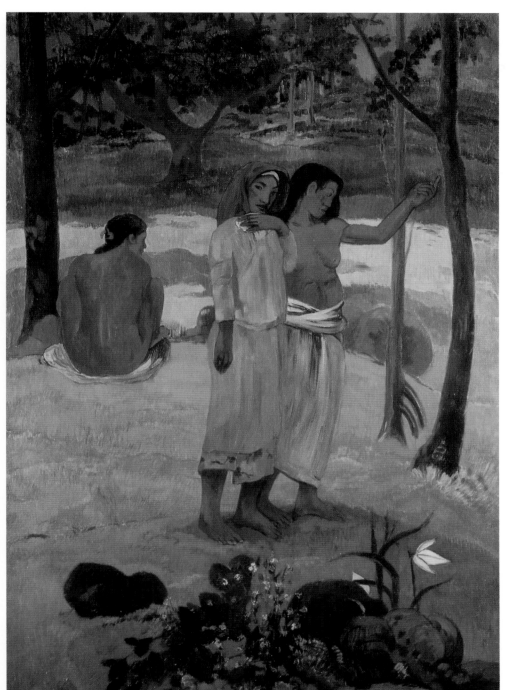

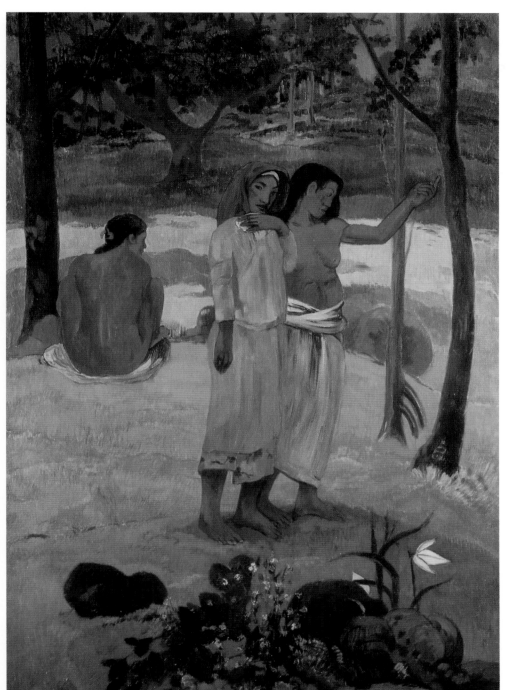 **7 · 40**

Paul Gauguin, *The Call (L'Appel)*, 1902. Oil on canvas, 51¼ × 35½ in (130.2 × 90.2 cm).

The Post-Impressionist painter Paul Gauguin established a basic unity by painting several broad areas of color – reds, oranges, greens, and blues. Small accents of the colors' complements are introduced into each zone for excitement and variety. Warm colors serve to establish the foreground and cool colors make the background recede.

Courtesy of the Cleveland Museum of Art, Cleveland, OH. (Gift of Hanna Fund.) 43.392.

CHAPTER EIGHT

Space

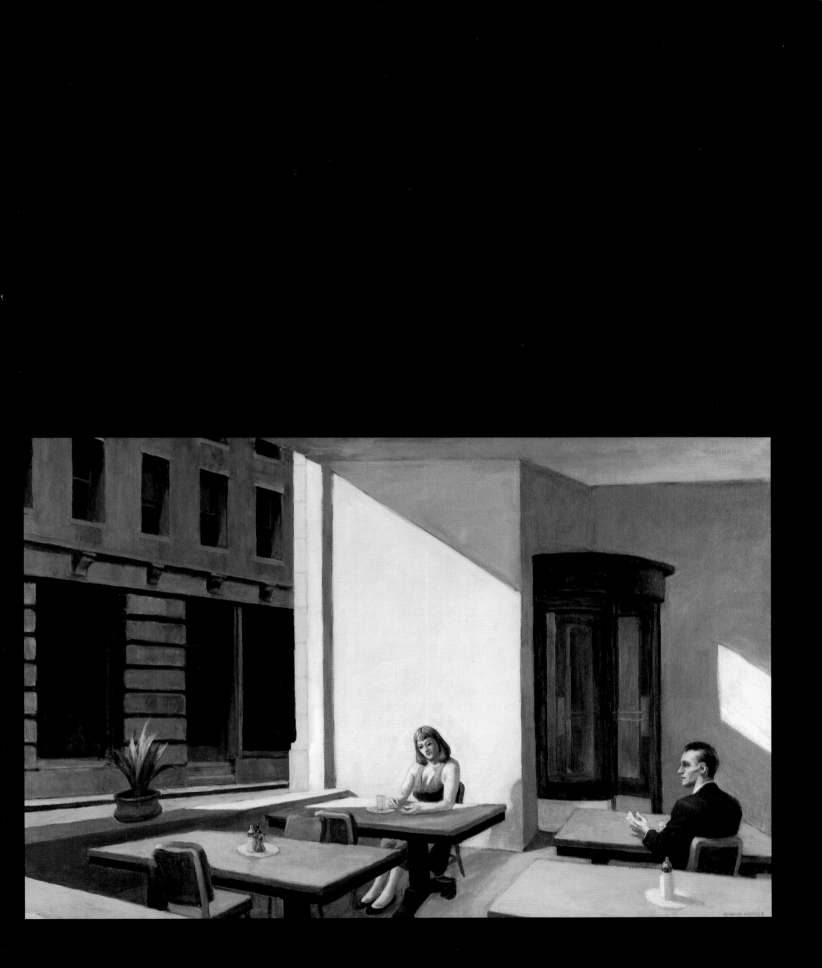

THE VOCABULARY OF SPACE

Space The interval, or measurable distance, between preestablished points or images.

atmospheric (aerial) perspective
The illusion of deep space produced in graphic works by lightening values, softening details and textures, reducing value contrasts, and neutralizing colors in objects as they recede (see **perspective**).

decorative (space)
Ornamenting or enriching but, more importantly in art, stressing the two-dimensional nature of an artwork or any of its elements. Decorative art (space) emphasizes the essential flatness of a surface.

four-dimensional space
A highly imaginative treatment of forms that gives a sense of intervals of time or motion.

fractional representation
A device used by various cultures (notably the Egyptians) in which several spatial aspects of the same subject are combined in the same image.

infinite space
A concept in which the picture frame acts as a window through which objects can be seen receding endlessly.

interpenetration
The movement of planes, objects, or shapes through each other, locking them together within a specific area of space.

intuitive space
The illusion of space that the artist creates by *instinctively* manipulating certain space-producing devices, including overlapping, transparency, interpenetration, inclined planes, disproportionate scale, fractional representation, and the inherent spatial properties of the art elements.

isometric projection (perspective)
A technical drawing system in which a three-dimensional object is presented two-dimensionally; starting with the nearest vertical edge, the horizontal edges of the object are drawn at a thirty degree angle and all verticals are projected perpendicularly from a horizontal base.

linear perspective (geometric)
A system used to develop three-dimensional images on a two-dimensional surface; it develops the optical phenomenon of diminishing size by treating edges as converging parallel lines. They extend to a vanishing point or points on the horizon (eye-level) and recede from the viewer (see **perspective**).

oblique projection (perspective)
A technical drawing system in which a three-dimensional object is presented two-dimensionally; the front and back sides of the object are parallel to the horizontal base; and the other planes are drawn as parallels coming off the front plane at a forty-five degree angle.

orthographic drawing
Graphic representation of two-dimensional views of an object, showing a plan, vertical elevations, and/or a section.

perspective
Any graphic system used in creating the illusion of three-dimensional images and/or spatial relationships on a two-dimensional surface. There are several types of perspective.

plastic (space)
1. The use of the elements to create the illusion of the third dimension on a two-dimensional surface. 2. Three-dimensional art forms such as architecture, sculpture, ceramics, etc.

shallow space
The illusion of limited depth. With shallow space, the imagery moves only a slight distance back from the picture plane.

three-dimensional (space)
To possess, or to create the illusion of possessing, the dimension of depth in addition to the dimensions of height and width.

transparency
A visual quality in which a distant image or element can be seen through a nearer one.

two-dimensional (space)
To possess the dimensions of height and width, especially when considering the flat surface, or picture plane.

INTRODUCTION TO SPACE

Some people consider space an element of *two-dimensional* art, while others see it as a product of the elements. But however categorized, the presence of *space* is felt in every work of art, and it is something that must concern every artist. In this text, space is conceived of as a product rather than a tool: it is created by the art elements. The importance of space lies in its function, and a basic knowledge of its implications and use is essential for every artist. Space, as discussed in this chapter, is limited to the graphic fields – that is, such two-dimensional surface arts as drawing, painting, and printmaking. The space that exists as an illusion in the graphic fields is actually present in the plastic areas of sculpture, ceramics, jewelry, architecture, and so forth. Their *three-dimensional space* concepts are discussed in Chapter 9.

SPATIAL PERCEPTION

All spatial implications are mentally conditioned by the environment and experience of the viewer. Vision is experienced through the eyes but interpreted by the mind. Perception involves the whole pattern of nerve and brain response to a visual stimulus. We use our eyes to perceive objects in nature and continually to shift our focus of attention. In so doing, two different types of vision are used: stereoscopic and kinesthetic. Having two eyes set slightly apart from each other, we see two different views of the object world at the same time. The term "stereoscopic" refers to our ability to overlap these two slightly different views into one image. This visual process enables us to see in three dimensions, making it possible to judge distances.

With kinesthetic vision we experience space in the movements of the eye from one part of a work of art to another.

While viewing a two-dimensional surface, we unconsciously attempt to organize its separate parts so that they can be seen as a whole. In addition, we explore object surfaces with our eyes in order to recognize them. Objects close to the viewer require more ocular movement than those farther away, and this changing eye activity adds spatial illusion to our kinesthetic vision.

MAJOR TYPES OF SPACE

Two types of space can be suggested by the artist: *decorative space* and *plastic space*.

Decorative space

The term "decorative space," although often needed as a convenience, is in fact a misnomer. Decorative space is the absence of real depth as we know it and is confined to the flatness of the picture plane. As the artist adds art elements to that plane (or surface), the illusion created may remain flat or "decorative;" but the space may be transformed to become shallow, deep, or infinite. In fact, a truly decorative space is inconceivable; any art element when used in conjunction with others will seem to advance or recede. Decorative space, though sometimes useful in describing essentially flat pictorial effects, is not accurate. Thus, decorative space for the artist is quite limited in depth (fig. 8.1; see fig. 5.15).

Plastic space

The term "plastic" is applied to all spatial imagery other than decorative. Artists base much of their work on their experiences in the objective world, and it is a natural conclusion that they should explore the spatial resources.

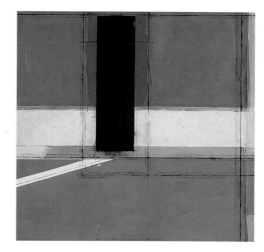

▲ 8 · I
Leonidas Maroulis, *68–388*, 1988. Oil on canvas, 5 ft 3 in × 5 ft (1.60 × 1.52 m). The planes in this work seem parallel to the picture surface. Spatial devices are missing except for the prominent white diagonal shape that fosters the illusion that the red shape on which it rests is tilted back into space.

Photograph courtesy of the Vorpal Gallery, San Francisco and New York.

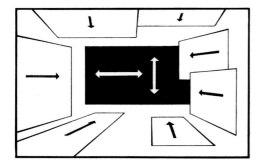

▲ **8·2**
Shallow space. As a variation on the concept of shallow space, artists occasionally define the planes that make up the outer limits of a hollow boxlike space behind the picture plane. The diagram shows this concept, although in actual practice, a return to the picture plane would be made through objects occupying the space defined. The back plane acts as a curtain that prevents penetration into deep space.

Divisions of plastic space

Artists locate their images in plastic space according to their needs and feelings, since infinite degrees of depth are possible. As a result, the categorizations of depth locations cannot be specific or fixed but must be broadened to general areas.

Shallow space Concentration on the picture surface usually limits the depth of a composition. Varying degrees of limited space are possible. Limited space – *shallow space* – can be compared to the feelings one might experience if confined to a box or stage. The space is limited by the placement of the sides or walls. For consistency, any compositional objects or figures that might appear in the boxlike or stagelike confines should be narrowed in depth or flattened (fig. 8.2). In the modern painting *The Studio* by Jacob Lawrence, the single figure has been flattened and placed in a confined room (fig. 8.3).

Asian, Egyptian, and Medieval artists used comparatively shallow space in their art. Early Renaissance paintings were often based on shallow sculptures which were then popular. Many modern artists

have elected to use shallow space because it allows more positive control and is more in keeping with the flatness of the working surface. Gauguin, Matisse, Modigliani, and Beckmann are typical advocates of the concepts of limited space (see figs. 5.15 and 10.25). For these artists, not having to create the illusion of deep plastic space allows more positive control of the placement of decorative shapes as purely compositional elements.

Deep and infinite space An artwork that emphasizes deep space denies the picture plane except as a starting-point from which the space begins. The viewer seems to be moving into the far distances of the picture field. This spatial feeling is similar to looking through an open window over a landscape that rolls on and on into infinity. This infinite quality is created using spatial indications that are produced by certain relationships of art form. Size, position, overlapping

▼ **8·4**
Jacob van Ruisdael, *Wheatfields*, c. 1670. Oil on canvas, 4 ft 3¼ in × 3 ft 3⅜ in (1.30 × 1 m).
Early Dutch landscape painting, which aimed at the maximum illusion of visual reality, emphasized the concept of infinite space. Diminishing sizes of objects and hazy effects of atmospheric perspective give the viewer a sense of seeing far into the distance.
Metropolitan Museum of Art, New York. Bequest of Benjamin Altman, 1913 (14.40.623).

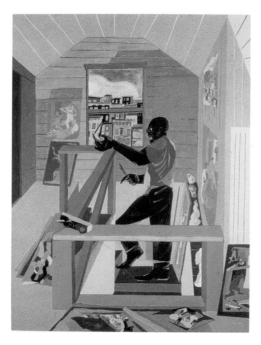

▶ **8·3**
Jacob Lawrence, *The Studio*, 1977. Gouache on paper, 30 × 22 in (76.2 × 55.9 cm).
The use of shapes with solid colors and values, generally lacking in traditional shading, creates an overall feeling of flatness. In addition, a stagelike effect arises from the shallow perspective.
Courtesy of Terry Dintenfass, Inc. © Jacob Lawrence/ DACS, London/VAGA, New York 1994.

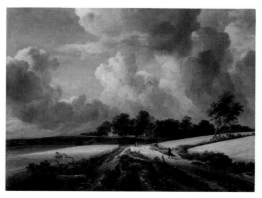

images, sharp and diminishing details, converging parallels, and perspective are the traditional methods of indicating deep spatial penetration (see fig. 6.20).

Infinite spatial concepts, allied with atmospheric perspective, dominated Western art from the beginning of the Renaissance (about 1350) to the middle of the nineteenth century. During this period, generations of artists, such as Botticelli, Ruisdael, Rembrandt, and Poussin, to name only a few, developed and perfected the deep-space illusion because of its obvious accord with visual reality (fig. 8.4). Present-day art is largely dominated by the shallow-space concept, but many contemporary artists work with strongly recessed fields. Any space concept is valid if it demonstrates consistent control of the elements in relation to the spatial field chosen.

SPATIAL INDICATORS

Artistic methods of spatial representation are so interdependent that attempts to isolate and examine all of them here would be impractical and inconclusive, and might leave the reader with the feeling that art is based on a formula. Thus, we will confine this discussion to fairly basic spatial concepts.

Our comprehension of space, which comes to us through objective experiences, is enlarged, interpreted, and given meaning by the use of our intuitive faculties. Spatial order develops when the artist senses the right balance and the best placement, then selects vital forces to create completeness and unity. Obviously, then, this process is not a purely intellectual one but a matter of instinct or subconscious response (see fig. 5.8).

Since the subjective element plays a part in controlling space, we can readily see that emphasis on formula here, as elsewhere, can quell the creative spirit. Art is a product of human creativity and is always dependent on individual interpretations and responses. Space, like

other qualities in art, may be either spontaneous or premeditated, but is always the product of the artist's will. If an artist has the impassioned will to make things so, they will usually be so, despite inconsistency and defiance of established principles. Therefore, the methods of spatial indication discussed in the following pages are those that have been used frequently and that guarantee one effect of space, though not necessarily one that is always exactly the same. These traditional methods are presented merely to give the student a basic conception of the more significant spatial forces (see fig. 4.15).

Size

We usually interpret largeness of scale in terms of nearness. Conversely, a smaller scale suggests distance. If two sailboats were several hundred feet apart, the nearer boat would appear larger than the other. Ordinarily we would interpret this difference in scale not as one large and one small image (although this could play a part in our perception), but as two vessels of approximately the same size placed at varying distances from the viewer (fig. 8.5). Therefore, if we are to use

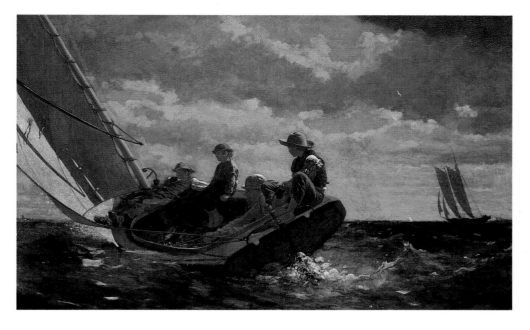

▲ **8 · 5**
Winslow Homer, *Breezing Up (A Fair Wind)*, 1876. Oil on canvas, 24⅛ × 38⅛ in (61.5 × 97 cm).
The horizon line in this painting separates the space into a ground plane below and a sky plane above. The smaller size and higher position of the distant boats help to achieve the spatial effect.

Gift of the W. L. and May T. Mellon Foundation. (© 1993 National Gallery of Art, Washington, D.C.)

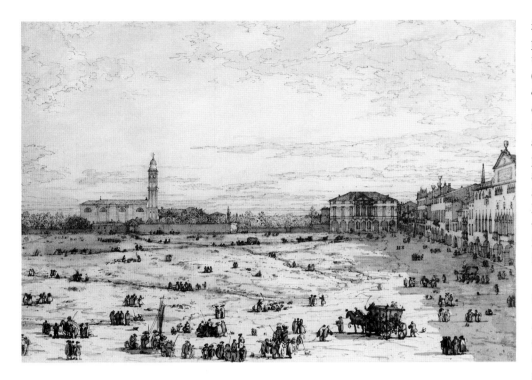

▲ **8 · 6**

Antonio Canaletto, *The Pra'della Valle at Padua with the church of the Misericordia* (detail), undated. Pen and watercolor with crayon outlines, 10⅝ × 14¾ in (27 × 37.5 cm).

In Canaletto's drawing, note how the figures gradually get smaller as they recede into the background areas. This, combined with the artist's command of linear perspective, gives the viewer a strong sense of depth.

The Royal Collection (© 1993 Her Majesty Queen Elizabeth II.)

indicates subsequently receding spatial positions (see fig. 8.5). Evidence suggests that this manner of seeing is instinctive (resulting from continued exposure to the objective world), for its influence persists even in viewing greatly abstracted and nonobjective work (fig. 8.7). The alternative, of course, is to see the picture plane as entirely devoid of spatial illusion and the distances of the visual elements as actually measurable across the flat surface. It is difficult to perceive in this way even when we discipline ourselves to do so, for it requires us to divorce ourselves entirely from ingrained environmental factors.

Overlapping

Another way of suggesting space is by overlapping planes or volumes. If one object covers part of the visible surface of another, the first object is assumed to be nearer. Overlapping is a powerful indication of space, because once used, it takes precedence over other spatial signs. For instance, one ball placed in front of a larger ball appears closer than the larger ball, despite its smaller size (fig. 8.8).

Transparency

The overlapped portion of an object is usually obscured from our view. If, however, that portion is continued and made visible through the overlapping plane or object, the effect of *transparency* is created. Transparency, which tends to produce a closer spatial relationship, is clearly evident in the upper triangle in the painting by Jack Brusca (fig. 8.9). It is most noticeable in the works of the Cubists and other artists who are interested in exploring shallow space (see figs. 4.8 and 10.38).

depth-scale as our guide, an object or human figure assumes a scale that corresponds to its distance from us, regardless of all other factors (fig. 8.6; see fig. 10.16). This concept of space has not always been prevalent. In many broad periods and styles of art, and in the works of children, large scale is assigned according to importance, power, and strength, regardless of spatial location (see figs. 8.12 and 2.48).

Position

Many artists and observers automatically assume that the horizon line, which provides a point of reference, is always at eye level. The position of objects is judged in relation to that horizon line. The bottom of the picture plane is seen as the closest visual point, and the degree of rise of the visual units up to the horizon line

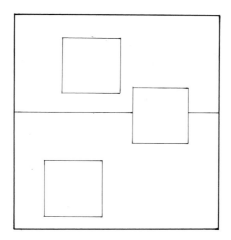

▲ 8 · 7

Placement of squares. A line across the picture plane reminds us of the horizon that divides ground plane from sky plane. Consequently, the lower shape seems close and the intermediate shape more distant, while the upper square is in a rather ambiguous position as it touches nothing and seems to float in the sky.

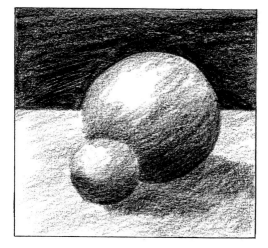

▲ 8 · 8

As an indicator of space, overlapping causes the object being covered to recede, regardless of size.

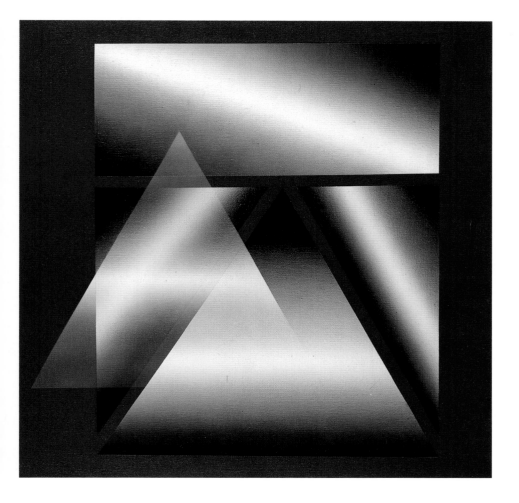

◀ 8 · 9

Jack Brusca, *Untitled*, 1969. Acrylic on canvas, 30 × 30 in (76.2 × 76.2 cm).
The precise, hard-edged geometric shapes in this work are a legacy of Cubism. However, notice that the implied triangular shapes overlap, remain transparent, and create a shallow space.

Courtesy of the Owens-Corning Collection. Owens-Corning Fiberglas Corporation, Toledo, OH.

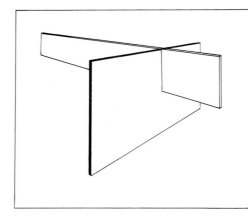

Interpenetration

Interpenetration occurs when planes or objects pass through each other, emerging on the other side. It provides a very clear statement of the spatial positioning of the planes and objects involved, and can create the illusion of either shallow or deep space (figs. 8.10 and 8.11).

◀ **8 · 10**

Interpenetrating planes. The passage of one plane or volume through another automatically gives depth to a picture.

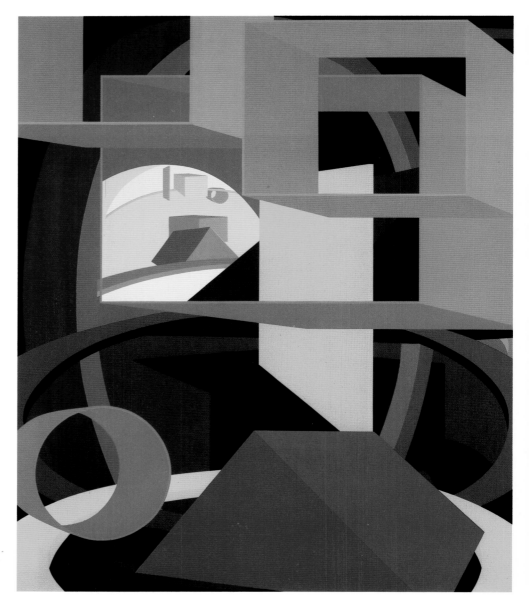

▶ **8 · 11**

Al Held, *Quattro Centric XIII*, 1990. Acrylic on canvas, 5 × 6 ft (1.52 × 1.83 m).

The effects in this work are quite subtle and do not follow any formal technique for generating space. Areas of overlapping and interpenetration contribute strongly to the overall sense of depth.

Courtesy of the André Emmerich Gallery, New York.

© Al Held/DACS, London/VAGA, New York 1994.

Fractional representation

Fractional representation can best be illustrated by studying the treatment of the human body by Egyptian artists. Here we can find, in one figure, the profile of the head with one eye visible, the torso seen front-on, and a side view of the hips and legs. This is a combining of the most representative aspects of the different parts of the body (figs. 8.12 and 8.13). *Fractional representation* is a spatial device revived in the nineteenth century by Cézanne, who used its principles in his still-life paintings (see "Plastic Images," p. 203). It was employed by many twentieth-century artists, most conspicuously Pablo Picasso. The effect is flattening in Egyptian work, but plastic in the paintings by Cézanne, since it is used to move us "around" the subjects.

Sharp and diminishing detail

Because we do not have the eyes of eagles and because we view things through the earth's atmosphere, we are not able to see near and distant planes with equal clarity at the same time. A glance out the window confirms that close objects appear sharp and clear in detail, whereas those at great distances seem blurred and lacking definition. Artists have long known of this phenomenon and have used it widely in illusionistic work. In recent times they have used this method and other traditional methods of space indication in works that are otherwise quite abstract. Thus, in abstract and nonobjective conceptions, sharp lines, clearly defined shapes and values, complex textures, and intense colors are associated with foreground or near positions. Hazy lines, indistinct shapes, grayed values, simple textures, and neutralized colors are identified with background locations. These characteristics are often included in the definition of *atmospheric perspective* (fig. 8.14).

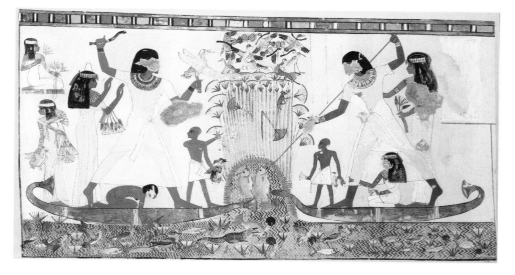

▲ **8 · 12**

Copy of Egyptian wall-painting (Thebes; tomb of Menena) *Fishing and Fowling,* **XVIII Dynasty, c. 1415 B.C. Copy in tempera, 39¾ × 35 in (101 × 89 cm) (1:1 scale with original).**

This work illustrates the Egyptian concept of pictorial plasticity: a combination of various representative views of the figure is combined into one image (fractional representation) and is kept compatible with the flatness of the picture plane. The arbitrary positioning of the figures and their disproportionate scale add to this effect.

Egyptian Expedition of the Metropolitan Museum of Art, New York. Rogers Fund, 1930 (30.4.48).

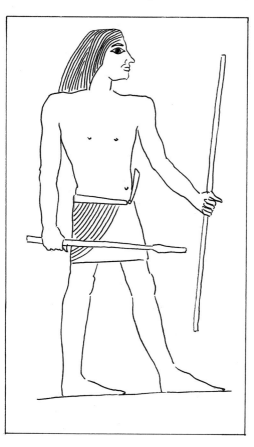

◄ **8 · 13**

This drawing illustrates the Egyptian technique of fractional representation of the human figure. The head is in profile, but the eye full-face. The upper body is frontal, gradually turning until the lower body, from the hips down, is seen from the side. This drawing combines views of parts of the body in their most characteristic or easily seen positions. In order to see all these views, one would have to move around the body.

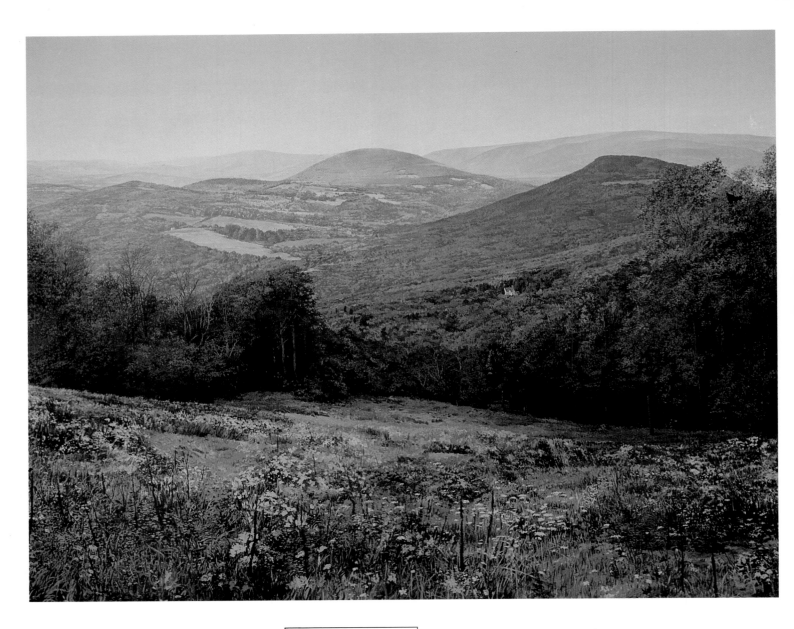

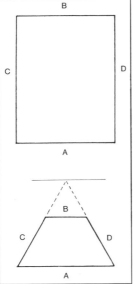

▲ 8 · 14
Doug Maguire, *Sleeping Eye*, 1987. Oil on linen, 4 ft 8½ in × 6 ft ½ in (1.44 × 1.84 m).
The clarity of the weeds, grasses, and flowers in the foreground and the darkness of the trees in the middleground, contrasted with the haziness of the background, contribute to the spatial effect of the atmospheric perspective.
Courtesy of the Katharina Rich Perlow Gallery, New York.

▶ 8 · 15
Converging parallels can make a shape appear to recede into the pictorial field.

Converging parallels

The space indicated by converging parallels can be illustrated using a rectangular plane such as a sheet of paper or a tabletop. By actual measurement, a rectangle possesses one set of short parallel edges and one set of long parallel edges (fig. 8.15). If the plane is arranged so that one of the short edges (A) is viewed head-on, its corresponding parallel edge (B) will appear to be much shorter. Since these edges appear to be of different lengths, the other two edges (C and D) that connect them must seem to converge as they move back into space. Either set of lines, when separated from the other set, would continue to indicate space quite forcefully. The principle of converging parallels is found in many works of art that do not abide by the rules of *perspective*. It is closely related to perspective, but the amount of convergence is a matter of subjective or intuitive choice by the artist. It is not governed by fixed vanishing points and the rules governing the rate of convergence (fig. 8.16).

Linear perspective

Linear perspective is a system for converting sizes and distances of known objects into a unified spatial order. It is based on the artist's/viewer's optical perception and judgments of such specific concepts as scale, proportion, placement, and so on. Its use involves the application of such spatial indicators as size, position, and converging parallels. The general understanding of perspective originated with the wave of scientific inquiry which swept many countries and which sowed the seeds of the Italian Renaissance – the

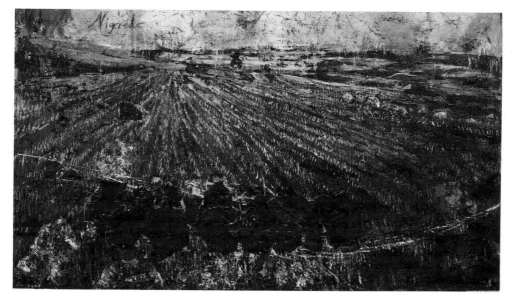

▲ 8 · 16
Anselm Kiefer, *Nigredo*, 1984. Oil, acrylic, emulsion, shellac, straw on photograph, mounted on canvas, with woodcut, 10 ft 10 in × 18 ft 2½ in (3.30 × 5.55 m).
Kiefer uses perspective as an aid to help him draw the viewer into the heart of his enormous canvas.
Philadelphia Museum of Art, PA.

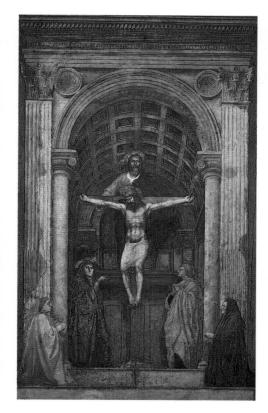

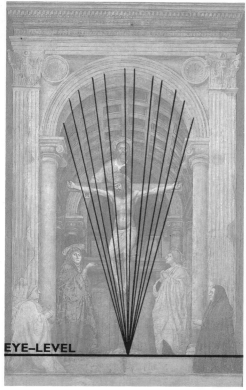

EYE–LEVEL

◄ 8 · 17A and B
Masaccio, *Trinity with the Virgin, St. John and Donors*, 1427. Fresco at Santa Maria Novella, Florence, Italy, 21 ft 10 in × 10 ft 5 in (6.65 × 3.18 m).
According to some art history experts, Masaccio's fresco is the first painting created in correct geometric perspective. The single vanishing point lies at the foot of the cross, as indicated by the overlay in figure 8.17B.
Photo Scala, Florence, Italy.

▶ **8 · 18A and B**
Sandro Botticelli, *Annunciation*, c. 1490. Tempera on wood, 9⅜ × 14⅜ in (23.8 × 36.5 cm).

In the tradition of much art of the Renaissance period, perspective in the form of receding planes creates space and directs our attention to the vanishing point (see fig. 8.18B).

Metropolitan Museum of Art, New York. Robert Lehman Collection, 1975 (1975.1.74).

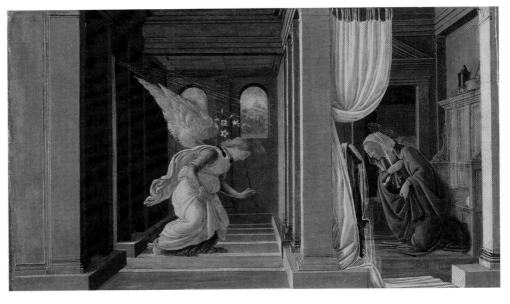

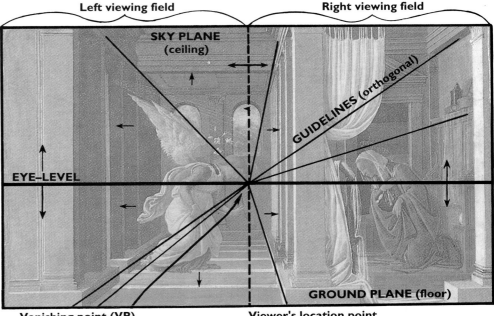

era that brought this spatial system to a point of high refinement. Artists focused their attention on one view, a selected portion of nature, seen from one position at a particular moment in time. The use of eye level, guidelines, and vanishing points gave this view mathematical exactitude (fig. 8.17A).

It has generally been agreed that perspective was invented by the Early Renaissance architect Filippo Brunelleschi (1377–1446), and was quickly adapted to painting by his contemporary, Masaccio

(1401–28) (see fig. 8.17A). Employing their knowledge of geometry (then one of the most important elements in the classical education of every student), Renaissance artists conceived a method of depicting objects in space, whether animate or inanimate, that was more realistic than any other that had appeared in Western art since the Romans. In their concept, the perspective drawing of shapes (fig. 8.18A) makes the picture plane akin to a view through an entry window; picture framing or matting defines the window

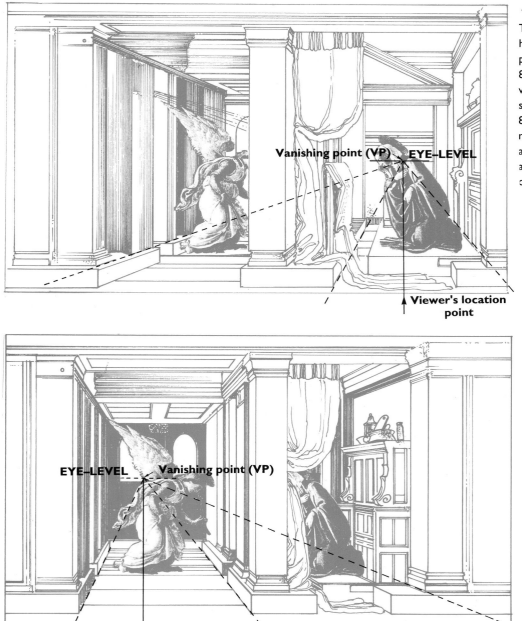

8 · 19A and B

These illustrations show how the interior might have changed if Botticelli had moved his location point left or right and up or down (see fig. 8.18A). Figure 8.19A indicates what Botticelli would have seen by moving to the right and standing directly in front of the Madonna. Figure 8.19B depicts the view he would have had by moving to the left, past the angel, and moving up a ladder one or two steps. Notice how the architectural elements change with each view, obscuring important parts of the image.

frame. In figure 8.18B imaginary sightlines or "orthogonals," called guidelines, are extended along the edges of the room's architectural planes to a point behind the angel's head.

The guidelines converge at a point on the eye level which is called the vanishing point (infinity). The eye level is synonymous with the horizon line (where the sky and ground meet) that is often seen in landscapes (see figs. 8.4 and 8.5).

While the eye level reveals the relative height of the observer's/painter's eyes, it also demarcates upper and lower divisions called ground plane (floor) and sky plane (ceiling). A vertical axis which can be seen through the vanishing point, behind the angel's head, establishes the location of the artist or viewer. This is known as the viewer's location point. Changing the latter will drastically alter the view of the room (figs. 8.19A and B).

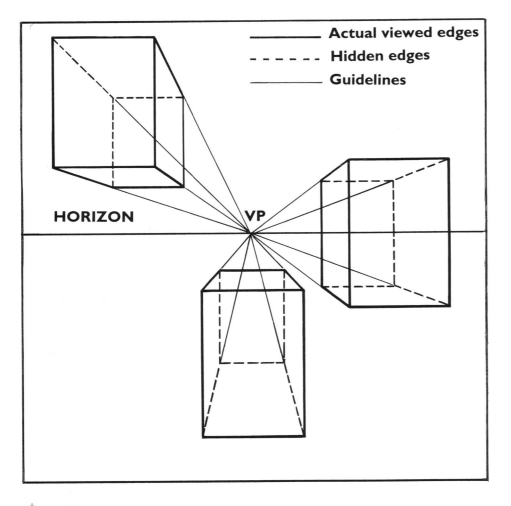

Actual viewed edges ——————
Hidden edges – – – – –
Guidelines ——————

HORIZON　　　　　　　　**VP**

▲ **8 · 20**
With one-point perspective the whole front or back plane of the subject is made to appear flat or parallel to the picture plane.

Major systems of linear perspective

There are three major systems of linear perspective: one-point, two-point, and three-point. All are relative to the way the artist views the subject or scene. Perspective is based on the assumption that the artist maintains a fixed position and in theory views the subject with one eye. In reality, unless immobilized by a plaster cast and fitted with blinders, most viewers will casually move either their eyes or their head as their focus moves from object to object within the image. While this may extend the viewer's ability to understand the subject, changing the

point of view to some extent works against the concepts of linear perspective.

Assuming a minimum of movement, the artist can view his subjects in one of three ways: 1. By taking a position directly in front of the image, the whole front plane of the subject is made to appear flat or parallel to the picture plane (one-point); 2. By moving so that an edge – instead of the whole flat plane – is closest and centrally located, all planes will then appear to recede because the top and bottom edges converge to vanishing points on either side (two-point); 3. Assuming a position very much above or below the subject will make the sides as

well as the top and bottom edges converge to distant points (three-point). In each of these examples the subject was thought of as stationary and the artist changed position. But the same concepts can be applied to still-life material, which can be altered or repositioned; a small box could be placed in each of the three locations relative to the artist's viewpoint.

One-point perspective One-point perspective is used when the artist views a flat surface or facing plane directly, or front-on. This flat plane will be drawn parallel to the picture plane and the horizon line. In this system, the artist first establishes the horizon line, which is on his or her eye level (fig. 8.20). It is placed low on the page if the artist is close to the ground, high on the page if the artist is on a ladder, or centered if the artist is standing. Next the vanishing point is located. It is usually centered on the horizon line. To make the composition less monotonous it is sometimes placed slightly to the right or left of center, so that the picture is not divided too symmetrically. In either case, the vanishing point represents a position directly in front of the viewer and at eye level.

After the vanishing point on the horizon line is established, the artist begins with the frontal plane of the geometric solid – that portion closest to the viewer. Guidelines drawn from the four corners of the front plane to the vanishing point will establish the theoretical position of the solid's side planes. They will appear to diminish in size as they recede in depth toward the horizon. In one-point perspective, all lines return to the same vanishing point except for those lines defining the original flat plane or any planes behind and parallel to it. Lines forming the front plane (horizontals or verticals) are at right angles to each other, remain constant, and are geometrically measurable. The lines forming these planes are parallel to the ground plane or perpendicular to it and establish their spatial location. Notice that the three geometric solids are located fairly close to the vanishing point. In reality, when viewing such solids, one sees the sides as foreshortened. The further away from the (centrally located) vanishing point the solids are drawn, the more distorted their side planes seem to appear. These far right and left locations are no longer seen as frontal and would more correctly be seen as a two-point perspective view. However, artists often employ such distortions for compositional and/or conceptual advantage.

Any subject with a flat frontal view, like the end of a room, hallways, long frontal views of the interior and exterior of buildings, streets, and lines of trees, lend themselves well to one-point perspective pictures, as seen in Canaletto's *The Piazza of St. Mark, Venice* (fig. 8.21).

Two-point perspective Two-point perspective is most often employed when the artist views a leading edge instead of a flat plane (fig. 8.22). This will cause the geometric solid to appear to be at an angle to the lines of sight; or, in other words, to appear to be at angular positions in depth on the surface of the picture plane. The artist begins by establishing the horizon line, as in one-point perspective, its placement in the drawing being relative to the height of the artist's viewing position. Next, vanishing points are located on the horizon line at the extreme left and right ends. In reality the vanishing points are so distant that they cannot be located on the picture plane, but for the convenience of drawing they are often located along the edge of the drawing format. Now, the artist draws the closest portion of the box – the vertical edge – as a vertical line. From the top and bottom corners of this vertical, guidelines are extended back to

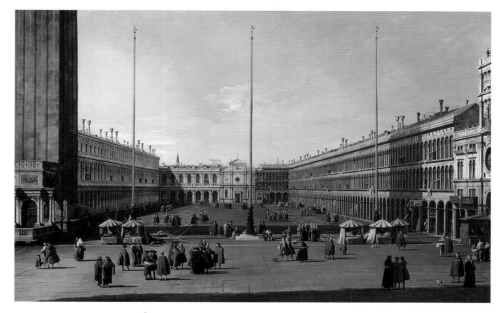

▲ **8 · 21**

Antonio Canaletto, *The Piazza of St. Mark, Venice, c.* 1735–45. Oil on canvas, 29⅞ × 46⅞ in (76 × 119 cm).

The appearance of planes and volumes in space determined by the systematic procedures of linear perspective is well illustrated in this painting by an eighteenth-century Venetian artist. It is basically in one-point perspective.

Detroit Institute of Arts, Detroit, MI. Founders' Society Purchase. General Membership Fund with a donation from Edsel B. Ford.

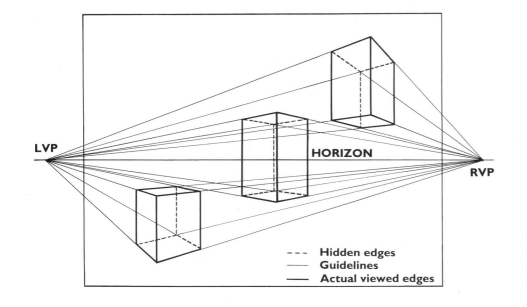

- - - **Hidden edges**
——— **Guidelines**
━━━ **Actual viewed edges**

◀ **8 · 22**

With two-point perspective, one vertical edge is closest and all top and bottom edges recede and converge at the left or right vanishing point.

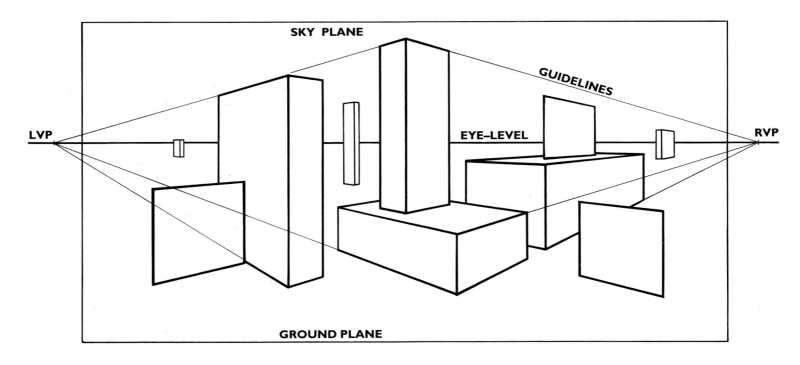

LVP   SKY PLANE   GUIDELINES   RVP

EYE–LEVEL

GROUND PLANE

▲ 8 · 23

A drawing showing the essential difference between planes and three-dimensional shapes. Planes are shapes having only two dimensions (height and width), whereas three-dimensional shapes, which are made up of planes, have the effect of solidity (height, width, and depth). The component planes (sides) of three-dimensional shapes may be detached and inclined at any angle. The drawing is also an example of two-point perspective. Object edges are shown as heavy lines, orthogonals (guidelines) as lighter lines. Vanishing points (LVP and RVP) show where object edges converge at the eye level or horizon line, which represents infinity. The eye level divides the picture space into planes which stand for the ground and sky.

both sets of vanishing points, tentatively establishing the side, top, and/or bottom planes of the geometric solid. These planes will appear to diminish as they recede toward the vanishing points. With two-point perspective, all lines except those that are vertical will return to the vanishing points. The verticals indicate the height of the volumes, stay parallel, and are perpendicular to the ground plane. Only the verticals may be measured and never converge.

Notice in figure 8.23 that multiple solids and planes create a sense of deep space. In addition, the vanishing points are placed outside the picture plane. Placing the vanishing points as far apart as possible eliminates the distortion of image that occurs when they are too close together.

Two-point perspective is most often employed in graphic artworks when objects, usually set in architectural settings, appear to be at an angle to the lines of sight, or when the artist wishes them to appear at angular positions in depth on the picture plane, as can be seen in the Hopper painting (fig. 8.24; see fig. 8.6).

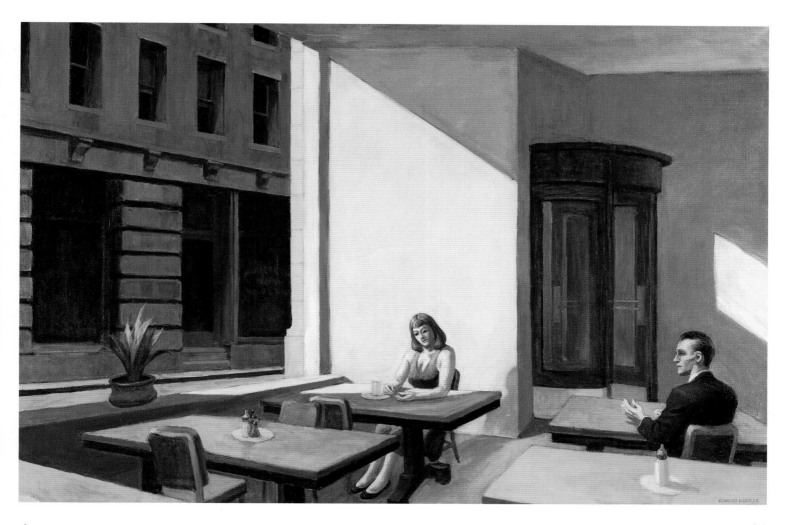

▲ 8 · 24

**Edward Hopper, *Sunlight in a Cafeteria*,
1958. Oil on canvas, 3 ft 4¼ in × 5 ft ⅛ in
(1.02 × 1.53 m).**
This nostalgic interior with an outside view is
painted in two-point perspective.

Yale University Art Gallery, New Haven, CT. Bequest
of Stephen Carlton Clark.

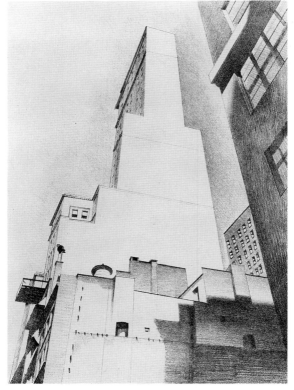

8 · 25
Charles Sheeler, *Delmonico Building,* **1926.
Lithograph, 9¾ × 6⅞ in (24.7 × 17.4 cm).**
This painting makes use of three-point
perspective – a "frog's-eye view."
Fogg Art Museum, Harvard University Art Museums,
Boston, MA. Gift of Paul J. Sachs.

8 · 26
Gene Bodio, *New City,* **1992. Computer
graphic created using Autodesk 3D Studio
Release 2.**
This is a bird's-eye view generated by a
computer. Though not strictly in three-point
perspective, the picture is an unusual variation in
the depiction of three-dimensional objects in
space.
Autodesk Inc., Sausolito, CA.

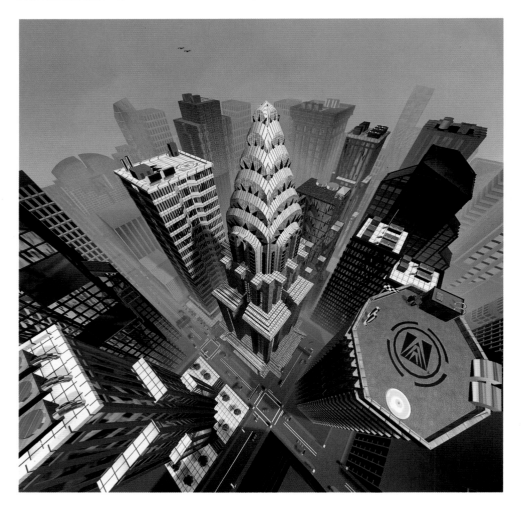

Three-point perspective

Three-point, or vertical, perspective is used
when an artist views an object from an
exaggerated position – lying on the
ground and looking up at a tree or
looking down from a skyscraper into the
center of the city. These are sometimes
referred to as a "frog's-eye view" (fig. 8.25)
and a "bird's-eye view" (fig. 8.26)
respectively.

The artist begins by locating the
horizon line which indicates the location
of the viewer's eyes and fixing the left
vanishing point (LVP) and the right
vanishing point (RVP) as far apart as
possible on the horizon line (fig. 8.27).
Usually the horizon line will be relatively
high or low on the picture plane. Next, a
third point called the vertical vanishing
point (VVP) is located anywhere along a
vertical axis coming perpendicularly off
the horizon line at a point representing
the viewer's location point. The further
away from the horizon line the third
point is located, the less exaggerated will
be the distortion of the solid. The image
is started by fixing the nearest corner (a)
of what will become a rectangular solid
that seems to be floating overhead. From

this point, guidelines (b) are extended to the RVP and to the LVP. This locates the leading front edges of the bottom plane. The width of both edges should be indicated and from those points new guidelines should be extended (c) again to the RVP and LVP. This completes the bottom plane and locates all four corners. The "verticals" (d) should now be drawn up and away from the three closest corners; but since there are no verticals in three-point perspective, these lines will have to converge to the VVP. Once the "verticals" are drawn, it should be decided how long the rectangular solid must be by gauging its length on the closest or center "vertical" edge (a–e). After marking this point (e), guidelines (f) are extended from it to the RVP and to the LVP. In certain cases the hidden back edges (g) could be added. This completes the drawing of the edges and fully defines the geometric solid as seen from below in three-point perspective.

Only in three-point perspective are the vertical (height) lines, as well as those receding to the left and right vanishing points, spatially indicated. All three guideline systems converge at vanishing points. They are not perpendicular nor parallel to one another, but at oblique angles (see fig. 8.25).

Perspective concepts applied

Whether using one-, two-, or three-point perspective, the artist is working with a system that allows the development of

items of known size and their placing at various distances into the picture plane. A one-point cube, as illustrated in figure 8.28A, shows a whole flat frontal plane (the closest part) and a receding top plane. The center of any front plane – square or rectangular – may be found by mechanically measuring the horizontal and vertical lengths and dividing them in half. Lines (a) drawn from those points parallel to the verticals and horizontals will divide the plane into quarters. However, this type of measurement only works on flat, frontal planes found exclusively with one-point perspective. It will not work on any plane with converging sides – one-, two-, or three-point – because the sides get smaller as they move away from the viewer and their changing ratio is not measurable on a ruler. Notice, on the front plane, that diagonals (b) drawn from corner to corner pass through the exact center found by mechanical measurement. The same type of diagonal lines drawn from corner to corner on the receding plane pass through the perspective center of the converging top plane. Lines drawn through this point parallel to the front edge (c) or to the vanishing point (d) create the equal division of the four edges of the receding plane. This concept of corner-to-corner diagonals may be applied to cubes or rectangles in one-, two-, and three-point to locate the perspective centers on any receding plane.

Using the center point of a cube's front square, a circle can be drawn with a

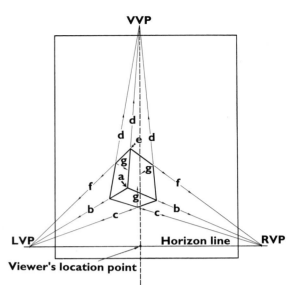

8·27
With three-point perspective a vantage point is assumed far above or below the subject. This will cause the sides, as well as the top and bottom edges, to converge to one of the three distant vanishing points.

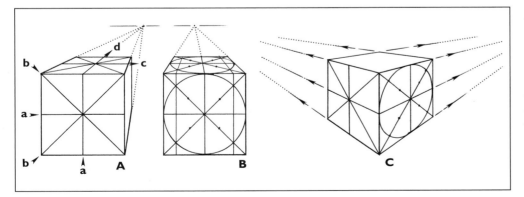

8·28A, B, and C
Subdividing a plane. These diagrams illustrate how to find the perspective center of a plane by crossing diagonals from corner to corner (A). To draw a circle on the same plane, divide each half of the diagonals into thirds. Draw the circle so that it passes through the outside "third" marks (closest to the corners) on the diagonals. The circle should also touch the middle points on the sides of the square. This concept may be applied to one- and two-point perspective (B and C).

compass which should fit into the square perfectly (fig. 8.28B). Notice that when the diagonals are divided in thirds from the center, the circle crosses the diagonal lines on approximately the outer third mark. With a compass, try to draw a circle that fits into the top receding plane. It cannot be done, because even though we know that it is a circle, it will appear as an ellipse. The appropriate ellipse can be drawn on the top receding plane when it passes through the third marks on the diagonals and touches the square on the center points of each side. This system may be applied to any receding plane – vertical or horizontal – in one-, two- or three-point perspective (fig. 8.28C).

Figure 8.29A shows the changing ellipses that could be located in a very tall rectangle. Occasionally an artist must draw the appropriate ellipse for the top and bottom of anything cylindrical relative to its position above or below the horizon line. Notice that the ellipses further away from the horizon line are less distorted and that the ellipses flatten as they get closer to the horizon line. Ellipses do not always have to be horizontal or vertical. Observe the ellipse drawn on the diagonal plane (fig. 8.29B). It is drawn using the same diagonal system for finding the center of the diagonal plane. In addition, the concept may be applied to drawing arches, bridges, and so on (fig. 8.29C). Although only the upper half of the ellipses are shown in the arch, it will be necessary to know the basic cube or rectangle they were found in and the perspective centers of their shapes.

Once a square or rectangle is created it may be easily turned into a pyramid, cylinder, or cone by finding the perspective center for the top and bottom planes of the new shapes (figs. 8.30A–D). For a pyramid (A), simply draw lines from the top plane's perspective center to the

▼ **8 · 29A, B, and C**

When seen from the side, a perfect circle looks like an ellipse. The ellipse flattens as it moves closer to the horizon line (A). It may be applied to an inclined plane (B) or used to create arches, tunnels, and so on (C).

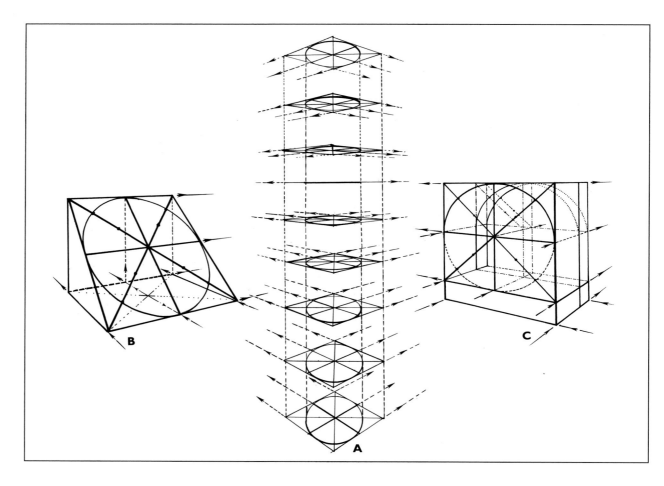

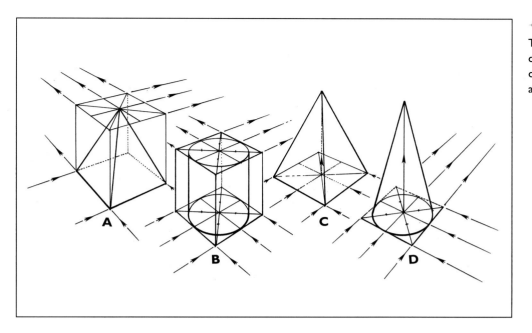

8 · 30A, B, C, and D
The concept of locating a plane's perspective center and the correct ellipse to indicate a circle can be extended to create pyramids, cylinders, and cones.

four corners on the bottom plane. For the cylinder (B), it will be necessary to first draw the proper ellipse on the top and bottom planes – as described earlier. Then draw vertical lines from the outermost limits of both ellipses. Also note that a second pyramid (C) and cone (D) can be drawn with only the establishment of the bottom plane. Find the perspective center of those planes and, from their points, draw lines perpendicular to the bottom planes at any desired length. Then from the end of this line draw the lines to the four corners for a pyramid and to the outer-edge points on an ellipse for a cone.

The system for finding the perspective center of a receding plane can be used to project known distances back or sideways into space at the proper diminishing rate or ratio. If a telephone company plants seven poles equally spaced down the road, how does an artist know exactly where they should be drawn on the picture plane? Study figure 8.28A, covering up one-half of the illustration. Note that the diagonal lines (b) stop at the center point. In the portion covered up, they continue on toward the upper and lower corners. Therefore, if the perspective center (vertical or horizontal plane) can be found, a known shape (half a unit) can be

projected into a space on the opposite side of the center mark by continuing the diagonals until they cross an extension of the top or bottom edge.

To draw the telephone poles equally spaced in perspective, simply draw the first pole and then extend guidelines from the top and bottom to the vanishing point (fig. 8.31, overleaf). Draw the second pole any distance you desire from the first and parallel to it touching the top and bottom guidelines. Next, find the center of the second pole by either measuring or by dividing the shape between the poles with diagonal lines. The point where the diagonals cross may be projected to the second pole by drawing a guideline from that point to the vanishing point. Now, remembering that diagonals cross on the midpoint, draw lines from the top and bottom of the first pole through the mid point found on the second pole, extending them until they touch the guidelines. Where they do, extend another vertical and it will locate the next pole at a perspective unit equal to the one just projected. A single diagonal line may be used to project through the center point on the new pole to find the location of the next pole. This process may be repeated as often as necessary until the

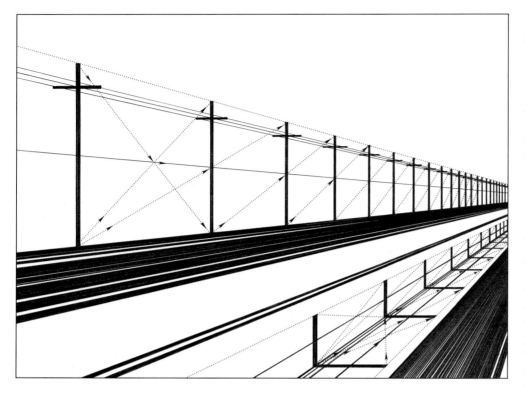

number of poles desired has been reached. Spacing may be projected horizontally as well as vertically. The same procedure has been applied to the guardrail poles in the lower right corner. In addition, horizontal projection may be applied to locate floor tiles, windows, and so on, or consistent spacing between architectural components (fig. 8.32).

A perspective drawing may also have several vanishing points other than those located on the horizon line (fig. 8.33). They are often used when it is desirable to show an angular or spatially receding plane within a perspective drawing, such as on a gable or truss-roofed house, or a door opening at an angle. In this case the roof is located first and its edges are extended back to their new vanishing point. Then any additional images that would be drawn on that receding plane – for example shingles and skylight windows – must be extended to that new point. A point may also be located as a source of light with all cast shadows

▲ **8·31**
Telephone poles showing vertical projection systems. A given unit – the distance between two telephone poles – may be projected. Extending a diagonal guideline from a corner through the midpoint of the next pole to the appropriate top or bottom guideline reveals the location of the next pole. Units may be projected on a vertical or horizontal plane.

▶ **8·32**
A room interior. Since horizontals and verticals in one-point perspective may be measured, all tile spacing was marked on the back edge of the floor. From the vanishing point, floor lines were extended through each of these points toward the viewer. After establishing the first row of tiles, a diagonal line was extended from corner to corner of one tile and beyond. Where the diagonal crossed each floor line, a horizontal line was drawn, thereby defining a new row of tiles. A second line, passing through the center of the edge of each tile, located points which were projected on to both walls to identify wall board spacing and window widths.

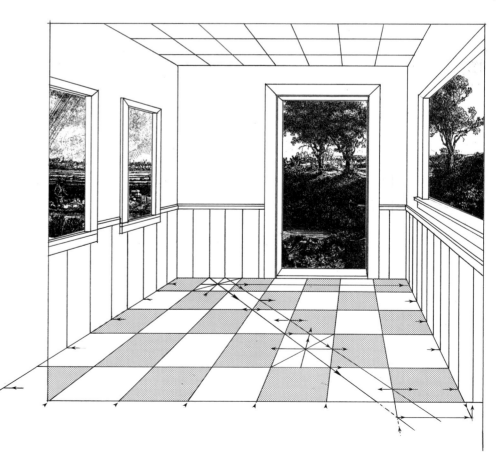

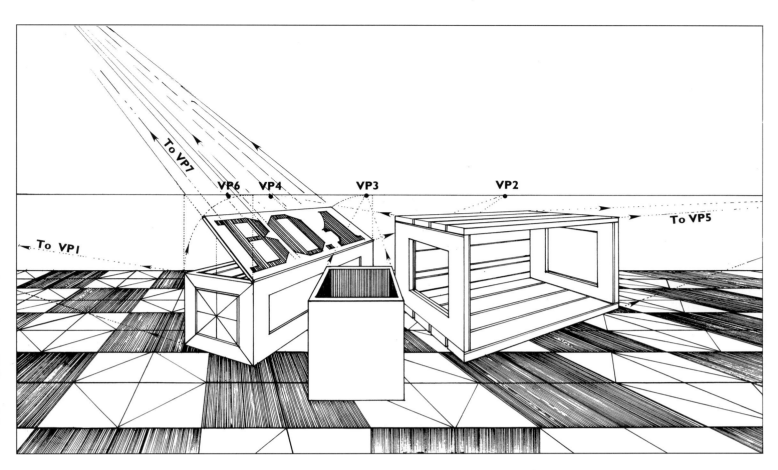

being indicated by guidelines projected from it to the ground plane. As a further complication, an artist may encounter situations where houses and other objects are not parallel to each other. One-, two-, and possibly three-point perspective systems may be used in the same drawing.

The disadvantages of linear perspective

Linear perspective has been a traditional drawing device used by artists for centuries. During that time the system has evolved and undergone modifications in attempts to make it more flexible or more realistic in depicting natural appearances. Some of these include multiple perspectives, with more than three vanishing points, and, at other times, the use of multiple eye levels. Linear perspective has been most popular during periods of scientific inquiry and reached its culmination in the mid nineteenth century. Despite its seeming

virtue of accurately depicting natural appearances, the method has certain disadvantages which, in the opinion of some artists, outweigh its usefulness. Briefly, the liabilities of linear perspective are as follows:

1. It is never an actual statement of shape or mass as they are known to be.
2. The only appearances that can be legitimately portrayed are those that can be seen by the artist/observer from one position in space.
3. The necessary recession of parallel lines toward common points often leads to monotonous visual effects.
4. The extreme reduction of scale within a single object, resulting from the convergence of lines, is another type of perspective distortion (see fig. 8.15. This diagram indicates that a rectangular tabletop depicted in perspective becomes a trapezoid and leaves spatial vacuums left of C and right of D).

▲ **8 · 33**

Seven in one. Seven vanishing points (VPs) were used to create this drawing. VPs 1 and 2 were used for the left box. VP 3 was used to create the center cube. VPs 4 and 5 were used for the open crate on the right. VP 6 was used for the floor tiles. VP 7 was used to define the inclined plane of the box lid and its lettering.

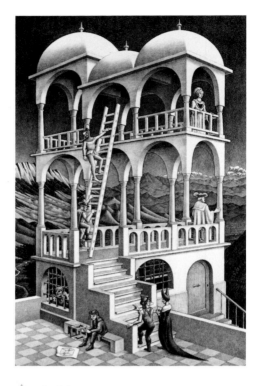

▲ 8·34

M. C. Escher, *Belvedere*, 1958. Lithograph, 18⅛ × 11⅝ in (46 × 29.5 cm).

From his early youth, Escher practiced the graphic technique of perspective and for many years strived to master that skill. Later he found ideas he could communicate by extending his perspective technique, and became fascinated with visually subverting our commonsense view of the three-dimensional world. In this print, Escher knew it was impossible to see the front and back of a building simultaneously, yet he managed to draw such an impossible building.

Courtesy of the Vorpal Gallery, New York. (Photograph by D. James Dee.)

These disadvantages are mentioned only to suggest that familiar modes of vision are not necessarily those that function best in a work of art. At various periods of time an intuitive use of perspective has supplanted systematic formulas for the indication of depth in pictorial forms of art.

To a certain extent, artists became prisoners of the system they had helped to produce. Because of its inflexible rules, perspective emphasizes accuracy of representation – an emphasis that does not favor creative expression. If, however, artists see perspective as an aid rather than an end in itself, as something to be used when and if the need arises in creating a picture, it can be very useful (see fig. 8.16). Many fine works of art ignore perspective or show "faults" in the use of the system. In such a case the type of spatial order created by traditional perspective is not compatible with the aims of the artist (fig. 8.34). Perspective, then, should be learned by artists simply so that it is available to them.

Other projection systems

Other systems that suggest objects spatially have been developed. They use parallel projecting lines (non-converging). Because they appear to "flatten" out objects when compared to traditional Western perspective systems that use vanishing points, they are of interest to designers, architects, and technical engineers.

Oblique projection looks at first glance to be related to one-point perspective, for both present a flat frontal view, which is always parallel to the picture plane (fig. 8.35A). For engineering and architectural applications, the front plane is always drawn at full scale. However, with oblique perspective all left or right side edges which would have converged at a singular vanishing point are drawn parallel. They come off the front plane at a forty-five degree angle. This type of non-converging parallel edges on receding planes is often seen in Asian art.

Isometric projection may be compared

▽ 8·35A

Oblique projection. This system for showing spatial relationships makes use of a flat frontal shape with nonconverging side planes drawn at a forty-five degree angle from the front plane.

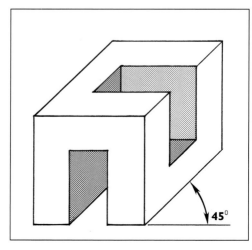

▽ 8·35B

Isometric projection features a vertical front edge and nonconverging side planes, which are drawn at a thirty degree angle to the left and right.

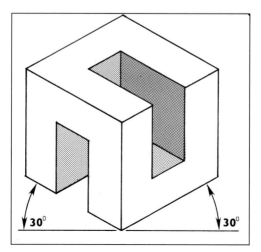

to two-point perspective in appearance. Both begin with a vertical frontal edge. Like oblique perspective, isometric work does not have any converging receding edges (fig. 8.35B). All edges that intersect at the vertical move away at a thirty degree angle, both to the left and to the right. For ease of drawing all three dimensions of the object use the same measurement system (scale) – there is no diminishing ratio on the receding planes. This system is often preferred to oblique perspective because all three faces are visible at the same time with less apparent distortion. No side of the image is drawn parallel to the viewer (picture plane). This system is used for technical *illustration* and drafting.

Orthographic drawing is perhaps less understood as a system for identifying objects in a spatial setting, but is used by engineers and architects to present blueprints and schematic layouts (see fig. 8.51). With this system all sides of the rectangular (geometric) object are drawn parallel or perpendicular to a base line and the measurements are scaled to an exact ratio. Artists, engineers, industrial designers, and architects employ this system.

The reverse perspective employed by traditional east Asian artists is a dramatic contrast to the linear perspective of the West. Ancient canons prescribed convergence of parallel lines as they approach the spectator. This type of presentation closes the space in depth so that the picture becomes a stage and the spectator an actor-participant in an active spatial panorama that rarely loses its identification with the picture plane (fig. 8.36A). Similar space concepts have been employed in the West during various historical periods. Ideas on pictorial space usually agree with the prevailing mental climate of the society that produces the art. In this sense, space is a form of human expression.

▼ **8 · 36A**

Kubo Shunman, *Courtesans Dreaming, c. 1790*. Print.

This Japanese artist, following his own (Asian) concept of space as moving forward toward the observer, employs – from a Western point of view – a kind of reverse perspective.

Metropolitan Museum of Art, New York. Bequest of Mrs. H. O. Havemeyer, 1929. The H. O. Havemeyer Collection.

▼ **8 · 36B**

A simple analysis of *Courtesans Dreaming* shows that if the lines defining the ends of the table are extended back toward the horizon line they will never meet as they would in the linear perspective of Western artists. However, if they are extended forward, following the Asian concept of space, they will converge. As a result, the near edge of the table is shorter than the back edge – which is characteristic of east Asian perspective.

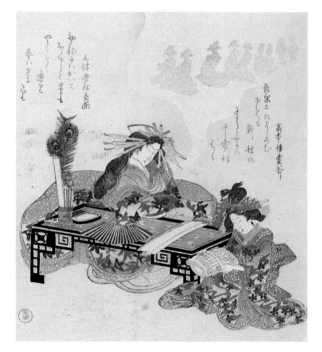

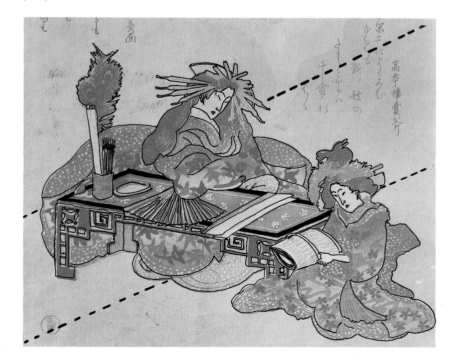

Intuitive space

Although planes and volumes play a strong part in creating illusions of space in linear perspective, they can also be used to produce *intuitive space*, which is independent of strict rules and formulae. Intuitive space is thus not a system, but a product of the artist's instinct for manipulating certain space-producing devices. The devices that help the artist to control space include overlap, transparency, interpenetration, inclined planes, disproportionate scale, and fractional representation. In addition, the artist may exploit the inherent spatial properties of the art elements. The physical properties of the art elements tend to thrust forward or backward; this can be used to define items spatially. By marshalling these spatial forces in any combination as needed, the artist can impart a sense of space to the pictorial image while adjusting relationships (fig. 8.37). The space derived from this method is readily sensed by everyone, although judged by the standards of the more familiar linear perspective, it may seem strange, even distorted. Nevertheless, intuitive space has been the dominant procedure during most of the history of art; it rarely implies great depth, but makes for tightly knit imagery within a relatively shallow spatial field (fig. 8.38).

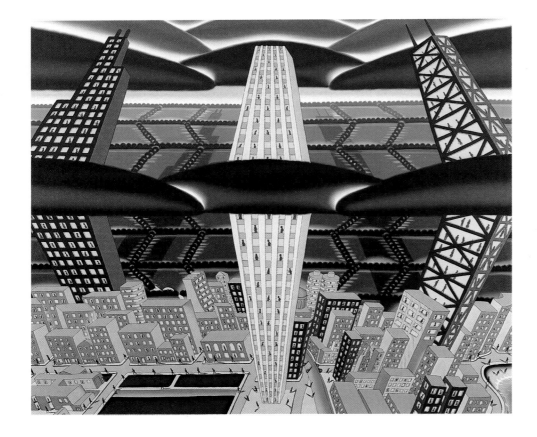

◀ **8·37**

Roger Brown, *Land of Lincoln*, 1978. Oil on canvas, 5 ft 11½ in × 7 ft (1.82 × 2.13 m). Certain contemporary artists employ individualistic devices to create unusual spatial effects. This painting by Roger Brown shows multiple viewpoints that seem to project backward and forward in a scale of unusual proportions.
Courtesy of Guy and Helen Barbier, Geneva, Switzerland.

▶ **8·38**

Lyonel Feininger, *Street: Near the Palace*, 1915. Oil on canvas, 39½ × 31½ in (100.3 × 80 cm). In this painting the artist has used intuitive methods of space control, including overlapping planes and transparencies, as well as planes that interpenetrate one another and incline into space.
The Norton Simon Foundation, Pasadena, CA. © DACS 1994.

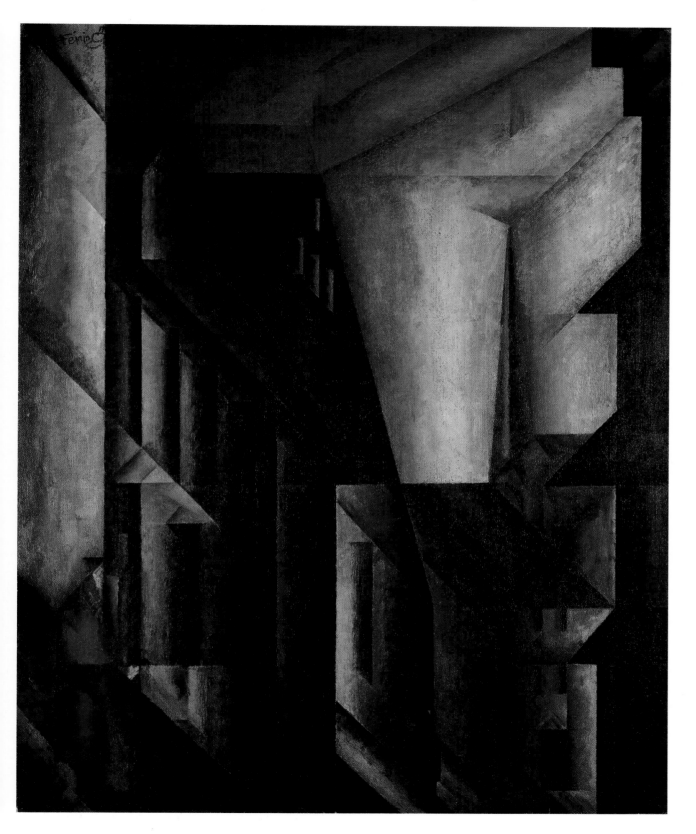

THE SPATIAL PROPERTIES OF THE ELEMENTS

The spatial effects that arise from using the elements of art structure must be recognized and controlled. Each of the elements possesses inherent spatial qualities, but the interrelationship between elements yields the greatest spatial feeling. Many types of spatial experiences can be achieved by manipulating the elements – that is, by varying their position, number, direction, value, texture, size, and color. The resultant spatial variations are endless (see fig. 3.22).

Line and space

Line, by its physical structure, implies continued direction of movement. Thus line, whether moving across the picture plane or deep into it, helps to indicate spatial presence. Since, by definition, a line must be greater in length than in breadth (or else it would be indistinguishable from a dot or a shape), it tends to emphasize one direction. The extension of this dominant direction in a single line creates continuity, moving the eye of the observer from one unit or general area to another. Line can be a transition that unifies the front, middle, and background areas.

In addition to direction, line contains other spatial properties. Long or short, thick or thin lines, and straight, angular, or curved lines take on different spatial positions and movements in contrast with one another. The indications of three-dimensional space mentioned earlier in this chapter are actively combined with the physical properties of line. A long thick line, for instance, appears larger (a spatial indication) and hence closer to the viewer than a short thin line. Overlapping lines establish differing spatial positions, especially when they are set in opposite directions (that is, vertical against horizontal). A diagonal line seems to

▶ **8 · 40**

Vivien Abrams, *Changing Dynamics*, 1984. Oil on masonite, 21¾ × 21½ × 21¼ in (55.2 × 54.6 × 54 cm).
The overlapping and convergence as well as the physical properties of the lines in this work have been orchestrated to create a strong illusion of space.
Louise Ross Gallery, New York.

move from the picture plane into deep space, whereas a vertical or horizontal line generally appears comparatively static (fig. 8.39). In addition, the plastic qualities of overlapping lines can be increased by modulating their values. The plastic illusion invariably suggests change of position in space.

The spatial indication of line convergence that occurs in linear perspective is always in evidence wherever a complex of lines occurs. The spatial suggestions arising out of this general principle are so infinitely varied that particular effects are usually the product of the artist's intuitive explorations. Wavy, spiral, serpentine, and zigzag line types adapt to all kinds of space through their unexpected deviations of direction and accent. They seem to move back and forth from one spatial plane to another. Unattached single lines define their own space and may have plastic qualities within themselves. Lines also clarify the spatial dimensions of solid shapes (fig. 8.40; see fig. 3.9).

Shape and space

Shape may refer to planes, solids, or volumes, all of which occupy space and are therefore entitled to consideration in this chapter. A plane, although physically two-dimensional, may create the illusion of three-dimensional space (fig. 8.41). The space appears two-dimensional when the plane seems to lie on the picture surface (fig. 8.42). The space appears three-dimensional when its edges seem to converge at a point toward the front or the back of the picture plane (fig. 8.43).

▼ **8 · 39**
Lines of various physical properties. Vertical, horizontal, and some diagonal lines often seem to occupy a fixed position in space. Wavy, spiral, serpentine, and zigzag lines appear to move back and forth in space. Alterations in line thickness also modify spatial position.

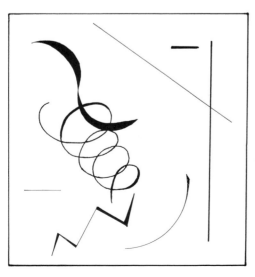

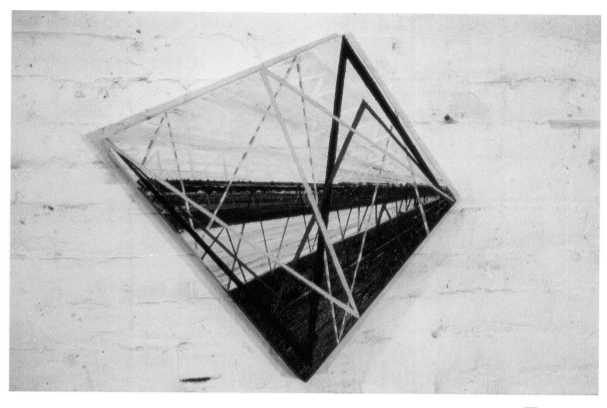

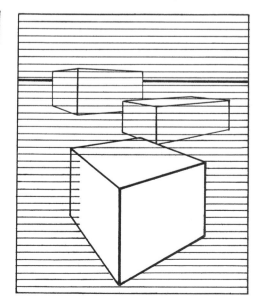

▼ 8·43

Planes and solids in space. The relationship of planes in this diagram describes an effect of solids or volumes that in turn seem to occupy space. The size, overlapping, and placement of these volumes further increase the effect of solidity. The horizontal shaded lines indicate an imaginary position for the picture plane, causing the near volume to project into the observer's space, or in front of the picture plane.

▼ 8·42

Flat planes. Since the shape outlines consist of horizontals and verticals repeating the essentially flat nature of the picture plane (as determined by the horizontals and verticals of the border), this diagram is an example of shape and space relationships that are two-dimensional.

▼ 8·41

Planes in space. In this example, the outlines of the two-dimensional shapes (or planes) are varied in thickness and placement, while two edges converge toward the back to give the effect of three-dimensional space. The overlapping planes enhance the effect of depth behind the picture plane.

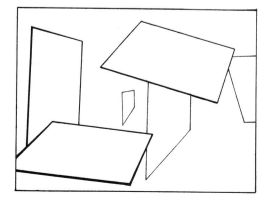

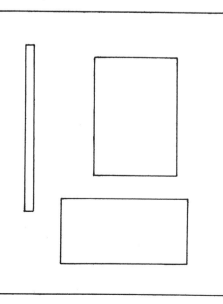

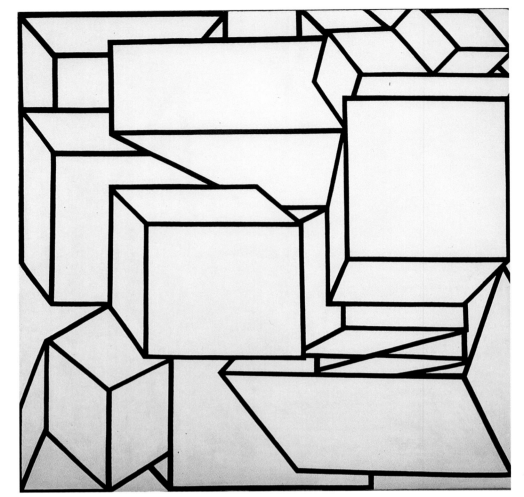

▶ **8 · 44**

Al Held, *B/WX*, 1968. Acrylic on canvas, 9 ft 6 in × 9 ft 6 in (2.90 × 2.90 m).
Although the physical properties of the lines in this work are consistent throughout, their arrangement causes the enclosed shapes to be seen in different spatial positions. This is somewhat similar to the program of Op art.
Albright-Knox Art Gallery, Buffalo, NY. Gift of Seymour H. Knox, 1969. © Al Held/DACS, London/ VAGA, New York 1994.

▼ **8 · 45**

Tony King, *Map: Spirit of '76*, 1976. Acrylic and newspaper on canvas, 7 × 8 ft (2.13 × 2.44 m).
The format, with its papier collé surface, is perfectly flat, but the use of light-and-dark values creates a strongly three-dimensional illusion.
Courtesy of the Owens-Corning Collection. Owens-Corning Fiberglas Corporation, Toledo, OH.

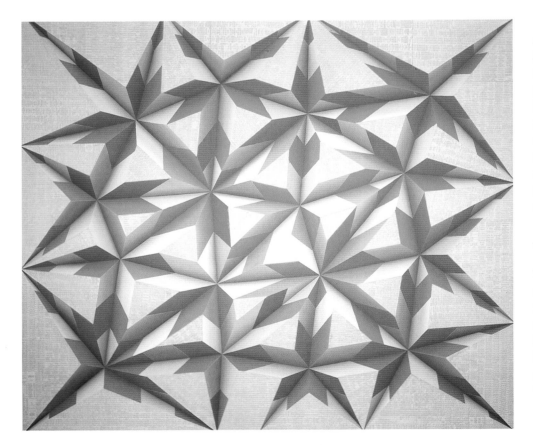

Solids, volumes, and masses automatically suggest three dimensions. Such shapes express the space in which they must exist and actually become a part of it. Planes, solids, and volumes can be made to take a distant position by diminishing their size in comparison to others in the frontal picture areas and by neutralizing their value, color, intensity, and detail (fig. 8.44). This treatment relates back to the indications of space outlined earlier in this chapter.

Value and space

The plastic effect of value can be used to control pictorial space. When a light source is assumed to be in front of a work, the objects in the foreground appear light. The middle and background objects become progressively dark as they move away from the picture plane (see fig. 10.2). When the light source is located at the back of the work, the order of values is reversed (see fig. 6.20). The order of value change is consistent in gradation from light to dark or dark to light.

In the natural world, foreground objects are seen with clarity and great contrast, while distant objects are ill-defined and gray. Therefore, neutral grays, when juxtaposed with blacks or whites, generally take a distant position (see fig. 8.14).

Cast shadows are sometimes helpful in describing plastic space, but they may be spatially confusing and even injurious to the design if not handled judiciously (see figs. 5.3A and 5.5).

Value-modeling can be abstract in the sense that it need not follow the objective natural order of light and dark. Many artists have totally ignored this natural order, using instead the inherent spatial position that results from the contrast of dark and light (fig. 8.45).

Texture and space

Because of the surface enrichment that texture produces, it is tempting to think of this element purely in terms of decorative usefulness. Actually, texture can have the plastic function of describing the depth position of surfaces. Generally speaking, sharp, clear, and bold textures advance, while fuzzy, dull, and minuscule textures recede. When modified through varied use of value, color, and line, texture significantly contributes to the total pictorial unity.

Texture is one of the visual signs used to produce the decorative surface so valued in contemporary art. The physical character of texture is related to allover patterned design and, as such, operates effectively on decorative surfaces. When patterned surfaces are repeated and distributed over the entire pictorial area, the flatness of the picture plane becomes vitally important. Many works of Pablo Picasso illustrate the modern use of surface textures to preserve the concept of the flat picture plane (fig. 8.46).

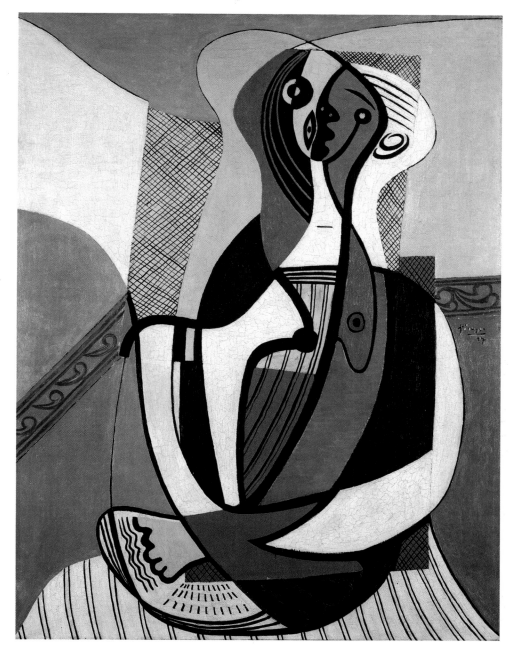

▲ 8 · 46

Pablo Picasso, *Seated Woman*, 1927. Oil on canvas, $51\frac{1}{2} \times 38\frac{1}{2}$ in (130.8 × 97.8 cm). Because of their obviously decorative quality, abstract textures emphasize the flatness of the picture plane. Background and foreground forms become closely integrated so that little sense of receding space is felt by the observer.

Art Gallery of Ontario, Toronto. Purchase, 1964. Acc. no. 63/44. (Photograph by Carlo Catenazzi, AGO.) © DACS 1994.

Color and space

One of the outstanding contributions of modern artists has been their reevaluation of the plastic potentialities of color. Color is now integrated directly into the form of the picture in a positive and direct manner in order to model the various spatial planes of surface areas (see Chapter 7, p. 156). Since the time of Cézanne, there has been a new awareness of the spatial characteristics of color in art. Prior to

▼ **8 · 47**
John Marin, *Sunspots*, 1920. Watercolor and charcoal on off-white wove paper, 16½ × 19¾ in (41.9 × 50.2 cm).
Marin used the watercolor medium to exhibit a free, loose style of painting. His play of color – sea against sunspots – helps to create tremendous spatial interaction.
Metropolitan Museum of Art, New York. Alfred Stieglitz Collection, 1949. (49.70.121).

then, deep space was considered as beginning with the picture plane and receding from it. Later, John Marin and others dealt with the spaces on or in front of the picture plane chiefly through the use of color (fig. 8.47). Hans Hofmann, the abstractionist, often used intense colors to advance shapes beyond the picture plane (fig. 8.48).

Analogous colors, because they are closely related, create limited spatial movement; contrasting colors enlarge the space and provide varied accents or focal points of interest. Both exploit the limitless dimensions of space.

RECENT CONCEPTS OF SPACE

Every great period in the history of art has espoused a particular concept of space. These spatial preferences reflect basic conditions within the civilization that produced them. Certain fundamental attitudes toward space seem to recur in varied forms throughout recorded history. When a new spatial approach is introduced, it is at first resisted by the public. Eventually, however, it becomes the standard filter through which people view things. During the period of their influence, these conventions become a norm of vision for people, gradually conditioning them to expect art to conform to certain general principles. The acceleration of change prompted by the cataclysmic revelations of modern science has now produced new concepts that are without precedent. Today, artists are groping for ways to understand and interpret these ever-widening horizons, and, as they do, their explorations are met by characteristic recalcitrance from the public (fig. 8.49).

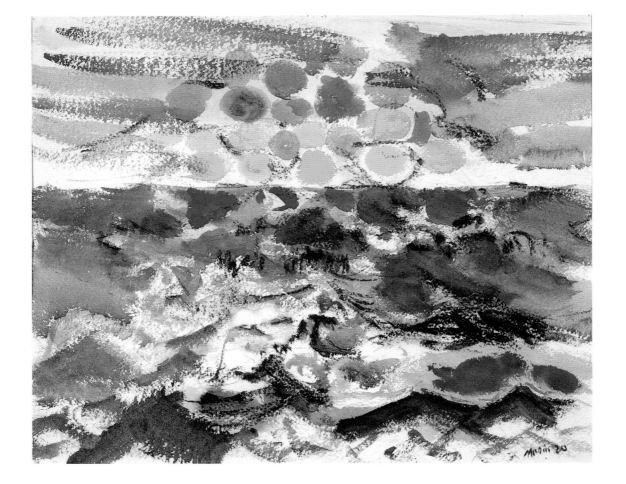

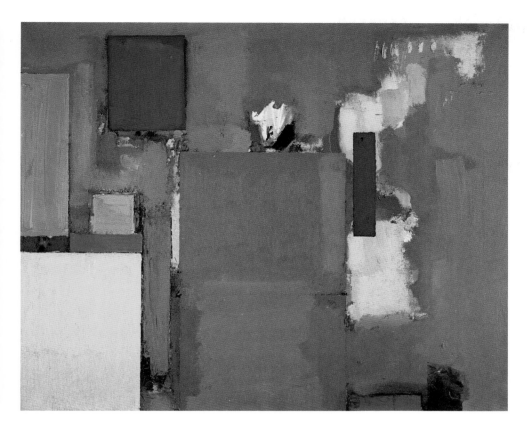

◁ **8 · 48**

Hans Hofmann, *The Golden Wall*, 1961. Oil on canvas, 4 ft 11½ in × 5 ft 11⅝ in (1.51 × 1.82 m).

The large areas of red in this painting unify the color scheme. A smaller area of green gives balance to the total color pattern. Complementary colors balance and enhance each other.

Art Institute of Chicago. Mr. and Mrs. Frank G. Logan Prize Fund, 1962.775.

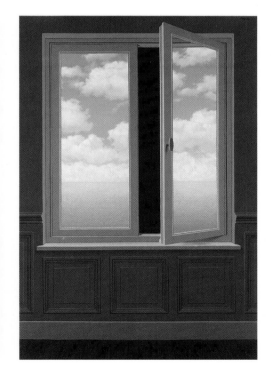

◁ **8 · 49**

René Magritte, *The Field-Glass*, 1963. Oil on canvas, 5 ft 9⁵⁄₁₆ in × 3 ft 9¼ in (1.76 × 1.15 m).

On close inspection one can see that this work is deliberately inconsistent in its use of space. As a Surrealist, Magritte often created ambiguous and unexpected effects to titillate our senses.

Hickey and Robertson, Houston. Courtesy of the Menil Foundation, Houston, TX. © ADAGP, Paris and DACS, London 1994.

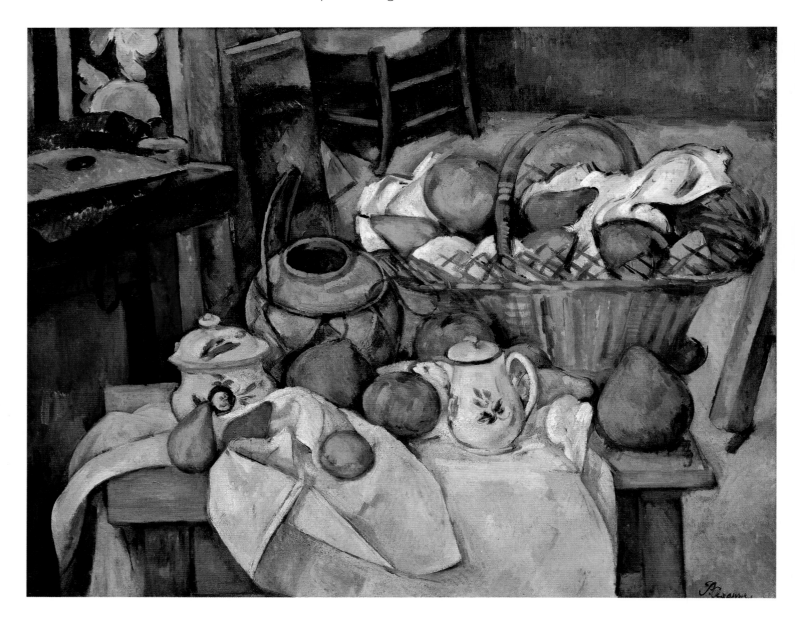

▲ **8 · 50**

Paul Cézanne, *Still Life with Basket of Fruit (The Kitchen Table)*, c. 1888–90. Oil on canvas, 25⅝ × 31⅞ in (65.1 × 81 cm).

Cézanne was concerned with the plastic reality of objects as well as with their organization into a unified design. Although the pitcher and sugar bowl are viewed from a direct frontal position, the rounded jar behind them is painted as if it were being seen from a higher location. The handle of the basket is shown as centered at the front, but it seems to become skewed into a right-sided view as it proceeds to the rear. The left and right front table-edges do not line up, and are thus viewed from different vantage points. Cézanne combined these multiple viewpoints in one painting in order to present each object with a more profound sense of three-dimensional reality.

Musée d'Orsay, Paris, France. (Photograph: RMN.)

The search for a new spatial dimension

Artists of the Renaissance, conditioned by the outlook of the period, set as their goal the optical, scientific mastery of nature. They sought to accomplish this by reducing nature, part by part, to a static geometric system. By restricting their attention to one point of view, artists were able to develop perspective and represent some of the illusionary distortions of actual shapes as seen by the human eye.

Modern artists, equipped with new scientific and industrial materials and technology, have extended the search into nature initiated by the Renaissance. They have probed nature's inner and outer structure with microscope, camera, video, and telescope. The automobile, airplane, and spacecraft have given them the opportunity to see more of the world than their early predecessors knew existed. The radically changed environment of the artist has brought about a new awareness of space. It has become increasingly evident that space cannot be described from the one point of view characteristic of the Renaissance, and the search continues for a new graphic vocabulary to describe visual discoveries. Since one outstanding feature of the modern world is motion, contemporary artistic representation must move, at least illusionistically. Motion has become a part of space, and this space can be grasped only if a certain period of time is allotted to cover it. Hence, a new dimension is added to spatial conception – the *fourth dimension*, which combines space, time, and motion, and presents an important artistic challenge. This challenge is to discover a practical method for representing things in motion from every viewpoint on a flat surface. In searching for solutions to this problem, artists have turned to their own experiences as well as to the work of others.

Plastic images

Paul Cézanne, the nineteenth-century Post-Impressionist, was an early pioneer in the attempt to express the new dimension. His aim was to render objects in a manner more true to nature. This nature, it should be pointed out, was not the Renaissance world of optical appearances; instead, it was a world of forms in space, conceived in terms of a plastic image (fig. 8.50). In painting a still life, Cézanne selected the most characteristic viewpoint of all his objects; he then changed the eye levels, split the individual object planes, and combined all of these views in the same painting, creating a composite view of the group. Cézanne often shifted his viewpoint of a single object from the right side to the left side and from the top to the bottom, creating the illusion of looking around it. To see these multiple views of the actual object, we would have to move around it or revolve it in front of us; this act would involve motion, space, and time.

The Cubists adopted many of Cézanne's pictorial devices. They usually showed an object from as many views as suited them. Objects were rendered in a type of orthographic drawing, divided into essential views that could be drawn in two dimensions, not unlike the Egyptian technique previously cited (see "Fractional Representation", p. 177, and figs. 8.12 and 8.13). The basic view (the top view) is called a *plan*. With the plan as a basis, the elevations (or profiles) were taken from the front and back, and the sections were taken from the right and left sides. The juxtaposition of these views in a painting showed much more of the object than would normally be visible. The technique seems a distortion to the lay spectator conditioned to a static view, but within the limits of artistic selection, everything is present that we would ordinarily expect to see (figs. 8.51 and 8.52).

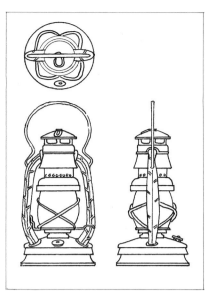

▲ 8·51
Tom Haverfield, *Kerosene Lamp* c. 1960. Pen and ink, 9 × 12 in (22.9 × 30.5 cm).
In this work objects are rendered in a type of orthographic drawing that divides them into essential views able to be drawn in two dimensions.
Courtesy of the artist.

▼ 8·52
Tom Haverfield, *Kerosene Lamp II, c.* 1960. Pencil on paper, 14 × 18 in (35.6 × 45.7 cm).
The juxtaposition of orthographic views illustrates all the physical attributes and different views of the object in one drawing. Such a composite drawing shows much more of an object than could normally be visible.
Courtesy of the artist.

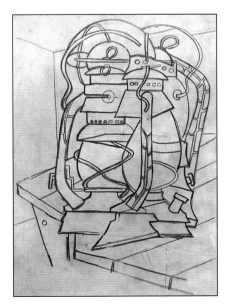

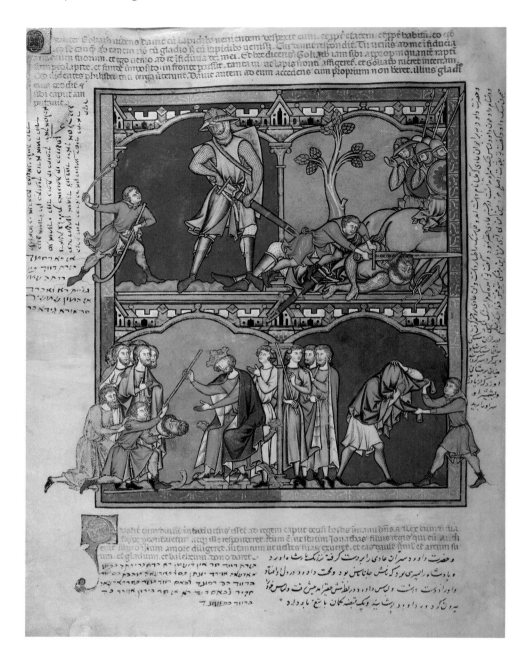

▲ **8 · 53**

**Unknown, *David and Goliath, c.* 1250.
Manuscript dimensions: 15⅜ × 11¾ in (39
× 30 cm).**

The element of time passing is present here, but
in a conventional episodic manner. The order of
events proceeds in a style similar to that of a
comic strip.

Pierpont Morgan Library, New York, M.638 f.28v.

In the works of the Cubists, we find
that a picture can have a life of its own,
and that the creation of space is not
essentially a matter of portrayal or
rendering. The Cubists worked step by
step to illustrate that the more a painted
object departs from straightforward
optical resemblance, the clearer is its
spatial order. Eventually, they developed
the concept of the "synthetically"
designed picture. Instead of analyzing a
subject, they began by developing large,

simple geometric shapes, divorced from a model. Subject matter suggested by the shapes was then imposed or synthesized into this spatial system (see fig. 4.8).

Pictorial representations of movement in time

From time immemorial, artists have grappled with the problem of representing movement on the stationary picture surface. In the works of prehistoric and primitive humans, the efforts were not organized, but were isolated attempts to show a limited phase of observed movement.

In an early attempt to add movement to otherwise static figures, Greek sculptors organized the lines in the draperies of their figures to accent a continuous direction. By means of this device, the eye of the observer is directed along a constant edge or line.

The artists of the Medieval and Renaissance periods illustrated biblical stories by repeating a series of still pictures. The representation of the different phases of the narrative (either in sequence or combined in a single work) created a visual synopsis of the subject's movement, the time period, and the space covered. These pictures were antecedents of modern comic-strip and motion-picture techniques whose individual frames, when projected at speed, provide the illusion of movement (figs. 8.53 and 8.54; see fig. 8.37).

Another representational device that suggests movement is the superimposition of many stationary views of the figure or its parts in a single picture. This technique catalogs the sequence of position of a moving body, indicating the visible changes. Twentieth-century artists have attempted to fuse the different positions of the figure by filling out the pathway of its movement. Figures are not seen in fixed positions but as moving paths of action. The subject in Marcel Duchamp's *Nude Descending a Staircase* is not the human body, but the type and degree of energy the human body emits as it passes through space. This painting

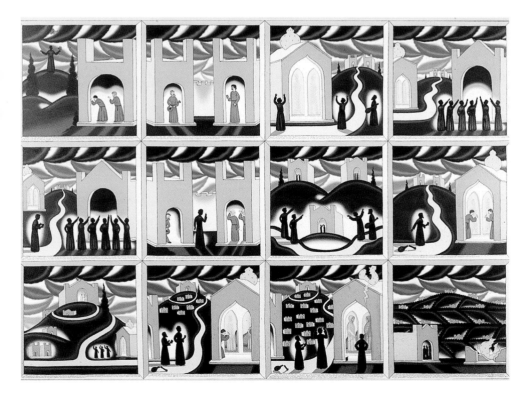

◀ **8 · 54**

Roger Brown, *Giotto and His Friends (Getting Even)*, 1981. Oil on canvas, 6 ft × 8 ft ⅜ in (1.83 × 2.45 m).

Contemporary artist Roger Brown has used the historical technique of segmental narrative. Each segment of the work is a portion of an unfolding story.

Private collection. Photograph courtesy of the Phyllis Kind Galleries, Chicago and New York. (Photograph by William H. Bengtson.)

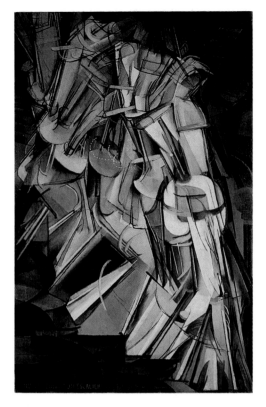

signified important progress in the pictorialization of motion, because the plastic forces are functionally integrated with the composition (fig. 8.55).

The *Futurists* (see Chapter 10, p. 264) were devoted to motion for its own sake. They included not only the shapes of figures and objects and their pathways of movement, but also their backgrounds. These features were combined in a pattern of kinetic energy. Although this form of expression was not entirely new, it provided a new type of artistic adventure – simultaneity of figure, object, and environment (figs. 8.56 and 8.57).

The exploration of space in terms of the four-dimensional space–time continuum is in its infancy. As research reveals more of the mysteries of the natural world, artists will continue to absorb and interpret them according to their individual experiences. It is reasonable to assume that even more

revolutionary concepts will emerge in time, producing great changes in art styles. The important point to remember is that distortions and unfamiliar forms of art expression do not occur in a vacuum – they usually represent earnest efforts to apprehend and interpret our world in terms of the latest frontiers of understanding.

Artists today may take advantage of the technological advances of our age. The hardware and software of computers can generate images that are preparatory, simulative or final art products. By means of animation the human form in motion may be studied. Video files make available a vast storehouse of information. The work of design agencies is greatly enhanced through the use of computer graphics. Video, film, and computer-generated interactive environments only hint at the unlimited potential for visual arts in the future.

▲ **8 · 55**

Marcel Duchamp, *Nude Descending a Staircase, No. 2,* **1912. Oil on canvas, 58 × 35 in (147.3 × 88.9 cm).**
The subject of Duchamp's painting is not the human body itself, but the type and degree of energy a body emits as it passes through space.
Philadelphia Museum of Art, PA. Louise and Walter Arensberg Collection. © ADAGP, Paris and DACS, London 1994.

▶ **8 · 56**

Giacomo Balla, *Dynamism of a Dog on a Leash,* **1912. Oil on canvas, 35⅜ × 43¼ in (89.9 × 109.9 cm).**
To suggest motion as it is involved in time and space, Balla invented the technique of repeated contours. This device soon became commonly imitated in newspaper comic strips, thereby becoming a mere convention.
Albright-Knox Art Gallery, Buffalo, NY. Bequest of A. Conger Goodyear and Gift of George F. Goodyear, 1964.

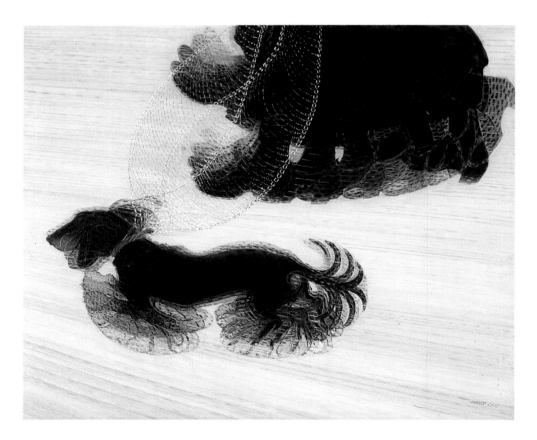

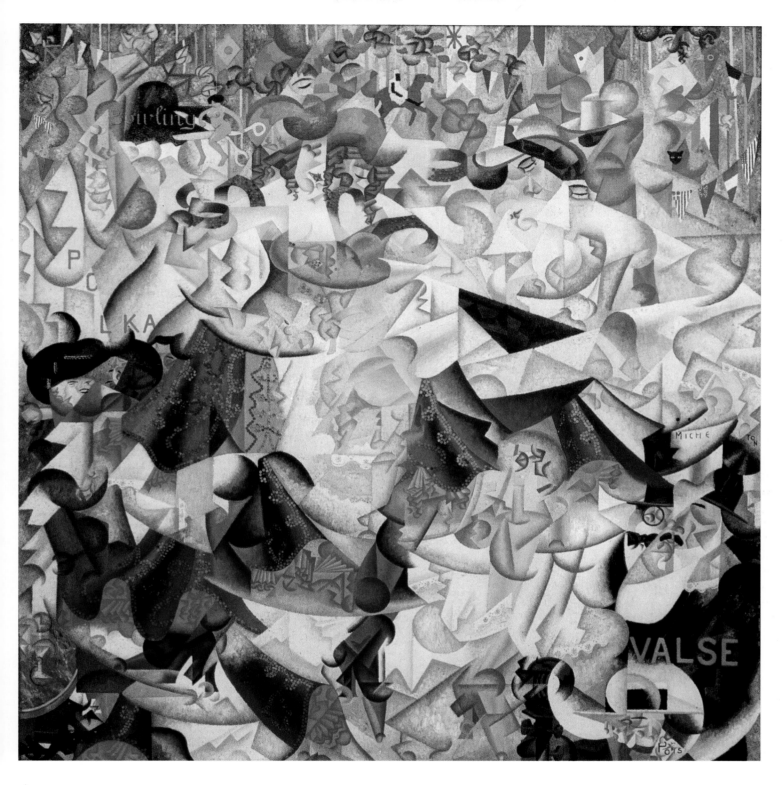

▲ **8 · 57**

Gino Severini, *Dynamic Hieroglyphic of the Bal Tabarin*, 1912. Oil on canvas with sequins, 5 ft 3⅝ in × 5 ft 1½ in (1.61 × 1.56 m).

The works of the Futurists were devoted to motion for its own sake. They included not only the shapes of figures and objects and their pathways of movement, but also their backgrounds. These features were combined in a pattern of kinetic energy.

The Museum of Modern Art, New York. Acquired through the Lillie P. Bliss Bequest. © ADAGP, Paris and DACS, London 1994.

The Art of the Third Dimension

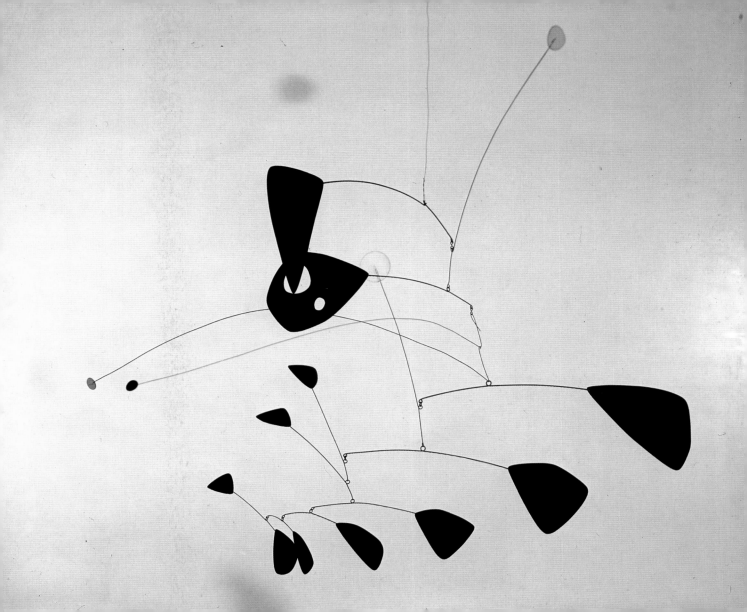

THE VOCABULARY OF THE THIRD DIMENSION

Three-dimensional To possess, or to create the illusion of possessing, the dimension of depth in addition to the dimensions of height and width.

addition
A sculptural term that means building up, assembling, or putting on material.

atectonic
Characterized by considerable amounts of space; open, as opposed to massive (or tectonic), and often with extended appendages.

Bauhaus
Originally a German school of architecture that flourished between World War I and World War II. The Bauhaus attracted many leading experimental artists of both two- and three-dimensional fields.

casting
A sculptural technique in which liquid materials are shaped by being poured into a mold.

glyptic
1. The quality of an art material like stone, wood, or metal that can be carved or engraved. 2. An art form that retains the color, tensile, and tactile quality of the material from which it was created. 3. The quality of hardness, solidity, or resistance found in carved or engraved materials.

manipulation
The sculptural technique which refers to the shaping of pliable materials by hands or tools.

mass (third dimension)
1. In graphic art, a shape that appears to stand out three-dimensionally from the space surrounding it, or appears to create the illusion of a solid body of material. 2. In the plastic arts, the physical bulk of a solid body of material.

mobile
A three-dimensional, moving sculpture.

modeling
A sculptural technique meaning to shape a pliable material.

patina
1. A natural film, usually greenish, that results from the oxidation of bronze or other metallic material. 2. Colored pigments and/or chemicals applied to a sculptural surface.

relief sculpture
An art work, graphic in concept, but sculptural in application, utilizing relatively shallow depth to establish images. The space development may range from very limited projection known as "low relief" to more exaggerated space development known as "high relief." Relief sculpture is meant to be viewed frontally not in the round.

sculpture
The art of expressive shaping of three-dimensional materials. "Man's expression to man through three-dimensional form" (Jules Struppeck, see Bibliography).

shape (third dimension)
An area that stands out from the space next to or around it due to a defined or implied boundary, or because of differences of value, color, or texture.

silhouette
The area between or bounded by the contours, or edges, of an object; the total shape.

substitution
In sculpture, replacing one material or medium with another (see also **casting**).

subtraction
A sculptural term meaning to carve or cut away materials.

tectonic
The quality of simple massiveness; lacking any significant extrusions or intrusions.

void
1. Area lacking positive substance; consisting of negative space. 2. A spatial area within an object that penetrates and passes through it.

volume (third dimension)
A measurable area of defined or occupied space.

BASIC CONCEPTS OF THREE-DIMENSIONAL ART

In the preceding chapters, our examination of art fundamentals has been limited mostly to the graphic arts. These art disciplines (drawing, painting, photography, printmaking, graphic design, and so on) have two dimensions (height and width), exist on a flat surface, and generate sensations of space mainly through illusions created by the artist. This chapter deals with the unique properties of *three-dimensional* artwork and the creative concepts that evolve from these properties.

In three-dimensional art, the added dimension is that of actual depth. This depth results in a greater sense of reality and, as a consequence, increases the physical impact of the work. This is true because a graphic work is limited to one format plan, always bounded by a geometric shaped picture frame, while a three-dimensional work is limited only by the outer extremities of its multiple positions and/or views. The three-dimensional format, although more complicated, offers greater freedom to the artist and greater viewing interest to the spectator.

Since actual depth is fundamental to three-dimensional art, one must be in the presence of the artwork to fully appreciate it. Words and graphic representations of three-dimensional art are not substitutes for actual experience. Two-dimensional descriptions are flat, rigid and representative of only one viewpoint; however, they do serve as a visual shorthand for actual sensory experiences. In this text, and particularly in this chapter, we use two-dimensional descriptions, by way of text and photographic reproductions, as the most convenient means of conveying the three-dimensional experience. But we emphatically encourage readers to put actual observation into practice when using this book.

Practicing artists and art authorities designate the three-dimensional qualities of objects in space with such terms as form, shape, mass, and volume. The term form can be misleading here, because its meaning differs from the definition applied in early chapters – the inventive arrangement of all the visual elements according to principles that will produce unity. In a broad structural sense, form is the sum total of all the media and techniques used to organize the three-dimensional elements within an artwork. In this respect, a church is a total form and its doors are contributing shapes; similarly, a human figure is a total form, while the head, arms, and legs are contributing shapes. However, in a more limited sense, form may just refer to the appearance of an object – to a contour, a shape, or a structure. *Shape*, when used in a three-dimensional sense, may refer to a positive or open negative area. By comparison, *mass* invariably denotes a solid physical object of relatively large weight or bulk. Mass may also refer to a coherent body of matter, like clay or metal, that is not yet shaped, or to a lump of raw material that could be modeled or cast. Stone carvers, accustomed to working with *glyptic* materials, tend to think of a heavy, weighty mass (fig. 9.1); modelers, who manipulate clay or wax, favor a pliable mass. *Volume* is the amount of space the mass, or bulk, occupies, or the three-dimensional area of space that is totally or partially enclosed by planes, linear edges, or wires. Many authorities conceive of masses as positive solids and volumes as negative open spaces. For example, a potter who throws a bowl on a turntable adjusts the dimensions of the interior volume (negative interior space) by expanding or compressing the clay planes (positive mass). The sculptor who assembles materials may also enclose negative volumes to form unique relationships (fig. 9.2, overleaf).

Looking more widely, most objects in our environment have three-dimensional

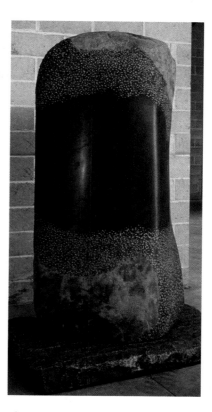

▲ 9 · 1

Isamu Noguchi, *The Stone Within*, 1982. Basalt, 75 × 38 × 27 in (190.5 × 96.5 × 68.6 cm).

The sculptor Noguchi has subtracted just enough stone in this work to introduce his concept of minimal form while preserving the integrity of the material and its heavy, weighty mass.

Isamu Noguchi Foundation. (Photograph by Michio Noguchi.)

▶ **9·2**
John Goforth, *Untitled,* **1971. Cast aluminum, 15¾ in (40 cm) high with base.**
The volume incorporates the space, both solid and empty, that is occupied by the work.
Courtesy of the artist.

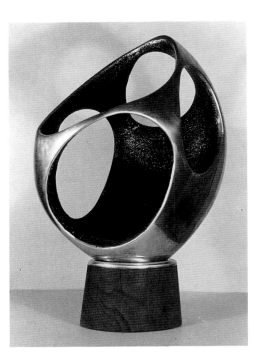

▼ **9·3**
Mark di Suvero, *Tom,* **1959. Wood, metal, rope, cable, and wire construction, 9 × 10 × 12 ft (2.74 × 3.05 × 3.66 m).**
Modern sculpture exploits every conceivable material that suits the intentions of the artist.
Courtesy of the Detroit Institute of Arts, Detroit, MI. Gift of Friends of Modern Art and Mr. and Mrs. Walter Buhl Ford II Fund.

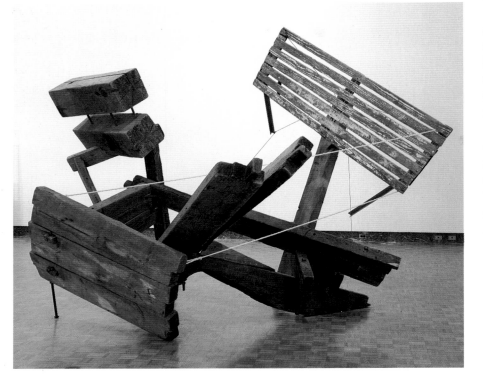

qualities of height, width, and depth, and can be divided into natural and human-made forms. Although natural forms may stimulate the thought processes, they are not in themselves creative. Artists invent forms to satisfy their need for self-expression. In the distant past, most three-dimensional objects were created for utilitarian purposes. They included such implements as stone axes, pottery, hammers and knives, and objects of worship. Nearly all these human-made forms possessed qualities of artistic expression; many depicted the animals their creators hunted. These historic objects are now considered an early expression of the sculptural impulse.

Sculpture

The term "sculpture" has had varied meanings throughout history. The word derives from the Latin verb *sculpere,* which refers to the process of carving, cutting, or engraving. The ancient Greeks' definition of *sculpture* also included the *modeling* of such pliable materials as clay or wax, to produce figures in relief or in-the-round. The Greeks developed an ideal standard for the sculptured human form which was considered the perfect physical organization – harmonious, balanced, and totally related in all parts. The concept of artistic organization was part of the definition of sculpture (see fig. 2.41).

Modern sculpture has taken on new qualities in response to the changing conditions of an industrialized age. Science and machinery have made sculptors more conscious of materials and technology, and more aware of the underlying abstract structure in their art.

Sculpture is no longer limited to carving and modeling. It now refers to any means of giving intended form to all types of three-dimensional materials. These means include welding, bolting, riveting, gluing, sewing, machine-hammering, and stamping. In turn, the three-dimensional artists have expanded their range of sculptural forms to include planar, solid, and linear constructions made of such materials as steel, plastic, wood, and fabric (fig. 9.3). The resulting sculptures are stronger (even though made of lighter materials) and more open. They also have expanded spatial relationships.

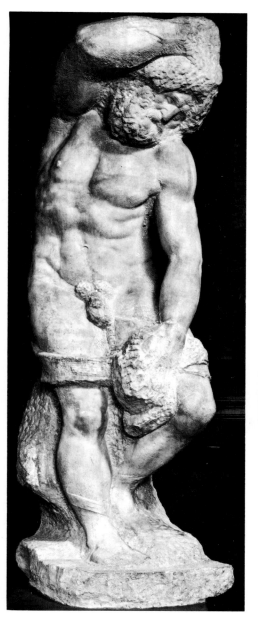

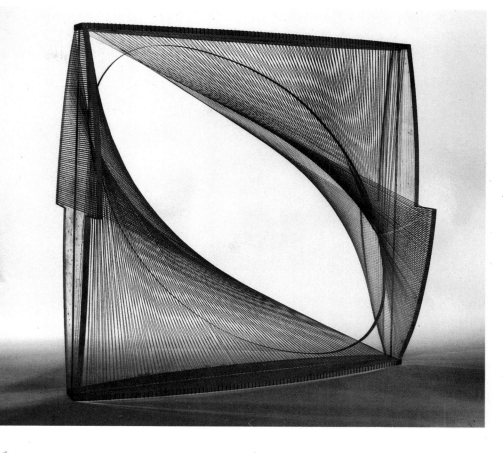

◀ **9 · 4**

Michelangelo Buonarroti, *The Bearded Captive*, date unknown. Marble, 8 ft 8¼ in (2.65 m) high.
Michelangelo developed the idea of heavy, massive sculpture and enlarged the sizes of human body parts for expressive purposes. The tectonic composition was in keeping with the intrinsic nature of the stone.

Accademia, Florence.

▲ **9 · 5**

Naum Gabo, *Linear Construction in Space No. 1 (Variation)*, 1942–43 (fabricated c. 1957–58). Plexiglas with nylon monofilament, 24¾ × 24¾ × 9½ in (62.9 × 62.9 × 24.1 cm).
Naum Gabo was an early pioneer in the Constructivist movement. He created sculptures free of traditional figures with such new materials as the sheet plastic seen here.

From the Patsy R. and Raymond D. Nasher Collection, Dallas, TX.

Three-dimensional forms like wire constructions and *mobiles* have changed the definition of sculpture that, prior to the nineteenth century, would have included only solid, heavy, and sturdy glyptic forms. Michelangelo Buonarroti, an innovative sculptor within his Renaissance time-frame, thought only in terms of massive materials and heavy figures (fig. 9.4).

The diversity of newfound materials and techniques has led to greater individual expression and artistic freedom. Sculptors experiment with new theories and have found new audiences and new markets (fig. 9.5).

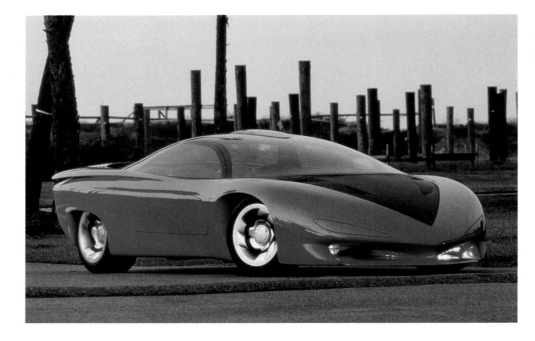

▲ 9·6
Pontiac Banshee concept car.
New concepts in automobile design are determined by advances in technology, engineering, economics, and visual appearance. The 1988 concept car for General Motors' Pontiac was the Banshee, a futuristic performance coupé with realistic design and engineering features.
Courtesy of public relations department/Pontiac Division/General Motors Corporation/Pontiac, MI.

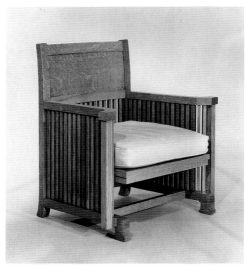

▲ 9·7
Armchair designed by Frank Lloyd Wright for the Ray W. Evans House, Chicago, c. 1908. Oak, 34¼ × 23 × 22½ in (86.9 × 58.5 × 57.1 cm).
To Wright, form and function were inseparable, so a chair, which functions for sitting, should be considered along with the whole architectural environment.
Art Institute of Chicago. Gift of Mr. and Mrs. F. M. Fahrenwald, 1970.435.

Other areas of three-dimensional art

The bulk of this book has addressed works of pure or fine art that have no practical function. But sensitivity to the sculptural (and/or artistic) impulse is not confined to the fine arts; it permeates all three-dimensional structures. The same abstract quality of expressive beauty which is the foundation for a piece of sculpture can underlie such functional forms as automobiles, television receivers, telephones, industrial equipment, window and interior displays, furniture, and buildings (fig. 9.6). Artist-designers of these three-dimensional products organize elements, shapes, textures, colors, and space according to the same principles of harmony, proportion, balance, and variety. Although form principles can be applied to such useful objects, the need for utility often restricts the creative latitude of the artist.

The famous architect Louis Sullivan made the oft-repeated remark that "form follows function." This concept has influenced several decades of design, changing the appearance of tools, telephones, silverware, chairs, and a vast

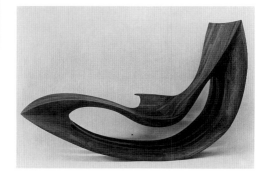

▲ 9·8
Michael Coffey, *Aphrodite* (a rocking lounge chair), 1978. Laminated mozambique, 4 ft 6 in × 7 ft 6 in × 28 in (137 × 229 × 71.1 cm).
A useful household article can be transformed by the style of contemporary sculpture.
Courtesy of the artist. (Photograph by Rich Baldinger, Schenectady, NY.)

array of other familiar and less familiar items. Sometimes this concept is misapplied. The idea of streamlining is practical when applied to the design of such moving objects as trains and cars, because it has the function of reducing wind resistance; but it has no logical application for the design of spoons and lamps. Although streamlining is helpful in eliminating irrelevancies from design, even simplification can be overdone. The *Bauhaus* notion of the house as a "machine for living" helped architects rethink architectural principles, but it also produced many cold and austere structures against which there was inevitable reaction.

Contemporary designers are very aware of the functional needs of the objects they plan. Consequently, they design forms that express and aid function. However, designers also know that these objects need to be aesthetically pleasing. All of this points out that the creator of functional objects must be able to apply the principles of fundamental order within the strictures of utilitarian need. Frank Lloyd Wright, the celebrated American architect, combined architecture, engineering, and art in shaping his materials and their environment. The unity of his ideas is expressed in the chair he designed for the Ray Evans House (fig. 9.7). The sophisticated design and formal balance which Wright incorporated into this ordinary object can be seen in his highly selective repetitions, proportional relationships, and detail refinement.

The balance that exists between design, function, and expressive content within an object varies with each creator. For instance, when designing his rocking lounge chair, Michael Coffey placed strong emphasis on expressive form without totally sacrificing the function of reclining comfort (fig. 9.8). At first glance, we are drawn in by the chair's dominant outer contour and by its open shape. This unique piece of furniture resembles many freely expressed contemporary sculptures.

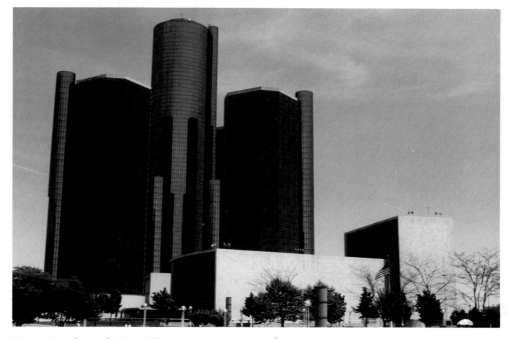

Expressive form follows function in a new and creative way.

Tremendous developments have taken place in the general areas of three-dimensional design in which works usually serve some functional purpose.

Architecture

Recent technological innovations and new building materials have given architects greater artistic flexibility. Thanks to developments in the steel and concrete industries, buildings can now be large in scale without projecting massive, weighty forms. With the advent of electric lighting, vast interior spaces can be illuminated. Because of air conditioning, buildings can be completely enclosed or sheathed in glass. Cantilevered forms can be extended into space. Sophisticated free-formed shapes can be created with the use of precast concrete. All of these structural improvements have allowed architects to think and plan more freely. Contemporary public buildings that demonstrate these developments include the Renaissance Center in Detroit (fig. 9.9), the Lincoln Center for the Performing Arts in New York, the Kennedy Center in Washington, D.C., the Jefferson Westward Expansion Memorial

▲ 9·9
John Portman, Renaissance Center, Detroit, Michigan, 1977.
Architect John Portman designed these high-level towers with steel, reinforced concrete, marble, and glass construction.
Photograph courtesy of the authors.

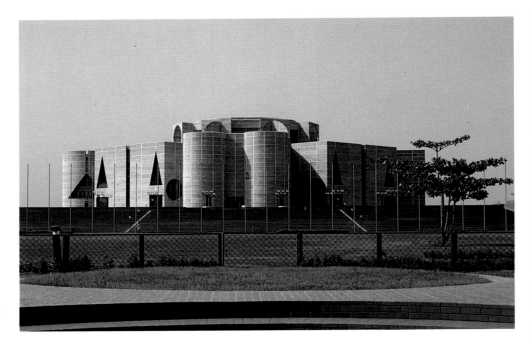

9·10
Louis I. Kahn, National Assembly Building at Sher-e-Bangla Nagar in Dhaka, Bangladesh, 1962–1983. Poured concrete, wood, brick.
Louis Kahn, an American architect, shows his unique use of geometry in a simple, massive sculpture-like structure. Classical and modernist ideals have been blended to create an unpretentious and stabilizing appearance.
Architectural Association Slide Library, London.

in St. Louis, and the Los Angeles City Hall and Civic Center. In many ways architects today are "building sculptors," and their designs require a thorough grounding in artistic principles as well as an understanding of engineering concepts (fig. 9.10).

Metalwork

Most of the changes in metalworking (jewelry, small bowls, and so on) have been in concept rather than technique. Although traditional techniques are still in use, modern equipment has made procedures simpler and more convenient. To a large degree, fashion determines the character of metalwork, but it is safe to say that contemporary work is larger and more oriented toward sculpture than most work of the past. Constant cross-fertilization occurs among the art areas, and metalwork is not immune to these influences. The metalworker benefits from studying the principles of both two- and three-dimensional art (figs. 9.11A and B).

9·11A and B
Harold Hasselschwert, (A) Pendant Necklace, 1972. Cast silvergilt with transparent enamel, cultured pearls, and a 55-carat rutilated kunzite; 4½ in (11.4 cm) height of pendant. (B) Obi Mock Urn, 1986. Copper enamel mounted on turned pine with gold leaf over venet-red and tied with cotton cord, c. 12 in (30.5 cm) high.
Articles of metalwork are sculptural in concept. The necklace is meant to be worn, while the urn is intended to be free-standing.
Courtesy of the artist.

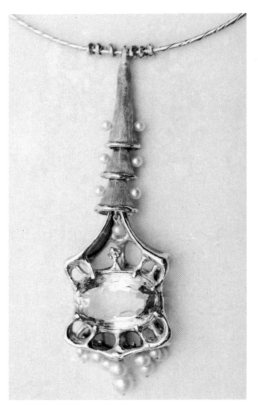

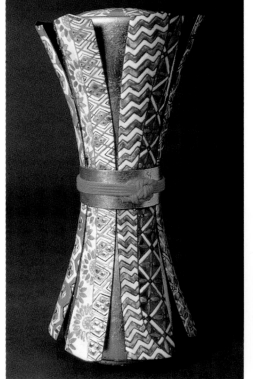

Glass design

Glassworking is similar to metalworking now that modern equipment has simplified traditional techniques. Designing glass objects, however, is very much an artform of recent times. Many free-form and figurative pieces have the look of contemporary sculpture. Colors augment the designs in a decorative, as well as an expressive, sense. Thus, the principles of art structure are integrated with the craft of the medium.

Ceramics

In recent years the basic shape of the ceramic object has become more sculptural as ceramic work has become, in many cases, less functional. The ceramist must be equally aware of three-dimensional considerations and of the fundamentals of graphic art, since designs are often incised, drawn, or painted on the surface of the piece (fig. 9.12).

Fiberwork

Fiberwork has undergone a considerable revolution recently. Three-dimensional forms are becoming increasingly common, particularly as the traditional making by hand of rugs and tapestries has diminished. Woven objects now include a vast array of materials incorporated into designs of considerable scale and bulk. Traditional as well as contemporary concepts of fiberwork require an understanding of both two- and three-dimensional principles (fig. 9.13).

Product design

A relative newcomer on the art scene, product design is usually concerned with commercial applications. The designer produces works that are based on function but geared to consumer appeal. To be contemporary in appearance and thus attractive to consumers, products must exploit all the design principles of the age. The designs of common objects in our daily environment are the products of the designer's training in these various principles.

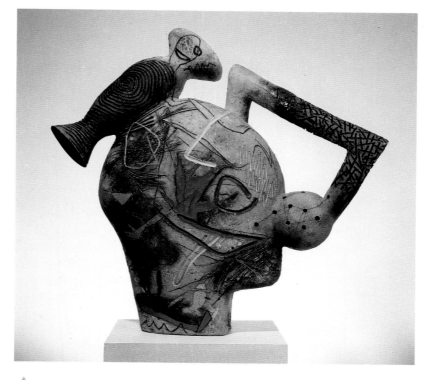

▲ **9·12**
Stan Welsh, *A Question of Balance*, no date. Terracotta clay, 45 × 47 × 16 in (114.3 × 119.4 × 40.6 cm).
The artist used low-temperature color glazes in conjunction with sandblasting to enhance the forms and strengthen the composition.
Courtesy of the artist.

▼ **9·13**
Kathleen Hagan, *Crocheted Series #5*, 1979. Largest shape, c. 8 × 10 in (20.3 × 25.4 cm).
Contemporary textile design frequently goes beyond its largely two-dimensional traditions.
Courtesy of the artist.

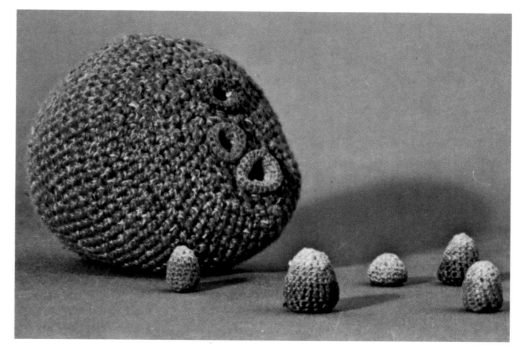

THE COMPONENTS OF THREE-DIMENSIONAL ART

Subject, form, and content – the components of graphic art – function in much the same manner in the plastic arts. The emphasis placed on each of the components, however, may vary. For example, sculptors use the components for expressive purposes. Architects, ceramists, and metalsmiths, while expressive, may also interpret form for the sake of utility and ornamentation.

Formal organization is more complex in three-dimensional art than in the graphic arts. Actual materials developed in actual space through physical manipulation exist in a tactile, as well as in a visual, sense. The resulting complexities expand the content or meaning of the form and add another whole aesthetic dimension.

Materials and techniques

Materials and techniques also play larger roles in three-dimensional art than in graphic art. In the last one hundred years the range of three-dimensional materials has expanded from basic stone, wood, and bronze to steel, plastic, fabric, glass, laser beams (holography), fluorescent and incandescent lighting, and so on. Such materials have revealed new areas for free explorations within the components of subject, form, and content. But they have also increased our responsibilities for fully understanding three-dimensional materials and their accompanying technologies. The nature of the materials puts limitations on the structures that can be created and the techniques that can be used. For example, clay modelers adapt the characteristics of clay to their concept. They manipulate the material with their hands, a block, or a knife to produce a given expression or idea. Modelers don't try to cut the clay with a saw. They understand the characteristics of their material and adapt the right tools and

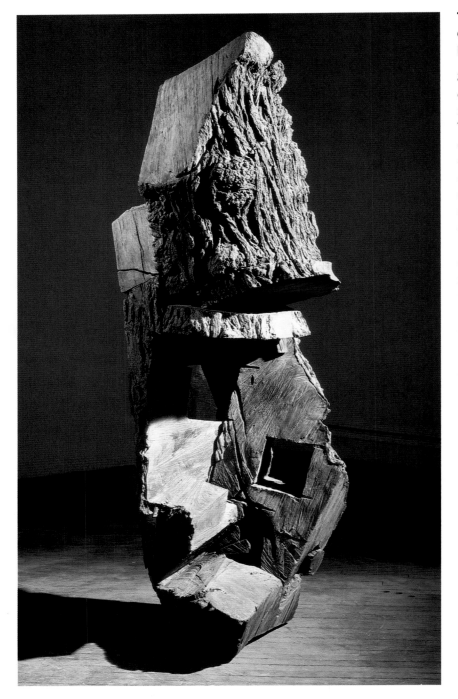

▲ 9·14

Mel Kendrick, *Osage with Two Squares (Bronze)*, 1990. Bronze, 73 × 28 × 28 in (185.4 × 71.1 × 71.1 cm).

This piece appears to be made of wood, but it is actually bronze that has been colored chemically to resemble weathered wood. The sculptor has to know his materials well to create this kind of *trompe l'oeil* effect.

Courtesy of the John Weber Gallery, New York.

techniques to control it. They also know that materials, tools, and techniques are not ends in themselves but necessary means for developing a three-dimensional work (fig. 9.14).

The four primary technical methods for creating three-dimensional forms are: *subtraction, manipulation, addition,* and *substitution.* Although each of the technical methods is developed and discussed separately in the following sections, many three-dimensional works are produced using combinations of the four methods.

Subtraction

Artists cut away materials capable of being carved (glyptic materials), such as stone, wood, cement, plaster, clay, and some plastics. They may use chisels, hammers, torches, saws, grinders, and polishers to reduce their materials (fig. 9.15). It has often been said that when carvers take away material, they "free" the image frozen in the material and a sculpture emerges. The freeing of form by the subtraction method, although not simple, does produce unique qualities that are characteristic of the artist's material.

Manipulation

Widely known as modeling, manipulation relates to the way materials are handled. Clay, wax, and plaster are common media that are pliable or that can be made pliable during their working periods. Manipulation is a direct method for creating form. Artists can use their hands to model a material like clay into a form that, when completed, will be a finished product. For additional control, special tools, such as wedging boards,

wires, pounding blocks, spatulas, and modeling tools (wood and metal), are used to work manipulable materials (fig. 9.16).

Manipulable materials respond directly to human touch, leaving the artist's imprint, or are mechanically shaped to imitate other materials. Although many artists favor the honest autographic qualities of pliable materials, others – especially those in business and manufacturing – opt for the economics of quick results and fast change. Techniques and materials are important since both contribute their own special quality to the final form.

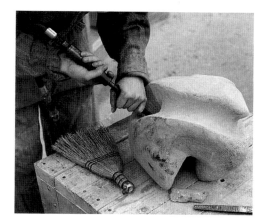

◀ 9·15
Subtracting stone. In the subtractive process, the raw material is removed until the artist's conception of the form is revealed. Stone can be shaped manually or with an air hammer, as above.
Photograph courtesy of Ronald Coleman.

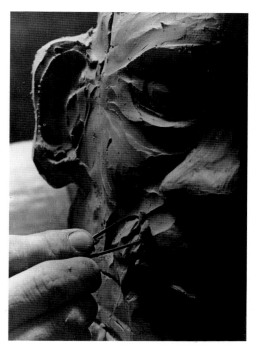

▶ 9·16
In this example of the manipulation technique, clay is removed with a loop tool. Clay may be applied to the surface with fingers, hands, or other tools.
Photograph courtesy of Ronald Coleman.

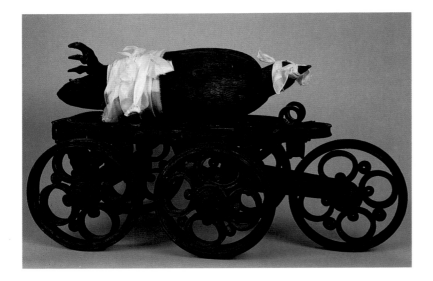

▲ **9 · 17**

David Cayton, *One Dead Tern Deserves Another*, 1990. Ceramics, primitive firing, 18 in (45.7 cm) high.

This is an example of clay that has been fired in a primitive kiln: the heavy reduction firing has caused the clay surfaces to turn black.

Courtesy of the artist.

▼ **9 · 18**

Welding. In the additive process, pieces of material are attached to each other and the form is gradually built up. Welded pieces such as the one illustrated are often, though not always, more open than other sculptural techniques.

Photograph courtesy of Ronald Coleman.

Because most common manipulable materials are not durable, they usually undergo further technical change. For instance, clay may be fired in a kiln (fig. 9.17) or cast in a more permanent material like bronze.

Addition

Methods of addition may involve greater technology and, in terms of (nonfunctional) sculpture, have brought about the most recent innovations. When using additive methods, artists add materials that may be pliable and/or fluid, such as plaster or cement (see figs. 9.21B and C). They assemble materials like metal, wood, and plastic with tools (a

welding torch, soldering gun, or stapler, and so on) and fasteners (bolts, screws, nails, rivets, glue, rope, or even thread) (fig. 9.18; see fig. 9.3).

Since three-dimensional materials and techniques are held in high esteem today, the additive methods, with great range, freedom, and diversity, offer many challenging three-dimensional form solutions.

Substitution

Substitution, or *casting*, is almost always a technique for reproducing an original three-dimensional model. Sometimes an artist alters the substitution process to change the nature of the cast. Basically, in this technique, a model in one material is exchanged for a duplicate form in another material, called the cast, and this is done by means of a mold. The purposes of substitution are first, to duplicate the model and second, to change the material of the model, generally to a permanent one. For example, clay or wax can be exchanged for bronze (fig. 9.19), fiberglass,

▼ **9 · 19**

Substitution technique. In the substitution process, molten metal is poured into a sand mold that was made from a model.

Photograph courtesy of Ronald Coleman.

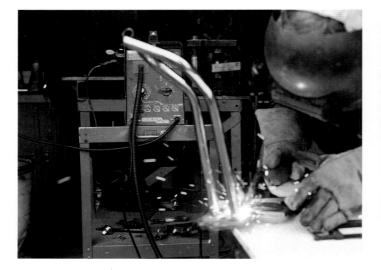

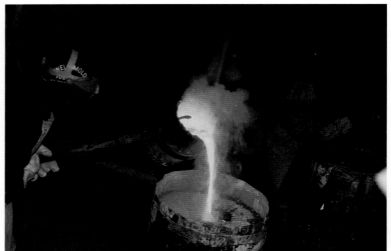

or cement. A variety of processes (sand casting, plaster casting, lost-wax casting, and so on) and molds (flexible molds, waste molds, piece molds, and so on) are used in substitution. Substitution is the least creative or inventive of the technical methods since it is imitative; the creativity lies in the original, not in the casting process.

Besides acquiring a knowledge of three-dimensional materials and their respective techniques, artists must also be aware of the elements of form.

The elements of three-dimensional form

Three-dimensional form is composed of the visual elements: shape, value, space, texture, line, color, and time (the fourth dimension). The order of listing is different from that for two-dimensional art and is based on significance and usage.

Shape

The artist working in three dimensions instinctively begins with shape. Shape, a familiar element in the graphic arts, takes on expanded meaning in the plastic arts. It implies the totality of the mass or volume lying between its contours, including any projections and depressions. It may also include interior planes. We can speak of the overall space-displacing shape of a piece of sculpture or architecture, of the flat or curved shape that moves in space, or of a negative shape that is partially or totally enclosed. These shapes are generally measurable areas limited by and/or contrasted with other shapes, values, textures, and colors. The three-dimensional artist should clearly define the actual edges of shape borders (fig. 9.20). Ill-defined edges often lead to viewers' confusion or monotony. Shape edges guide the eye through, around, and over the three-dimensional surface.

In three-dimensional art the visible shape depends on the viewer's position. A slight change of position results in a change in shape. A major contour is the outer limit of the total three-dimensional work as seen from one position (figs. 9.21 A–C). Secondary contours are perceived

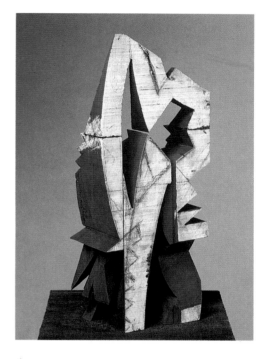

▲ **9 · 20**
Mel Kendrick, *White Wall*, 1984. Oiled mahogany, gesso, pencil, 16 × 5 × 6½ in (40.6 × 12.7 × 16.5 cm).
The shape of this three-dimensional piece has edges that have been clearly defined.
Courtesy of the John Weber Gallery, New York.

▼ **9 · 21A, B, and C.**
Major and secondary contours. In figure A the major contour surrounds the silhouette, or the total visible area, of the work. Secondary contours enclose internal masses. In figures B and C, each change in position reveals new aspects of a sculpture in the round.

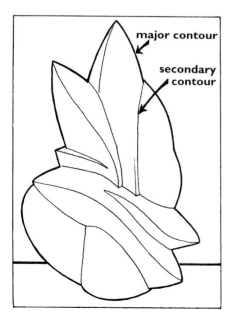
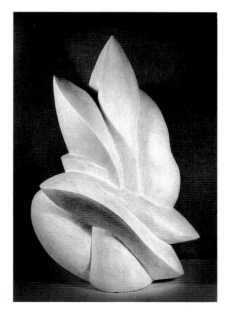
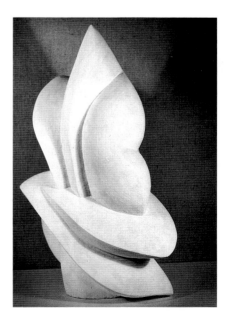

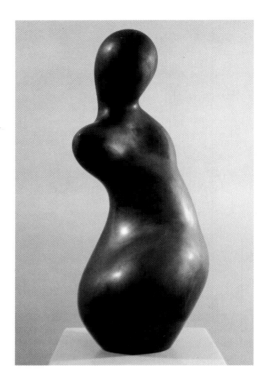

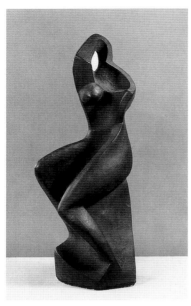

edges of shapes or planes that move across and/or between the major contours. Some three-dimensional works are constructed so that the secondary contours are negligible (fig. 9.22).

A shape might be a negative space – a three-dimensional open area that seems to penetrate through or be contained by solid material. Open shapes can be areas that surround or extend between solids. Such open shapes are often called *voids*. Alexander Archipenko and Henry Moore, prominent twentieth-century sculptural innovators, pioneered the use of void shapes (fig. 9.23). Voids provided new spatial extensions for these artists; they revealed interior surfaces, opened direct routes to back sides of the sculpture, and reduced excessive weight. Void shapes should be considered integral parts of the total form. In linear sculpture, enclosed void shapes become so important that they often dominate the width, thickness, and weight of the materials that define them (fig. 9.24).

Value
As the artist physically manipulates three-dimensional shapes, contrasting values appear through the lights and shadows produced by the forms. Value is the

▲ 9 · 22
Jean Arp, *Torsifruit*, 1960. Bronze (edition of ten), 29 × 12 × 11½ in (73.7 × 30.5 × 29.2 cm).
The major contour of *Torsifruit* is its outermost edge. Secondary contours are nonexistent or, at best, minimal.
Courtesy of Kent Fine Art, New York. © DACS 1994.

▲ 9 · 23
Alexander Archipenko, *Woman Doing Her Hair*, c. 1958. Bronze casting from plaster based on original terracotta of 1916, 21⅝ in (55 cm) high.
This is a significant example of sculptural form where the shape creates negative space, or a void. Archipenko was one of the pioneers of this concept.
Courtesy of the Kunst Museum, Dusseldorf, Germany.

▶ 9 · 24
José de Rivera, *Brussels Construction*, 1958. Stainless steel, 3 ft 10½ in × 6 ft 6¾ in (1.18 × 2 m).
The concept of attracting observers to a continuous series of rewarding visual experiences as they move about a static three-dimensional work of art led to the principle of kinetic or mobile art, as with this sculpture set on a slowly turning motorized plinth.
Art Institute of Chicago. Gift of Mr. and Mrs. R. Howard Goldsmith, 1961.46.

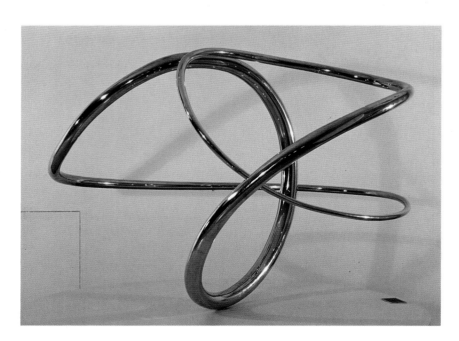

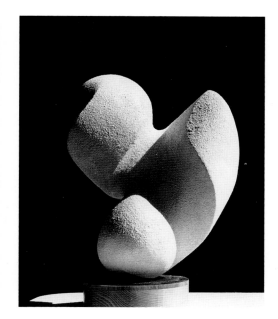

▲ **9 · 25**
**Student work, *Untitled*, c. 1970. Plaster,
approx. 18 in (45.7 cm) high.**
A piece of sculpture "paints" itself with values.
The greater the projections and the sharper the
edges, the greater and more abrupt the
contrasts.

Photograph courtesy of Ronald Coleman.

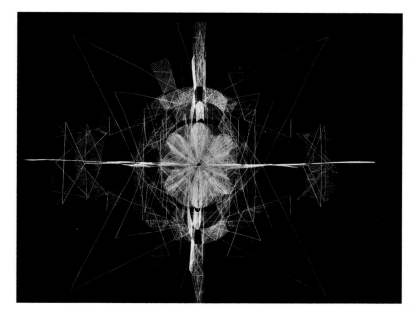

▲ **9 · 26**
**Richard Lippold, *Variation within a Sphere,
No. 10, the Sun*, 1953–56. 22-carat gold-
filled wire, 11 × 22 × 5½ ft (3.35 × 6.70
× 1.68 m).**
Development of welding and soldering
techniques for use in sculpture made the shaping
and joining of thin linear metals possible, as in
this work by Lippold.

Metropolitan Museum of Art, New York. Fletcher
Fund, 1956.

quantity of light actually reflected by an object's surfaces. Surfaces that are high and facing a source of illumination are light, while surfaces that are low, penetrated to any degree, or facing away from the light source appear dark. Any angular change of two juxtaposed surfaces, however slight, results in changed value contrasts. The sharper the angular change, the greater the contrast (fig. 9.25).

When any part of a three-dimensional work blocks the passage of light, shadows result. The shadows change as the position of the viewer, the work, or its source of illumination changes. If a work has a substantial high and low shape variation and/or penetration, the shadow patterns are more likely to define the work, regardless of the position of the

light source. Sculptors who create mobiles typify artists interested in continuously changing light and shadow. The intensity of light markedly changes the shadow effect as the object moves.

Value changes can also be affected by painting a three-dimensional work. Light values strengthen the shadows, while dark values weaken them. The lighter values work best on pieces that depend on secondary contours; darker values are most successful in emphasizing the major contours. Thin linear structures that depend more on background contrast appear as strong dark or light silhouette (fig. 9.26).

Space
Space may be characterized as a boundless or unlimited extension of occupied areas.

When artists use space, they tend to limit its vastness. They may mark off extensions in one, two, or three dimensions, or measurable distances between preestablished elements. Three-dimensional artists use objects to displace space and to control spatial intervals and locations. Rectangular and ovoid shapes control space effectively, because their weight is felt and established by the flat or rounded dimensions of the planes (fig. 9.27). The two shapes seen together create a spatial interval. Although the two solids illustrated are three-dimensional, their spatial indications are minimal. Greater interest and, in turn, greater spatial qualities could be added to the two shapes by manipulating their surfaces. If material were cut away, the space would move inward and if material were added, the

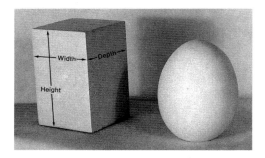

▲ **9 · 27**

The rectangular and ovoidal solids are examples of two minimal objects that can be formed from displaced, boundless space. The flat and rounded planes in these positions define their special characteristics and spatial intervals.

space would tend to move outward.

In figure 9.28A the four bricks have been arranged in a very restricted manner to form a large, minimal rectangular solid. The individual bricks are distinguished only by the line of crack-like edges visible in the front and side planes. These linear edges are reminiscent of graphic linear renderings.

The four bricks illustrated in figure 9.28B are separated by indentations similar to the mortar joints used by masons. These gaps, although relatively shallow, nevertheless produce distinctively clearer and darker edges than those shown in figure 9.28A. Although the darker edges indicate greater three-dimensional variation than the first stack of bricks

shown, they still have decided limitations. Many shallow-*relief sculptures* function in a similar way (fig. 9.29).

The bricks in figure 9.28C utilize even more space. They are positioned so that the planes moving in depth are contrasted with the front and side planes, moving toward and away from the viewer. The light that strikes the grouping produces stronger shadows and more interesting value patterns. This arrangement can be compared to the qualities of high-relief sculpture. The play of deep shadows against the lights on projecting parts of a high-relief sculpture can increase the work's expressive or emotional qualities (fig. 9.30).

Although still in a compact and closed

▶ **9 · 28A–E**

The figures show four bricks that have been arranged and rearranged to illustrate an increasing level of visual complexity within the third dimension – this is achieved by interactions between the *positive* objects and *negative* sculptural spaces.

A Stacked bricks
B Separated bricks
C Crooked bricks
D Slanted bricks
E Crossed bricks

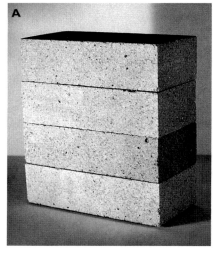

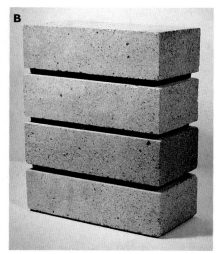

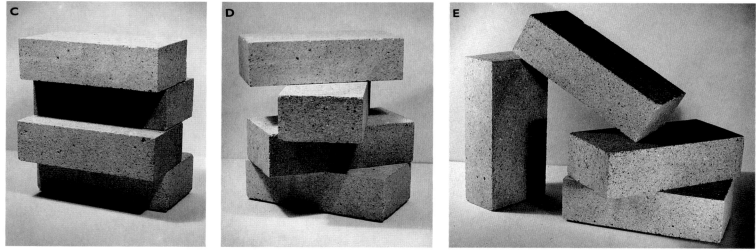

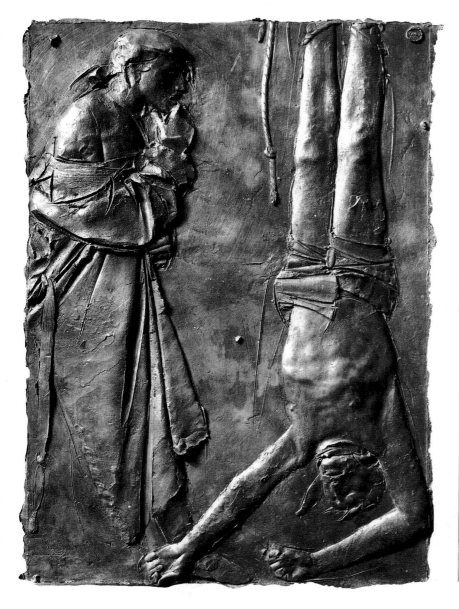

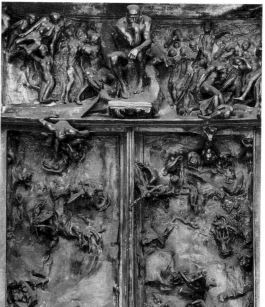

9 · 29

Giacomo Manzu, *Death by Violence*, 1963. Bronze cast from clay model, 36⅝ × 25¼ in (93.5 × 64 cm).

This is a study for one of a series of panels for the doors of St. Peter's. The confining spatial limitations of relief sculpture are evident. To create a greater feeling of mass, Manzu used sharply incised modeling that is similar to the engraved lines of the printmaker's plate. The crisp incising creates sharp value contrasts that accentuate movement as well as depth.

Exhibited at the XXXII Venice Biennale in 1964.

9 · 30

Auguste Rodin, *The Gates of Hell* (detail), begun 1880. Bronze, 20 ft 8 in × 13 ft 1 in (6.3 × 3.99 m).

In this high relief, the forms nearly break loose from the underlying surface.

Rodin Museum, Philadelphia, PA. Gift of Jules E. Mastbaum.

arrangement, the rotation of the bricks in figure 9.28D makes possible new directions and spatial relationships. The work is becoming more truly sculptural as contrasts of movement, light, and shadow increase. In a way, this inward and outward play of bricks is similar to what the sculptor creates in a free-standing form. Such works are no longer concerned with simple front, side, and back views, but with multiple axes and multiple views. Although all the brick illustrations are actually free-standing, or in-the-round, the first two examples show surface characteristics closer in spirit to

the condition of relief sculpture, as was previously indicated. Some authorities use the terms "free-standing" and "sculpture in-the-round" interchangeably when referring to any three-dimensional work of art not attached to a wall surface (see fig. 9.25).

The variety of brick positions in figure 9.28E, particularly the diagonally tipped brick, creates far greater exploitation of space than other groupings. The void, or open space, emphasizes the three-dimensional quality of the arrangement by producing a direct link between the space on each side.

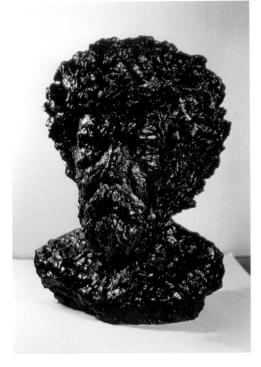

▲ 9·31

Paul Nesse, *Portrait of Ron Russel*, 1974. Painted plaster, life size.

Artists select a surface character for their work that expresses their conception of the subject's character and/or physical characteristics.

Courtesy of the artist.

▼ 9·32

Isamu Noguchi, *The Opening*, 1970. French rose and Italian white marble, 30¾ × 32 × 8 in (78.1 × 81.3 × 20.3 cm).

This sculpture is enriched by the artist's choice of materials in contrasting colors and variegated graining.

Courtesy of the artist.

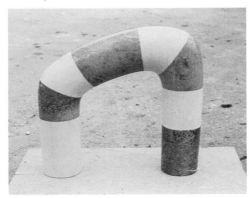

Texture

Textures enrich a surface, complement the medium, and enhance expression and content. Textured surfaces range from the hard glossiness of glass or polished marble to the roughness of fingerprinted clay or painted plaster (fig. 9.31; see fig. 6.3). Certain surfaces are inherent to certain media, and, traditionally, these intrinsic textures are respected. The artist usually employs texture to encapsulate the distinctive qualities of the subject. The sleek suppleness of a seal, for example, seems to call for a polished surface, while the character of a rugged, forceful person calls for a more rough-hewn treatment. However, artists sometimes surprise us with a different kind of treatment. The actual, simulated, and invented textures of graphic artists are also available to plastic artists and are developed from the textures inherent in the materials which plastic artists use.

Line

Line is a phenomenon that does not actually exist in nature or in the third dimension. It is primarily a graphic device used to indicate the meeting of planes or the outer edges of shapes. Its definition might be broadened, however, to include the main direction or thrust (axis) of a three-dimensional shape whose length is greater than its width. Line, then, can be used to refer to the thin shapes of contemporary linear sculpture comprising wires and rods. Development of welding and soldering techniques made possible the shaping and joining of thin linear metals in sculpture. Such artists as José de Rivera and Richard Lippold have expanded the techniques of linear sculpture (see figs. 9.24 and 9.26).

Incising line in clay or in any other soft medium is similar to the graphic technique of drawing. In three-dimensional art, incised lines are used to accent surfaces for interest and movement. The Italian Giacomo Manzu employed such lines to add sparkle to relief sculpture (see fig. 9.29).

Color

Color is also an inherent feature of sculptural materials. Sometimes it is pleasant, as in the variegated veining of wood or stone (fig. 9.32), but it can also be bland and lacking in character, as in the flat chalkiness of plaster. Paint is often added when the material needs enrichment or when the surface requires color to bring out the form more effectively. The elements of value and color are so interwoven in sculpture that artists often use the two terms interchangeably. Thus, an artist may refer to value contrasts in terms of color, actually thinking of both simultaneously. Many applications of color are an attempt to capture the richness and form-flattering qualities of the *patina* found on bronzes oxidized by exposure to the atmosphere. This approach stresses color that is subordinate to the structure of the piece. In certain historical periods (for example, early Greek art) application of bright color was commonplace. Some revival of this technique is evident in contemporary works. In every case the basic criterion for the use of color is compatibility with the form of the work (fig. 9.33).

Time (the fourth dimension)

Time is an element unique to the spatial arts. It is involved in graphic arts only insofar as contemplation and reflection on meaning are concerned. The physical act of viewing a graphic work as a totality requires only a moment. However, in a plastic work, the additional fourth dimension means that the work must turn or that we must move around it to see it completely.

The artist wants the time required to inspect the work to be a continuum of rewarding visual variation. Each sequence or interval of the viewing experience must bring out interesting relationships and lure the observer further around the work, extending the time he or she spends on it.

In the case of kinetic sculpture, the

artwork itself, not the observer, moves. Such works require time for their movements. Mobiles, for example, present a constantly changing, almost infinite series of views (fig. 9.34; see fig. 10.93).

▶ **9 · 33**
Marisol, *Women and Dog*, 1964. Mixed media, 72 × 82 × 16 in (182.9 × 208.3 × 40.6 cm).
This example of Pop art reveals the willingness of some contemporary artists to use bright color to heighten the three-dimensional characteristics of form at the same time that it enriches surfaces. The form has its roots in previous twentieth-century styles, while the use of combine-assemblage tends to fuse the media of sculpture and painting into one.
Collection of the Whitney Museum of American Art. Purchase, with funds from the Friends of the Whitney Museum of American Art, 64.17. © Marisol/DACS, London/VAGA, New York 1994.

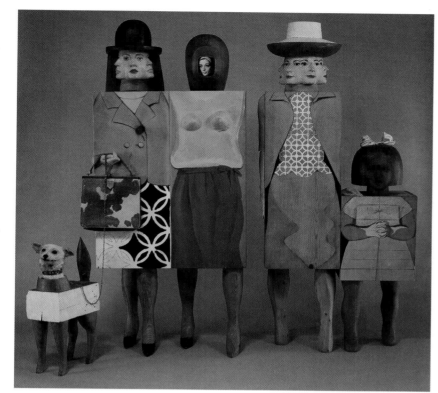

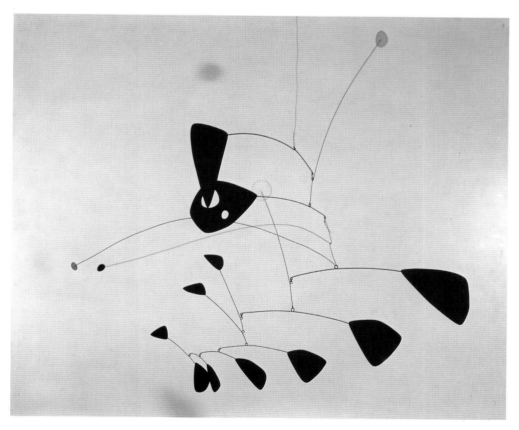

◀ **9 · 34**
Alexander Calder, *Antennae with Red and Blue Dots*, 1960. Metal kinetic sculpture, 3 ft 7¾ in × 4 ft 2½ in × 4 ft 2½ in (1.11 × 1.28 × 1.28 m).
This noted artist introduced physically moving sculptures called mobiles. Movement requires time for observation of the movement, thereby introducing a new dimension to art in addition to height, width, and space. The result is a constantly changing, almost infinite series of views of parts of the mobile.
Tate Gallery, London. © ADAGP, Paris and DACS, London 1994.

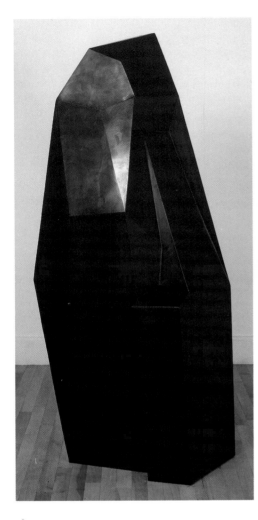

▲ **9·35**

James De Woody, *Big Egypt*, 1985. Black oxidized steel, 72 × 30 × 30 in (182.9 × 76.2 × 76.2 cm).

In this example of a tectonic arrangement, James De Woody has cut planes that project in and out of his surfaces without penetrating voids or opening spaces. This is sometimes referred to as "closed" composition.

Courtesy of the Arthur Roger Gallery, New Orleans, LA.

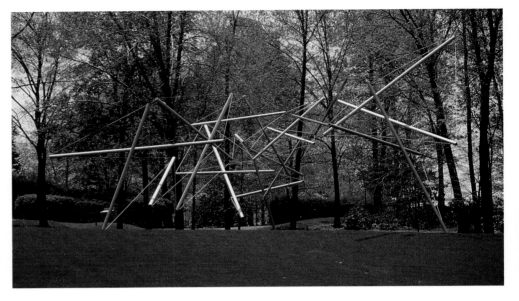

▲ **9·36**

Kenneth Snelson, *Free Ride Home*, 1974. Aluminum and stainless steel, 30 × 60 × 60 ft (9.14 × 18.28 × 18.28 m).

Kenneth Snelson has developed sculptures that are "open" or atectonic.

Storm King Art Center, Mountainville, NY. Purchase 1975.64. (Photograph by David Finn.)

Principles of three-dimensional order

Organizing three-dimensional art is the same as organizing two-dimensional art. However, three-dimensional forms, with their unique spatial properties, call for somewhat different applications of the principles.

Three-dimensional artists deal with forms that have multiple views. Composing is more complex. What might be a satisfactory solution for an arrangement with one view might be only a partial answer in the case of a work seen from many different positions. Adjustments are required in order to totally unify a piece. Compositionally, a three-dimensional work may be *tectonic* (closed, massive, and simple) with few and limited projections, as in figure 9.35, or *atectonic* (open, to a large degree), with frequent extensive penetrations and thin projections, as in figure 9.36. Both tectonic and atectonic arrangements can be found in nearly all three-dimensional art, and

each of these arrangements can be used individually to achieve different expressive and spatial effects.

Balance

When considering balance and the extension of spatial effects in three-dimensional art, some special conditions should be examined. For example, the symmetrical balance of a three-dimensional piece exists only when it is seen from back or front. A work that appears symmetrical from front or back could not be symmetrical from certain top or side positions. Two types of balance are possible in actual space: asymmetrical balance (fig. 9.37) and radial balance (fig. 9.38). Of the two, radial balance is more formal and regular. Radial balance is spherical, with the fulcrum in the center. The parts that radiate from this point are usually similar in their formations. However, more artists make use of asymmetrical balance because it provides the greatest individual latitude and variety.

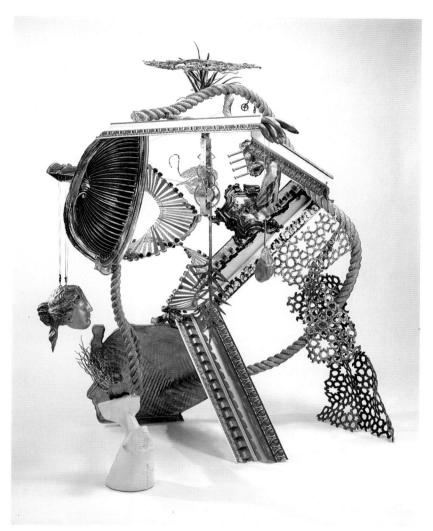

◁ **9·37**

Nancy Graves, *Unending Revolution of Venus, Plants, and Pendulum*, 1992. Bronze, brass, enamel, stainless steel, and aluminum, 8 × 7 × 4 ft (2.44 × 2.13 × 1.22 m).

In this sculpture we see a variety of form parts. We also see an excellent example of an asymmetrically balanced sculpture.

Created at Saff Tech Arts. © Saff Tech Arts/Nancy Graves 1992. (Photograph by Sam Kwong.) © Nancy Graves/DACS, London/VAGA, New York 1994.

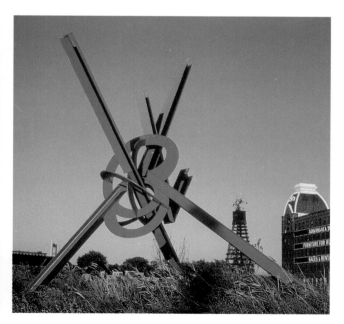

◁ **9·38**

Mark di Suvero, *For Veronica (Erk Thru Able Last)*, 1987. Steel, 21 ft 9 in × 35 ft 2 in × 39 ft (6.63 × 10.72 × 11.89 m).

The center of this sculpture is the fulcrum identified by the contrasting rounded, curled parts. All of the diagonal beams radiate in outwardly thrusting directions.

The Rene and Veronica di Rosa Foundation, Napa, CA. (Photograph: Oil & Steel Gallery, Long Island City, NY.)

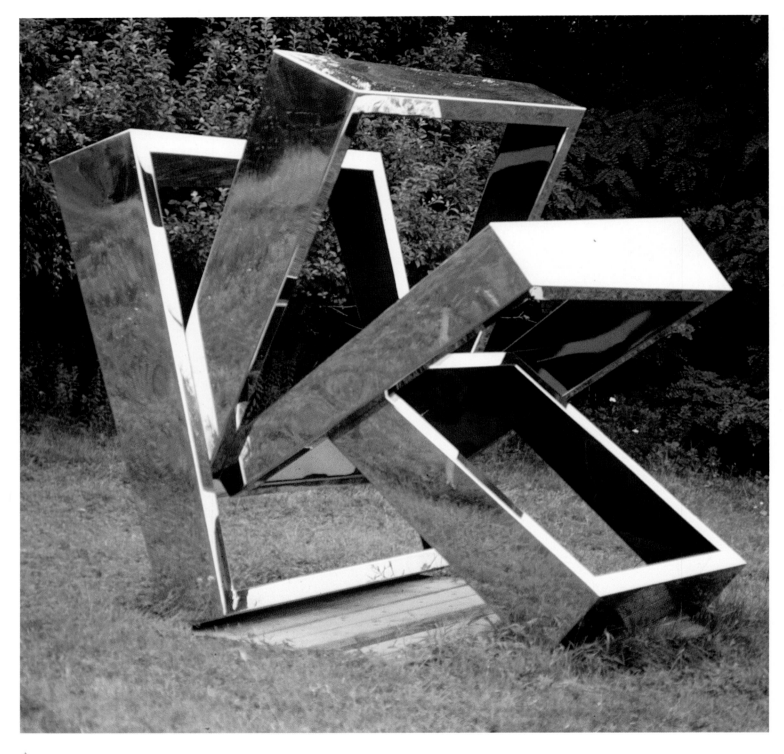

▲ **9 · 39**
**Beverly Pepper, *Ventaglio*, 1967. Stainless
steel with blue enamel, 8 ft (2.44 m) high.**
The rhythmical repetition of the frames in
Beverly Pepper's sculpture creates an exciting,
flowing movement.
Courtesy of the André Emmerich Gallery, New York.

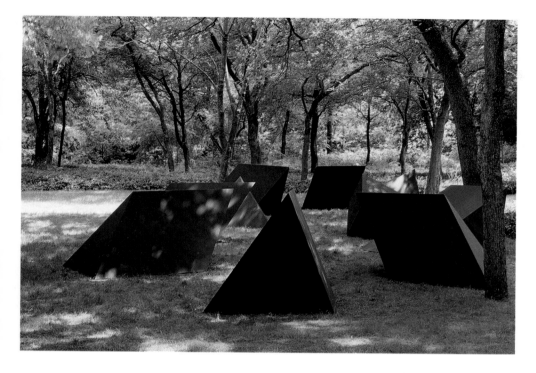

▲ **9 · 40**
Tony Smith, *Ten Elements*, 1975–79 (fabricated 1980). Painted aluminum, tallest element 4 ft 2 in (1.27 m), shortest element 3 ft 6 in (1.07 m).
Tony Smith has created many artworks that represent nothing more than large-scale, starkly simple geometric shapes. In this backyard group, he has repeated ten different shapes that interact spatially. The economic means of Smith, a Minimalist, unify a complex arrangement.
Patsy R. and Raymond D. Nasher Collection, Dallas, TX.

Proportion

When viewing a three-dimensional work, the effect of proportion is of crucial significance. The one-on-one relationship of actually experiencing a three-dimensional work brings out a special feeling for tension, balance, and scale. Proportion is involved in determining the basic form; it sets the standard and permeates the other principles. Repetition and rhythm have relationships that include proportional similarities. Predictable rhythm incorporates proportional transitions that aid in giving flow to a work (fig. 9.39).

Economy

Included within the group known as Primary Structurists or Minimalists are three-dimensional artists who emphasize the principle of economy in their works, because they, like their fellow painters, want to create stark, simple, geometric shapes. These Minimalists strip their shapes of any emotional, psychological, or symbolic associations and eliminate physical irrelevancies. For further emphasis they also tend to make a feature of large size. Tony Smith has reduced his shapes to simple geometric forms (fig. 9.40), while Donald Judd aligns his primary shapes in vertical and horizontal rows, thereby interrelating economy with repetition and rhythm (fig. 9.41).

▶ **9 · 41**
Donald Judd, *Untitled*, 1978. Brass, ten boxes, 6 × 27 × 24 in (15.2 × 68.6 × 61 cm).
Judd is primarily interested in perceptually explicit shapes, reflective surfaces, and vertical interplay.
Courtesy of the artist.

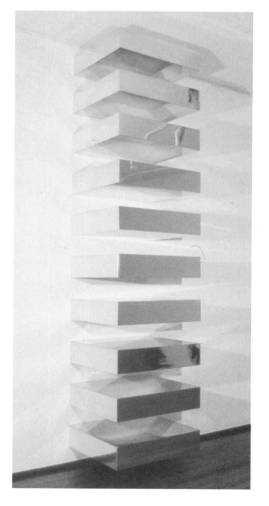

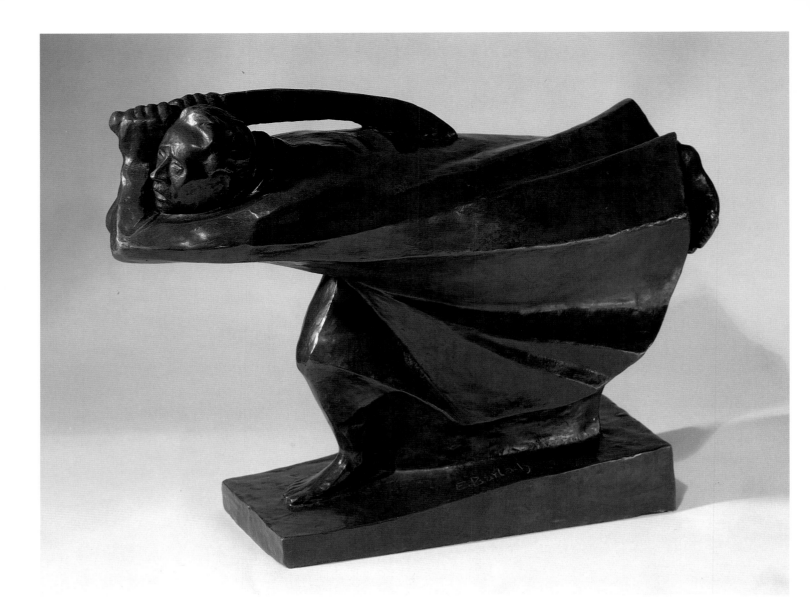

Ernst Barlach, *The Avenger*, 1914. Bronze, 17¼ × 22¾ × 8 in (43.8 × 57.8 × 20.3 cm).

This figure is not actually moving, but it does depict a powerful forward thrust. Movement is implied by the long sweeping horizontal and diagonal directions made by the edges of the robe, and the projection of the head and shoulders.

Tate Gallery, London.

Movement

Two types of movement are used by three-dimensional artists. Implied movement, the most common type (fig. 9.42; see fig. 9.39), is illusionary, but actual movement is special and involves the total work. Actual movements that take place in kinetic art are set into motion by air, water, or mechanical devices. Alexander Calder, the innovator of mobile sculptures, at first used motors to drive his pieces but later used air currents generated by human body motion, wind, air conditioning, or heating (see figs. 9.34 and 10.73). George Rickey, a contemporary sculptor, works with wind and air propulsion (see fig. 10.93). Water has been used as a propellant in other three-dimensional works. Jean Tinguely, José de Rivera and Pol Bury propel their sculptures with motor drives (fig. 9.43; see figs. 9.24 and 10.92). Computer-activated kinetics are now being marketed. The principle of movement is inherently related to the art elements of time and space.

When properly combined, the principles of order produce vibrant forms. In the three-dimensional field, new conceptual uses of time, space, and movement have changed definitions and meanings that had endured for centuries. The prevailing thought of the past, that sculpture was a step-child of the graphic arts, needs no longer be true.

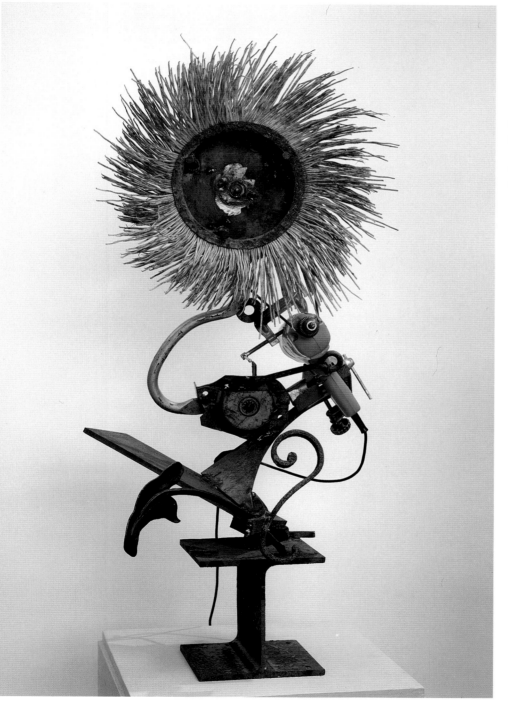

◀ **9 · 43**

Jean Tinguely, *O Sole Mio*, 1982. Metal, steel; paint, plastic, drill, clamp; 40⅛ × 22 × 20 in (102 × 56 × 51 cm).

For Jean Tinguely, the machine was an instrument for the poet/artist. He produced machine-driven sculptures that involve kinetic anti-machine ironies, mechanical breakdowns, and appropriate rattling noises.

Detroit Institute of Arts, Detroit, MI. Gift of the City of Montreux, Switzerland, Detroit Renaissance, and the artist. © ADAGP, Paris and DACS, London 1994.

CHAPTER TEN

Content and Style

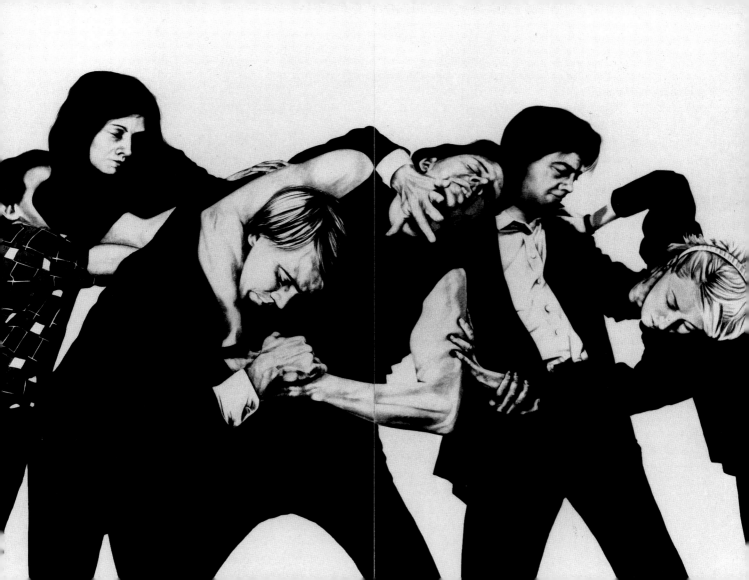

INTRODUCTION TO CONTENT AND STYLE

This chapter is concerned with the third component of a work of art, which we call *content*. It would be worthwhile for the reader at this point to reread the introductory chapter as it provides an analytical view (or review in this case) of the factors producing content. This chapter is also concerned with style, which may be defined in terms of the widespread practices of artists living in a particular area and period of history; alternatively, style can refer to the ideas and techniques of an individual artist or group of artists – an increasingly valid definition for modern times.

In our role as teachers, as well as authors, we felt that it would be useful to include this chapter, because a study of the content and style of art traditions might help in students' training – serving as a stimulating guide, a source of ideas, and a groundwork for some of their practice. Hence, since space is limited, we can provide only a brief account of the last two centuries of art. Only the most important styles, or movements, are given; and there is a limited coverage of the artists who helped to create those styles. We have also made some effort to include the works of innovative photographers, as well as other developments in the arts.

An overview of historical developments may be found in the timeline or Chronological Outline of Western Art following this chapter, while short definitions of the styles and movements of nineteenth- and twentieth-century Western art may be found in the Glossary.

NINETEENTH-CENTURY STYLES

Most nineteenth-century styles contributed in some degree to the character of art in the present century. On the one hand, twentieth-century Western art can generally be considered a reaction to all art since the latter half of the eighteenth century; but on the other, it hinged on, indeed owed a great deal to, those past traditions.

Until the middle of the last century, artists were still directly inspired by the appearance of the world around them. The invention of the camera stemmed from developments which took place over a number of centuries, beginning with the *camera obscura* in the Renaissance (though it was already known of in Ancient Greece). The process culminated in the development and fixing of an image on a surface between the 1830s and 1850s, and made possible the exact imitation of natural appearances in a permanent image – the *photograph*. The efforts of Daguerre, Niépce, Fox Talbot, and others were responsible for the first photographic images (fig. 10.1). By the end of the century, partly through the impact of the photographic image, and partly from the growth of realism in the graphic arts from the Renaissance forward, the old problem of representing reality was so completely resolved that artists were compelled to search for new expressive directions. Some turned to ancient styles, to those of the Middle Ages, for example. The growth of photography also gave artists the opportunity to examine contemporary and past art in hitherto unknown, or little-known, places; this, combined with sociological and other matters, enhanced the search for new directions.

Economic conditions, which continue to be potent influences today, played a part in this search for new principles of expression. From about the time of the High Renaissance (the 1600s in Italy) until the 1850s, artists came to depend more frequently for their economic welfare on the patronage of a wealthy middle-class clientele. Some artists actually adopted the dubious aesthetic tastes of their patrons, rather than learn to sell their art in the same milieu as the merchandise produced by the Industrial Revolution, or to assert their own inventiveness. Such artists were happy to supply works of art designed to satisfy and flatter the vanity of their patrons. The more daring and discerning ones dared to fight the tide of conventional popularity and prejudice, drawing their inspiration from their surroundings and society, or from subjects that seemed to have more universality.

Neoclassicism

The *Neoclassical* style, like so many others until almost the middle of the twentieth century, originated in France. France had been the recognized epicenter of the arts in Europe since the seventeenth century. Neoclassicism began in the 1700s but lasted well into the 1800s. By mid-century it became the approved manner of the government-supported École des Beaux-Arts (School of Fine Arts), and its *Salons* (exhibits). The founding of the French Royal Academy of Arts and Letters in 1648, which promoted rules for producing "correct" works of art, led to the strength of French art, but by the 1900s resulted in a stifling, academic style, which dominated French art through most of the 1800s.

The Neoclassicists were forming just before the French Revolution. They were beginning to seek artistic freedom from royal patronage, much as the French proletariat sought freedom from human bondage. The principal artist of Neoclassicism was the painter Jacques-Louis David. He founded a new Classical style, based on the ancient Greek ethics of a high moral order, which reflects to some extent the rise of the middle class up the social scale. David came to be identified with the Revolution, and was considered its archetypal painter. His style grew out of an excellent knowledge of Greek and Roman literature, from which he often borrowed titles. It also owed its form to a somewhat faulty knowledge and understanding of Greek and Roman art. Rome's seeming virtues, before it became an empire, were likened to those of the Revolution and post-Revolutionary period, and the high moral tone of his work stemmed from an equation between the two eras.

The strength, firmness, and controlled compositions of his works, often stressing a strong horizontality, were probably based in their relief-like effect on Roman relief sculptures and frescos. In *The Oath of the Horatii* (fig. 10.2), the clarity and realistic details seem to anticipate the art of photography, while foreshadowing the interest in the two-dimensional nature or surface of paintings, which was to be so significant in the next century.

After the Revolution there developed an increasing taste among the middle class for simulated views of objects which

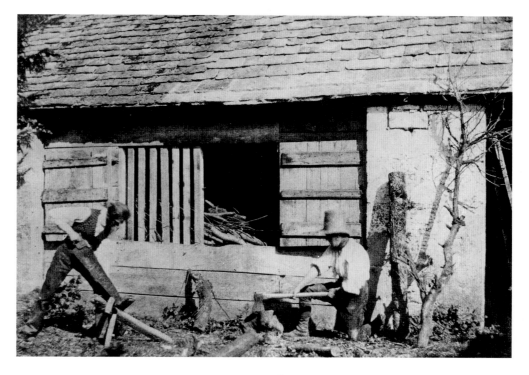

▲ **10 · 1**

William Henry Fox Talbot, *Workmen, One Chopping, One Sawing, at Lacock,* not dated. Calotype.

This is an example of a photograph by one of the medium's earliest pioneers, the English aristocrat Fox Talbot. His system, using sensitized paper negatives from which many prints could be made (calotype), was one of the key foundations of modern photography. Because of the long exposure time needed, "action" shots like this would have involved posing motionless for some minutes.

The Royal Photographic Society, Bath, England.

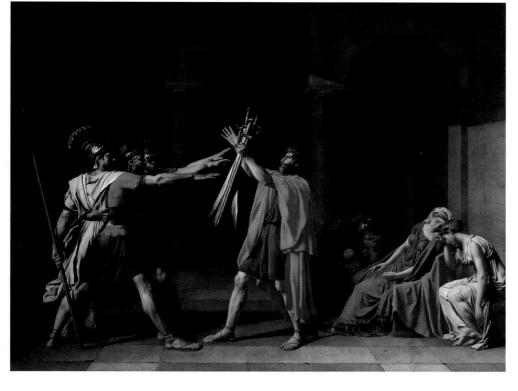

◀ **10 · 2**

Jacques-Louis David, *The Oath of the Horatii,* 1786. Oil on canvas, approx. 14 × 11 ft (4.27 × 3.35 m).

A cold, formal ordering of shapes, with emphasis on the sharpness of drawing, characterized the Neoclassical form of expression. Both style and subject matter are strongly influenced by ancient Greek and Roman sculpture.

The Louvre, Paris, France. (Photograph: RMN.)

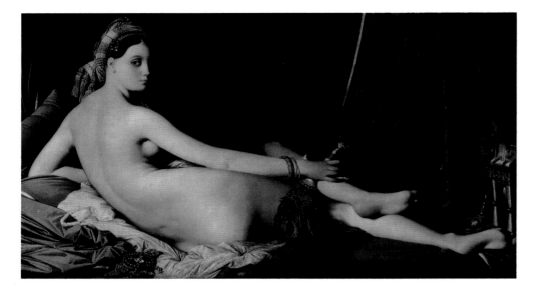

△ 10·3

Jean-Auguste-Dominique Ingres, *La Grande Odalisque*, 1814. Oil, 35¼ × 63¾ in (89.5 × 161.9 cm).

Neoclassicist Ingres, while being a doctrinaire follower of Classical expression, often tended toward romantic subjects with their attendant sensual expression or content. "Odalisque" was a term meaning harem girl, or concubine, in a Turkish seraglio.

The Louvre, Paris, France. (Photograph: RMN.)

accompanied their materialistic outlook on the world. This helped to lead to the invention of photography.

Jean-Auguste-Dominique Ingres, a later Neoclassicist, was in essence a doctrinaire follower of Neoclassicism, but introduced a more ornamental, curvilinear style, owing much to the High Renaissance classicism of Raphael. He also had a romantic interest in exotic lands and people, which reflected a desire by society and artists to escape from the growing materialism of the time. This aspect of Ingres, and his academic followers, foreshadowed the replacement of Neoclassicism by a newer artistic style, called *Romanticism*. As the long-serving head of the École des Beaux-Arts in Paris, however, Ingres had much to do with the domination of officially approved styles in art until past the middle of the century (fig. 10.3).

Romanticism

The first group who rejected artistic servitude to the tastes of the middle class, or those of aristocratic survivors of the Revolution, were the Romantics. With the restoration of the monarchy from 1814 to 1830, aristocrats dominated officialdom, and Romantic artists unfortunately had to find their clients amongst them. The Romantics became the first true revolutionaries of modern times, because they ceased to abide by their patrons' wishes and tastes, focusing, instead, on the intrinsic worth of the work of art itself. True revolutionaries realize that they do not always have to seek an audience. If there are values worth expressing, people will eventually be convinced by their views. This has become one of the fundamental principles underlying modern art. On the other hand, artists now had to market their art as a product, since they could not suit all their potential clients' tastes, and had to learn to sell their art to the general public. But the Romantic revolt did free creative artists to express their ideas, often in nontraditional ways.

The most important artists of the Romantic movement were Eugène Delacroix of France, Francisco Goya of Spain, and J. M. W. Turner of England. Goya is the earliest Romantic, emerging from the Spanish Rococo of the late 1700s, and preceding the movement, which was largely championed by the French. These artists' works share a feature common to all Romantic art: a frequent dependence on dramatic and exotic literary subjects, provided by novels, news sources, and history (figs. 10.4, 10.5, and 10.6).

Technically, the Romantics exploited the juicy and bold textures of oil paint, its ability to produce bright exciting hues and stirring value contrasts. These techniques shifted the emphasis away from choice of subjects toward an attention to form and the artist's materials – an emphasis which was to prevail throughout much of the twentieth century. This Romantic approach to painting contrasts with that of the Neoclassicists, who used a smooth, glazed surface technique, surviving from the Renaissance. The Romantics tended to be more excited by the bold painting manner and asymmetrical compositions of seventeenth-century artists like Rubens or Rembrandt (see fig. 5.11).

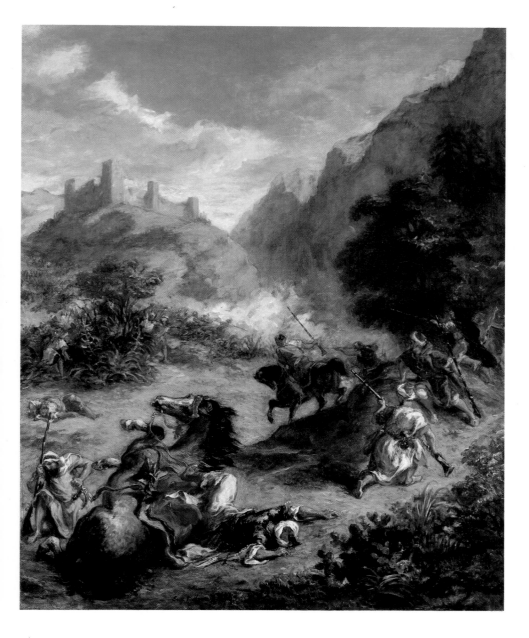

▲   10 · 4

Eugène Delacroix, *Arabs Skirmishing in the Mountains*, 1863. Oil on linen, 36³⁄₈ × 29³⁄₈ in (92.4 × 74.6 cm).

Subject matter depicting violent action in exotic foreign settings was often found in paintings of the Romantic movement. Although relaxed in style, they were generally bold in technique, with an emphasis on bright colors.

Chester Dale Collection. (© 1993 National Gallery of Art, Washington, D.C.)

▶ **10·5**
Francisco Goya, *The Famous American Mariano Ceballos, c.* 1815. Print (etching), 12¼ × 15¾ in (31.1 × 40 cm).
The romanticism of Goya is displayed in both his choice of subject matter and his dramatic use of light and dark values.
Philadelphia Museum of Art, PA. The McIlhenny Fund.

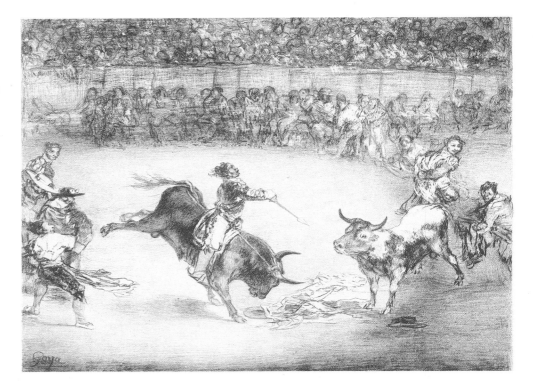

▶ **10·6**
J. M. W. Turner, *Keelmen Heaving in Coals by Moonlight, c.* 1835. Oil on canvas, 36¼ × 48¼ in (92.1 × 122.6 cm).
A historical theme and a seminarrative presentation of subject are qualities found in many works of the Romantic movement. By using color to produce atmospheric effects, Turner anticipated the techniques of later Impressionists. Like them, he placed less emphasis on formal organization.
Widener Collection. (© 1993 National Gallery of Art, Washington, D.C.)

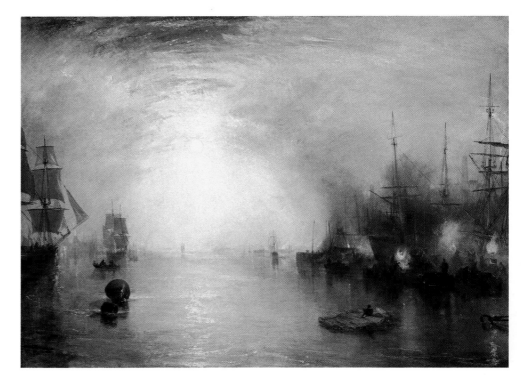

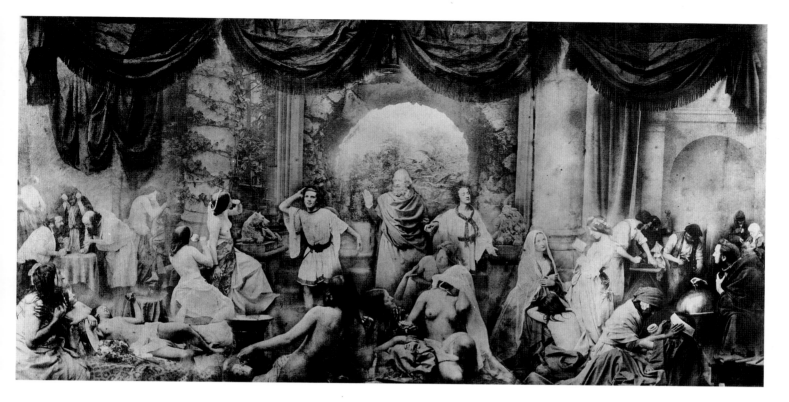

In the meantime, painting-conscious Romantic photographers like Oscar Rejlander (fig. 10.7) could assemble out of many prints a colossal, superficially Romantic work and exhibit it in the Salon des Beaux-Arts in 1857. This set in motion one aspect of photographical research called *Pictorialism*, which was opposed by those who believed that there should be no additional manipulation of the image, either in the taking or the developing process. These were designated *straight*, or sometimes *Realist*, photographers.

Realism and naturalism

The art of the Romantics had been a reaction to the pseudoclassical and academic formulas of Neoclassicism. The Realist movement in its turn was a reaction against the exotic, escapist, literary tendencies of Romanticism. The Realists were stimulated by the prestige of science, particularly the technological revolution epitomized by photography, but opposed to the kind of superficial pictorial Romantic-Realism embraced by Rejlander. At the same time they avoided mere surface appearances, such as the camera usually provided, and gave, instead, a philosophical or expressive quality to their art. Yet they also tried to impart a sense of the real-life immediacy they found missing in the idealistic content of Neoclassical and Romantic art. Because the Realists believed their clients shared their way of viewing the world, it might be thought that their art would have been immediately acceptable. Instead because they often chose to depict working-class subjects, the Realists were more often seen by their upper-class clientele as subversive, and were for a long time regarded with disfavor.

The most extreme form of Realist art is *naturalism*, a term invented by the writer Emile Zola near the end of the century. The naturalistic artist, according to Zola, closely accepted the optical veracity of the world, much of which was provided by the camera image. Artists of similar sensibilities, in turn, thought this kind of

△ 10·7
Oscar J. Rejlander, *The Two Ways of Life*, 1857. Combination albumen print.
A photographer trained as a painter, Rejlander tried to create a great mural out of hundreds of photographs. His approach to image manipulation is a Romantic one that is called "Pictorialism" in photography.

Courtesy of the International Museum of Photography at George Eastman House, Rochester, NY.

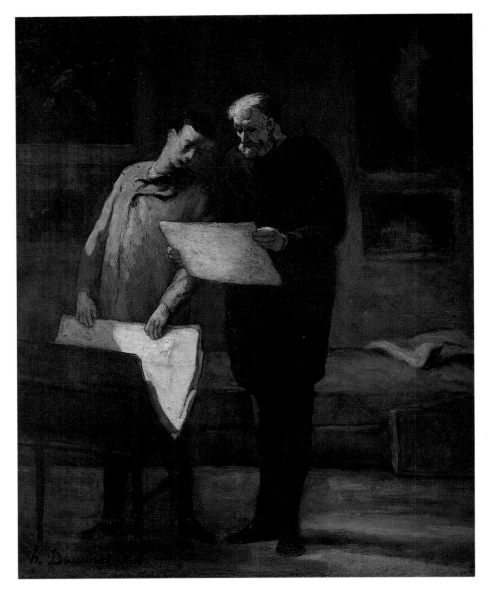

▲ 10·8

**Honoré Daumier, *Advice to a Young Artist*,
probably after 1860. Oil on canvas, 16⅛ ×
12⅞ in (41 × 32.7 cm).**

Influenced by a climate of scientific positivism,
the artists of the Realist movement tried to
record the world as it appeared to the eye, but
also wished to interpret it so as to record
timeless truths. This painting by Daumier
suggests not so much the particular appearance
of costume and setting but rather the universal
quality in the subject – the idea of wisdom being
passed on from one generation to another.

Gift of Duncan Phillips. (© 1993 National Gallery of
Art, Washington, D.C.)

descriptive form was the way most people
regarded reality. Thus they attempted to
paint a visual copy of the objective world,
without investing their art with the more
universal meanings associated with
Realism. The major difference between
realistic and naturalistic art, therefore, lies
in the degree of emphasis placed on
natural detail and in the particularizing
of specific times and conditions (of
weather, for example) in the visual world.
Among the important Realist/Naturalist
artists were Honoré Daumier and Gustave
Courbet in France and Winslow Homer
in the United States (fig. 10.8; see figs.
3.26 and 8.5).

Technological developments in photography

At the same time, photographers were also developing their own kinds of artistic expression. Photographers could not escape the longer-standing traditions of painting and its sought-after qualities, so the Pictorialists often tried to imitate some of the outward effects of lighting and atmosphere. Technical experiments and research led to fairly rapid improvements in cameras, lenses, and in the quality of printing surfaces, which enabled photographers to experiment in new ways of creating pictures. Among some of the technical developments were: the faster lenses invented in the 1840s; the "wet plate" (or collodion) process in 1851 and the "dry plate" process in 1871; and the development of films to replace glass and metal plates for the exposure process in the late 1890s/early 1900s. In 1888, George Eastman invented the first camera that could be mass-produced (the "Kodak"), without the need for the amateur to develop the film or make print copies. From that point on, the widespread popularity of the medium was assured.

Because of these technical improvements, photographic experimenters could more frequently create images of artistic quality, as well as exploit the medium's ability to record reality faithfully. This ability not only favored the honesty of straight photography but, despite the size and amount of the early equipment required, generated a notable record of human and natural phenomena everywhere in the world. For instance, by mid-century, cameras were recording the face of mass conflict, such as the Crimean War and the American Civil War. Mathew Brady, originally a New York portrait photographer, organized a team of photographers which left us an outstanding record of the latter (fig. 10.9). Others gave us fascinating views of the

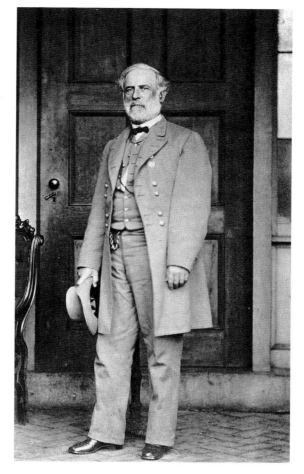

▲ **10 · 9**

Mathew Brady, *General Robert E. Lee*, 1865. Photograph.
Despite the bulky equipment needed in the "wet-plate" process, by the 1860s photographers were busily documenting wars, nature and exotic locations all over the world. The portraitist Mathew Brady assembled such a troop of photographers and left us an amazing record of the American Civil War. Brady himself took this photograph, reluctantly posed for by the great Southern general, just a week after the surrender at Appomattox Court House.
Reproduced from the Collections of the Library of Congress, Washington, D.C., #309737.

ruins of ancient cities and contemporary foreign cities, of nature, and particularly the American "Wild West" (fig. 10.10). From such images, many graphic artists, even when they could not actually travel themselves, became familiar with exotic places, and cultures past and present, which they often sought as subjects. Out of both the technical improvements and the photographic record cited came the first illustrations leading to photogravure, which in its turn hastened the development of photojournalism. The rapid expansion of photographic images

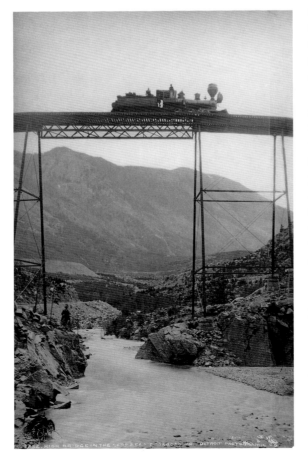

▼ 10 · 10

William Henry Jackson, *High Bridge, Georgetown Loop, c. 1889. Collodion print.* Jackson was one of the earliest photographers of Western scenery in the United States. This is one of the many superb studies he made as the West was being opened up after the Civil War. His work foreshadows the great landscape photography of, for example, Edward Weston and Ansel Adams.

Courtesy of the Colorado State Historical Society. WH J# 1852.

in newspapers, magazines, and journals was devoted to all kinds of specific topics, among which was photography itself. Photojournals, like the documents issued by the other graphic media in the late nineteenth and early twentieth centuries, helped to gain acceptance of, and appreciation for, the formal qualities of the medium.

Among other important discoveries were those in color photography. Daguerre had experimented with color, but very little progress was made in recording colored images until James Clerk Maxwell demonstrated in 1860 that all color could be reduced to three primary colors. This was followed a decade later by Dr. Hermann Vogel's discovery that dye colors could be made sensitive to light and thus the sensitivity of silver emulsions could be extended into both panchromatic and orthochromatic areas of the spectrum.

Impressionism

It is interesting to note, and significant for its relationship to photography, that the first independently arranged Impressionist exhibit was held in the studio of the eminent Realist portrait photographer Felix Nadar in 1874. However, despite the Impressionists' concern with recording reality, they wanted to do it in a new way. Their style indicates a strong shift toward the modern view that the form of a work (materials and methods) is more important than the subject matter. Where previous movements had developed the trend towards freedom of choice in subject, the Impressionists contributed a new technical approach to painting, which underlined the importance of the art object itself, as well as achieving a new way of conveying the appearance of natural phenomena. It is in this respect that the Impressionists represented the transition between tradition and revolution in art. For while still wishing to represent the essential appearance of a subject, they developed revolutionary and controversial techniques for doing so.

The Impressionists' interest in light and atmosphere required them to make a fairly intensive study of the scientific light theory of color and of the effect of light on the color of objects. The technique of juxtaposing complementary hues in large areas for greater brilliance, and the interpretation of shadows as being composed of the hue of the object casting those shadows, was of tremendous significance. To achieve the vibrating character of light, they revived the old technique of tachiste painting, in which pigment is put on the canvas in thick spots or dabs that catch actual light and reflect it from the surface. The tachiste method of painting can be seen in the work of earlier exponents, from Titian (see fig. 5.9) to that of Goya and Delacroix in later times. The Impressionists' use of complementary hues in the dabs of pigment, however, was the important breakthrough. When seen from a distance, these spots or dabs tend to form tones fused from the separate hues.

Local color was very important to secure the effects of sunlight, shade, and shadows, and all kinds of weather conditions. Thus landscape, actually painted outdoors (— *plein air*), directly from the subject to the canvas ("wet-on-wet" or *alla prima*), became the Impressionists' favorite subject for painting and method of recording it.

Traditional methods of composition were challenged when the Impressionists discovered the fascinating possibilities of high or unexpected angles of composition. The new photographic views of the natural scene were often different from the conventional eye-level arrangements that had been used by artists for many years. Japanese block prints, imported into France for the first time, also encouraged new views. These prints often placed a dramatic decorative emphasis on high-angle views or on views looking down on landscape subjects and people. Often used merely to wrap up goods being shipped to Europe, these prints were frequently cropped, resulting in curious truncated compositions. These odd-angled views had also appeared in landscape photography, inspiring those that typified Impressionist painting. The camera was now also able to capture human and animal figures stopped in action, in the midst of walking, or running.

Some of the coloristic effects of weather were not yet reproducible by the camera, since only black-and-white photography was possible. But this was soon to begin changing with the invention in 1906 of the first commercially feasible color process; this was not dependable, however, until the 1930s.

The most important Impressionist artists in France were Claude Monet, Camille Pissarro, and Pierre-Auguste Renoir (figs. 10.11 and 10.12; see figs. 4.3, 7.28, 7.29, and 7.30). Edgar Degas is sometimes included as an Impressionist of

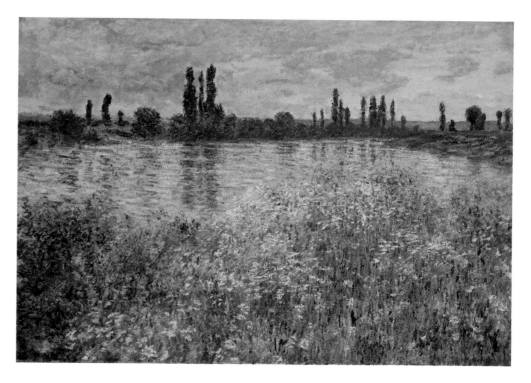

▲ **10 · 11**

Claude Monet, *Banks of the Seine, Vetheuil,* 1880. Oil on linen, 28⅞ × 39⅝ in (73.3 × 100.6 cm).

The selection of subject in this painting is typical of the Impressionist movement. The bright weather and the shimmering water offered an opportunity to express light and atmosphere through a scientific approach to the use of color.

Chester Dale Collection. (© 1993 National Gallery of Art, Washington, D.C.)

movement, or of "stop-action" painting (fig. 10.13). Degas, in fact, was well acquainted with photography, sometimes using photographs to achieve his high-angle views and the sense of motion in his ballet dancers and other subjects. He preferred working in his studio to painting out-of-doors, however. Edouard Manet also shows the impact of the photograph in his depiction of the impression of movement, but is usually regarded as a representative of the transition from Realism to Impressionism

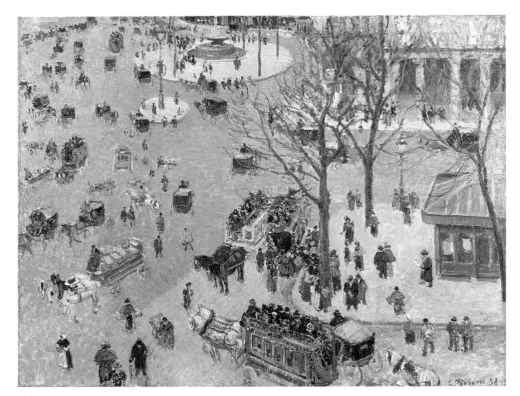

▲ 10·12
Camille Pissarro, *La Place du Théatre Français*, 1898. Oil on canvas, 28½ × 36¼ in (72.4 × 92.1 cm).
In this painting the Impressionist Pissarro shows a high-angle view of the Parisian street, a technique that was influenced by both Japanese prints and photography.
Los Angeles County Museum of Art, CA. Mr. and Mrs. George Gard De Sylva Collection, M.46.3.2.

Manet's *Race Track near Paris*, painted in 1872, with the photographs of horses in motion ("scientifically considered") taken by the Anglo-American photographer Eadweard Muybridge in 1878–79 (figs. 10.14 and 10.15).

By 1888, some of the Impressionists were beginning to realize that there were certain deficiences in the movement's theory and innovations, causing some to pursue individual directions. The key innovation of the 1860s and 1870s, as we have seen, was the perceptual recording of light, color, and atmospheric effects. But some artists, for example Cézanne and van Gogh, felt that these effects were now being executed superficially, in an automatic manner. The principal flaw, which irritated most of them, was the loss of shape and design resulting from an acceptance of surface illusion alone. The effect of light and atmosphere in Impressionist painting appeared to make objects evaporate or become indistinct. The Post-Impressionists, as they were to be called, also objected to the way in which outdoor lighting affected the way they saw color. In strong sunlight it was difficult to avoid making greens too raw, and there was a tendency to overload the canvas with yellows.

(see fig. 10.14). His technique of an even, but painterly application of paint once again accentuated the growing interest in the painting surface; but it also pointed up a startling difference from the textural use of paint by such contemporaries as the now aged Courbet and the Impressionists. It is also oddly fascinating to compare

▶ 10·13
Edgar Degas, *Four Dancers*, c. 1899. Oil on canvas, 4 ft 11½ in × 5 ft 11 in (1.51 × 1.80 m).
Two aspects of the Impressionist artist's recording of natural form can be found in this painting. First, it demonstrates the customary interest in the effects of light. Second, the painting shows a high-angle viewpoint of composition derived either from Japanese prints or from the accidental effects characteristic of photography.
Chester Dale Collection. (© 1993 National Gallery of Art, Washington, D.C.)

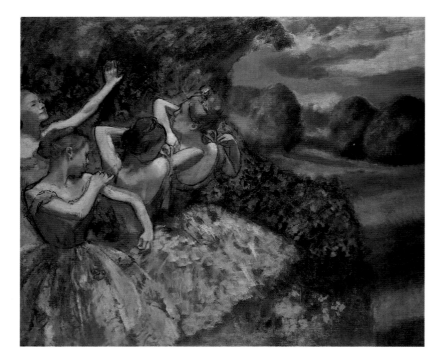

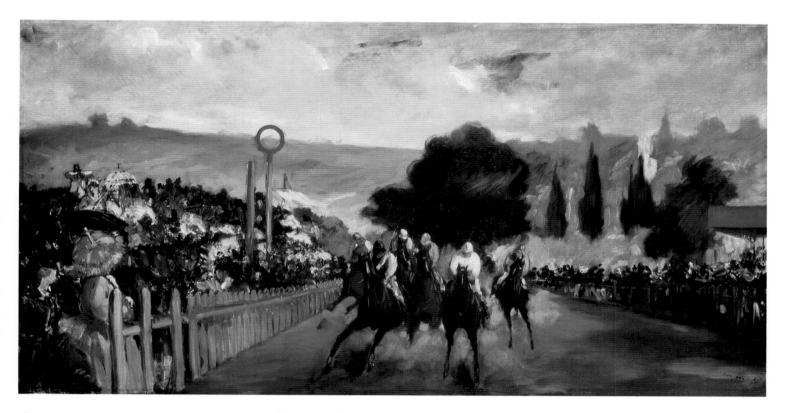

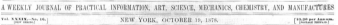

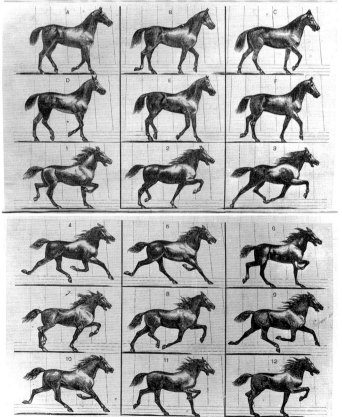

▲ **10 · 14**

Edouard Manet, *Race Track near Paris*, 1864. Oil on canvas, 17¼ × 33¼ in (43.9 × 84.5 cm).

The artist Manet reveals the Impressionists' concern to capture movement realistically, as part of their desire to render perceptual reality in a new way. Photographic studies like those of Muybridge (see fig. 10.15) may have benefited Manet.

Art Institute of Chicago. Potter Palmer Collection 1922.424.

▶ **10 · 15**

Eadweard Muybridge, *A Horse's Motion Scientifically Considered*. Engravings after photographs, 1878.

An American rancher friend and supporter of Muybridge encouraged his studies of horses in motion, which proved that at some point mid-gallop all four hooves leave the ground (note the fourth row down from top, numbers 4 and 5). The photographer took the series with some of the earliest fast-action cameras and went on to influence Manet (see fig. 10.14), Degas, and later artistic students of motion.

Muybridge Collection, Kingston Museum and Heritage Service, Surrey, England.

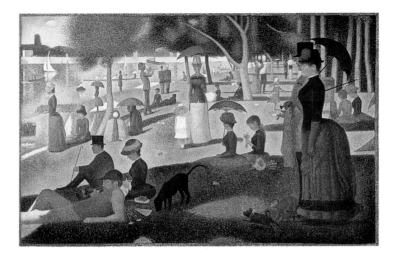

▲ 10·16

Georges Seurat, *A Sunday on La Grande Jatte – 1884*, 1884–86. Oil on canvas, 6 ft 9¾ in × 10 ft 1¼ in (2.08 × 3.08 m).
Seurat is classified as a Post-Impressionist, but his technique set him apart from all other artists. He applied his color in a manner that he considered scientific, using dots of broken color that are resolved and harmonized by the eye of the observer. Though a remarkable achievement, "Pointillism" had only a brief stylistic life.

Art Institute of Chicago. Helen Birch Bartlett Memorial Collection, 1926.224.

Post-Impressionism

The most important artists near the end of the nineteenth century had once been inspired by Impressionist theories, but now began to abandon them. These were Georges Seurat, Paul Cézanne, Paul Gauguin, and Vincent van Gogh. From these pioneers stem the major directions and styles of twentieth-century art. At the same time, their styles were all individualistic and completely different from each other's. The ambiguous title given to these artists – Post-Impressionists – does not indicate this, nor does it point to their significance for the future of art.

These artists had some common objectives, since they all sought: (1) a return to the structural organization of pictorial form; (2) an increased emphasis on the picture surface for the sake of pictorial unity and the unique patterns that might result; and (3) a more or less conscious exaggeration of natural appearances for emotionally suggestive effects, which is popularly called distortion (see fig. 8.50). Stylistically, Seurat and Cézanne on the whole illustrate the first of these aims; Gauguin, the second; and van Gogh, the third. Each, however, incorporated some aspect of the others' objectives in his stylistic form. It is these similarities which, despite the artists' individuality, caused the Post-Impressionists to be grouped in the same stylistic movement.

In 1886, at the last Impressionist exhibit, there appeared Georges Seurat's masterpiece *A Sunday on La Grande Jatte – 1884* (fig. 10.16). This painting, with its methodically dotted canvas, in many ways defines the moment when Impressionism began to be supplanted by Post-Impressionism. Seurat had been trained in the academic manner of the École des Beaux-Arts. He admired the Classical modes of the Early Renaissance, eighteenth-century painters like Nicolas Poussin (see fig. 5.16), and, from his own century, Ingres (see fig. 10.3). Yet in the 1830s he became associated with, and influenced by, the Impressionists, particularly Camille Pissarro (see fig. 10.12). From these influences he developed his own style, which he called Divisionism, but which others came to call Pointillism or Neo-Impressionism. Seurat's achievement came from his merging of the earlier academic/Classical influences with the newer techniques and theories of the Impressionists, as seen, for instance, in the *Grande Jatte*. In its interrelationship between people and object shapes, it is Classical, while in its textured pigment and use of precisely arranged complementary colors, it is Impressionist. Seurat's sense of classical monumentality and reserve also contrasted with the lighter-hearted mood or content of Impressionism. This combination foretells much about the abstract art of the following century.

Like Seurat, Paul Cézanne – by general agreement, the paramount artist of the Post-Impressionist movement – remains close in spirit to Classicism. He, too, sought a way out of the patently haphazard organization and ephemeral forms of the Impressionists, seeing a work of art in terms of the interrelationship of all its parts. In this he foreshadowed the *Gestalt* psychologists' theories a short time later (see Chapter 4, pp. 87–8). While retaining the individual dabs of color of the Impressionists, Cézanne used them more as building blocks in the total physical structure of his paintings, while not becoming as rigidly precise as Seurat (see figs. 2.45A and 7.27). Although Cézanne might be called an analyst rather than a recorder of reality (as both the Realists and Impressionists had been), he went beyond mere analysis. Reality for him was not the object in nature from which he drew his inspiration, but all of the artistic interpretations of the object, brought to fruition in the completed work. He conceived of reality as the totality of expression derived from the appearance of nature as it was transformed by the artist's mind and hand. Therefore, although Cézanne found his starting-point in nature, as was traditional, he became the first artist of modern times to consider the appearance of his pictorial form more important than the "realistic" representation of the subject.

In searching for his own kind of reality, Cézanne looked beneath the surface matter of the world for universal changeless form. He once wrote to a friend that he found that all nature was reducible to such simple geometric shapes as cones, spheres, and cubes. The essential character of such forms seemed more permanent to Cézanne than the transient effects of nature (fig. 10.17). Because of the intellectual processes involved in his realizations of form, he is considered a Classicist in spirit. Nevertheless, he was the forerunner of modern Cubism as well as other intellectualized abstraction in the twentieth century.

In comparison to the Classical, architectural character of Cézanne and Seurat, the works of Paul Gauguin show the invention of a vivid, symbolic world of decorative patterns (see figs. 2.11, 4.19, and 7.40). The patterns owe part of their particular character to the types of expression Gauguin gleaned from Medieval carvings, mosaics, and manuscripts. Some of these carvings he saw on roadside chapels while living in Brittany, France, in the 1880s. While many of his later themes (1890s) were inspired by more exotic places, particularly Tahiti in the Pacific, Gauguin's work always demonstrates a sophistication typical of French art. An underlying suavity tempers Gauguin's work and gives to it a quality reminiscent of an old master's painting, in spite of his brilliant color and free patterns. The decorative style of the early twentieth-century French *Fauves* stems primarily from the work of Paul Gauguin.

The work of Vincent van Gogh, the fourth pioneer, represents the beginning of a new, highly charged, subjective expression which we find in many forms of modern art. The character of Expressionism in the early 1900s owes a great deal to the impetuous brushstrokes and dramatic distortions of color and

objects first used by Vincent van Gogh. He was mostly self-taught as an artist, having turned to art after failures at other careers. It was van Gogh's failures, however, which were the root of his impassioned style, now marked by history as one of the greatest and most distinctive. His way of vibrantly meshing his emotions with his subjects, be they portraits, landscapes, or still-life paintings, goes far beyond the perceptual starting-point and final forms of the Impressionists (see figs. 1.13, 3.1, and 6.6).

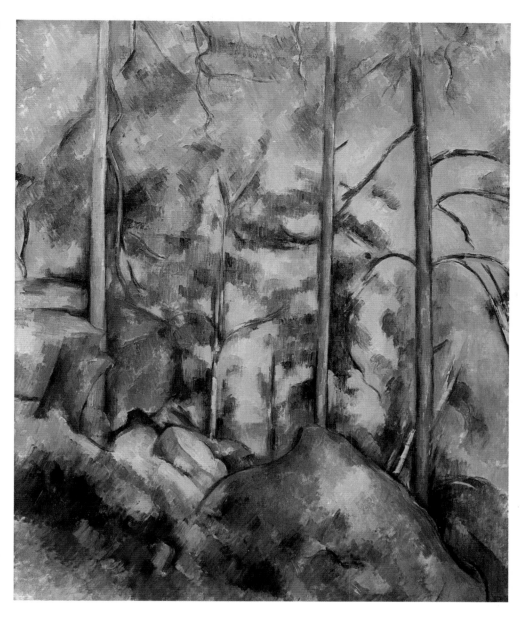

▲ 10·17
Paul Cézanne, *Pines and Rocks* (Fontainebleau?), 1896–99. Oil on canvas, 32 × 25¾ in (81.3 × 65.4 cm).
Cézanne tried to show the essence of natural forms rather than mere surface description. In this painting he simplified the tree and rock shapes to produce a solid compositional unity.
The Museum of Modern Art, New York. Lillie P. Bliss Collection.

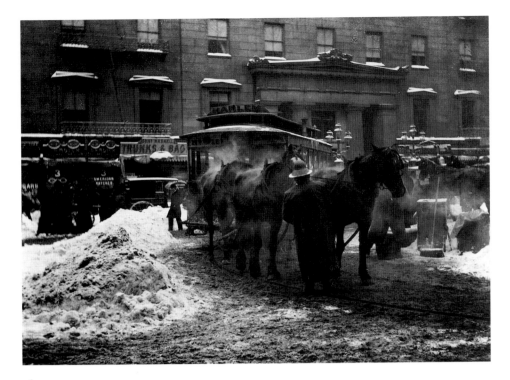

Modernist trends in photography

In the meantime, certain Pictorialist
photographers were working in an
Impressionist or Post-Impressionist vein,
while others were following the
Symbolists (see fig. 10.22), whose style
sought to achieve ultimate reality by
intuitive or inward spiritual experiences of
the world. Many of these artists, like their
counterparts in painting, always worked
directly from nature and yet, increasingly,
were making perception a way of learning
about composition and an evocative
expression. They also seem to have had an
awareness that there was something
beyond the mere recording of a moment.
Some of these Pictorialists did not
approve of the fuzzy focus and film
manipulation which their colleagues used
to attain their effects. They began to
experiment instead with the natural
effects of light and atmospheric effects, as
had the Impressionist painters. The fusing
of experimental Pictorialism with a
Realist point of view, then, seems to have
been influenced by the theories of both
Post-Impressionism and, to some extent,
Symbolism. Many of these modernist
photographers grouped together, leading
to the foundation in London in 1892 of
the so-called Linked Ring. From this early
group, the Royal Photographic Society of
England branched off shortly after, while
various "Linked-Ring" groups spread to
the major cities of Europe. By the end of
the nineteenth century many of these
photographers were scrupulously
promoting the artistic worth of the
camera image through exhibits and
documents. They were also calling
themselves Photo-Secessionists, and by
likening themselves to those painters who
had held "secessionist" exhibits of their
rejected works in defiance of the École des
Beaux-Arts, the photographers deliberately
declared their affinity to them and the
similarity of their aims.

It was in great part due to the
photographer Alfred Stieglitz that

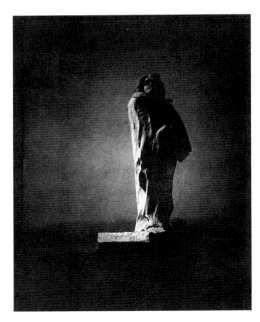

progressive modernist directions in art came to America. Born in New Jersey, Stieglitz originally went to Germany to study engineering, but came under the influence of photography and immediately adopted it as his career. His early work in that medium had an affinity with late nineteenth-century painting, but through his affiliation with Edward Steichen (fig. 10.19), Stieglitz was to become a connoisseur of avant-garde painting and sculpture in Europe, even after his return to New York in 1890. While his picture *The Terminal* of *c.* 1892 (fig. 10.18), photographed shortly after his return, shows Stieglitz's awareness of Impressionist "slices-of-life" under atmospheric conditions, it also indicates that he was a Pictorialist experimenting in a straight manner. But, despite his working in a Realist manner, Stieglitz strongly believed in the autonomous value of the camera image. Moreover, in articles written for the New York Camera Club, and in his later magazine – *Camera Work*, set up in 1903 – Stieglitz joined all the Pictorialists in maintaining that their works should be displayed and regarded for their intrinsic artistic qualities, like other nonphotographic media. In 1905 Stieglitz established the Little Galleries of the Photo-Secession at 291 Fifth Avenue, in order to exhibit the work of his group and to promote photography as a unique form of art.

Nineteenth-century sculpture

At this point we turn to nineteenth-century sculpture to trace the way in which twentieth-century sculpture developed from preceding times. Just as the direction of painting changed course in the second half of the nineteenth century, so too did the sculptural values – changes, moreover, that resounded into the twentieth century. But first we should reiterate at least two of the differences between the media. These differences have been treated more extensively in Chapter 9, "The Art of the Third Dimension," so here we only need to point out that the major differences are in the kinds of materials used and in the differing concepts of space.

Painters work with flexible materials in an additive manner. They invent not only their own illusion of space, but also the kinds of three-dimensional shapes that occupy that space. By contrast, sculptors work with tangible materials which are usually more resistant, creating objects with actual mass and/or volume in real space.

Obviously, the thinking of sculptors would normally be dominated by the weight and mass of the materials they employ. Yet, paradoxically, the spirit of nineteenth-century sculpture was primarily painterly, or additive. This was partly because clay modeling, an additive rather than a subtractive process, was dominant during that time.

During the early 1900s, a key development that occurred in sculpture, as well as in painting, was the gradual overcoming of the conservative reluctance towards change. The continued authoritarianism of the European academies was a primary cause for this lack of change, in all the arts. The lingering preference in sculpture for allegorical ideals, which use the human figure to symbolize spiritual values, whether from Classical mythology and/or religion, was largely responsible. Another reason was that in the preceding century, more so than in painting, commissions to sculptors were awarded on the basis of fidelity to nature. This attitude was influenced mostly by the actual three-dimensionality of sculpture, but was partly nurtured by the popularizing of the photographic image. Is it any wonder that the best sculptural talent was submerged by such strictures, or that sculptors, more than contemporary painters, lost sight of the older values so fundamental to their craft?

For these reasons, there was a void in innovative sculpture during the

▼ **10·20**
Antonio Canova, *Perseus with the Head of Medusa*, c. 1808. Marble, 7 ft 2⅝ in (2.20 m) high.
Although he was the best of the Neoclassical sculptors, Canova's great technical facility lacked the streak of individualistic meaning that would have made his art truly outstanding. He repeated themes that were centuries old and hackneyed.
Metropolitan Museum of Art, New York. Fletcher Fund, 1967 (67.110).

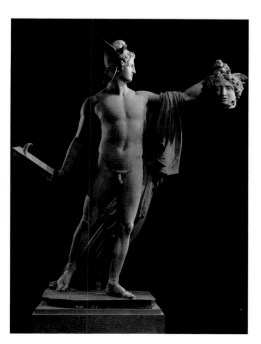

nineteenth century. True, there were gifted sculptors who were skilled in the tools of sculpture, handling with virtuoso dexterity resistant materials like marble, and creating some memorable works. Such a sculptor was Antonio Canova, an Italian Neoclassicist (fig. 10.20), who was almost as closely connected to the post-Revolutionary Napoleonic regime as the painter David. Others, like the Romantic sculptor Antoine Louis Barye, employed, more imaginatively than Canova, malleable materials such as clay and plaster (from which bronzes are usually cast) (fig. 10.21). Yet while Barye seems more original in his grasp of the essentially dynamic, monumental, and ferocious character of animal life, his allegorical subjects conform to the recommendations of the academies. Barye was reworking an old romantic tradition of evoking human emotions by parallels with animal nature or the vagaries of the

weather. It had originally been expounded in the 1600s by the great Dutch philosopher Baruch Spinoza. So old values and thinking were merely being repeated, while no one was searching for new forms to express actual human conditions in contemporary life.

Of all nineteenth-century sculptors, only Auguste Rodin can be adjudged an important figure. Rodin looked to the future as well as to the past. Historically, he was the link between traditional forms of representation and the modern trend of exploiting form, materials, and expressive content for their own inherent values.

Although he was never a direct follower of the Impressionist movement, Rodin worked in a similar manner. But Rodin went far beyond Impressionism. His search for new ways to express emotional states directly through sculptural form epitomized a crucial development of the early twentieth

▼ **10 · 21**
Antoine Louis Barye, *Tiger Devouring an Antelope*, 1851. Bronze, 13 × 22½ × 11⅝ in (33 × 57.1 × 29.5 cm).
Barye's emotionalized romantic form is similar in dynamism to the intense coloristic qualities of Romantic painters such as Delacroix and Turner. Philadelphia Museum of Art, PA. W. P. Wilstach Collection.

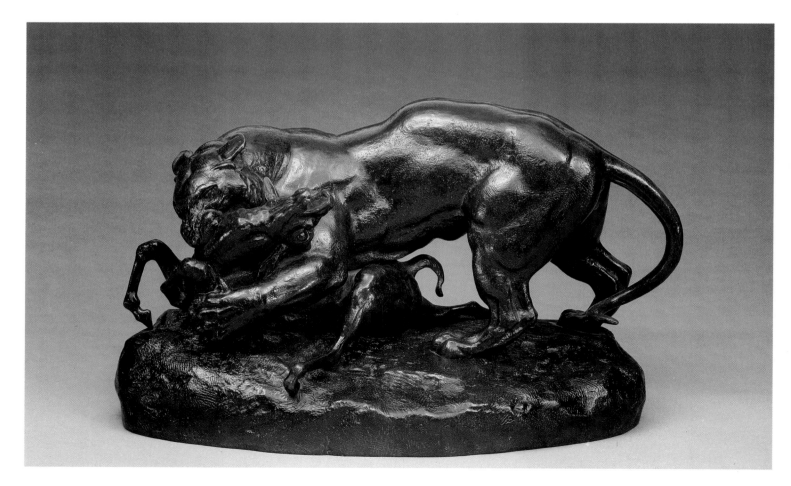

century. In this respect, Rodin's attitude is similar to the endeavors of expressionistic Post-Impressionist painters like van Gogh and Toulouse-Lautrec (see figs. 6.6 and 3.6).

Rodin's Impressionist effects derive from the way light falls upon his figures to suggest musculature and bone structure. He expanded this impression of form to express the inner condition of humanity, as it was then conceived. This was a favorite theme of the Symbolists, such as Pierre Bonnard (fig. 10.22), who followed in the footsteps of Paul Gauguin. Rodin's Impressionist effects were also influenced by photography, particularly the "stop-action" effect of movement, even though Rodin detested attempts at capturing movement on camera, saying it produced distortions of reality. He always said that photography lied and that only the artist could produce the impression of movement. He was not entirely against photography as a document or record of his work, however, since he asked the young Edward Steichen to photograph some of his work later on (see fig. 10.19). Throughout his life Rodin paid a great deal of attention to the idea of movement, trying to express drama and emotive effect in static sculptures. Rodin's interest in movement was very probably influenced by such painters as Degas (see 10.13) more than photographers, and he may have also been influenced by the great seventeenth-century sculptor Giovanni Lorenzo Bernini, whom he regarded highly.

Some critics have argued that his irregular surfaces were not Impressionist in conception, but were done with almost expressionistic emotion as he gouged and worked the clay. His sources included the Renaissance sculptors Donatello and Michelangelo, and the carvers of Gothic cathedrals in the Middle Ages. While he was repelled by most of the academic sculpture of his time, he did not hesitate to make use of literary, heroic, and allegorical themes. Employing such a theme is the *Gates of Hell*, which was

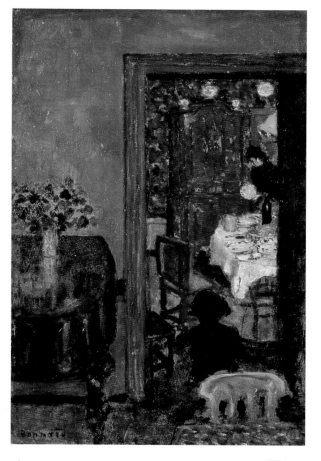

△ **10·22**

Pierre Bonnard, *The Lessons*, 1898. Oil on board, 20¼ × 13¼ in (51.4 × 33.6 cm). This capturing of the inner life of humanity on canvas is typical of the Symbolists, and it is similar to the kind of psychological approach that we can find in Rodin's work.

North Carolina Museum of Art, Raleigh, NC. © ADAGP/SPADEM, Paris and DACS, London 1994.

▽ **10·23**

Auguste Rodin, *Danaïde*, 1885. Marble, 14¼ × 28 × 20⅞ in (36 × 71 × 53 cm). This example of the sculptor's later work reflects Michelangelo's influence in its partially revealed form emerging from the roughly finished stone (see fig. 9.4).

Musée Rodin, Paris #5.1155. (Photograph by Bruno Jarret © ADAGP, Paris and DACS, London 1994.)

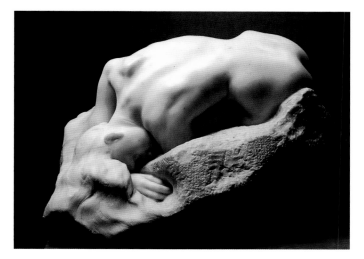

unfinished at Rodin's death in 1917 (see fig. 9.30).

Stung by criticism that his early work was so natural that it must have been cast in bronze, Rodin in his later work moved away from Naturalism toward the expression of psychological or emotional states. But it was mostly in admiration of Michelangelo that Rodin tried to restore sculptural values which he felt had been lost since that great artist's time. These values included a sense of the heft and texture of stone, and of the contrast between highly polished surfaces and unfinished roughness, as seen in his *Danaïde* of 1885 (fig. 10.23). Rodin also reintroduced the technique of having a figure, or its parts, fractionally emerging from blocks of stone. He also sculpted fragmentary human forms, producing an effect of humanity striving against fateful forces (see fig. 9.4). Moreover, it was in the unusual effects of torsion, dimension, fractional presentation, and the potency expressed in his figures that he predicted the future. These effects paved the way for twentieth-century sculptors to escape the naturalistic inhibitions imposed by the academies on so much nineteenth-century art. Rodin's career also confirms once more the fact that the individual genius most often leads the way to new ideas and forms. Most artists, substantive though they may be, usually profit mainly from only one or two of the directions foreseen by the genius.

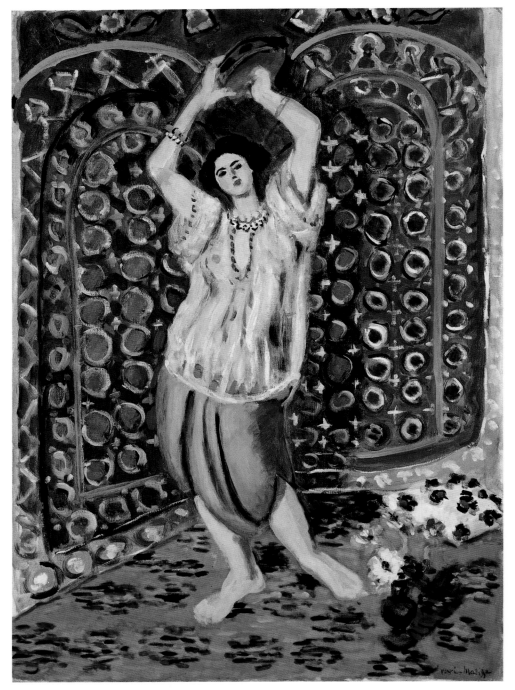

▲ 10 · 24

Henri Matisse, *Odalisque with Tambourine (Harmony in Blue)*, 1926. Oil on canvas, 36¼ × 25⅝ in (92.1 × 65.1 cm).
The Fauves, led by Matisse, tried to show the emotional essence of a subject rather than its external appearance. Matisse also exhibits the characteristically decorative, colorful, spontaneous, and intuitive qualities of this French Expressionist style.
Norton Simon Art Foundation, Pasadena, CA. © Succession H. Matisse/DACS 1994.

EARLY TWENTIETH-CENTURY STYLES

Expressionism

French and German Expressionism, perhaps the most significant phase in the evolution of newer art forms, came into being around 1910. The young artists of this movement were the first to declare so forcefully their rightful freedom to paint a subject in accord with their feelings. Expressionism is a form of art that tries to arrive at the emotional essence of a subject rather than to show its external appearance. As previously mentioned, similar ideas were being put forward by the Photo-Secessionist groups (see p. 250).

In a sense, these artists were merely more liberal Romantics. However, it was possible to be more liberal only after the intervening period of change, driven by Post-Impressionism – a period which had introduced new ways of seeing and feeling.

But it was the early 1900s that saw the greatest growth of a new awareness in art. Cézanne, Seurat, Gauguin, and van Gogh had opened the door through which hosts of young artists were eager to pass, anxious to explore a new world of artistic sensations, diversions, and mysteries. The shape of this new artistic world was signaled by an explosion of color and an exciting style of drawing which ranged from the graceful curves of Henri Matisse to the bold slashings of Oskar Kokoschka.

French Expressionism: the Fauves

The members of the earliest Expressionist group were called *Les Fauves* (The wild beasts), because of the wild appearance of their paintings after the academic formalism that was still expected by the general public. Whereas the public had been only dimly aware of Cézanne and van Gogh as revolutionaries, they could not ignore this host of new young painters, who threw Paris into a turmoil with group exhibitions, pamphleteering,

and other forms of personal publicity. At first the Fauves seemed to be trying to live up to their name. However, within a period of only seven years they had lost their original vigor and were considered rather sedate compared to the newer movements that were evolving. While it sought to evoke the emotional essence of a subject, rather than its appearance, the Fauve manner was decorative, colorful, spontaneous, and intuitive. When an Expressionist artist's emotional excitement was communicated to the spectator, the work of art could be called successful.

The color, brilliance, and winning sophistication found in the work of Henri Matisse, nominal leader of the Fauvist group, was largely influenced by Persian and Middle Eastern art (fig. 10.24; see figs. 4.7 and 5.15). The group as a whole registered similar influences, often searching for patterns in museums of

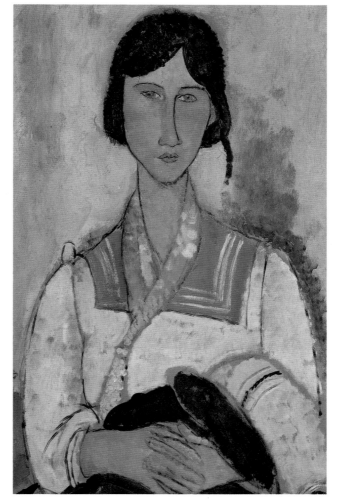

▼ **10 · 25**
Amedeo Modigliani, *Gypsy Woman with Baby*, 1919. Oil on canvas, 45⅝ × 28¾ in (115.9 × 73 cm).
The artist's painting stresses sensitive shape arrangement and subtle modeling of form within a shallow space. His interpretation of the figure reminds us of the influence of Gothic and African sculpture.
Chester Dale Collection. (© 1993 National Gallery of Art, Washington, D.C.)

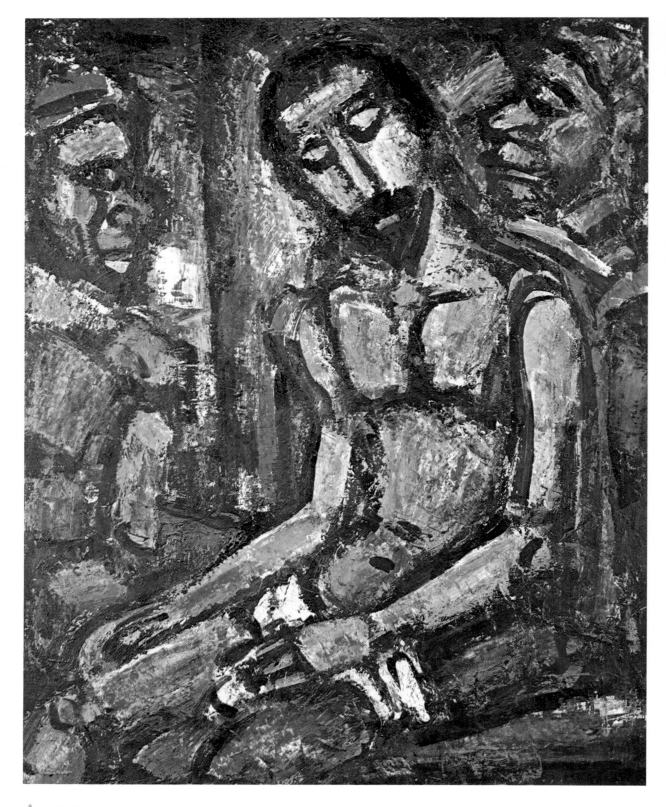

▲ 10 · 26

Georges Rouault, *Christ Mocked by Soldiers*, 1932. Oil on canvas, 36¼ × 28½ in (92.1 × 72.4 cm).

In this Expressionist contrast of clashing complements, the pattern is stabilized by heavy neutralizing lines of black reminiscent of Medieval stained glass.

ancient artefacts. The Fauves were inspired by the work of the Byzantines, the Coptic Christians, and archaic Greek artists, as well as by the tribal art of Africa, Oceania, and that of Native Americans. The influence of African masks and sculpture can be detected in the stylized, impersonal human faces found in Matisse's paintings. Behind this impersonal but enigmatic effect lies a sense of mystery or threat.

The Expressionists Matisse, Utrillo, and Modigliani, despite their general preference for strong, vibrant color, painted charming, decorative structures that in fact continued the long tradition of Classical restraint found in French and Italian art (fig. 10.25; see fig. 7.36). Georges Rouault, on the other hand, was an exception among the French Fauve Expressionists, his work being as harsh and dramatic as that of his German counterparts. His paintings express a violent reaction to the hypocrisy and materialism of his time through characteristic use of thick, crumbling reds and blacks. His images of Christ are symbols of man's inhumanity to man, as his *Christ Mocked by Soldiers* reveals (fig. 10.26); while his paintings of judges are comments on the crime and corruption of his time. Rouault's artistic comments on the French leaders of the day were anything but complimentary.

German Expressionism

German artists of the early nineteenth century felt that they, as prophets of new, unknown artistic values, must destroy the conventions that bound the art of their time. The foundation of painting in Europe for the next fifty years was provided by three groups of German artists: *Die Brücke* (*The Bridge*), *Der Blaue Reiter* (*The Blue Rider*), and *Die Neue Sachlichkeit* (*The New Objectivity*). The Expressionism of these artists, drawn from an environment that seemed complacent toward social and political injustices, was ultimately an art of protest, but it was also an attempt to assert as

directly as possible their basic urge for expression. The resulting art forms had a vehemence, drama, gruesomeness, and fanaticism never completely captured by the rationality of French art.

The German Expressionists often identified with the religious mysticism of the Middle Ages, with the tribal arts of primitive peoples, and with the psychotic expression of the mentally ill. Others followed the manner of children, with a naïve, but direct emotional identification with the environment. For example, the art of Emil Nolde is similar in feeling to the mystic art of the Middle Ages (see fig. 7.32). The Norwegian Edvard Munch, a pioneer of Expressionism living in Germany, was introducing a style of emotional instability based on his own tragic childhood (fig. 10.27). Munch was also partly influenced by folk art, tales from the Middle Ages, and by African tribal art.

The Austrian Oskar Kokoschka revealed that even in portraiture it was not the external likeness that counted, but once again the emotional significance and mood of the artist and model (fig. 10.28). Kokoschka in his later years turned to an increasingly romantic kind of Impressionist-Abstraction in which he tried to infuse cities in different parts of the world with an emotional, personal character.

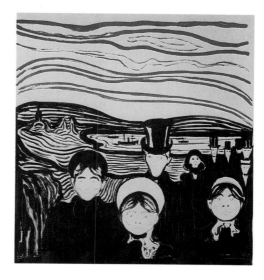

▲ 10 · 27

Edvard Munch, *Anxiety from L'Album des Peintres-Graveurs,* **Paris, Ambroise Vollard, 1896. Lithograph, printed in color, 16⅜ × 15⅜ in (41.6 × 39.1 cm).**

The angst-ridden life of this artist is reflected in his emotional and distorted pictures. Childish terrors and Medieval superstitions are interwoven in a form expressive of frightful conditions.

The Museum of Modern Art, New York. Abby Aldrich Rockefeller Fund. © Edvard Munch/Munch Estate/ BONO, Oslo/DACS, London 1994.

▶ 10 · 28

Oskar Kokoschka, *Self-Portrait,* **1917. Oil on canvas, 31⅛ × 24¾ in (79 × 63 cm).**

The Expressionism of Kokoschka is manifested by his tortured forms and violent ribbons of paint.

Von der Heydt Museum, Wuppertal, Germany. © DACS 1994.

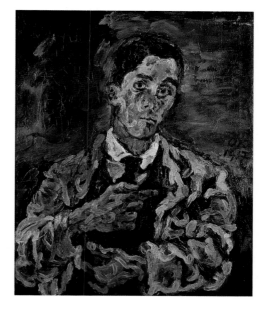

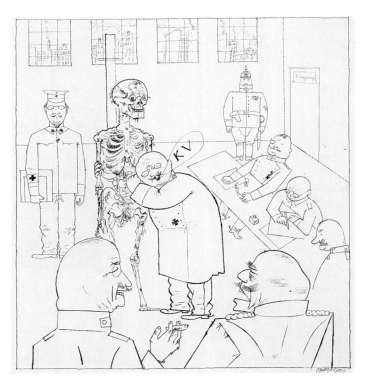

▲ **10 · 29**

George Grosz, *Fit for Active Service*, 1916–17. Pen, brush, and india ink, 20 × 14⅜ in (50.8 × 36.5 cm).

In this work, characteristic German emotionalism is pressed into the service of satire. Expressionism, which shows moral indignation at its peak, now becomes an instrument of social protest, as the artist comments bitterly on his experiences of World War I. Niceties of color are ignored in favor of harsh, biting black lines.

The Museum of Modern Art, New York. A. Conger Goodyear Fund. © DACS 1994.

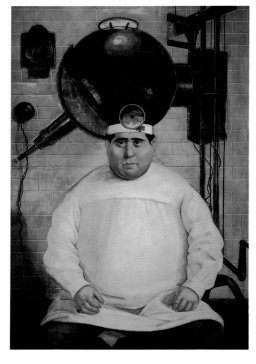

▶ **10 · 30**

Otto Dix, *Dr. Mayer-Hermann*, 1926. Oil and tempera on wood, 58¾ × 39 in (149.2 × 99.1 cm).

The German Expressionists, with whom Dix is grouped, were highly critical of German society after World War I. Their paintings of people of that period were either tinged with satire or savage with invective.

The Museum of Modern Art, New York. Gift of Philip Johnson.

▶ **10 · 31**

Max Beckmann, *Departure*, 1932–33. Oil on canvas, triptych: center panel 7 ft ¾ in × 3 ft 9⅜ in (2.15 × 1.15 m); both side panels 7 ft ¾ in × 3 ft 3¼ in (2.15 × .997 m).

Here style is emotionally intensified through strong contrasts of value and the impasto with which the artist has applied his pigment. However, the intensity of expression is partially modified by the cool, orderly arrangement derived from Cubism.

The Museum of Modern Art, New York. Given anonymously (by exchange). © DACS 1994

Following World War I, protests against Prussian jingoism, and the failures of the Weimar Republic (which led to the rise of the Nazis), became the subject matter of the New Objectivity painters, such as George Grosz and Otto Dix (figs. 10.29 and 10.30). Max Beckmann, although not a part of any organized Expressionist group, followed a path close in spirit to the work of the New Objectivity. While his work similarly satirized the swampy, degraded underworld of political society, he modified Expressionism's emotional bite by way of a calming, geometric order, learned from Cubism. This quality gives a certainty of execution to his manner of painting that is reminiscent of the work of the old masters (fig. 10.31).

Expressionism in the United States and Mexico

The expressionistic style had adherents in the Americas as well as in European countries. The Great Depression of the 1930s influenced such artists as Max Weber and Ben Shahn, both of whom spent the war years in Paris, where they were affected by Fauvism and Cubism. They returned home to make mournful and sometimes mildly satirical comment on the American society of the Depression period (see figs. 2.29 and 6.9). Jack Levine, an expressionistic artist working in the late forties and early fifties, made similar

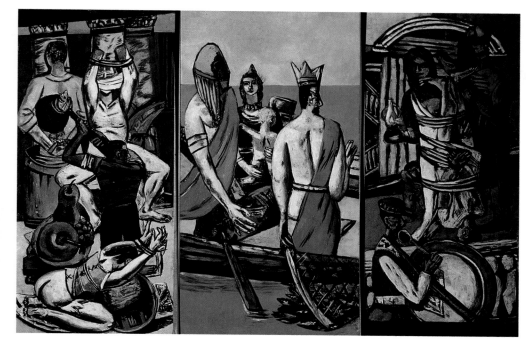

Post-Impressionist and Expressionist sculpture

New concepts in painting remained ahead of those in sculpture until about the 1950s, but a continuous interchange of ideas guaranteed that lines of development were parallel in the two groups.

By 1900, revolutionary changes were discernible as sculptors began to react to contemporary thought and experience rather than to ancient myth and legend. Sculpture then took three general directions: (1) the human figure was retained but simplified to express only the essential structure and material used; (2) forms were abstracted from nature, or new forms of a highly structural character were invented; and (3) experimentation with new materials produced new shapes and techniques.

No Post-Impressionist movement took place in sculpture, but the works of such artists as Aristide Maillol, Gaston Lachaise, and Wilhelm Lehmbruck suggest a new interest in the totality of form and an accent on the intrinsic beauty of materials – trends that are similar to the new synthesis of form from nature in Post-Impressionist painting.

commentary on the world situation during the social and political confusion of the Cold War years. His subjects were frequently plump politicians, at play or celebrating their victories (fig. 10.32).

Mexico, during the 1920s and 1930s, underwent an artistic renaissance. Many artists there found fruitful ground in an expressionistic style which identified with the problems of the Indian and *mestizo* (mixed) classes. José Orozco, whose art evolved during this period, became the greatest exponent of Expressionism in the Western hemisphere. Inspired by the rapidly changing social order in Mexico, he produced work similar in its dark, tragic vision to that of Rouault in Europe (see fig. 2.17A).

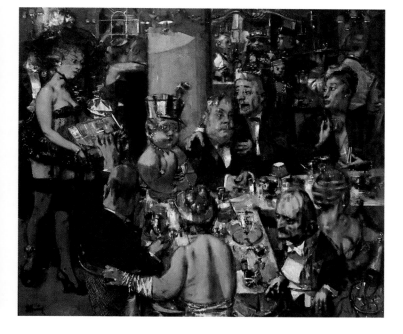

◀ **10 · 32**

Jack Levine, *Election Night*, 1954. Oil on canvas, 5 ft 3⅛ in × 6 ft ½ in (1.60 × 1.84 m).

Preoccupied by the social and political problems of the post-World War II period, the artist arrived at a distinctive manner that combines a complicated and glowing technique with an expressionistic pungency of feeling.

The Museum of Modern Art, New York. Gift of Joseph H. Hirshhorn. © Jack Levine/DACS, London/VAGA, New York 1994.

Maillol, while maintaining a classical sense of serenity indicative of the paintings of Cézanne and Seurat, pioneered a simplification of figural form. He wanted to recover a sense of sculptural monumentality that would reassert the essential blockiness of stone and the agelessness suggested by bronze and lead. He also generated a trend away from academic representation of the human figure by using slightly exaggerated proportions.

Gaston Lachaise, a Franco-American sculptor, created weighty, voluminous female figures that evoke the sensuous through exaggerated, but rhythmically balanced proportions. At times his sense of poise imbued his figures with a feeling of aerial suspension seemingly at odds with their weightiness; but this contradiction was resolved by his exquisite sense of balance and the finish he gave to metal (fig. 10.33).

▲ 10 · 33
Gaston Lachaise, *Standing Woman*, 1927. Bronze, 73 × 28 in (185.4 × 71.1 cm); base 17¼ × 21 in (43.8 × 53.3 cm).
This ponderous figure was given a feeling of lightly balanced poise.
Art Institute of Chicago. Friends of American Art Collection, 1943.580.

▶ 10 · 34
Wilhelm Lehmbruck, *Standing Youth*, 1913. Cast stone, 7 ft 8 in × 33½ in × 26¾ in (233.7 × 85.1 × 68 cm), including base.
This work is a good example of the mildly expressionistic style that dominated the pioneering phase of contemporary sculpture in the early twentieth century.
The Museum of Modern Art, New York. Gift of Abby Aldrich Rockefeller.

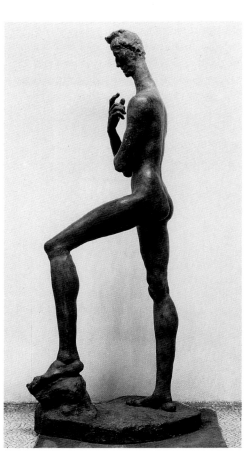

▲ 10 · 35
Marino Marini, *Horse and Rider*, c. 1947. Bronze, 39 × 27 in (99 × 68.6 cm).
In this work, a formal tension is created by allying the time-honored tradition of equestrian sculpture with twentieth-century abstraction.
Art Institute of Chicago. Gift of Mrs. Wolfgang Schoenborn, 1971.881. (Photograph by Robert Hashimoto.) © DACS 1994.

Lachaise and Lehmbruck both worked in a manner reminiscent of the more emotional aspects of Post-Impressionism, comparable in some ways to Gauguin or van Gogh. Lehmbruck evolved a style of elongated figures that was suavely charming or nostalgic and melancholic. Like Lachaise, he distributed the masses of his figural forms rhythmically; but he used a strong vertical axis, unlike Lachaise's variable axis. Where Lachaise used rounded masses, Lehmbruck created relatively sparse forms that were almost stripped of flesh (fig. 10.34).

Just as there was no clearly defined Post-Impressionist movement in sculpture, neither was there a clearly perceivable Expressionist school. Several sculptors worked in a manner similar to that expressed by the "Blaue-Reiters" in Germany – stripping away surface reality to arrive at underlying truths. Generally speaking, however, such sculptors were less disposed than Expressionist painters toward violent distortion of form to reveal the psyche. Lachaise and Lehmbruck are sometimes called Expressionists because of their moderate distortion of human form.

In the 1940s and 1950s sculptors like the Italian artist Marino Marini continued to work in this mildly expressionistic idiom reminiscent of early twentieth-century sculpture. A slight distortion characterizes his best-known works – the equestrian figures. The subtly abstract shapes of horse and rider may be related to Wassily Kandinsky's rider series of 1909–10 and seem to convey Marini's concern with the impersonality of modern life (fig. 10.35). Marini's sculpture became increasingly abstract in later years.

The rise of color photography

In 1907, when the Lumière brothers made it commercially possible to create color images with the autochrome, photographers began to experiment. Although the process used in the autochromes – coating a plate with tiny grains of starch loaded with light spectrum colors – gave images with good color fidelity, some found the coarseness of these grains objectionable. Yet interestingly this graininess, in conjunction with the Pointillism of Seurat, was a major influence on the Fauve painters' method of working.

Another drawback to early experiments with color photography was the instability of the color dyes, which had a tendency to bleed into the layers of emulsion. In 1935, with Kodak's development of Kodachrome film, which left the dyes to the color process, more dependable color images, with less graininess, could be made. This film also made it possible for anyone who could successfully expose black-and-white film to make colored photographs, and it was

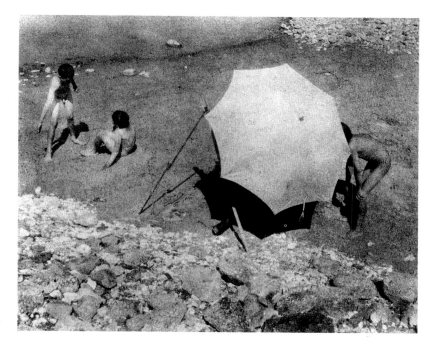

soon being employed not only by photographers, but also by amateur movie makers. Then the 35-millimeter camera was developed, and became the favorite means for shooting both black-and-white and color photographs. Eventually, newer color films increased the speed with which exposures could be made in weaker light and cameras could stop fast action in color. All these technological advancements naturally led to a growth of experimentation in photography, paralleling similar efforts in painting and sculpture to express a freedom from past ideas. Most professional photographers, however, continued to explore monochromatic photography, rather than color, and this has been the case until recent times. This was due to the more abstract quality of black-and-white images and the departure from simulated reality which they provided, not to mention the ephemeral quality of color dyes used in color films and printing papers.

The two graphic media of painting and photography have had a long history of mutual influence. This has been almost continuous, from Daguerre's first discovery in 1839 to the present day. We

▲ 10·36
Heinrich Kuehn, *The Artist's Umbrella*, 1910. Hand-printed photogravure on heavy wove paper, 9½ × 11⅝ in (23 × 28.9 cm).
As late as 1910, the photographing of nudes in unusual settings was a rebellion against the vestiges of Victorian prudery. This, in itself, marks out Kuehn as a modernist, but so does the use of a high-angled shot, which has the effect of flattening space.
Metropolitan Museum of Art, New York. The Alfred Stieglitz Collection, 1949. (49.55.193)

also noted how the grainy texture of early autochromes influenced the Fauves. The German Expressionists were also indebted to photographers' experiments, and contributed to them too. The work of German photographers may have affected the New Objective portraits of certain compatriots like Otto Dix, for example. By contrast, photographer Heinrich Kuehn was apparently influenced by the Expressionist painters to take candid, unidealized shots of his nude models in bright natural light, which are reminiscent of the Brücke artists (fig. 10.36).

Abstract art

Cubism

Around 1906 in Paris, a new attitude toward the world was observed in the work of certain artists. Before Cézanne, European artists tended to see nature and objects in terms of material surfaces. Cézanne began the trend toward the search for a reality (the universal unvariables) that lay beneath these material things. He observed and emphasized the basic structure of the world around him. This new way of seeing developed gradually over a period of about twenty-five years, paralleling the changing concepts of reality in science and photography. Cézanne had stated, for instance, that the artist should seek the universal forms of nature in the cube, the cone, and the sphere. Artistic exploration founded directly on this concept evolved in the styles of certain Fauve Expressionists and finally resulted in a new approach to art, termed Cubism.

Among the most active of the young artists in the Fauve movement from 1903 to 1906 was the Spaniard Pablo Picasso

(see figs. 2.37 and 7.35). Because of his admiration for the work of Paul Cézanne, and his desire to challenge Henri Matisse's leadership of the Fauves, Picasso had begun to look for new possibilities of form expression. He based his explorations on volumetric illusions and an analysis of spatial structure. Like Cézanne, Picasso had become dissatisfied with the contemporary emphasis on the external characteristics of objects and sought a method whereby he could express their internal structure. By 1907, in his painting *Les Demoiselles d'Avignon*, Picasso had begun to develop a formal style which showed the structure of objects in space by portraying many facets of them at the same time – a principle called *simultaneity* (fig. 10.37). Many of his ideas for this type of pictorial expression are traceable not only to the influence of Cézanne, but to the style characteristics of such *primitive art* as archaic Greek sculpture or traditional African tribal sculpture. By 1910–11, the sophistication of this style – called Analytical Cubism – culminated in such works as *Man With Violin* (fig. 10.38; see fig. 8.46 for

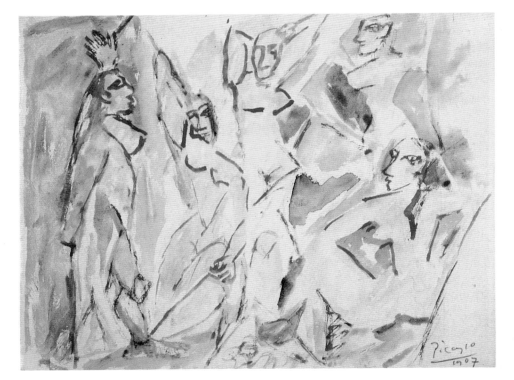

Picasso's art after his Cubist period).

One of the most noticeable aspects of Analytical Cubist paintings by Picasso and his collaborator, Georges Braque, is the cubelike rendering or geometric faceting of the people and objects they painted. Another feature of these works is that different views from different positions in space – say, a back, front, and high-angle view – are all superimposed simultaneously, thereby preserving a sense of the two-dimensional picture plane. By these methods, the Cubist artists, as well as their chief followers, tried to arrive at a more permanent order than that found in a standard representation of natural forms – an idea certainly stimulated by Cézanne. At the same time, Cubists set about reordering the traditional illusion of space in order to create a more stable form of spatial relationships, independent of the vagaries of light and the distorting effects of linear perspective.

In his concern with arriving at a new aesthetic view of the structure of matter, Picasso often stripped away many aids to expression – for example, richness of color. Moreover, in this process of reduction, he formulated an artistic language that put an end to the adherence to surface appearance which had been dominant in most art since the time of the Renaissance. Paintings began to emphasize image-making devices for their own sake rather than as a means for imitating nature. Traditional renderings of natural appearances began to give way to expressions of pure artistic form. This new value placed on the art elements as builders of artistic form and expression in their own right led to a new set of terms to explain what the artist was trying to achieve as the goal of art. Abstract art and nonobjective art were two of the terms applied to these new forms. Cubism, a semiabstract art form, was the forerunner of all the later forms of abstraction, whether they were semiabstract or totally abstract. In semiabstract art we can usually still recognize certain objects from nature; the transformation of such forms

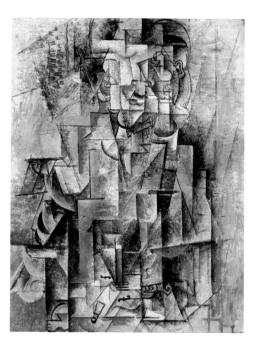

Pablo Picasso, *Man with a Violin*, 1911. Oil on canvas, 39¼ × 28⅞ in (99.7 × 73.3 cm). The shapes in Picasso's facet-Cubist style are component planes coaxed forth from subject forms and freely rearranged to suit the artist's design concept. Some facets are retained in their original position, and certain elements of the figure are only fleetingly recognizable.
Philadelphia Museum of Art, PA. Louise and Walter Arensberg Collection. © DACS 1994.

in the process of abstraction is meant to convey the artist's sensibilities, and convictions, about life and the material universe. Conversion of material forms in art became a matter of degree that varied from the semiabstract styles of Cubism and Futurism to the pure abstraction of Wassily Kandinsky and Piet Mondrian.

Cubism, as the beginning of abstract art, was of major importance. It was introduced to the world not only in the works of Picasso, but also in those of Georges Braque, a French artist who shared a studio with Picasso between 1910 and 1912. Braque added a uniquely expressive quality to the Cubist approach of Picasso by attaching non-painted, textured materials to the surface of his canvases – a technique called papier collé or, more generally, collage (see fig. 6.7). On the whole, Braque remained true to the tradition in French art of reason and charm in content, despite his use of the new Cubist forms. This contrasted with the more forceful, even explosive quality seen in some of Picasso's work. The sense of relaxed beauty in those of Braque's works executed during the peak of Cubist expression (1911–18) was engendered by his restrained manipulation of tasteful

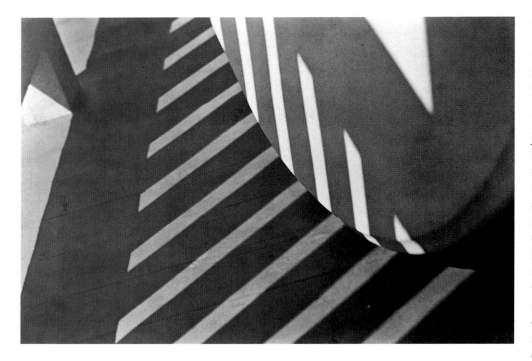

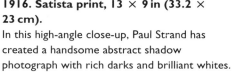

10·39

Paul Strand, *Shadows (Porch Abstraction)*, 1916. Satista print, 13 × 9 in (33.2 × 23 cm).

In this high-angle close-up, Paul Strand has created a handsome abstract shadow photograph with rich darks and brilliant whites.

Art Institute of Chicago. The Alfred Stieglitz Collection, 1949.885.

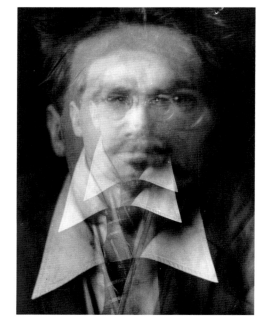

10·40

Alvin Langdon Coburn, *Portrait of Ezra Pound*, 1916. Photograph.

Strongly influenced by Cubism, the diversely talented photographer Coburn produced this multiple image of the poet Ezra Pound.

Courtesy of the International Museum of Photography at George Eastman House, Rochester, NY.

color and value patterns. The patterns were developed in terms of the finite volume of space, one of the chief Cubist idioms (see fig. 4.17A for Braque's painting after Cubism).

Two other Cubists of note were Fernand Léger, another French artist, and Juan Gris, a countryman of Picasso. These two preferred the rather austere expression of Picasso to his more violent side. Léger and Gris developed individual form qualities within the Cubist idiom that set them apart as important creators in their own right. Inspired by the impact of industry on society, Léger took the machine as his central motif (see fig. 4.28). Gris, on the other hand, stayed close to nature, treating material masses as decorative shape patterns suggestive of recognizable objects (see fig. 4.8). But Gris developed these patterns without aiming to merely imitate appearances.

There were also some photographers who worked within the Cubist idiom, such as Paul Strand and Alvin Langdon Coburn, who were members of Stieglitz's Photo-Secession group in New York (figs. 10.39 and 10.40). They worked either with close-up camera shots from above a subject, or used overlapping multiple effects to produce decoratively formal photographic images.

Futurism

Futurism, like Cubism, remained a "submovement" within the overall field of abstraction. Futurism is a form of Cubism remodeled by certain Italian artists who had been in Paris during the excitement caused by the new artistic ventures of Picasso and Braque. Among these was Gino Severini, who was instrumental in getting a French journal to publish the poet/critic Filippo Marinetti's Futurist Manifesto. The most important artists in this movement, besides Severini, were Giacomo Balla and Umberto Boccioni (fig. 10.41). Balla was the oldest adherent and seems to have led the way for the others in his paintings (fig. 10.42; see figs. 8.56 and 8.57). These artists either studied in France, or were very much influenced by its visual arts. Marinetti's manifesto belligerently denounced the old classical tradition in the fine arts (Italy's chief source of tourism), while extolling the virtues of the new age of machinery, physical well-being, and aggressive force. Under the sway of Marinetti's arguments the abovementioned artists soon wrote their own manifesto, forming a union of ideas with Marinetti. Their expression was inspired by the ceaseless activity of modern machinery, the speed and violence of contemporary life, and the psychological effects of this ferment on human life. The artists tried to show both the activity and what they perceived as the beauty of modern machinery at work. Using sheaves of lines and planes, they created an effect of dynamic movement and tension within the canvas. The Futurists were preoccupied with attempts to interpret contemporary incidents of violence – such as riots, strikes, and war – and their effects for the future.

Arguably, however, the fervor of the Futurists does not really match up to their artistic contributions. They merely energized the somewhat static geometry of Cubism and brought back richer coloring. Perhaps the group's attention to the machine was its most important contribution, for other artists and the public became more aware of the mechanized nature of their society. In contrast to the traditional mission of art to portray timeless truths, the art of the Futurists consciously expressed the age in which it was created.

Again it appears that photography and the other graphic arts had a mutual impact on one another. In Italian Futurism, for example, the influence of early photographers such as Muybridge and Eakins is implicit, not only on painters such as Marcel Duchamp and Giacomo Balla, but on photographers like Anton Bragaglia in Italy (fig. 10.43) and Alvin Langdon Coburn in the United States (see fig. 10.40).

▼ 10·41

Umberto Boccioni, *Unique Forms of Continuity in Space*, 1913. Bronze (cast 1931), 43⅞ × 34⅞ × 15¾ in (111.4 × 88.6 × 40 cm).
Boccioni was a leading founder and member of the Futurist group. An accomplished painter and sculptor, he was preoccupied for much of his career with the dynamics of movement.
The Museum of Modern Art, New York. Acquired through the Lillie P. Bliss Bequest.

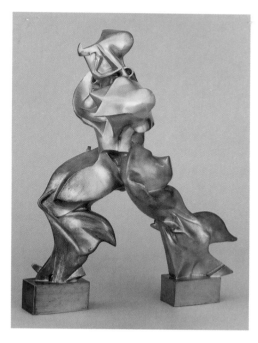

▼ 10·42

Giacomo Balla, *Speeding Automobile*, 1912. Oil on wood, 21⅞ × 27⅛ in (55.6 × 68.9 cm).
This artist's handling of the image of a speeding machine is characteristic of the Futurist idiom. Incorporated into the dynamic form is a sense of the hysteria, violence, and sheer tension in modern life.
The Museum of Modern Art, New York. Purchase.

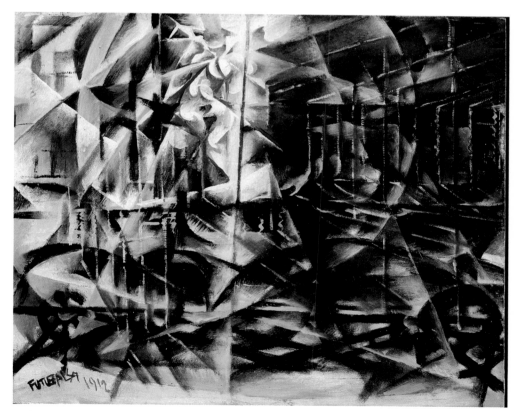

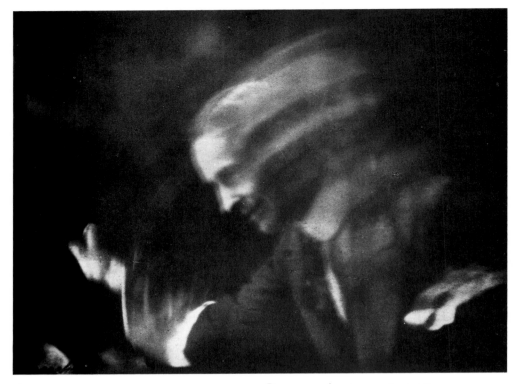

▲ 10·43

Anton Giulio Bragaglia, *Greeting*, 1911. Fotodinamica.

Within the milieu of Italian Futurist painting, Bragaglia made this time exposure of a man in the midst of greeting someone with a broad gesture. He coined the term "photo-dynamic" to describe pictures of this kind.

Centro Studi Bragaglia, Rome. Collection of A. Vigliani Bragaglia.

Pure abstract art

During the period from 1910 to 1918, the chief motivation of many artists throughout Europe was to completely eliminate nature from art. Inspired primarily by the experiments of Picasso, artists explored pure, or total abstraction in two main directions. Some, like the Russian Wassily Kandinsky, preferred an emotional, sensuous, expressionist abstraction, which later influenced American abstract painting. Others, such as the Dutch artist Piet Mondrian, preferred the cold precision of geometric abstraction.

Kandinsky's earliest, and perhaps best work featured powerful rhythms and loose biomorphic shapes that had a sense of great spontaneity (fig. 10.44). Although it was rarely evident, Kandinsky's paintings usually originated from specific conditions or circumstances. After turning to abstraction from his earliest more Romantic-Realist landscapes, Kandinsky attempted eventually to interpret his responses to nature in terms of a bold visual language without reference to outward appearances. His loose, direct manner remained essentially that of a romantic, and it is not insignificant that he was closely connected with the Blaue Reiter Expressionists, while gradually moving toward abstraction. After his experiments with biomorphic abstraction, Kandinsky underwent another conspicuous change in manner in 1919 after joining the German Bauhaus (a design institute that stressed the unity of all art in terms of design). At that time, influenced by some teachers there, Kandinsky's style became more geometrically abstract.

The most representative exponent of geometric abstraction was Piet Mondrian. Like Kandinsky, Mondrian also eventually dealt with the pure or most basic elements of form but, unlike Kandinsky, purged them of any emotional qualities. Although Mondrian came only gradually to pure abstraction, once he did, he pushed the unemotional qualities of shape, value, and color to a state of total optical purity (see fig. 1.3). In such work, meaning or content is inherent in the precise relationships established between the horizontal and vertical lines creating rectilinear shapes, and the sole use of primary colors. This direction seemed sterile and shallow to both artists and critics when it first appeared. That it was, instead, momentous and rich in possibilities is proven by its tremendous impact on hundreds of artists. Believers were soon finding metaphysical and mystical content in the purely optical harmonies of geometric abstraction, while the critics who were ridiculing his art were soon in the minority.

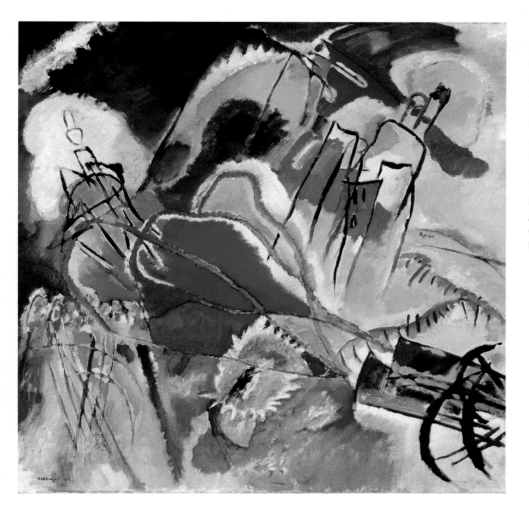

Wassily Kandinsky, *Improvisation No. 30 (Cannons)*, 1913. Oil on canvas, 3 ft 7 in × 3 ft 7¼ in (1.09 × 1.10 m).

About 1910, the Russian Wassily Kandinsky began to paint freely moving biomorphic shapes in rich combinations of hues. His characteristic early style can be seen in this illustration. Such an abstract form of expression was an attempt to show the artist's feelings about object surfaces rather than to describe their outward appearances.

Art Institute of Chicago. Arthur Jerome Eddy Memorial Collection, 1931.511. © ADAGP, Paris and DACS, London 1994.

Nonobjective art

The abstract art discussed so far in this chapter originated from nature. The next development was so-called nonobjective art, which presumed to divorce itself from nature altogether, originating entirely (insofar as this can be determined) within the mind of the artist. The differences between pure abstraction and nonobjective works of art are not readily apparent; perhaps an attempt to differentiate is of theoretical interest only. Both concepts opened up a new realm of aesthetic endeavor, and exploration in this area continues to this day. The term "nonobjective" does not mean that the artist has no objective. The artist definitely attempts to communicate, but without resorting to an objective account of external reality. Ideas about the use of the elements of form, unencumbered by recognizable objects, became subjects for nonobjective artists. A certain amount of pure abstract and nonobjective work lacks originality, for it is easy to produce synthetic abstract art that is an end in itself. However, where abstraction is part of a genuinely creative process, great powers of thought and expression are required of the artist (see fig. 10.44).

Many elements of the human-made world today derive their personality from the continuing influence of abstraction. Modern designers have readily assimilated abstract theories of form in buildings, furniture, textiles, advertising, and machines, to name only a few areas. The gap between fine art and art of a commercial or industrial nature has gradually narrowed. This may be due in part to the fact that abstract art developed out of an environment in which the practical function of the machine had become both an implicit and a conscious part of life. In a sense, the abstract artist created a machine-age aesthetic.

Abstraction in photography

Abstract art was also making its influence felt in the experimental work of photographers. So photography, too, began to be freed from its former role as a recorder of reality and to explore a whole new language of patterned design. We saw this process beginning to some extent with photographers inspired or stimulated by Cubist and Futurist painting, such as Paul Strand (see fig. 10.39) and Alvin Langdon Coburn (see fig. 10.40). These artist-photographers had been determined to work in the Realist or straight tradition without manipulating focus, negatives, or the process of development.

Coburn is particularly interesting because of his involvement with Percy Wyndham Lewis's Vorticist movement in England just before World War I. While he had concentrated mostly on portraiture at first, Coburn later became a member of the "Linked-Ring" brotherhood in England, and the New York "Photo-Secession" group of Stieglitz. Under these influences he had become increasingly experimental in attitude. Coburn's images (fig. 10.45) illustrate how he and his fellow Vorticists reacted to the avant-garde movements on the Continent as a way of trying to rid England of its academic traditionalism. Coburn invented a system of multiple, complex images by reflecting his subjects in three mirrors, giving him the distortions and abstract point of view he wanted to achieve. As can be seen in his portrait of Ezra Pound (see fig. 10.40), Coburn had already absorbed Cubist representations of multifaceted images before he arrived at his vortographs. A sense of motion was achieved through hallucinatory repetitions – an idea derived not only from Cubism, but also probably from Futurism.

Abstract art in the United States

Abstract art was slow in coming to America, but shortly after World War II the movement gathered momentum. The influence of European emigré artists was an important factor. Actually, during the period between the two world wars, many American artists were affected by the structural order of Cubism. John Marin, Lyonel Feininger, and Max Weber were among the early pioneers of abstraction in the United States (see figs. 8.47, 8.38, and 6.9). In a peculiarly American way, however, this early generation of abstractionists refrained from surrendering completely to pure abstraction and retained a strong personal vision of their own. This may have been due to the strong hold which, since the nineteenth century, various American

▼ **10 · 45**
Alvin Langdon Coburn, *Vortograph number 1*, 1917. Silver print, 7⅞ × 5¾ in (20 × 14.6 cm).
As was already evident in the portrait of *Ezra Pound*, (fig. 10.40), before coming to his pure-abstract "vortographs" Coburn had invented a method of recording multiple images of people. In the vortographs, the image was recorded from the manifold refractions of objects from three mirrors, which were arranged in an open triangle around the objects.
The Museum of Modern Art, New York. Gift of the photographer.

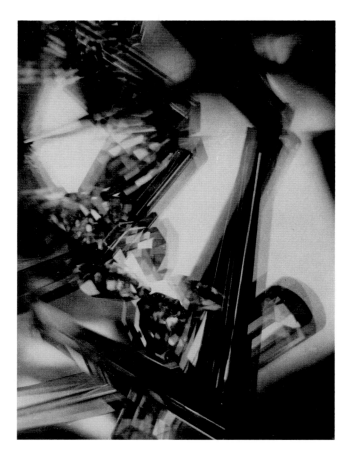

realist schools still had on national tastes. It was in this milieu that young, experimental artists like Grant Wood, Edward Hopper, and Charles Burchfield – among the best of the so-called Regionalists – had to find their way (see figs. *2.32A, 8.24,* and *4.24*). By the mid 1940s, through the influence of the earlier abstract pioneers, a still younger group of American artists had renounced their last ties with nature. Representative of this pure abstract group were Mark Tobey and Mark Rothko (figs. *10.46* and *10.47*). These men moved on to become *Abstract Expressionists,* or to strongly influence that movement.

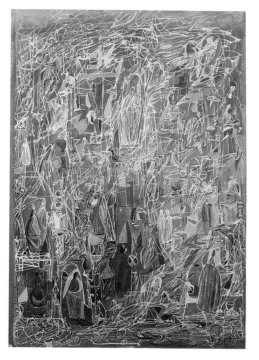

◀ **10 · 46**

Mark Tobey, *Threading Light*, 1942. Tempera on cardboard, 29⅜ × 19½ in (74.6 × 49.5 cm).

Tobey was not directly a member of the small group of young Americans who founded the Abstract-Expressionist movement in the immediate post-World War II years, but he seems to be formally related. He originated his own method of linear expression in painting (called "white writing"), which has bunches of lines wavering on the edge of shape recognition and slipping off into a controlled tension between surface and space.

The Museum of Modern Art, New York. Purchase. © DACS 1994.

▶ **10 · 47**

Mark Rothko, *No. 10*, 1950. Oil on canvas, 7 ft 6⅜ in × 4 ft 9⅛ in (2.30 × 1.45 m).

Using apparently simple masses of color on a large scale, the artist is able to evoke emotional sensations in the observer. Rothko was one of the American artists who worked in the pure abstract idiom.

The Museum of Modern Art, New York. Gift of Philip Johnson.

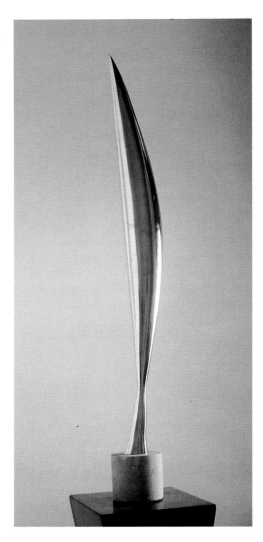

▲ **10·48**

Constantin Brancusi, *Bird in Space*, 1928. Bronze (unique cast), 54 × 8½ × 6½ in (137.2 × 21.6 × 16.5 cm).

Brancusi abstracted down to essential forms, and showed great concern for the properties of his medium.

The Museum of Modern Art, New York. Given anonymously. © ADAGP, Paris and DACS, London 1994.

Abstract sculpture

Picasso's Cubist collages and constructions of 1912–14 opened the way for a wide range of abstract sculptural forms. Perhaps the most important early abstract sculptor was the Franco-Romanian Constantin Brancusi. As early as 1913 he chose to free sculpture from mere representation. Such works as the *Bird in Space* of 1928 (fig. 10.48) reveal an effective and sensuous charm through their flowing, geometrical poise and emphasis on beautifully finished materials. Brancusi usually preferred to work in a semiabstract mode, but always considered the shape, texture, and handling of materials to be more significant than the representation of subject.

Another pioneer abstract sculptor, the Russian-born Alexander Archipenko, belonged to the so-called School of Paris during the Cubist period of Picasso and Braque. His significant contribution was the use of negative space (the void) in sculpture, as in *Woman Doing Her Hair* (see fig. 9.23), in which a hollow replaces the face. Archipenko also explored the use of new materials and technology, occasionally incorporating machine-made parts into his work.

The same Cubist intellectual and artistic ferment that led Archipenko to explore human-made materials, and Brancusi to pioneer the use of power tools, also led the Russian brothers Naum Gabo and Antoine Pevsner to develop their very important Constructivist concepts. This movement was founded in pre-Communist Russia by Vladimir Tatlin, but it is usually associated with Gabo and Pevsner because they issued the definitive manifesto in 1920, proclaiming pure abstraction as the new realism in art. Gabo was the more exciting of the two, inventing both nonobjective and nonvolumetric forms (three-dimensional forms that do not enclose space but interact with it) (see fig. 9.5). Pevsner worked more with solid masses, nearer to sculpture of a traditional

kind. Many artists were connected with the Constructivist movement: Joseph Albers (see fig. 4.25) and Lázsló Moholy-Nagy, to name two, were forced to come to the United States, like Gabo and Pevsner, to carry on their careers during World War II.

The common denominator in the work of all abstract sculptors during the period of 1900–30 was an approach that emphasized materials and blurred the division between the fine arts and the functional arts. This was essentially the point of view held by both the Constructivists and the Bauhaus movement.

Realist photography in the United States

Under the aegis of Alfred Stieglitz and Edward Steichen (pp. 250–51), the New York-based 291 gallery (as it was known) became between 1905 and 1917 a meeting place for American and international pioneers of avant-garde photography, painting, and sculpture. Among the painters and sculptors introduced by the gallery were Cézanne, Rodin, Rousseau, Matisse, Toulouse-Lautrec, Brancusi, Picasso, Duchamp and Picabia, along with such American artists as John Marin, Georgia O'Keeffe (whom Stieglitz married), and Marsden Hartley. Among the photographers exhibited were Edward Steichen, Gertrude Kasebier, A.L. Coburn, and Stieglitz's protégé Paul Strand.

The exhibits of these photographers, although they were of less enduring importance than the artists in the other media, gave photography a credibility which meant that the artform itself could not be dismissed without at least an artistic evaluation. It is also interesting to note that photographers from the United States were far more respected in Europe than its artists in other media. They seemed to be more inventive than their European counterparts and often took the prizes in photographic exhibits in the first two decades of the twentieth century.

As an exponent of straight photography, despite some Pictorialist leanings that lingered, Stieglitz in his later years created some daring photographs of cloud patterns that were very abstract and evocative, predicting American Abstract-Expressionist painting in the 1940s. They were entitled *Songs of the Sky*, but Stieglitz said they were *Equivalents* (fig. 10.49), intended to be seen not merely as clouds alone, but gateways to more profound emotional experiences.

Edward Steichen, Stieglitz's ingenious compatriot, was born in Luxembourg, but came to the United States in 1880. His early work in Europe was for Auguste Rodin, as we have seen (see fig. 10.19). A Pictorialist by persuasion, Steichen became a straight photographer after his experiences as an aerial photographer during World War I, and his association with the 291 gallery. With the closing of 291, and the dissolution of the magazine *Camera Work* in 1917, Steichen turned to fashion photography, becoming chief photographer for *Vogue* and *Vanity Fair*. From about 1923 to 1938 his outstanding portraits of luminaries and fashion models frequently appeared in the two magazines (fig. 10.50). Steichen also served with the U.S. Navy in World War II as director of its Photographic Institute. In 1947 Steichen was put in charge of photography at the Museum of Modern Art in New York, where he mounted, in 1955, a famous exhibit of photographs from all over the world, known as "The Family of Man." Steichen was also an accomplished painter.

Paul Strand, the young protégé of Stieglitz, was also a practitioner of straight photography. By using sharp focus and close-ups, his photographs of natural objects fill the picture format, and in so doing he achieved almost abstract effects (see fig. 10.39). Also noted for his studies of ordinary New Yorkers, he worked as an X-ray technician with a medical team during World War I, and

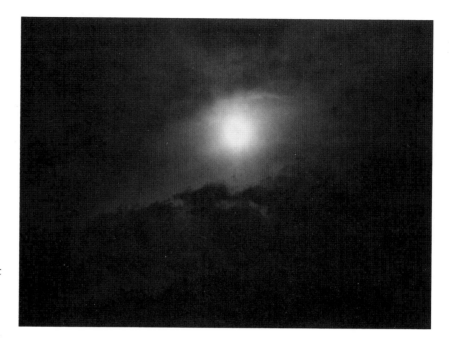

▲ 10 · 49

Alfred Stieglitz, *Equivalent*, 1929. Chloride print, 3⅝ × 4⅝ in (9.2 × 11.6 cm).
Stieglitz reacted to the criticism that he could only create powerful portraits by producing completely straight abstract images of cloud patterns, anticipating Abstract-Expressionist painting of the forties.
Art Institute of Chicago. The Alfred Stieglitz Collection, 1949.791.

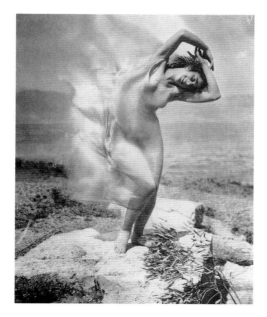

◄ 10 · 50

Edward Steichen, *Wind Fire: Thérèse Duncan*, 1921. Gelatin-silver print, 16⁹⁄₁₆ × 13⅝ in (42 × 34.6 cm).
This magnificent portrait of the dancer Thérèse Duncan, daughter of Isadora Duncan, is one artist's tribute to another. Steichen, in Athens to photograph Isadora's dance troupe, wrote about the garments flickering like flames in the wind when he took this photograph.
The Museum of Modern Art, New York. Gift of the photographer. Reprinted with permission of Joanna T. Steichen.

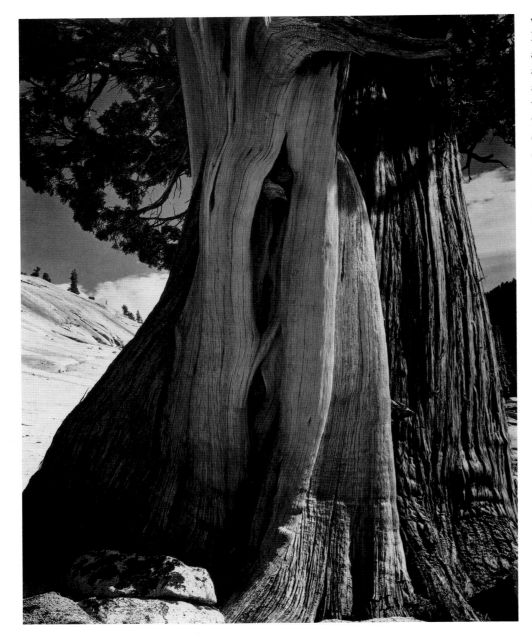

▲ **10 · 51**

Edward Weston, *Juniper, Lake Tenaya, 1938*, 1938 (Yosemite National Park). Gelatin silver print.
The hypnotic play of dark and light values and the contrast between the textures of bark, stone and clouds are indicative of Weston's artistic accomplishments.

© 1981 Center for Creative Photography, Arizona Board of Regents.

was a movie maker for a time afterwards. He eventually returned to photography and did much traveling, creating an album of photographs taken in Mexico, and wrote several books on the subject with other authors. He died in France, where he had gone to live toward the end of his life. In 1932 a photographic group calling themselves Group f-64, because they used the smallest aperture (the f-64) to provide good depth of field, was being set up in the western United States. Charter members of the group were: Edward Weston, Imogen Cunningham, and Ansel Adams. Edward Weston was already famous for his sharply focused, detailed images, which were produced with minimum equipment and without cropping the negatives. Much earlier he had opened a studio in California and had already achieved international fame for his soft-focused, Pictorialist portraits of Hollywood personalities. Later, after meeting Stieglitz and winning a Guggenheim fellowship, Weston became noted for his beautifully detailed studies of people, nature, and structures typical of "the American scene" (fig. 10.51). In this respect he shared the preoccupations of Regionalist painters like Grant Wood and others (see fig. 2.32A).

Another photographer carrying on the Stieglitz credo after World War II was Ansel Adams. Adams, like Weston, changed from earlier Pictorialist imagery to straight, after coming under the influence of Paul Strand. By 1936, Adams had become so well known for his scenes of the West, with their dramatic dawn or sunset lighting, that Stieglitz exhibited his work at the American Place, a new gallery opened to replace the earlier 291 (see fig. 2.3). Adams was also very important as a teacher of workshops, through the books he published, and for his "zonal system," used to translate the values of nature to those of the photographic image. Adams worked for periods as a commercial photographer, and served as an advisor to the Polaroid Company.

Fantastic art

The third major direction for twentieth-century art became apparent about 1914, the first year of World War I. The war had evidently begun to raise questions about human alienation in a mechanized society, and it was suggested that individual freedoms might actually be destroyed in an age of technology. As a kind of antidote to the machine cult in abstract art, certain writers, poets, and artists began to extol artistic forms that reemphasized the emotional, intuitive side of creativity. During the period of World War I, which marked the end of early twentieth-century experiments, Picasso moved away from the monumental style of early Cubism and began to make new experiments that were to become the basis for Dadaism's destructive, cynical, and absurd parodies on the cult of materialism in society. Just before the war, while he and Braque were still collaborating, Picasso had established the collage technique, and Braque, papier collé, both of which finally freed art from any necessary dependence on the "reality" of appearances. On the eve of the war in 1914, Picasso revealed his developed conception of Cubist reality in a three-dimensional form that opened the way for the Constructivists in Russia (fig. 10.52). In other forms of plastic art, from assemblage to found art, Picasso also proved a pioneering spirit. Then, in the mid 1920s, he became an exponent of *fantastic art* forms, leading his followers, and those he had influenced, by the examples we have cited (see fig. 8.46).

Artists had devoted their energies to fantastic art in the past. The centaurs of the ancient Greeks; the beast symbols of human sin in Medieval manuscripts and sculpture; the superstitions and alchemical nightmares of Hieronymous Bosch in the early sixteenth; and the fantasies of Goya in the late eighteenth and early nineteenth – these are a few of the prototypes of twentieth-century fantasy.

Dadaism

The World War I years nurtured the growth of an art that emphasized the irrational side of human behavior. Neutral Switzerland had become the mecca for poets, writers, artists, liberals, and political exiles who sought refuge there from persecution or the terrors of modern warfare. *Dada* arose out of an intellectual milieu characterized largely by disillusionment with the role of reason in society and art. Dada was a semiphilosophical creed that ridiculed and protested against the conventional morality of the social order, which its proponents believed had degenerated and brought the world to war. Thus the Dadaists maintained that a complete destruction of accepted institutions and conventions was needed; only on completely virgin soil could humanity rebuild a more desirable society. The Dadaists, therefore, embarked on a programmatic undermining of traditional civilized mores by cynically deriding all of society's most firmly held beliefs, among which were beliefs about the role of artists and art.

Marcel Duchamp, Max Ernst, and others began to fashion machinelike forms that depicted humans as unthinking robots. Later, they created biomorphic images that discredited Kandinsky's romanticized abstract art (fig. 10.53; see fig. 2.22). These inventions were meant to show disrespect toward the new experimental art forms and shock a public already disturbed by a visual revolution. One of the most complex and intelligent of the Dadaists, Marcel Duchamp, established in Dada a form of art that was to have an impact on the rest of the century – ready-mades or found art, here illustrated by the *Bicycle Wheel* (fig. 10.54). These commonplace items were given an "artistic" value when they began to be exhibited and bought by museums and collectors, even though they were intended to satirize all conventional aesthetic values.

▼ **10 · 52**
Pablo Picasso, *Glass of Absinthe*, spring 1914. Painted bronze with absinthe spoon, 8½ × 6½ × 3⅜ in (21.6 × 16.4 × 8.5 cm); diameter at base, 2½ in (6.4 cm).
In constructions such as this, which were produced during the same period as his Cubist paintings, Picasso opened the door for many developments in the plastic arts, such as assemblage and "found" art.
The Museum of Modern Art, New York. Gift of Mrs. Bertram Smith. © DACS 1994.

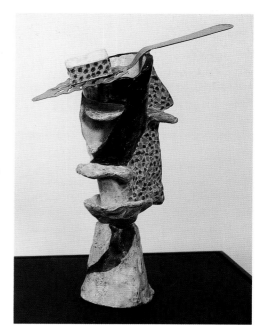

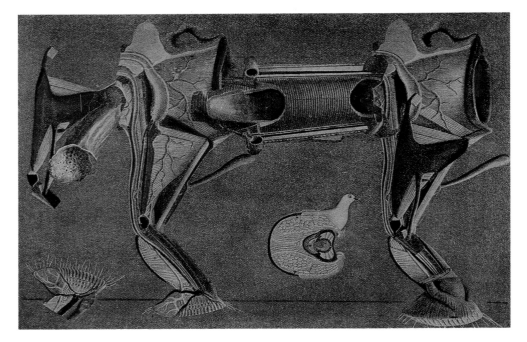

Dada thus provided its adherents with an intellectual license to attack the old social and artistic order. In principle, there was no limit to the disorder that might be unleashed on painting, poetry, and general social behavior. Consequently, Dadaism created a backlash against modern art among much of the public. For many years people tended to classify all twentieth-century works of art in terms of the outlandish forms created by the Dadaists. Actually, the disorder of the movement eventually led to its demise. Dada was pure nihilism, an exhibitionism of the absurd. Being against art, its only medium was a kind of outrage, publicly displayed to discredit all forms of sense. Its main value today is historical, since it was the principal source of Surrealism and a new liberator of expressive freedom. But it was also a precursor of much absurdity found in modern art to the present, and continually raises public and official hackles – witness present-day attempts by conservative legislators to divert public taxation away from the arts.

Individual fantasists

Fantasy in art seemed to be a general tendency in Western Europe during the period of Dada satire. This fantasy followed individual, but quite influential, directions in the hands of certain artists who were not part of the Dada movement. The Italian Giorgio de Chirico painted incongruous modern machines in ancient shadowed plazas (see fig. 5.5). Using the vaguely Classical image of silent squares inhabited by statuesque remnants of an unknown people, he seemed to be commenting on the decadence of the modern world. The frozen, trancelike effect of his images evokes a wistful desire to recover the past.

The Swiss artist Paul Klee created an idiom using witty, abstract imagery based on Expressionism and Cubism. His work pokes gentle but penetrating fun at the cult of the machine and smiles shyly at human pretensions. The implication is that there is more to extrasensory

▲ **10 · 53**

Max Ernst, *The Horse, He's Sick*, 1920. Collage (pasted paper, pencil, and ink), $5\frac{3}{4} \times 8\frac{1}{2}$ in (14.6 × 21.6 cm).

As part of the Dadaists' debunking of all twentieth-century art forms, a natural organism is here turned into a mechanical absurdity. At the same time, the use of pasted photoengravings is a nonsensical twist of the collage technique first invented by Braque.

The Museum of Modern Art, New York. Purchase. © SPADEM/ADAGP, Paris and DACS, London 1994.

▶ **10 · 54**

Marcel Duchamp, *Bicycle Wheel*, 1951 (third version, after lost original of 1913). Assemblage, metal wheel, $25\frac{1}{2}$ in (63.8 cm) in diameter, mounted on painted wood stool $23\frac{3}{4}$ in (60.2 cm) high; overall, $50\frac{1}{2}$ in × $25\frac{1}{2}$ in × $16\frac{5}{8}$ in (128.3 × 63.8 × 42 cm).

Duchamp was one of the most complex and inventive of the Dadaists. After having become disillusioned with Cubism and Futurism, he was forever questioning the aesthetic viability of art. With this piece he gave birth in 1913 to the concept of "ready-made" art, which was to be a profound influence.

The Museum of Modern Art, New York. The Sydney and Harriet Janis Collection. © ADAGP, Paris and DACS, London 1994.

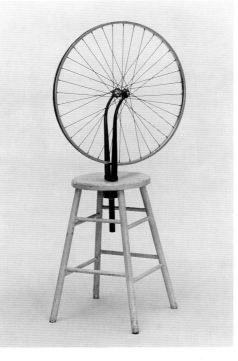

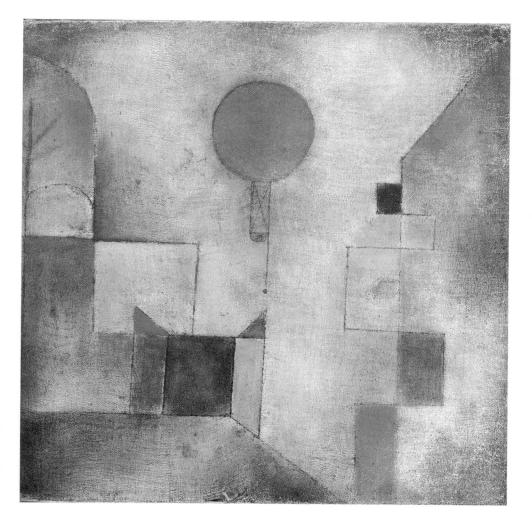

Paul Klee, *Red Balloon*, 1922. Oil (and oil transfer drawing?) on chalk-primed linen gauze, mounted on board, 12½ × 12¼ in (31.7 × 31.1 cm).

Many artists developed fusions of twentieth-century concepts that defy ready classification. This reproduction is a refined synthesis of relaxed Cubist forms allied to the naïve charm of children's art.

Solomon R. Guggenheim Museum, New York. (Photograph by David Heald; © The Solomon R. Guggenheim Foundation, New York; 48.1172 × 524.)

perception than modern humanity's addiction to practicality allows us to believe (fig. 10.55).

Marc Chagall, born in Russia but in later life a resident of France and the United States, originally worked in an Expressionist manner. His stay in France brought him within the sphere of Cubism. Eventually, he made fantasy and Cubism join forces, creating a brand of romanticized poetic art that has an Alice-in-Wonderland quality. Chagall showed people's interior organs and let them float on air in a gravity-free world. The first contact with Chagall usually brings a chuckle to the spectator. On better acquaintance, his underlying warmth and humanity are revealed (fig. 10.56).

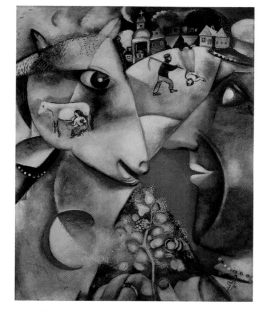

Marc Chagall, *I and the Village*, 1911. Oil on canvas, 6 ft 3⅝ in × 4 ft 11⅝ in (1.92 × 1.51 m).

The fairy-tale world of the imagination is found in this example by an artist who evades fixed classification. Recent technological concepts (x-rays and flight) are reflected in the freely interpreted transparent objects and in the disregard for gravity.

The Museum of Modern Art, New York. Mrs. Simon Guggenheim Fund. © ADAGP, Paris and DACS, London 1994.

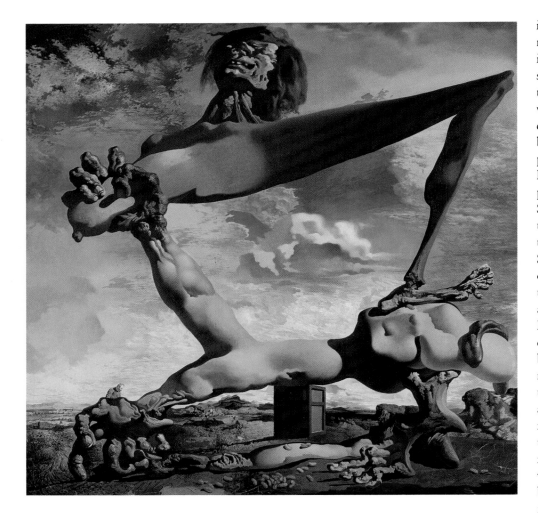

▲ 10·57

Salvador Dali, *Soft Construction with Boiled Beans: Premonition of Civil War*, 1936. Oil on canvas, 39⅜ × 39 in (100 × 99.1 cm). A naturalistic technique combined with strange abstractions gives a nightmarish mood to the political commentary in this painting. This approach to form is typical of Surrealist artists in the early 1920s.

Philadelphia Museum of Art, PA. Louise and Walter Arensberg Collection. © DEMART PRO ARTE BV/ DACS 1994.

Surrealist painting

Surrealism evolved about 1924 from the art of the individual fantasists and Dadaists, becoming a way of life for its members. With the end of World War I, there came a semblance of stability, and the public became complacent about the ills of modern society. The Surrealists reacted to this by following a Dadaist program designed to preserve the life of the imagination against the pressures and tensions of the contemporary world.

Whereas the Dadaists had tried to debunk meaning in what they saw as a stale art tradition propped up by a corrupt society, the Surrealists tried to build a new art out of works that fused the conscious and unconscious levels of human awareness. Generally speaking, both Dadaism and Surrealism were a continuation of the counterattack (first

instigated by the Romantics in the nineteenth century) against an increasingly mechanized and materialistic society. The Romantics had often created the same kind of hallucinatory images in which the Surrealists delighted. In so doing, they gave evidence of the growing belief that humanity could not solve every problem by means of science, and that little-known, seemingly insoluble problems existed within the human mind. Sigmund Freud's theories of dreams and their meanings lent strong credence to this belief. Operating on this thesis, Surrealist artists created a new pantheon of subconscious imagery that was claimed to be more real than that generated by activities and behavior on the conscious level. The Surrealists believed that only in dreams, which arise in the mind from below the conscious level, could humans retain their personal liberties. In their art the Surrealists cultivated images that arose unbidden from the mind. These images were recorded through automatic techniques of drawing and painting. Such images bring to attention the arbitrary way in which our senses construct reality, by exploring incongruous relationships of normal objects in abnormal settings, and vice versa. The Surrealists juxtaposed commonsense notions of space, time, and scale in unfamiliar ways.

Max Ernst in his *frottages* (invented about 1925) employed the Surrealist technique of shutting off the conscious mind. Frottages were rubbings made on rough surfaces with crayon, pencil, or similar media. In the resulting impressions the artist would search for a variety of images while in a state of feverish mental intoxication. A process bordering on self-hypnosis was embraced to arrive at this heightened state. No doubt some artists used drugs and alcohol. Such artists as Salvador Dali affected a similar creative fever but used a meticulous, naturalistic technique to give authenticity to their improbable, weird, and shocking images (fig. 10.57). Yves Tanguy employed a method similar to

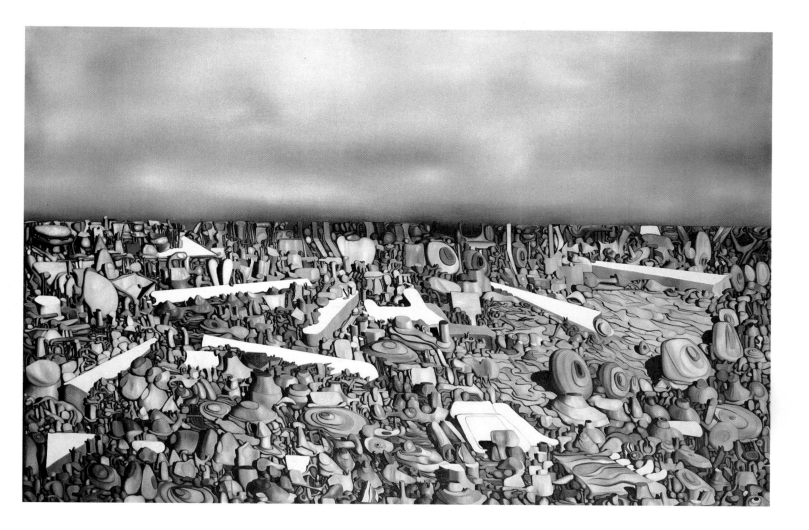

that of Ernst. Allowing his hand to wander in free and unconscious doodlings, he created strange landscapes consisting of nonfigurative objects that suggested life. Tanguy's pictorial shapes have the appearance of sentient, alien organisms living in a mystical twilight land (fig. 10.58; see fig. 4.6).

There were many Surrealists, but Ernst, Dali, and Tanguy were the most influential, thanks to their unflagging invention of arresting images. A great number of other painters, even where they did not hold with the strictures of André Breton's Surrealist manifesto of 1924, fell under the sway of these outstanding artists. Some of those influenced followed the ideas of the group, while planning and designing in a traditional manner (an approach disdained by orthodox Surrealists).

Surrealist sculpture

The effect of Surrealism on the work of many artists was variable – certainly, not many twentieth-century sculptors were pure Surrealists when we consider the character of their work. Generally, however, the trends of the first two decades merged to such an extent that classification into specific categories is rarely possible. This tendency increased after the middle of the century and led to the complex, interwoven movements of the 1960s, 1970s, and 1980s.

Alberto Giacometti, a Swiss sculptor/painter who spent much of his career in France, was perhaps one of the greatest Surrealist artists of this century. The evolvement of his personal style was affected by such diverse influences as Lehmbruck's mild Expressionism, Cubism, and Constructivism. Like other

▲ 10·58

Yves Tanguy, *Multiplication of the Arcs*, 1954. Oil on canvas, 3 ft 4 in × 5 ft (1.02 × 1.52 m).

Working with nonfigurative objects in a polished technique, the Surrealist Tanguy invents a world that appears to be peopled by lifelike gems.

The Museum of Modern Art, New York. Mrs. Simon Guggenheim Fund. © DACS 1994.

twentieth-century sculptors, Giacometti was fascinated not only by the effects of new materials, but also by the effect of light and space on form. By 1934 he had reached his mature style of elongated, slender figures pared away until almost nothing remained of substantial form. In their arrested movement, these figures suggest poignant sadness and isolation

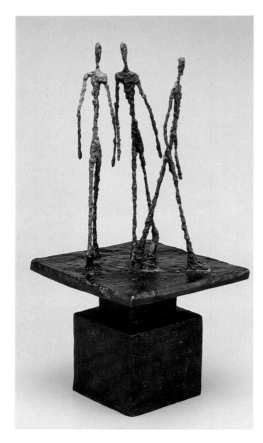

Alberto Giacometti, *Three Walking Men*
1948/49. Bronze, 29½ in (74.9 cm) high.
Giacometti emphasizes the lonely vulnerability of
humanity by reducing his figures to near-
invisibility and by emphasizing the spaces
between them.

Art Institute of Chicago. Edward E. Ayer Endowment
in memory of Charles L. Hutchinson, 1951.256. ©
ADAGP, Paris and DACS, London 1994.

▶ 10·60
Julio González, *Cactus Man #1*, 1939–40.
Bronze, 25½ in (64.8 cm) high.
Expressively textured surfaces appealed greatly
to this Spanish artist, who was the earliest
modern sculptor to introduce welding as part of
his repertoire.

Purchase, Horsley and Annie Townsend Bequest. The
Montreal Museum of Fine Arts Collection. © ADAGP,
Paris and DACS, London 1994.

(fig. 10.59). Giacometti's indirect method
of approaching content stemmed from
Surrealism and was related to the stream-
of-consciousness theory supported by early
twentieth-century psychologists.

The first sculptor to explore direct
metal sculpture (welding) was the Spanish
artist Julio González. In the late 1920s,
under the influence of Picasso, González
began to substitute outlines for masses
and planes, and even allowed the tendrils
of metal to stop short so that they were
completed by implication alone. His sense
of the dematerialization of form is similar
to Giacometti's but is more often infected
with a humor that teeters on the edge of

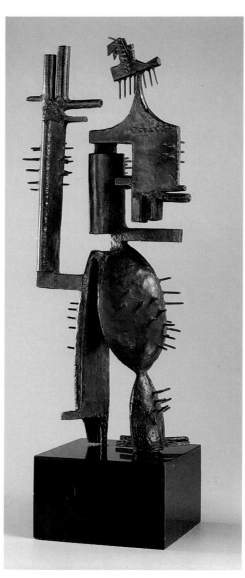

the subconscious. The influence of
González's work could be seen in Picasso's
sculptural experiments of the 1930s, but
the influence worked both ways (fig.
10.60).

The Alsatian artist Jean Arp also
explored the Surrealist preoccupation with
preconscious suggestion and the effect of
the unexpected, or surprising, form.
Before this shift of direction, Arp had
explored most of the avant-garde
movements of the early twentieth
century: Cubism, the Blaue Reiter, Dada
(he was a cofounder of the Zurich branch
in 1916), and Constructivism. He was well
known for his abstract collages and reliefs,
arranged according to the laws of chance,
such as *Mountain Table Anchor Navel* of
1925, before turning to ovoidal sculptural
forms in the 1930s. These later works
reveal the influence of Brancusi and the
prehistoric sculpture of the Cycladic
Islands. In fact, Arp's ovoidal shapes
became so famous that almost all kinds of
rounded, organic shapes were called "Arp
shapes" for a time (see fig. 9.22).

Surrealism and photography

While only a few Dadaists and Surrealists
seemed to use photography as a source for
their images, the medium's power to
distort reality proved a way for some to
free themselves from traditional image-
making. Arp, for example, may have used
the cut-and-paste method of creating
accidental arrangements of shapes in his
reliefs, known as photomontage. This
technique, arguably invented by George
Grosz, was directly descended from the
Cubist papier collé or collage techniques.
Although we know Dali profoundly
admired Vermeer, the Dutch Baroque
painter, and the nineteenth-century
Romantic-Naturalist Messonieri, he did
call his weirdly delineated paintings
"hand-painted dream photographs,"
hinting that he was as much influenced
by that medium. Along with Spanish
director Luis Buñuel he created two
Surrealist art movies, *Un Chien Andalou*

and *L'Age d'Or*, using the distinctive advantages of the medium to create unusual Surrealist effects.

Two photographers liberated by Surrealism were the American Man Ray and the Frenchman Henri Cartier-Bresson. Duchamp and Man Ray were invited to exhibit at Gallery 291 by Stieglitz, and were important for introducing Dada and later Surrealism to New York. Man Ray took up photography at Stieglitz's instigation, and a long, successful career ensued. He is credited with inventing a photographic technique, independent of cameras, which he called the Rayograph. This consisted of placing objects on or near sensitized paper and exposing it to light, thereby creating "chance" or "automatic" photographic images (fig. 10.61). These have been popular ever since. Man Ray was also a painter, and his aerographs saw in 1922 the introduction of the first spray techniques used in the medium. Similarly, he was able to create an unearthly halo effect in his photographic solarizations, which were made by exposing the film to light halfway through the development time to fog it. About 1920 Man Ray went to Paris where he lived until the end of his life, photographing artists, art, and fashions.

Henri Cartier-Bresson, the French photographer partly influenced by Surrealism, was famous for his "chance" photographs of people engaged in their day-to-day activities. His pictures attempted to seize the moment, and his aim was "to 'trap' life ... as it unrolled itself before my eyes." Although he was basically a photojournalist, his images have a character that goes far beyond the mere record of an incident, and are creative in terms of their organization and dramatic lighting. He was also among the first to use the recently introduced 35-millimeter Leica, a format that became the most popular amongst professionals and amateurs alike (fig. 10.62).

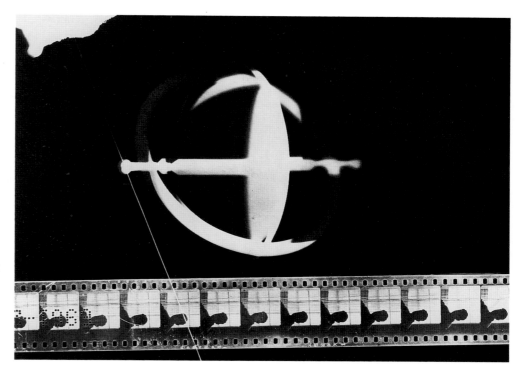

▲ 10·61
Man Ray, *Rayograph*, 1924.
This photograph involves the technique, developed by Man Ray, of placing objects on sensitized paper which is then exposed to light.
Courtesy of the International Museum of Photography at George Eastman House, Rochester, NY.

▼ 10·62
Henri Cartier-Bresson, *An Old Customer, San Remo, Italy*, 1953. Photograph.
This "chance" photograph of a genteel woman, caught at the moment of downing the last of her drink, was typical of this great photographer's semisurreal "accidental" images.
© Henri Cartier-Bresson/Magnum.

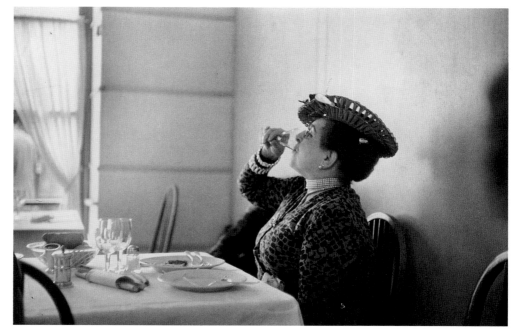

▶ **10 · 63**
Joan Miró, *Person Throwing a Stone at a Bird*, 1926. Oil on canvas, 29 × 36¼ in (73.7 × 92.1 cm).
Miró here combines sophisticated color and biomorphic shapes with simple childlike images – in many respects, the painting is similar to Klee's *Red Balloon* (see fig. 10.55). The Abstract Surrealism of Miró is, in general, semirepresentational in character.
The Museum of Modern Art, New York. Purchase. © ADAGP, Paris and DACS, London 1994.

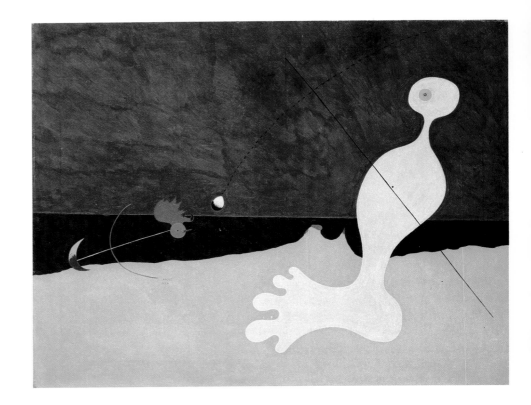

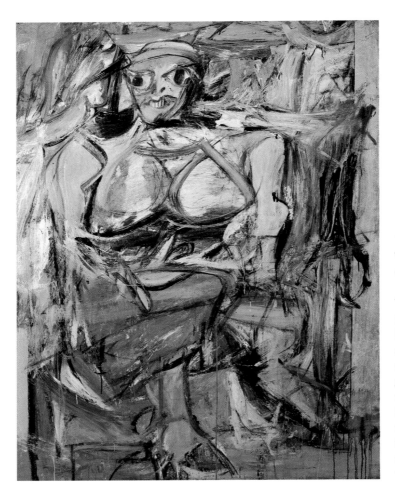

◀ **10 · 64**
Willem de Kooning, *Woman, I*, 1950–52. Oil on canvas, 6 ft 2⅞ in × 4 ft 10 in (1.90 × 1.47 m).
This artist summarizes most aspects of the romantic, or Action, group of Abstract Expressionism: revelation of the ego through the act of painting; neglect of academic or formal organization in favor of bold, direct, free gestures that are instinctively organized; and willingness to explore unknown and indescribable effects and experiences. Even though de Kooning's subject is ostensibly the figure, its representational value is subordinated to the motivating activity of pure painting.
The Museum of Modern Art, New York. Purchase.

ART FORMS OF THE 1940s AND EARLY 1950s

A host of artists mixed certain aspects of the three major movements of the early twentieth century. Generally speaking, these artists found pure abstraction too impersonal, mechanical, and dehumanizing. On the other hand, they felt that Surrealism disregarded the desire for order that was traditionally fundamental to most art.

Abstract-Expressionist painting

The forerunners

Generally speaking, the precursors of Abstract Expressionism had managed to combine the harmonious shape relationships of Abstraction with the unbidden imagery of Surrealism. Most important among these are: Joan Miró of Spain, Rufino Tamayo of Mexico, Roberto Matta Echaurren of Chile, Mark Tobey of the United States; and the ex-Europeans Willem de Kooning of Holland, Arshile Gorky of Turkish Armenia, and Hans Hofmann of Germany. The latter three, in particular, by living in the United States after World War II, helped to pioneer the first wholly American art movement, Abstract Expressionism (figs. 10.63, 10.64, and 10.65; see figs. 4.1, 4.5, 10.46, and 8.48).

The Abstract-Expressionist movement

Abstract Expressionism was a coalescence of the three major movements that had peaked in the 1930s – Expressionism, Abstraction, and Surrealism – though some deeper roots could trace the influence of Post-Impressionism. Essentially the Abstract Expressionists wanted to state their individual emotional and spiritual state of being without necessarily referring to representational

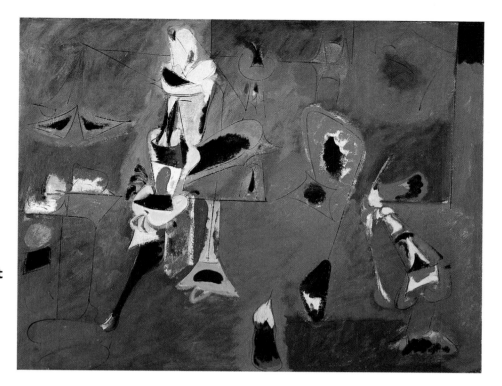

▲ 10·65

Arshile Gorky, *Agony*, 1947. Oil on canvas, 3 ft 4 in × 4 ft 2½ in (1.02 × 1.28 m).
A combined engineering and artistic background in his student days, plus the stimulation of Surrealism's unconscious imagery, led this artist into the emotionalized phase of Abstract Expressionism. Gorky's career followed a downward spiral of bad luck and tragedy, which seems to be mapped out in his work. His early paintings are precise and stable, gradually becoming more unsettled and unsettling in the later work. Gorky was an important influence on the younger generation of American Abstract Expressionists.
The Museum of Modern Art, New York. A. Conger Goodyear Fund. © ADAGP, Paris and DACS, London 1994.

form. But one should stress that Abstract Expressionism was a movement without a common style: each artist expressed his or her experiences independently.

Works of art which would be loosely gathered under the banner of Abstract Expressionism began to coalesce in the early 1940s. By 1951, the exhibit in New York's Museum of Modern Art "Abstract Painting and Sculpture in America," made the arrival of the new style official. The artistic founders of the group were primarily painters concentrated in New York toward the end of World War II, but by the mid 1950s, there were artists working in various media in this manner all over the United States, as well as in Western Europe, Japan, and Latin America. As the movement developed, it divided roughly into two groups, though there was significant overlap: a generally romantic group (often called "Action painters") and a more classical or restrained group, who explored large, unified color fields of personally conceived shapes or signs. The first group found its origins in the "automatic" works of such artists as Matta, Gorky, and Tobey, and in the biomorphic abstractions of Wassily Kandinsky (see figs. 4.5, 10.46, and 10.44). Those in the second group were more closely allied to the branch of pre-World

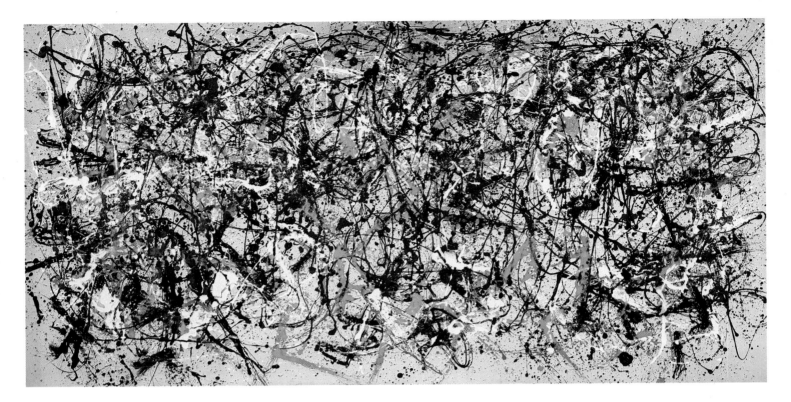

▲ 10 · 66

Jackson Pollock, *Autumn Rhythm*, 1957. Oil on canvas, 8 ft 9 in × 17 ft 3 in (2.67 × 5.26 m).

This artist is considered the prime example of youthful Abstract-Expressionist Action painters in the late 1940s. He is noted primarily for creating swirling nonrepresentational images in linear skeins of fast-drying paint which are dripped directly onto canvases through controlled gestures of his tools.

Metropolitan Museum of Art, New York. George A. Hearn Fund, 1957. © 1994 The Pollock-Krasner Foundation/ARS, NY.

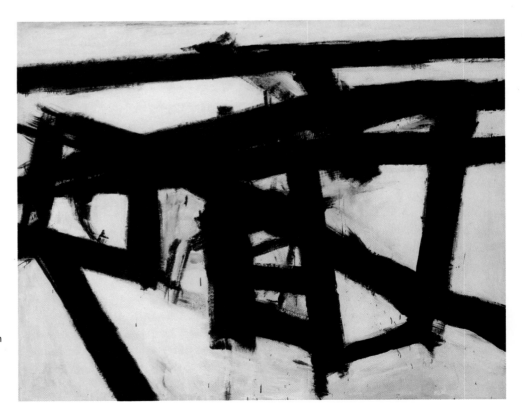

▶ 10 · 67

Franz Kline, *Mahoning*, 1956. Oil on canvas, 6 ft 8 in × 8 ft 4 in (2.03 × 2.54 m).

The artist was more interested in the actual physical action involved in this type of expression than in the character of the resulting painting.

Collection of the Whitney Museum of American Art, New York. Purchase, with funds from the Friends of the Whitney Museum of American Art, 57.10.

War II geometric abstraction, whose overriding influence in the United States was Piet Mondrian (see fig. 1.3). Hans Hofmann also played a major influential role (see fig. 8.48).

The Action group Jackson Pollock and Franz Kline were two of the outstanding artists of the "Action" group. They worked in a way that was reminiscent not only of Kandinsky's prewar biomorphic expressionism, and of Surrealism, but also, in their brush technique, of Impressionism. Confusion, fear, and uncertainty about humanity's place in a world threatened by thermonuclear holocaust may have led such painters to reject most previous forms of twentieth-century art and, as a kind of personal catharsis, to express their belief in the "value of doing" at the expense of disciplined design. For example, Jackson Pollock is frequently cited as the sole originator of the "gesture," on which *Action painting* was founded. His swirling,

nonrepresentational images, created out of linear skeins of fast-drying paint dripped directly onto large canvases, expressed through the direct act of creation the reality of self (fig. 10.66).

Franz Kline followed a slightly different course but with a similar intention of expressing self through direct contact with the forms created. His drawings were made with gestures of a brush on newsprint, then cut up and reassembled to provide a sense of power, movement and an intensified personal rapport. Kline used these "sketches" as guides and enlarged them with loaded brushes on large canvases without directly copying them. Applied with a house painter's brush, his savage slashings in black and white, or sometimes color, became monumental projections of inward experiences (fig. 10.67).

The daring and willingness to explore the unknown self that such artists displayed were also expected of the viewer. This conscious attempt to involve the spectator in art is, perhaps, the leitmotif

of the second half of the twentieth century, going far beyond a similar endeavor in much previous art. Perhaps one of the reasons for recent efforts among artists to involve the viewer is the increased awareness of the pressures and aberration caused by urban life; art serves as a tonic for helping people to escape, if only momentarily, their sordid surroundings. We must remember that the early careers of many of these New York artists had been marked by neglect and deprivation.

▼ **10 · 68**

Robert Motherwell, *Elegy to the Spanish Republic #131*, 1974. Oil on canvas, 8 × 10 ft (2.44 × 3.05 m).
Motherwell's work is characterized by an intimacy and heroic scale commonly found in Abstract Expressionism.
Detroit Institute of Arts, Detroit, MI. Founders Society Purchase. W. Hawkins Ferry Fund. © Estate Robert Motherwell/DACS, London/VAGA, New York 1994.

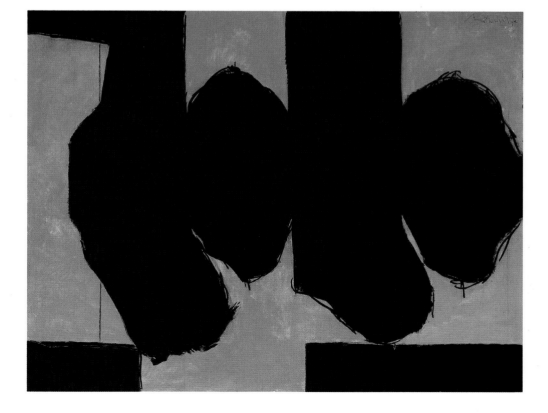

The Color Field group The second group of artists within Abstract Expressionism, known as the *Color Field painters*, appear to have been concerned primarily with reducing form to the sensations produced by color-filled canvases. Shape, value, line(s), and combinations of elements often played a role in this type of painting. Typical of this group were Robert Motherwell, Barnett Newman, Morris Louis, and Ad Reinhardt (figs. 10.68, 10.69, and 10.70; see figs. 2.15 and 10.47). (Ad Reinhardt will be considered later as part of the Minimalist group, for artists frequently move on to other ways of working.) Many artists in Color Field painting drew not only on Piet Mondrian and Hans Hofmann, but were also motivated by the subtle color relationships of Joseph Albers, who, like Kandinsky, was a former teacher at the Bauhaus (see fig. 4.25).

Both Action and Color Field paintings are meant to enwrap the spectator, and make him or her a part of the painting through shared sensation. The work of Color Fieldists was not as emotionally fervid as that of their Action painting counterparts, aiming, instead, for quieter insinuations on the viewer's being. Barnett Newman later went on to identify himself with Hard-Edge Abstraction, paralleling Reinhardt's move to Minimalism (see fig. 10.69). Morris Louis is considered another important Color Field painter because of his novel method of staining canvases by pouring handsome tones of color in overlapping thin washes. These paintings came close to approximating the "gestures" of the Action group (see fig. 10.70). Helen Frankenthaler also explored this technique, modifying it somewhat by using unprimed canvases into which her brilliant colors soaked (see fig. 4.27).

Surreal and Abstract-Expressionist sculpture

Many sculptors worked in forms allied to Surrealism, but with a greater degree of formality. These ranged from the organically sleek figures of the Englishman Henry Moore (fig. 10.71) to the built-up, open-wire, and welded sculptures prefigured by the forms of González and Picasso in the 1930s. Among those influenced by wire or linear sculpture was the maker of mobiles, Alexander Calder. González, as the pioneer of welded sculpture, must also be credited with influencing a younger generation of sculptors like Theodore Roszak and David Smith. Their extension of González's technique came as close as their medium of bronze, iron, and steel permitted to the Action painting of the Abstract-Expressionist painters. Dadaism and Surrealism influenced the Neo-Dadaist or "junk" sculpture of men like John Chamberlain, Richard Stankiewicz and Robert Mallary in the late fifties and sixties.

Henry Moore merged the vitality and expressive potential of González and Arp with such older traditions as Egyptian, African, and pre-Columbian sculpture, which he had discovered as a student.

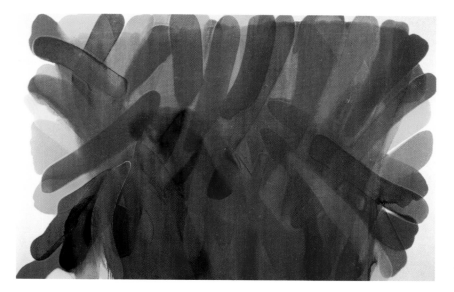

△ 10·70
Morris Louis, *Number 99*, 1959. Acrylic on canvas, 8 ft 3 in × 11 ft 10 in (2.51 × 3.61 m).
The Color Field painter Morris Louis pioneered the technique of flooding the canvas with liquid pigments, which rendered his stripes and shapes soft-edged and almost intangible. Louis was also one of the earliest painters to explore spray-painting.
Contemporary Collection of the Cleveland Museum of Art, 68.110, Cleveland, OH.

▽ 10·71
Henry Moore, *Reclining Figure*, 1939. Carved elm wood, 37 × 79 × 30 in (94 × 201 × 76 cm).
Moore's work is a synthesis of influences from primitive sculpture, Surrealism, and a lifelong study of the forms of nature.
Detroit Institute of Arts, Detroit, MI. Gift of Dexter M. Ferry, Jr., Trustee Corporation.

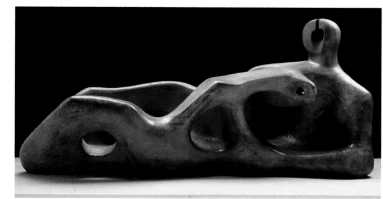

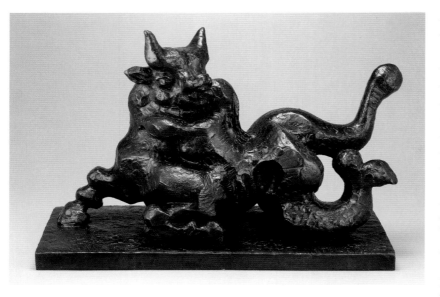

▲ 10 · 72

Jacques Lipchitz, *Rape of Europa*, 1938. Bronze, 16 × 23 in (40.6 × 58.4 cm).

After an early exposure to Cubism, Lipchitz developed his unique sculptural shapes and personal symbolism, but his Cubist background always served as a disciplinary force.

Art Institute of Chicago. Gift of an anonymous donor, 1943.594. © Estate Jacques Lipchitz/DACS, London/ VAGA, New York 1994.

▼ 10 · 73

Alexander Calder, *Oscar*, 1971. Painted steel, 25 × 25 ft (7.62 × 7.62 m).

A late work by the famous inventor of movable sculpture combines portions of moving (mobile) and static (stabile) forms.

Toledo Museum of Art, Toledo, OH. Gift of Dayton Hudson Department Store Company. © ADAGP, Paris and DACS, London 1994.

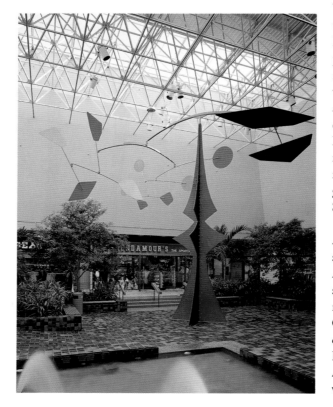

Moore's objective over the years was to create lively, though not lifelike, forms. His sculptures emphasize the natural qualities of the selected materials; only secondarily do they resemble human forms. In this respect, his frequently repeated theme of the reclining nude seems to retain in stone a geologically inspired character, and in wood a sense of organic growth and an emphasis on the natural grain. Moore was primarily responsible for reestablishing British art on the international scene and laid the basis for the great vitality British art has shown in the twentieth century.

The Lithuanian sculptor Jacques Lipchitz, who worked in France before World War I and was strongly influenced by Cubism at the time, began to be concerned with the Surrealist idiom in the 1930s. He developed a highly robust configuration of freely flowing, knotted, and twisted masses that evoke at times the agonies of birth, death, and psychic torment, and at others nameless new species of mythological monsters. The horrors of the Jewish holocaust in World War II were in the minds of many of these artists. From Surrealism Lipchitz had also gleaned the semiautomatic principle, kneading his favorite sketching medium of clay into shapeless blobs without forethought. Then, through the accident of suggested form, he would construct the finished piece (fig. 10.72). Lipchitz, whose fame became international, came to the United States in 1941 and strongly influenced a younger generation of American Abstract-Surrealist sculptors.

Certainly one of the most significant American pioneers of Surreal-Abstract sculpture was the Philadelphia-born Alexander Calder. Calder's father was a sculptor working in a conservative nineteenth-century Realist style. At first, Calder reacted to this academic conservatism by training as an engineer. However, he was soon ensconced at the Art Students League in New York, from where, in 1926, he left for Paris. There he began to create the wire sculptures of animals that won him almost immediate recognition. In the late 1920s he was mingling in Dada, Surrealist, and abstract circles, meeting people like Miró, Duchamp, Mondrian, Arp, and González. These new associations led him to drop figurative work for free-form abstract shapes of sheet metal and wire, and by 1930 he had created the first of his mobiles. His earlier kinetic assemblages had been powered by motors and pulleys; but the delicate balance and perfect engineering of the mobiles needed only air currents to create rhythmic, varied motion, producing ever new compositions and relationships of shapes in space (see fig. 9.34). Thus, Calder was able to express the fourth dimension of time and movement in space, for which artists, with their implied kinetics, had been searching since the beginnings of Impressionism.

Calder evolved three basic types of assemblage (a term invented by Marcel Duchamp in 1950):

1. The *stabile* is usually attached to a base, can rest on the ground, and does not move. However, some later ones were made with moving parts.
2. The *mobile* hangs in the air, usually from a ceiling.
3. The *constellation* is a form of mobile that is usually suspended on one or more arms from a wall.

Mobiles are probably one of the most popular forms of modern art, and Calder is thus considered by many as among the most important American artists of the twentieth century. From 1933 until his death in 1976, Calder divided his time between farms in Connecticut and France, where he created, toward the end of his career, monumental stabiles and stabile/ mobiles of welded iron, some of which were architectural in scale (fig. 10.73).

Some of the most interesting new shapes and techniques in sculpture of the late 1940s and early 1950s suggested an affinity with Abstract-Expressionistic painting. One artist whose creations highlight this link is the Polish-born sculptor Theodore Roszak. Roszak began his career before World War II as a Constructivist of severely geometric shapes, but later underwent a complete change. He became engrossed in portraying the conflict inherent in natural phenomena as a metaphor for humanity's potential to destroy itself. Roszak employed coarse, eroded, scarred, and pitted textures, as in *Mandrake* (1951), which, with its spiked and anguished skeletal angularities, expresses some of the terror of the nuclear age (fig. 10.74).

The promising career of David Smith, an Illinois native who studied painting at the Art Students League in New York during the late 1920s and early 1930s, was cut short by a fatal automobile accident in 1965. In the thirties, pictures of González's and Picasso's Surrealist sculptures awoke his interest in creating similar Surreal-Abstract forms. Their influence helped him to originate welded sculpture, and he was reportedly the earliest American artist to employ this technique. Smith usually investigated linear sculptures and volumetric shape systems at the same time. Smith's use of such materials as welded sheets of

▼ **10 · 74**

Theodore Roszak, *Mandrake*, 1951. Steel brazed with copper, 25½ × 40 × 11¾ in (64.8 × 101.6 × 29.8 cm).

In sculptural forms that paralleled the Action painting of the late 1940s, artists like Roszak employed welding techniques to capture, through spiked angular shapes and corroded porous surfaces, some of the anxieties of the nuclear age.

Cleveland Museum of Art, Cleveland, OH. Gift of the Cleveland Society for Contemporary Art, 64.4.

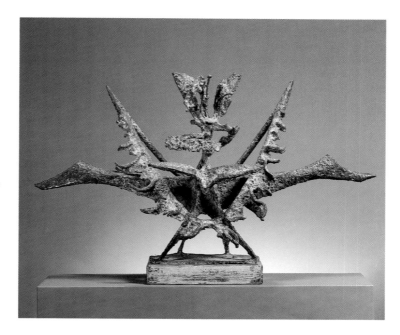

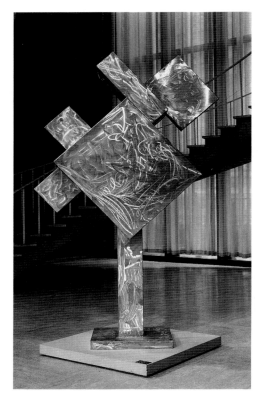

wrought iron and steel give his sculptures an undeniable power, reminiscent of both Cubism and Constructivism and the Action painting of Franz Kline. The slashing diagonals of his linear forms and metal cubes, in particular, remind one of Kline's black diagonals against their flat white-canvas surfaces. Smith's last cubic style before his death influenced the next generation of sculptors, who, like their counterparts in painting, broke away from the metaphysical subjectivism of Abstract Expressionism (fig. 10.75).

Other artists often used organic formations with varying degrees of openness or closedness, suggesting an involvement with Surrealist preconscious imagery resolved by Cubist, Constructivist,

or abstract formality. Among such sculptors was Reuben Nakian (fig. 10.76). Nakian, however, appears to be more closely related to the free-form manner of such earlier twentieth-century artists as Gaston Lachaise, his teacher, while avoiding their more obviously representational effects. Jacques Lipchitz was one of the Abstract-Surrealist sources Nakian might have drawn upon, and he seems to have preferred the more porous surfaces used by his peers in the 1950s to the smoothly refined surfaces of Lachaise or earlier abstractionists like Brancusi.

Another distinguished international sculptor is the Japanese-American, or Nisei, Isamu Noguchi, who studied in New York, Japan, and France. He was in

▲ **10 · 75**

David Smith, *Cubi VII*, 1963. Stainless steel, 9 ft 3⅜ in (2.83 m) high.
Smith was rarely concerned with likeness to natural objects. Instead, he used nonobjective forms and tried to give them a life of their own through his animated arrangement.
Art Institute of Chicago. Grant J. Pick Purchase Fund, 1964.1141. © Estate of David Smith/DACS, London/ VAGA, New York 1994.

▼ **10 · 76**

Reuben Nakian, *Goddess of the Golden Thighs*, 1964–66. Metal, bronze cast, 8 ft 8½ in × 12 ft (2.64 × 3.66 m).
Nakian roughcast his sculptural forms to take full advantage of the emotion-evoking qualities of the resulting texture, rather than use the more smoothly finished forms employed by his teacher, Gaston Lachaise (see fig. 10.33). His abstractions also invoke surreal inward forces that have a life of their own.
Detroit Institute of Arts, Detroit, MI. Founders Society Purchase, W. Hawkins Ferry Fund.

▼ **10 · 77**

Isamu Noguchi (and Shoji Sadao), *California Scenario*, located at Two Town Center, Costa Mesa, California, 1981–82.
The work of the great Japanese-American sculptor Isamu Noguchi ranged from pure abstract through Surreal-Abstract and Minimalist styles, but he is equally well-known for his architecturally oriented plazas in various parts of the world.
Courtesy of the Isamu Noguchi Foundation Inc., Long Island City, NY. (Photograph by Gary McKinnis.)

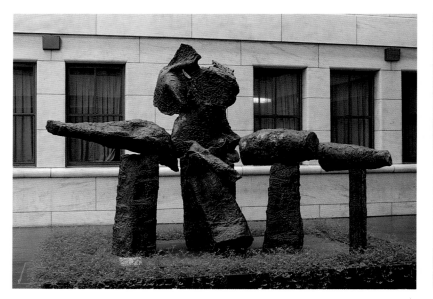

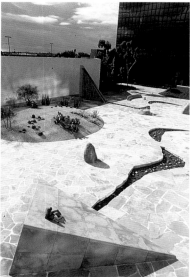

Paris on a Guggenheim fellowship at the height of Cubist and Surrealist domination. Particularly important was his study with Brancusi; he also became acquainted with Calder while in France. His first exhibit, of Constructivist-like sculpture, took place in New York in 1929. Noguchi was soon widely recognized as an important sculptor, but over his career also pursued interests in architectural landscape, furniture, and theatrical design. Always aware of both his Asian heritage and Western origins, his sculpture, with a sense of grace and elegance, makes use of a kind of Surreal-Abstract biomorphics. Noguchi's style, however, ranged from near Surrealism to something approaching Minimalism (see fig. 9.1). One of Noguchi's distinguished landscape designs and sculptures can be seen in the Plaza at Costa Mesa, California (fig. 10.77). Perhaps through his association with Brancusi, Noguchi has always shown an inclination for a complete mastery of craft, which entails the use of beautiful materials. His preferred taste was for stone, which shows how Noguchi cherished color. Color adds an inestimable charm to his works, whether small or very large.

Abstract Expressionism and photography

In the years after World War II there were at least two photographers whose work continued to show the straight photographic influence of Stieglitz and his group, while bearing a resemblance to the Abstract-Expressionist painting then developing. The most important of these photographers was Minor White. His background of psychology and religious studies provided a basis for the expressive sensitivity seen at work in his photography. White also wrote poetry and sometimes used it in conjunction with photographs to enhance their meaning. Although he generally created straight images of a Realist kind (see fig. 1.15), White often favored two forms tending towards abstraction – the *Equivalents*, based on those of Stieglitz (fig. 10.78), and the *Sequences*, which he invented. The *Sequences* appear to draw upon organic natural forms, and while often obscure in form and meaning, generally seem to concern White's own feelings, as do the *Equivalents*. His photographs were often metaphysical, expressive of the fears and tensions of his time, and were probably a form of personal catharsis. White's imagery was masterly and beautiful in its use of detail,

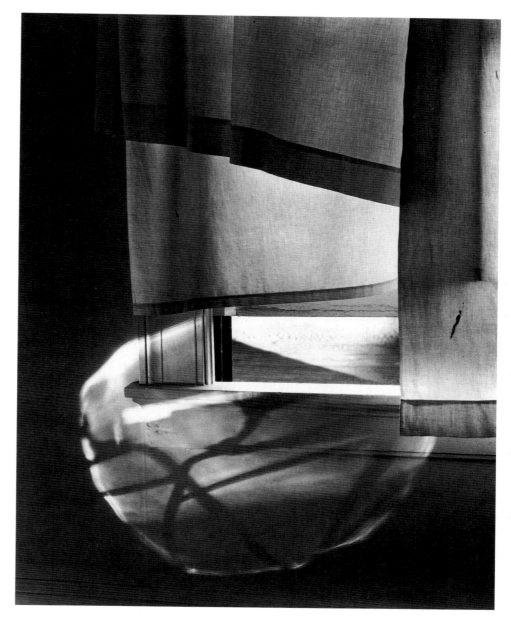

▲ **10·78**

Minor White, *Windowsill Daydreaming*, 1958. Photograph.

A follower of Stieglitz's straight photography, White applied his knowledge of religion and psychology to his photography. His study of early morning sunlight pouring through a window has an almost mystical sensitivity.

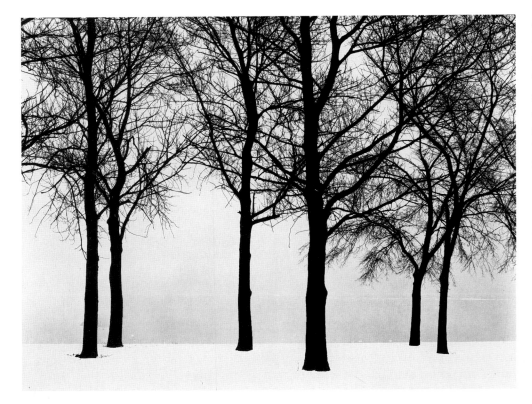

▲ **10·79**

Harry Callahan, *Chicago*, **1950.**
Photograph.
Callahan's work always reveals a concern with pattern and is notable for its strong values, sparse realism and poetic simplicity. The linear starkness of the trees superimposed on an almost featureless background is reminiscent of the Color Field Abstract Expressionists.
© Harry Callahan. Courtesy of the Pace/MacGill Gallery, New York.

texture, and value relationships, or luminosity. The reasons for his importance as a force in creative photography are multiple: the frequent exhibits of his work; his association as a staff member of the George Eastman House; his editing of the influential *Aperture* journal; his teaching and workshops, held at technological institutes across the country – all contributed to his respected position.

A second post-World War II photographer whose work sometimes seems akin to Abstract-Expressionist painting was Harry Callahan. Early in his

career, he became interested in pattern and design, creating images reminiscent of Paul Strand and Edward Steichen. Callahan's main source of inspiration was the second generation of Stieglitz-influenced photographers – Ansel Adams and Edward Weston. To some degree, he also emerged from the Bauhaus tradition of Moholy-Nagy at the Chicago Institute of Design (sometimes called the American Bauhaus). From the 1940s on he worked in a multitude of styles which always showed his interests in form; his subjects ranged from nudes and street photographs to multiple-exposure abstractions. Callahan's more abstract works are often akin to those of the Color Field painters – even the realistic trees of *Chicago*, 1950, can conjure up the stark lines of a Newman or Noland against a single color ground (fig. 10.79). It is this range from dark to light, this sparse realism and lyrical simplicity, which make Callahan's work notable. Like White, Callahan was a teacher, setting up the later highly admired and popular program at the Chicago Institute of Design.

ART FORMS OF THE LATE 1950s, 1960s, AND 1970s

Throughout history new generations of artists have become dissatisfied with the route taken by their elders and, therefore, struck out in new directions. The feeling that inherited methods and media have reached a state of perfection or exhausted their possibilities has been especially keen among artists of the twentieth century and increasingly so since mid-century. Among the strong motivations for change have been the development of motion pictures and other technological advances in photography, machinery, electronics, and space flight.

Drawn by these technological innovations, artists have often met the desire for change by refusing to observe the separate categories of painting and sculpture, instead merging the two in assemblages. This mixture of hitherto separate disciplines has its closest parallel in Baroque art of the seventeenth century, in which a similar intermingling of traditionally separate media and disciplines took place. Some artists have explored film, video, dance, and theater, and, more recently, laser- and computer-generated art. A fusion of computer technology with video, particularly, has been of great significance.

▷ **10·80**

Kenneth Noland, *Wild Indigo*, **1967. Acrylic on canvas, 7 ft 5 in × 17 ft 3 in (2.26 × 5.26 m).**
Noland's Hard-Edge, nonobjective painting is descended from Cubist works like Léger's. Without the benefit of any representation, the meanings we intuit in such a work are less obvious and appeal to the intellect. Compared to a biomorphic work such as Matta's *Listen to Living* (see fig. 4.5), with its soft edges and emotional implications, we must seek meaning in Noland through a more cerebral approach.
Albright-Knox Art Gallery, Buffalo, NY. Charles Clifton Fund, 1972. © Kenneth Noland/DACS, London/ VAGA, New York 1994.

Hard-Edge and Minimalist art

The first serious challenge to the dominance of Abstract Expressionism after World War II was among a group of painters known as the Post-Painterly Abstractionists. This category of painting breaks down into Hard-Edge painters, Color Field painters, and Minimalists. All owe a debt to early twentieth-century geometric abstraction, particularly that of Joseph Albers. After coming to the United States, Albers, a product of the German Bauhaus tradition, did a series of paintings during the 1930s called *Homage to the Square* (see fig. 4.25). In this series his interest in *Gestalt* psychology is expressed through the effects of optical illusion. He created passive, free-floating square shapes which had just enough contrast of value, hue, and intensity with surrounding colors to be able to emerge slightly from the background.

Albers's successors, Hard-Edge painters like Ellsworth Kelly, stress definition of edges or shapes that are set off more explicitly than in the work of the earlier Color Field Abstract Expressionists (see

fig. 2.10). Color Field painting continued in the hands of such artists as Kenneth Noland, Frank Stella, and Larry Poons (fig. 10.80; see fig. 2.12). Most of them use stripes or bands of color moving in different directions, or spots and shapes of various kinds – specific combinations of these are trademarks of their individual styles.

Minimalists, of whom the nonconformist New Yorker Ad Reinhardt was a key figure in the late 1950s, painted pictures in such close values that only after intense concentration could the spectator determine that any shapes or lines or other elements of form were present at all (fig. 10.81).

Another characteristic of Post-Painterly Abstraction was the tendency either to thin down the pigments to stain, to soak the canvas in color, or to lay color on in such thin layers that the work seems to be entirely without texture except for that of the canvas support (ground) on which it was painted. Morris Louis's *Number 99* (1959) is an example (see fig. 10.70); and Helen Frankenthaler, as mentioned earlier, used a very similar technique (see fig. 4.27).

▲ 10 · 81

Ad Reinhardt, *Abstract Painting, Blue 1953*, 1953. Oil on canvas, 50 × 28 in (127 × 71.1 cm).

This Reinhardt work is an example of Minimalist painting, in which the values are so close that only intense scrutiny can reveal differences of shape within.

Collection of the Whitney Museum of American Art, New York. Gift of Susan Morse Hilles 74.22.

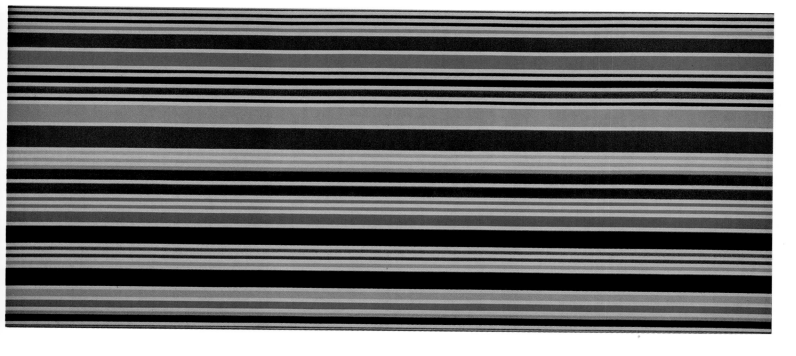

Neo-Dada, Assemblage, Pop art, and Performance art

Neo-Dada, another branch of Post-Painterly Abstraction, led directly to a significant trend of the 1950s and 1960s: Pop art. Robert Rauschenberg was one of the first to drift away from pure Abstract Expressionism. He combined pure, fluid brushwork in pigments with foreign materials like old mattresses, wireless sets,

▼ **10 · 82**

Robert Rauschenberg, *Monogram with Ram*, 1955–59. Construction (free-standing combine), 3 ft 6 in × 5 ft 3¼ in × 5 ft 4½ in (1.07 × 1.61 × 1.64 m).

In this combine-painting which merges into three-dimensional assemblage, one can witness the drift away from the pure painting of the 1950s. Such work provided a platform for the Pop art movement which followed shortly.

Courtesy of the National Museum, Stockholm, Sweden. © Robert Rauschenberg/DACS, London/ VAGA, New York 1994.

photographic images and stuffed animals attached to the canvas. From Rauschenberg's combine-paintings also came much of the new art of assemblage (fig. 10.82; see fig. 6.10), a term used before in relation to Calder's distinctive works.

Jasper Johns, an American artist more satirical in his approach than Rauschenberg, was equally important in pointing the new direction away from Abstract Expressionism. He chose as his chief motif single images of commonplace objects that had lost their effectiveness, such as the United States flag, targets, and the like (see fig. 7.33).

The trend away from Abstract Expressionism in various forms culminated in the early 1960s in a movement called *Pop art*. The term Pop stands for "popular art" or even for "pop bottle art," judging by the frequency with which such mundane objects appeared. The movement as a whole originated in England in the fifties and then naturally filtered through to the United States. In it, images made popular by mass-media

advertising and comic strips, and other everyday objects, such as pop bottles, beer cans, and supermarket products, are presented in bizarre combinations, distortions, or exaggerations of size. The original human-made object is always rendered faithfully, however. Such works as Andy Warhol's Campbell's soup cans or Roy Lichtenstein's grotesquely magnified comic-strip heroes and villains are capable of startling the viewer – the shock of the familiar in a new context (figs. 10.83 and 10.84). As with Abstract Expressionism, the observer is involved directly in the work of art, if only because of the frequency with which the observer sees these commonplace items. The blurring between art and real life in Pop art is more pronounced in the Pop-originated Happening. Happenings were a form of participatory art in which spectators, as well as artists, were engaged. They have been defined as an assemblage on the move, bringing in concepts of motion, time, and space. More recently this type of art has been called *Performance Art*, expanding its approach to include theater, dance, cinema, and video.

Happenings were based on the ancient concept of drawing spectators into the heart of a work of art so that they can experience the work more directly. This concept reached its first climax in Baroque art of the seventeenth century when, as mentioned earlier in this chapter, the disciplines overseen by the Medieval guilds had finally lost their technical control over the artist. From the Renaissance on, the religious iconography and media used by artists were intermingled in an artistic fabric (the church building) that was unified within itself. However, the completion of this unifying process was dependent on the spectator's participation in the artistic experience.

Since similar experiences were promoted by the Dadaists in 1916, some of the Pop artists were also called Neo-Dadaists. But whereas Dada was nihilistic, self-exterminating, and satirical,

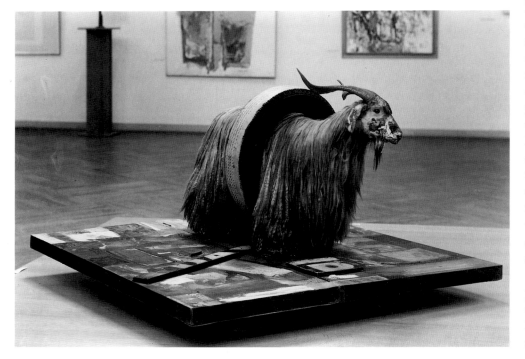

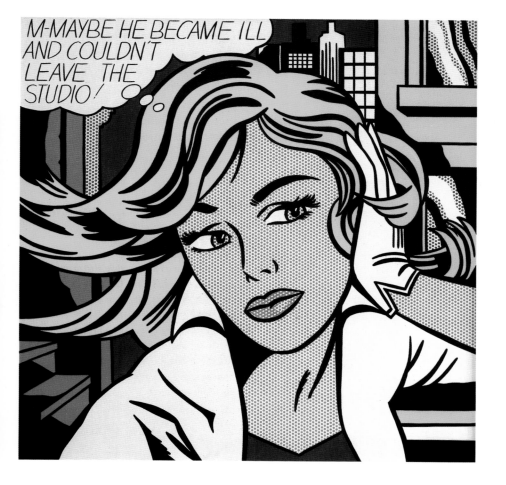

◀ **10 · 83**

Andy Warhol, *100 Cans*, 1962. Oil on canvas, 6 ft × 4 ft 4 in (1.83 × 1.32 m).
Warhol's *100 Cans* beats a repetitive visual tattoo whose power derives from the insistence of similar commercial imagery in our daily lives. Repetition of a more or less monotonous kind was one of the principles of form exploited first by the Pop artists.

Albright-Knox Art Gallery, Buffalo, NY. Gift of Seymour H. Knox, 1963.

◀ **10 · 84**

Roy Lichtenstein, *M-Maybe*, 1965. Oil and magna on canvas, 5 ft × 5 ft (1.52 × 1.52 m).
Lichtenstein's use of magnified comic-strip heroes and heroines is typical of Pop art's playful treatment of popular culture.

Ludwig Gallery, Cologne, Germany. (Photograph: Rheinisches Bildarchiv.) © Roy Lichtenstein/DACS 1994.

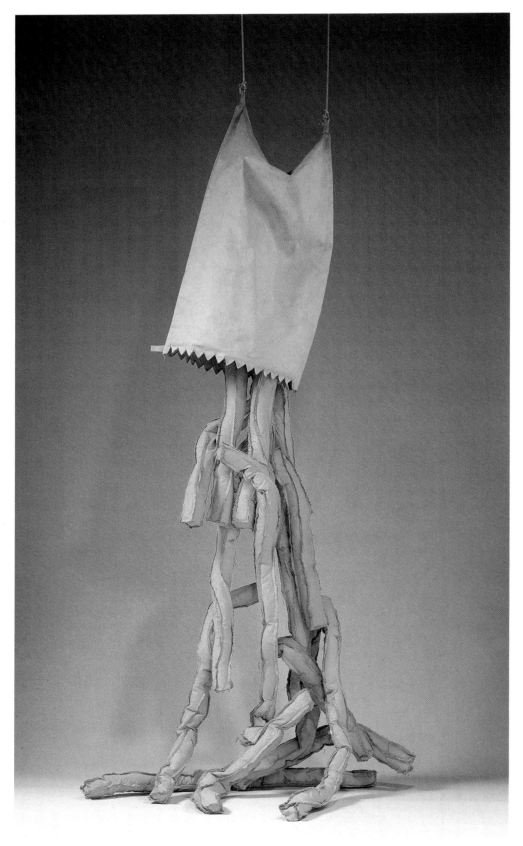

Pop art had little of this purpose. Instead, it encouraged an awareness and acceptance of the fact that mass media communications have a tremendous impact on our daily lives. There was a kind of joyful enthusiasm for exploring the possibilities thrown up by the daily images and objects of a metropolitan culture. From billboards to bar interiors, from grocery-store cans and boxes to the bathtubs and sinks of the average house interior came the realist subjects of Pop art – a reaction, in part, to the inwardly directed and cerebral art of Abstract Expressionism.

Significant artists of the Pop persuasion, besides Warhol and Lichtenstein, are: Robert Indiana, Tom Wesselmann, Claes Oldenburg, Marisol Escobar, and George Segal (see figs. 2.6 and 2.57). The latter three are sculptors or assemblers, fields in which Pop art made as many inroads as painting (figs. 10.85 and 10.86). The Venezuelan-born Marisol, in particular, reveals how Pop art carried over into environmental art. Marisol often uses her own image as a foundation for her gawky, part humorous, part melancholic assemblages of wood, plaster, paint, and other materials (see fig. 9.33). The environmental concept was an important development in the 1960s. We shall see that it continued into the 1970s and 1980s with renewed vigor.

◀   10 · 85

Claes Oldenburg, *Shoestring Potatoes Falling from a Bag,* **1966. Canvas, kapok, glue, acrylic, 9 ft × 3 ft 10 in × 3 ft 6 in (2.74 × 1.17 × 106.7 m).**

Pop artists generally disregard all form considerations, which they believe create a barrier between the observer and the everyday objects that serve as subjects. Pop art is an art rooted in the present.

Collection of the Walker Art Center, Minneapolis, MN. Gift of the T. B. Walker Foundation, 1966.

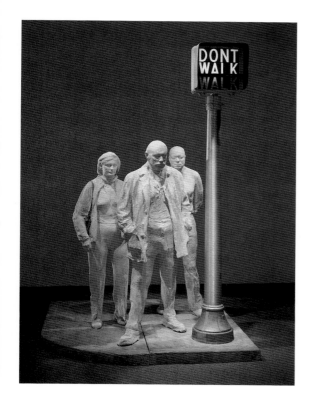

◄ **10·86**

George Segal, *Walk, Don't Walk*, 1976. Plaster, cement, metal, painted wood, and electric light, 8 ft 8 in × 6 ft × 6 ft (2.64 × 1.83 × 1.83 m).

In 1961, this artist began to win fame for his plaster-casts of living people. Dressing them in ordinary clothing and placing them in everyday situations, Segal was able to break down the barriers between life and art – a familiar preoccupation with Pop artists.

Collection of the Whitney Museum of American Art, New York. © George Segal/DACS, London/VAGA, New York 1994.

The popularity of assemblage and the enhancement of the Dada idea of the "found object" led to a revival of "junk" sculpture. The Dadaists – as well as Picasso – can be said to have pioneered the use of "found objects" as works of art – see Marcel Duchamp's *Bicycle Wheel* (fig. 10.54) and Picasso's work from about 1914 on (see fig. 10.52); but ultimately, all similar forms of art stem from Picasso's and Braque's experiments with collage in the early part of the century. It is not too surprising to find, therefore, that the "junk" that later twentieth-century artists used, drawing as they did on these earlier experiments, often included scrapped fragments of such industrial forms as automobiles, farm machinery, factory parts, airplanes, tubes, and pipes. There was a satire implicit in the use of many of these items: they were often the cast-offs of an overly affluent and wasteful society. John Chamberlain's sculptures, made from the parts of wrecked automobiles, and those of Richard Stankiewicz, created by welding together old boilers, sinks, and the like, are a kind of comment on consumer culture that can also be found in Pop art (fig. 10.87). The artists just

mentioned are American, but Europeans like César work along similar lines.

Edward Kienholz's works, which he calls tableaux, also fall into the category of assemblages. His varied combinations of materials have something of the shock value of Dada art, making pungent comment on the sickness, tawdriness, and melancholy of modern society (fig. 10.88).

Early in her career, Louise Nevelson was using smooth abstract shapes in a way comparable to Henry Moore. Later, when she moved toward assemblage, she developed her own distinct style by fitting together ready-made wooden shapes, such as knobs, bannisters, moldings, and posts gleaned from demolished houses and old furniture. These fragments were articulated into boxlike compartments – various-sized rectangles and squares that became large screens or freestanding walls. These complex pieces were usually painted a uniform color, which stressed the unified relationship between the parts. The relationships and complexities of Nevelson's forms seem in keeping with a recent trend toward Process Art, but her final results are often more exciting than those of artists like the Minimalists, who

▼ **10·87**

John Angus Chamberlain, *Untitled*, 1958–59. Painted and welded metal, 32½ × 26½ × 24 in (82.6 × 67.3 × 61 cm).

The popularity of assemblage, enhanced by the Dadaist idea of the "found object," led to the junk ethos of metal and other material form combinations. During the 1950s and 1960s, artists of this persuasion, like Chamberlain, who worked with bent and crushed metal from old automobiles, were dubbed Neo-Dadaists.

Cleveland Museum of Art, Cleveland, OH. Andrew R. and Martha Holden Jennings Fund, 73.27.

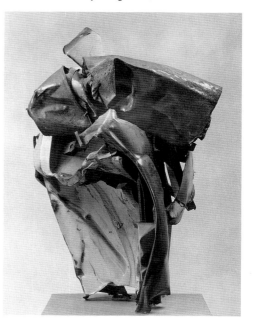

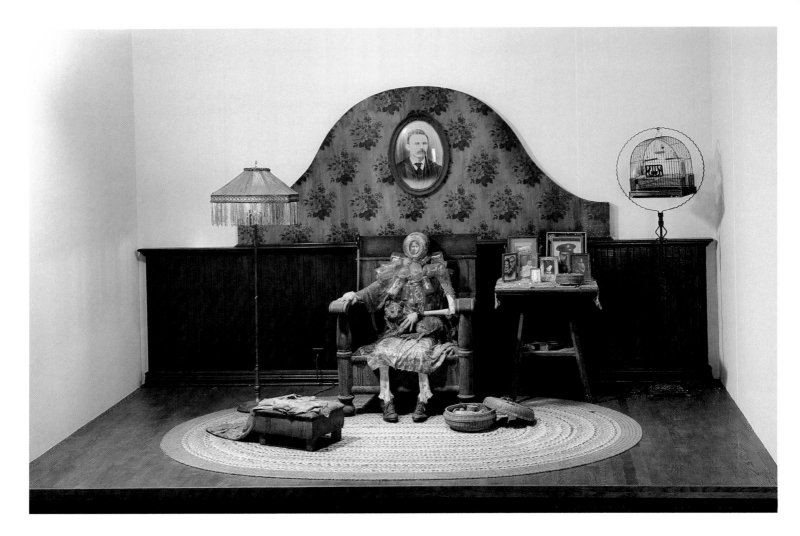

▲ **10 · 88**

Edward Kienholz, *The Wait*, 1964–65. Mixed media (tableau), 6 ft 8 in × 12 ft 4 in × 6 ft 6 in (2.03 × 3.76 × 1.98 m).

This artist belongs to a branch of assemblage art sometimes known as environments. His tableaux of the old, the derelict, and the mentally ill are comments on the sickness, tawdriness, and melancholy of modern society.

Collection of the Whitney Museum of American Art, New York. Gift of the Howard and Jean Lipman Foundation, Inc., 66.49.

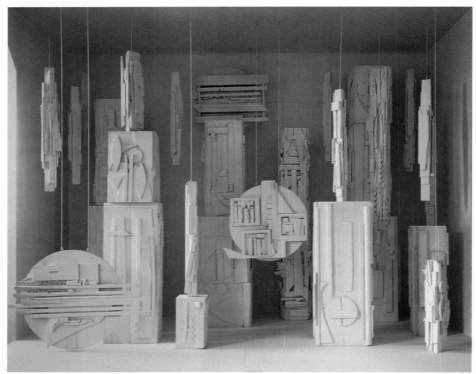

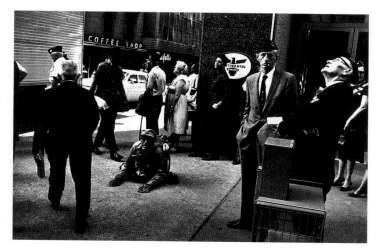

often emphasized process over form or content (fig. 10.89).

In the late fifties and sixties, accompanying the tongue-in-cheek irony and humor of Pop art's new look at rampant consumerism in the United States, came a related way of photographing American life. It was introduced by a Swiss-born American, Robert Frank, through his photographic book entitled *America*. In a style descended from the direct social commentary of the Farm Security Administration photographers during the Depression, Frank was able, through a Guggenheim grant in 1955, to travel with his camera throughout the country. Frank took a somewhat detached, if critical, view of the triviality, banality, and apparent isolation of the individuals he

saw on his travels. His apparently random "snapshots" of events are undergirded, however, by a tight structure, and were carefully planned to intensify the rather crude and harsh quality of people's circumstances. Frank influenced a new generation of photographers, epitomized by the work of Garry Winogrand (fig. 10.90). But his style has become so widely employed in recent times that it no longer seems so novel or fresh a vision.

Op art

The "Op" in Op art is an abbreviation of "optical." This form of art is primarily graphic, although it merges into three-dimensionality when the colors used in paintings provide the illusion of relief. Op art is, once more, an extension and modification of earlier twentieth-century geometric abstraction and nonobjectivity. Even while some artists were opposing the relative obscurity of meaning in modern abstraction, others chose to send abstract art in yet another direction. Among the artists who chose to do this were the kinetic and light sculptors, the New Realists, the Minimalist or Primary Structurist sculptors, and the Op artists themselves. Significant members of the Op movement (many again influenced by Albers) included Victor Vasarely, Richard Anuszkiewicz, Agam (Yaacov Gipstein),

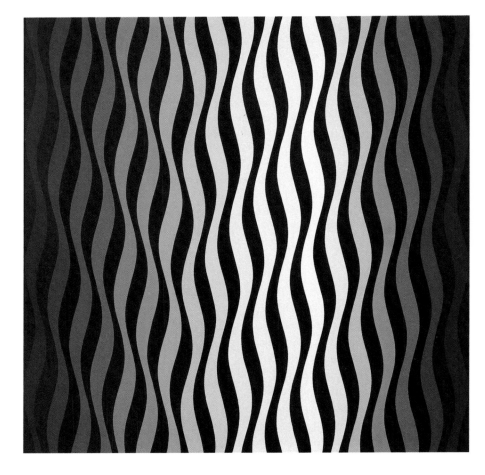

▲ 10·91
Bridget Riley, *Drift No. 2*, 1966. Acrylic on canvas, 7 ft 7½ in × 7 ft 5½ in (2.32 × 2.27 m).

Op artists generally use geometric shapes, organizing them into patterns that produce fluctuating, ambiguous, and tantalizing visual effects very similar to those observed in moiré patterns, such as in door or window screens.

Albright-Knox Art Gallery, Buffalo, NY. Gift of Seymour H. Knox, 1967.

and Bridget Riley (fig. 10.91; see figs. 2.24 and 2.34). These artists employed precise shapes, sometimes wriggly lines, or concentric patterns which have a direct impact on the physiology and psychology of vision. They explored wavy patterns that seem dedicated more to the scientific investigation of vision than to its evocative expression in art.

Kinetics and light

Kinetic forms of art are those that create movement, while those that create light may take various forms – from incandescence and fluorescence to reflectiveness. Light sculptures often combine materials: "assemblage" might, therefore, be a more appropriate term for such artworks.

Obviously kinetics are partly derived from Calder's motor-driven, wire and wood circus of the 1920s and later mobiles, but they also owe their origins to Dadaism and Op art. Dadaists, under the aegis of their antitraditional and destructive credo, created the first examples of actual movement or kinetics in art. The earliest examples can be found in the work of Marcel Duchamp. For a short period in the twenties, he became fascinated by the swirling designs produced by phonograph turntables or disks driven by other rotating means. Duchamp, however, soon lost interest in movement, unlike Calder.

Many kinetic artworks use a mechanical means to make the art object move, as in the example by Polish-born Pol Bury (fig. 10.92). Other pieces, such as those by George Rickey, use wind to produce motion, as did those of Calder. Nonetheless, Rickey's style is imaginatively distinct from Calder's, and a distinguished accomplishment in its own right (fig. 10.93). While kinetics owes something of its origins to Op Art, the latter remains primarily a static form, using various realistic devices to suggest movement. Kinetic art is thus another form deriving from a concern with space and time which began with elements of Impressionism in the late nineteenth century and continued with Futurism, Dadaism, and Calder's Surreal-Abstract mobiles in the early twentieth century.

Present-day kineticists use mechanical or electronic means, as well as random movement, to achieve their ends. Jean Tinguely created large, slack, junky contrivances that outdid the imaginary cartoons of Rube Goldberg in the 1920s and 1930s. Tinguely's pieces sometimes moved about, but more often merely stood and shook, as if they were about to scatter the gears and cogs that ran them. In fact, Tinguely's most famous kinetic construction of this kind, called *Homage to New York*, did just that, destroying itself in 1960 in the garden of the Museum of Modern Art in New York (see fig. 9.43 for an existing example of a Tinguely).

The sculptors or assemblers of light forms, such as Chryssa and Dan Flavin, explore lighted objects, sometimes combining them with movement and electronically produced sounds to create kinetic fantasies. Both artists use mainly neon light in their fluorescent kinetics (fig. 10.94).

Another artist producing a slightly different kind of lighted sculptural form is Richard Lippold. Primarily seen as a pioneer of welded sculpture, he did not actually light his sculptures, but constructed them from such bright materials that they take on a mystic luminescence when lit up by external sources. He created some distinctive linear forms of this kind that are compatible with such monumental architectural settings as churches and commercial buildings (see fig. 9.26).

▼ **10 · 92**
Pol Bury, *The Staircase*, 1965. Wood with motor, 78⅝ × 27 × 16¼ in (200 × 68.6 × 41.3 cm).
Here is an example of an art form in which the components (the ball shapes) actually move. Today a growing number of technologically oriented artists exploit the possibilities of such kinetic art.
Collection, the Solomon R. Guggenheim Museum, New York. (Photograph by Robert E. Mates; © The Solomon R. Guggenheim Foundation, New York; 65.1765.) © ADAGP, Paris and DACS, London 1994.

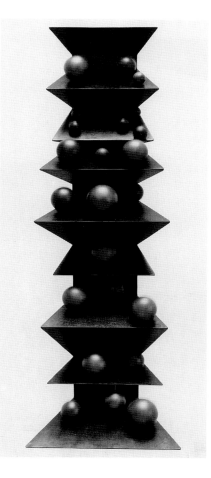

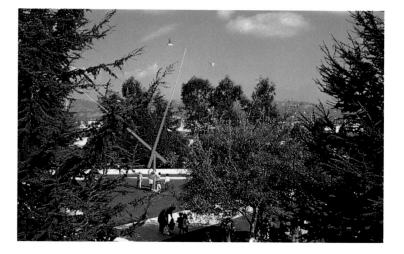

▲ **10 · 93**
George Rickey, *Two Red Lines II*, 1966. Painted steel, 37 ft × 30 in × 8 in (11.28 m × 76.2 cm × 20.3 cm).
Many of Rickey's works are kinetic, having been constructed to make use of the wind and so to provide constantly changing aspects.
Collection of the Oakland Art Museum, CA. © George Rickey/DACS, London/VAGA, New York 1994.

▼ **10 · 94**
Dan Flavin, *Untitled* (in memory of my father, D. Nicholas Flavin), 1974. Daylight fluorescent light (edition of three), 8 × 48 ft (2.44 × 14.63 m).
One of the artists who has devoted much of his career to light sculptures or assemblages, Don Flavin represents a branch of artists working with static assemblies of fluorescent lights, as opposed to the moving, or kinetic, forms of others.
Leo Castelli Gallery, New York.

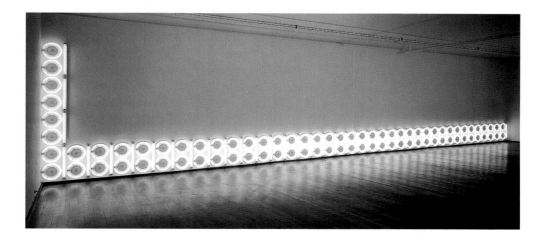

Minimalist/Primary-Structurist sculpture or ABC art

In sculpture the Post-Painterly Hard-Edge Abstractionists are paralleled by a group of artists which includes Tony Smith, Anthony Caro, Lila Katzen, Tony Judd, and others. They have transformed the late mechanomorphic cubes of David Smith into blunt sculptures of simplified geometric volumes that seem stripped of all psychological or symbolic content. These artists have been variously labeled as Primary Structurists, Minimalists, and sometimes, due to the simplicity of their forms, ABC artists. Quite often they rejected metal and welding for materials hitherto uncommon in sculpture, such as cardboard, masonite, plywood, plastics, and glass. Some, like Larry Bell, used hard sheet plastic (plexiglas) or tinted glass to create transparent volumes that enclose space (fig. 10.95). While a few such artists, like James De Woody, still preferred the abstract mass or solid (see fig. 9.35), most of the Primary Structurists apparently wanted to obliterate the core, creating simple volumes of enclosed space, or opening up numerous voids. Some of these pieces are merely boxes of gigantic size. (Large size is a characteristic of much twentieth-century sculpture, as well as painting.) Donald Judd, another proponent of Minimalism, constructed a repeated sequence of loaf-shaped boxes hung on a wall, relief fashion (see fig. 9.41). Later he turned to making sculptures of identical large, open-centered concrete boxes. Whether repeated either in the same or different materials, Judd's and others' sculptures were often laid out in rows, or stacked up vertically. In the 1970s, when a considerable number of such "repeats" were laid out on the floor of a gallery, they were named scatterworks or floorworks, or indoor siteworks, as in Larry Bell's 1989 work *First and Last*, with its repetition of several glass units coated with inconel (see fig. 10.95). At other times, when such works were placed outdoors, they were called siteworks, examples of which may be seen in figures 9.36, 9.38, 9.39 and 9.40. This repetition of similar forms seems a continuation of a characteristic Pop conceit, for example Warhol's *100 Cans* (see fig. 10.83).

In their stress on totally simplistic forms, the Minimalists rejected the belief that humans count for much in the work of art. This is a reminder of antecedents from the 1930s to 1950s – purists like Mondrian and the painters of the nonobjective movement (see "Pure Abstract Art" and "Nonobjective Art", pp. 266–8). The lack of content in Minimalist art was most likely a reaction to the psychological suggestivity found in welded sculpture, particularly the Abstract-Expressionist kind.

There is, however, another branch of the Primary Structurist movement that preferred open spatial forms to the simplified volumes of the first group considered. They have been variously termed Minimalists, Neoconstructivists, and Environmentalists. Their main distinction from the enclosed-shape or volumetric Minimalists was their liking for large, spatially opened, rectilinear, and curvilinear forms. Sometimes these sculptures featured beamlike arms or girderlike extensions into space, and at other times curving planes, or flat planes with curving edges that are interrelated. These sculptures were often related to the walls, floor, or ceiling of a room just like

▼ **10 · 95**

Larry Bell, *First and Last*, 1989. Ten pieces of 12-mm float glass coated with inconel. The Primary Structurists make use of simple, monumental forms exploiting a wide variety of materials.

Musée d'Art Contemporain, Lyon, France. © Larry Bell. (Photograph courtesy of the artist.)

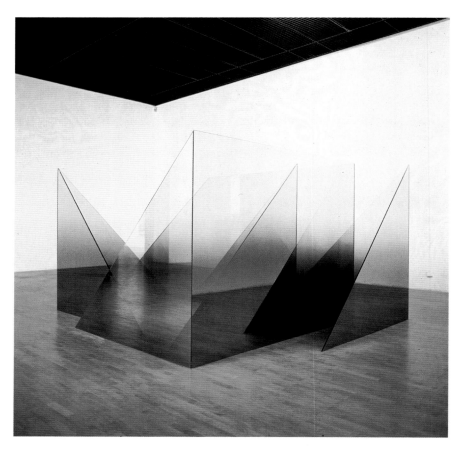

those of the simpler volumes of the other Minimalists. They were also often made on a scale appropriate for an outdoor environment, becoming public monuments in parks, or in conjunction with architecture (especially in the 1970s). Like the boxier, volumetric work of the Primary Structurists, these artists' creations also seem to reject any connotations of human expression. Attention is concentrated on a mechanical impersonality that is apparently a part of our cultural heritage. However, the free, spatial play of these works' components can bring with it a stronger sense of human intervention.

A dominant characteristic of all 1960s sculpture is its preoccupation with size and space – not merely in terms of the work itself, but the work's relationship with its surrounding environment. Space may be incorporated as an element within the sculptural pieces, or it might be involved with a flow or thrust into the natural environment. Many such works, as mentioned, became public monuments, related in various ways to such public buildings as museums, city office buildings, and those on college campuses.

Examples of this trend can be found in Tony Smith's work (see fig. 9.40). We can also witness it in Lila Katzsen's large, open-rolled, sheet-metal forms (fig. 10.96); in Mark di Suvero's variously angled I-beam girder structures (see fig. 9.38), and in Kenneth Snelson's hanging tubes with cables (see fig. 9.36).

A few of the open boxes, and occasionally some of the enclosed rectilinear sculptures, stress brightly colored surfaces, while others are neutral or devoid of color. Without doubt, many such pieces make a powerful impact as we come on them in public places; however, some of these Minimalist forms often transmit a feeling of sameness or monotony and, to younger artists growing to maturity in the sixties, often seem without perceivable content. In addition, the creative process of constructing such objects seemed more

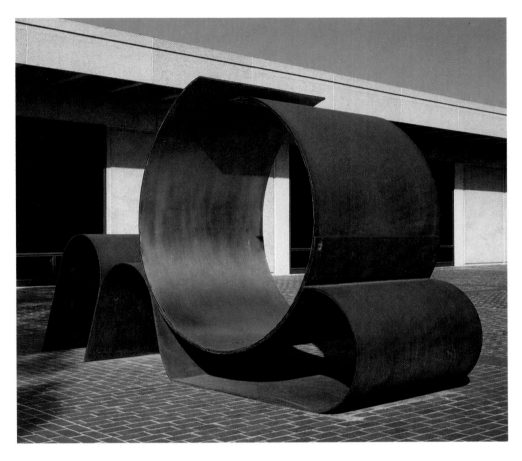

▲ 10 · 96
Lila Katzsen, *Oracle*, 1974. Corten and stainless steel, 11 × 17 × 5 ft (3.35 × 5.18 × 1.52 m).
These flowing sheet-metal forms, set in outdoor space, are typical of the works of Katzen.
University of Iowa Museum of Art, Museum purchase, 1976.88. © Lila Katzsen/DACS, London/VAGA, New York 1994.

important at times than its form or final effect on the response of the observer.

The strictly sculptural use of the assemblage concept had a great influence on sculptors in the 1960s and 1970s, as did the creation of Environmental works, and the attendant trend toward gigantic size. All the approaches mentioned above merged to various degrees in the decades following the 1960s. It is this virility of forms, and the lively crosscurrents between them, that is the characteristic of modern sculpture.

Postmodernism: the reaction to earlier modern art

Postmodernism is the term applied to a new mode of art created mostly by a younger generation of artists, although there are some older artists identified with it. It signalled a reaction to what was perceived as a paucity of content or expression in early modern art from abstraction to Minimalism. The term is given to the variety of styles and movements that have arisen since the late 1960s and early 1970s. All art of the last thirty years which appears to be looking either for a new means of expression, or of near-realistic figurative form, can be said to lie within the Postmodern sphere. Most figurative art had been cast in the shadows by the dominance of formal abstraction. Many artists therefore returned to art that had for long been considered out of the mainstream. A new

▼ **10·97**

Richard Estes, *Helene's Florist*, 1971. Oil on canvas, 4 × 6 ft (1.22 × 1.83 m).
The meticulously rendered images of Richard Estes attempt to reach the degree of reality found in photography.
Toledo Museum of Art, Toledo, OH.

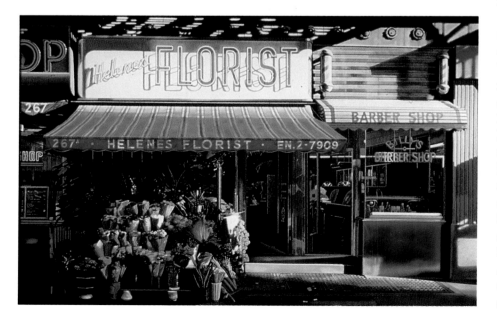

kind of eclecticism which expressed itself through an outright copying of previous art, from recent to ancient, came into play. Artists who took this course modified the older works by changes in scale or relationships, however, so they were viewed in a new way. New materials or media continued to be introduced.

Other notable characteristics of Postmodernism were the reintroduction of decoration, such as could be found in Islamic manuscripts; a diversity of novel techniques as required by new media; and even a return to literary sources, a procedure adopted before by the nineteenth-century Romantics. From early modernism there has been a constant switching back and forth between styles and media, so that it is difficult to make clear distinctions as to the categories in which many artists belong. Because of this, it would make no sense to say that Postmodernism means that all the practices of early modernism were abandoned; so the term is loosely used to encompass all the styles that have come into being as reactions to *some* of the early modern "dogmas." There was also a growing desire to "clean the slate and start over again," that perennial attitude that has arisen when accepted art forms become exhausted and bled of new ideas.

New Realism (Photorealism)

The style that began the Postmodernist reaction to the paucity of content in early modern art, and a general trend from the late 1960s to the 1970s, was New Realism. It was, in a sense, a new kind of Pop art that dealt for its style in verisimilitude, but of a more matter-of-fact kind. While it emerged from Pop art, its stress on meticulously rendered images of reality had little of the wit, humor, and sly jibes of Pop. For a century representation had been an anathema to abstract and Abstract-Expressionist artists, as their values had been based on the rejection of anything suggesting an objective mapping of reality. Now representation, or realism, returned "with a vengeance." The movement was led by such artists as Richard Estes, Chuck Close, Philip Pearlstein, and Gary Schumer (fig. 10.97; see figs. 2.50, 5.4, and 6.11).

The New Realists were sometimes referred to as New Illusionists or Photorealists. They depended on both photography and images taken from commercial advertising to gain their meticulous artistic ends; although some, like Pearlstein, maintain that they do not paint from projected images, or photographs, but rely upon painstaking observation of their model(s). By and large, however, all the New Realists show average people involved in everyday activities; there is little or no evocative content. Many feature photolike renditions of city streets, store fronts, and the like.

The New Realists were preceded, clearly, by the continuing high level of interest in realistic art throughout the twentieth century, particularly in the United States. This can be witnessed not only in the unabated popularity of Andrew Wyeth, but the recurring interest in artists like Grant Wood, Edward Hopper, and Ben Shahn from the earlier part of the century (see figs. 2.32, 8.24, and 2.29). On occasion, nineteenth-century Realism, from the Pre-Raphaelites to the Impressionists, has also returned to favor. Even Picasso, that towering genius of the century, in the midst of all his Expressionist, Abstract, and Surrealist explorations, continually returned to realistic idioms.

Like Pop art, New Realism has its sculptural participants. The sculptors refined the styles of Segal and Oldenburg and made even more lifelike images in fiberglass and resins. Very popular in this area during the late 1960s and early 1970s were Frank Gallo, John De Andrea, and Duane Hanson (fig. 10.98). *Trompe l'oeil* verisimilitude reached a new level of virtuosity in such three-dimensional illusions.

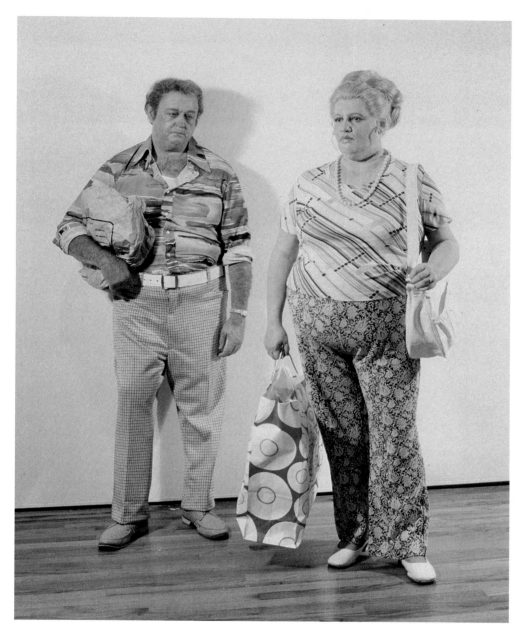

▲ 10 · 98

Duane Hanson, *Couple with Shopping Bags*, 1976. Polyvinyl/polychromed in oil, life size.

This work belongs in the context of photorealist painting, but it incorporates more illusions than any painting could. Duane Hanson's three-dimensional, lifelike, life-sized figures are cast in colored polyester resin and fiberglass to look like real skin and are clothed in real garments. His human reproductions are so meticulously detailed that one reacts to them first as real people, and only later as sculpture.

Courtesy of O. K. Harris Works of Art, New York.

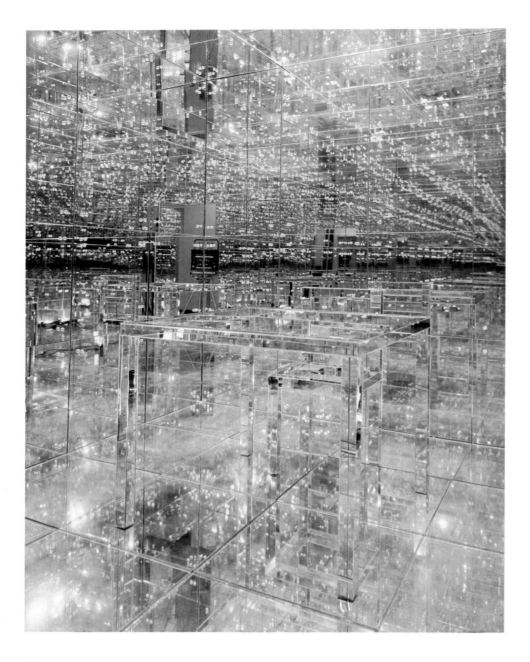

▲ 10·99

**Lucas Samaris, *Mirrored Room*, 1966.
Mirrors on wooden frame, 8 × 8 × 10 ft
(2.44 × 2.44 × 3.05 m).**
This is an example of environmental art, which,
by its size and structure, may actually enclose
the observer within the form of the work.
Albright-Knox Art Gallery, Buffalo, NY. Gift of
Seymour H. Knox, 1966.

Environmental art

Environmental art takes its name from
the fact that the environment surrounds
the spectator. The artwork becomes a slice
of (artificial) life, which is completed by
spectators because of the stress placed on
the details of the created forms around
them. Environmental artists believe that
not only should spectators' vision be
engaged in works of art, but their whole
bodies, including the senses of touch,
smell, and hearing. Although Dadaists
like Kurt Schwitters and Marcel
Duchamp created the first twentieth-
century Environments, the Pop artists

must be credited with renewing this form
of art in the 1960s and 1970s. While Lucas
Samaris was primarily a Pop artist, his
Mirrored Room is also a good example of
that particular form of an Environment
called an inside sitework (fig. 10.99). Such
a work contains the seeds of the
Postmodernist revolt against the death of
the artistic personality which was so
much a part of art into the late 1960s.
The desire to express pure form in a work
of art, rather than to project the artist's
character, was a continual ideal until
Postmodernism, and still lingers on in
much recent art (New Realism, for
example).

Environments in various materials
emerged from the static assemblages of
the 1950s and 1960s, as well as from the
Pop art concept of bombarding the
spectator with mundane images from the
everyday world. The manner in which
Pop art took the most commonplace
items in our culture out of their normal
context and gave them the legitimacy of
fine art has been considered. With such
enclosed Environments, spectators became
involved in the principle of space/time –
the action involved in either creating or
looking at works of art – which involves
the fourth dimension. This has been a
continuous concern for many generations
and remains so in recent work.

Among the artists who produce
Environments, while also creating other
kinds of art, are Christo, Oldenburg, and
Robert Morris. Christo has continuously
explored the environment, from the great
balloons featured at the Whitney
Museum in 1968, to the surrounding of
islands off the coast of Florida with pink
sheet plastic in the early 1980s. One of
Christo's most recent works, *The
Umbrellas*, was preceded by drawings and
paintings which he uses as working
models for the final Environmental
projects. These are sold to raise money for
the supplies and helpers required to
execute Christo's monumentally scaled
art. In a sense, the accomplishment of an
Environmental form also takes on the

character of a Happening or performance. Christo's colorful umbrellas, placed on hillsides in California and Japan in 1992, are one of his most charming projects (see fig. 1.14A and B).

Another pioneer of Environmental works is the sculptor Robert Smithson, whose *Spiral Jetty*, created at Great Salt Lake, Utah, in 1970, played an important part in such large-scale Environments (fig. 10.100). Claes Oldenburg, the well-known Pop artist, also explored Environments, as in his gigantic designs of lipstick tubes and other forms for various parks.

The Minimalist/Primary Structurist emphasis on the large scale of their "pure" forms also helped lead to those branches of Environmental art called earthworks and siteworks. The latter term refers not only to indoor sites, as mentioned in regard to Samaris's *Mirrored Room*, but to works out-of-doors. The displacement of the natural and/or prepared land and space necessary for the setting or exhibiting of large-scale public sculptures drew attention to the places where they would be situated. Some artists soon conceived that the manipulation of the setting, or natural environment itself, was a significant artwork in its own right. Another source for the idea of earthworks or outdoors art lies in the indoor siteworks of Minimalist sculptors. When the Minimalists chose to take the commonplace materials of their craft out of the studio and scatter them on the floors of old factories, public buildings, and galleries, scatterworks and floorworks were born, and suggested the shaping of the outdoors in the same way.

The exact birth of earthworks in art is difficult to pinpoint, although its roots have existed in landscape painting, sculptural monuments, and landscape or park design for at least three centuries. As a movement in modern times it appears to have developed in the late 1960s. In 1967, for example, Claes Oldenburg dug holes which he called "invisible sculptures," in New York's Central Park. Michael Heizer dug five twelve-foot trenches that he lined with wood in the Black Rock Desert of Nevada in 1969 (fig. 10.101). The concept of "bigger is better" has also taken hold in earthworks, since cranes and power shovels have been used by the artist/directors to produce their works.

Part of the reason artists took their work outdoors in the first place was to escape from the dominance, the hyperbole, and reverential attitude displayed by galleries marketing artists' works. Ironically, in spite of the desire to escape institutional domination on the part of scatterwork or site artists, some of these works are possessed by art museums today. It is impossible to miss these collections of wood, rope, cloth, metal, and so forth, that, because of their size, monopolize large parts of a museum floor or walls.

▼ 10·100

Robert Smithson, *Spiral Jetty*, Great Salt Lake, Utah, 1970. Rock, salt crystals, earth, algae, coil, 1,500 ft (457 m).
Students of art must be willing to concede the possible validity of many unfamiliar forms of individual expression.

Estate of Robert Smithson. Courtesy of the John Weber Gallery, New York. (Photograph by Gianfranco Gorgoni.)

▼ 10·101

Michael Heizer, *Double Negative*, Mormon Mesa, Overton, Black Rock Desert, Nevada, 1969–70. 240,000-ton displacement in rhyolite and sandstone, 1,500 × 50 × 30 ft (457 × 15 × 9 m).
Some of the artists producing Environments – in this case, an earthwork – were looking to escape the high-pressure commercial world of galleries and museums. Antecedents for Environments are found in landscape architecture and painting, while the modern desire for works on a monumental scale also played a part.

© Michael Heizer. (Photograph courtesy of the artist.)

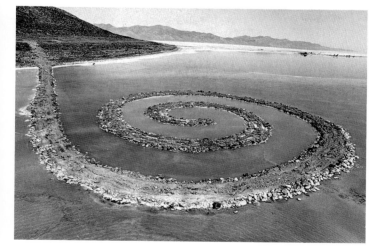

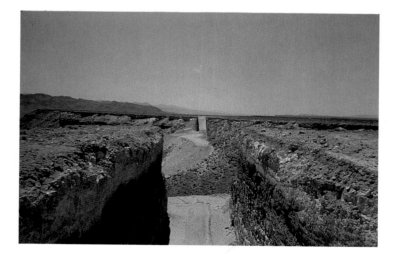

Process and Conceptual art

As we have found, the Minimalists/ Primary Structurists of the 1960s and 1970s emphasized purity of form in simple volumes, with obscure content (although faithful believers saw it as transcendental in meaning). Earlier the Abstract Expressionists had promoted this lack of content – as the Postmoderns saw it – by raising the creative act in importance over the form of the finished artwork. In these movements a great deal of artistic energy had been expended toward exploring the creative process and the conception of ideas. The forms called Process and Conceptual Art are the results of this kind of thinking carried to its logical conclusion, where the "process" or "idea" become ends in themselves. To Postmoderns at least, both seemed to conceal somewhat the importance of artistic personality, or expression, as well as the final art object, which even in early modern art had served as the goal in art.

The Process artists believed that art is experienced primarily in the act of producing. The interpretations given to the final form do not seem important to them, as is suggested by, for example, the exposure of their works to the natural effects of the weather. This is, perhaps, a logical extension of the belief that the analysis of critics and connoisseurs goes beyond, yet somehow fails to measure up to, the artistic experience and the fruits of that experience. Process and Conceptual art are, therefore, transitional between earlier forms and full-blown Postmodernism. As has been indicated, Postmodernism was foreshadowed in Pop art as early as the late 1950s, and expanded into all kinds of new art alongside the older avant-garde.

The German Process artist Joseph Beuys in his *Rescue Sled* (fig. 10.102) uses clearly recognizable objects as subjects, but states that the ideas behind the work and its production are more important than the medium or form. He claimed that every act of society is a work of art. The blanket rolls, pieces of animal fat, and flashlights that appear in this work, while not the ordinary media of traditional artists, are meant to express complex, deep-seated personal, and symbolic meanings. These objects are symbols of Beuys's survival during World War II, when his airplane was shot down and he was saved by nomadic Crimean Tartars on just such a sled. His art is moreover a continuing reference to the catastrophic brinkmanship of our times – times afflicted by nuclear weapons, the resulting Cold War, and the destruction of our environment.

The most significant notion behind Conceptual art, perhaps, is that almost anything a person picks up can be called a "work of art" and almost anybody can be called an artist. This aesthetically anarchic view of art ultimately stems from Dada and Duchamp's notion of "found" and "ready-made" objects. Conceptual artists, therefore, believed that neither the act of making nor completing an art object was

▼ **10 · 102**

Joseph Beuys, *Rescue Sled*, 1969. Wood, metal, rope, blanket, flashlight, wax, 13¾ in (35 cm).

Process artists, such as Joseph Beuys, believe that the ideas behind, and production of, an artwork are more important than its medium or form. His commonplace objects often entail a complex symbolism springing from personal experiences. Here, for example, the sled and objects with it refer obliquely to his rescue by nomadic Tartars after his plane was shot down in World War II.

Art Institute of Chicago. Twentieth Century Purchase Fund, 1973.56. © DACS 1994.

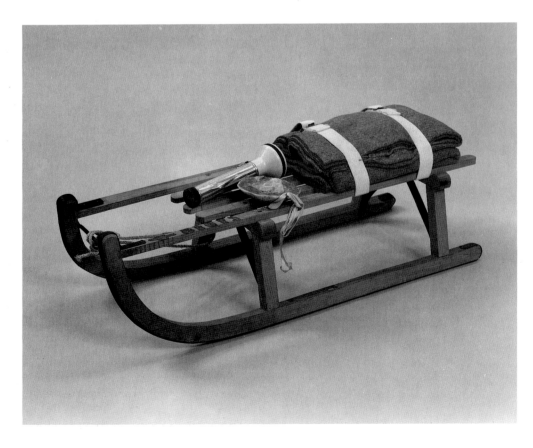

as important as the idea, or concept, that lay behind it. The most extreme representatives of this point of view were the artists who conceived of filling the air with oxygen or steam vapor in the early 1960s. This they called "universal art," because the vapors would expand endlessly into the universe. They were also the forerunners of what we now call Conceptual art. Today this form of art, like Process art, often involves action by the artist alone, but more often involves helpers and/or an audience. In one sense, Christo's Environments can be considered Conceptual forms of art since they require a "director," who has conceived of the work, and those who assist or participate in the recording of the idea in whatever form it may take. However, most Concept art was on a smaller scale and began to take on the respectable veneer of "fine art" once it was exhibited in galleries.

An early example of Conceptual art is found in Joseph Kosuth's *One and Three Chairs* of 1965 (fig. 10.103). Kosuth took a "found object" or "ready-made," in this case a chair, added a photograph of the chair, and next to that a dictionary definition of a chair. Rapidly, during the late 1960s and early 1970s, similar items were being exhibited and given the status of aesthetic objects. When they were put on display, it was much to the discomfiture of the artists involved, since such ideas were intended to squash the idea of art-as-precious-object and the control exerted over artists by galleries, museum officials, and private owners. Many Conceptual works were just displays of typed or handwritten words, explaining theories of art, the sciences, topology, or anything else that might seem of interest to someone. Photographs, plus cinematic and video images, were often used to record these concepts, so they could also be seen in terms of processes and performances. Nam June Paik was the first artist to display video ensembles, which are examples of both Process and Performance art (fig. 10.104). He now has several followers.

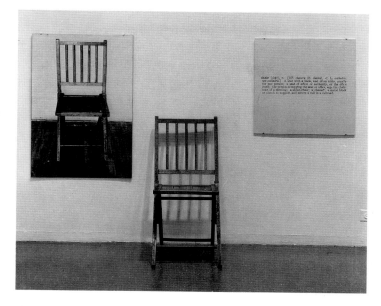

▲ 10 · 103

Joseph Kosuth, *One and Three Chairs*, 1965. Wooden folding chair, photographic copy of a chair, and photographic enlargement of dictionary definition of a chair; chair, 32⅜ × 14⅞ × 20⅞ in (82 × 37.8 × 53 cm); photo panel, 36 × 24⅛ in (91.5 × 61.1 cm); text panel, 24 × 24⅛ in (61 × 61.3 cm).

In this example of Conceptual art, the idea of one actual or "ready-made" chair is triplicated by a photograph of a chair and a dictionary definition of a chair.

The Museum of Modern Art, New York. Larry Aldrich Foundation Fund.

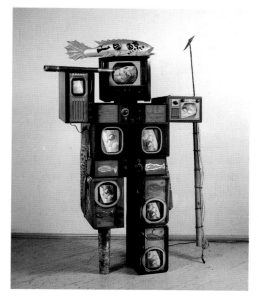

◄ 10 · 104

Nam June Paik, *Captain Ahab*, 1990. Video sculpture, 89 × 58 × 27 in (226.1 × 147.3 × 68.6 cm).

Process, Conceptual, and Performance art are closely related, often overlapping, art forms. The Korean-American artist Nam June Paik, who mostly produces video installations – which he pioneered – bridges the slight differences between the forms. He has several followers who also explore the impact of technology on modern society.

Courtesy of the Holly Solomon Gallery, New York.

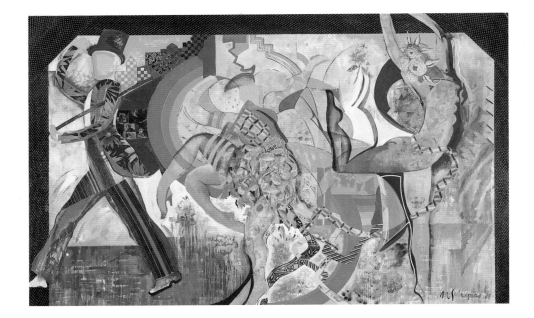

▲ 10 · 105
Miriam Schapiro, *I'm Dancin' as Fast as I Can*, 1985. Acrylic and fabric on canvas, 7 ft 6 in × 12 ft (2.29 × 3.66 m).
This artist became well-known in the late 1960s for her *Femmages*, which incorporate into collage sewing and quilting materials and techniques. Using the same basic techniques, she has recently propelled her work in a figurative direction, though the content remains disturbing and ambiguous. Her work is a good example of recent Postmodernist directions in art.
Collection of Dr. and Mrs. Harold Steinbaum. Courtesy of the Steinbaum Krauss Gallery, New York.

Postmodernist reactions to Conceptualism

New Content/ Figurative art

The highly simplistic and rarefied content of Minimalism, capped by Conceptualism, continued to lead new painting and sculptural styles in the 1970s. The matrix of styles which evolved seemed to have no common thread for a time, so it is difficult to supply any one all-encompassing label. For this reason, the term "Postmodernism" has been used to designate the art of the late 1960s to the 1980s. It is no more satisfactory, of course, than the designation of "Post-Impressionism" at the end of the nineteenth century.

Most of this art is the expression of individuals. Yet some of them reject the notion of individualism and want to return art to the anonymity which dominated most historical styles before the Renaissance. In the context of art today, this is probably an impossibility.

One common denominator detectable in many works of art from the 1970s onward is the strong desire to bring back recognizable content or meaning to works of art. There have been attempts to give a name to some of the different ways in which this new concern for a more representational approach has manifested itself; but the attempt flounders because of the individualistic approach, apart from any "movements," adopted by many of today's artists.

Miriam Schapiro, a Canadian-born artist based in New York, was important in the late 1960s for introducing new patternmaking media. The new media consisted of materials used in the home, for quilting and sewing, and Schapiro employed the old collage method of mounting materials on a support, including cloth, sequins, thread, paper, and paint. Schapiro had been involved in Abstract Expressionism and Hard-Edge Abstraction before turning to a decorative approach. Some of these previous influences rubbed off and became part of her formal approach when she developed her quilt- and collage-based *Femmages* (fig. 10.105). Schapiro has continued through the 1980s to create lively, colorful images with discernible, but sometimes ambiguous content.

In the late 1960s, when Philip Guston, the well-known Abstract-Expressionist painter, gave up that style and developed a semiabstract, almost cartoonlike, figurative approach, many younger artists were inspired to head down the same road. Guston explained his switch by saying that he was "tired" of "purity of form" and wanted to tell stories once again. The artists who were excited by this new approach were reacting to what they felt was the lack of content in Minimalism and Conceptualism, and wanted to find a new way through the clutter of modernist styles which preceded them. Many paths were followed in this process of shaking off the past. While to some extent it involved older artists like Guston, and some artists who had never abandoned a representational approach altogether, most of the younger artists selfconsciously sought out methods and manners different than had existed before. Or were they different? The question is raised because some took a peculiar delight in eclectically borrowing from recent and distant art, turning "everything on its ear," so to speak. These particular ideas were mixed and combined in such a way that "new" images resulted. Many also chose to take old and newer techniques and media, mixing them up in random fashion to produce unusual combinations, as in the case of Schapiro's *Femmages*. And although they also chose to narrate, their stories are usually oblique and often ambiguous, unless we know their source(s).

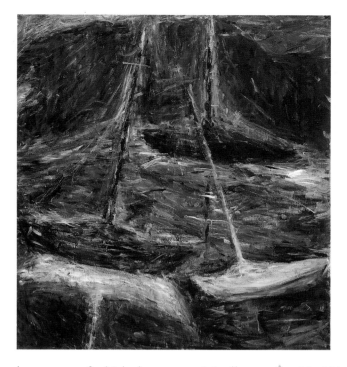

Other artists that may be included in the 1970s Postconceptual group are so numerous that we can only cite a very few. Susan Rothenberg and Donald Sultan, both painters, along with the sculptor Joel Shapiro, are worth mentioning here. They continue to work to this day, although there have been changes in their styles from time to time. Rothenberg became known for her heavily impastoed, monochromatic horse paintings in the 1970s. These retained a sense of the flat painting surface, through the use of a slashing diagonal, or vertical, across the canvas which split the shallow space behind it, including the horse, into two uneven, but visually balanced parts. By the mid 1980s she was painting other subjects, including the human figure, that are partially blurred into the deeper space provided. Her images of this kind became increasingly Expressionist (fig. 10.106; see fig. 3.16).

Joel Shapiro was born, raised, and educated in New York. He started working as a Process artist with different materials, but turned to producing miniature clay, glass, copper and lead works, shaped in an objective manner. Clusters of these small, geometric pieces were spread out on the floor of galleries, an important element being the actual space in which they were placed. These floorworks gave way in the 1980s to large-scale stick figures that in their precarious balance update and geometricize Gaston Lachaise's work of the twenties and thirties. They are cast in metal, but retain a sense of the tools used on the wood

beams out of which they were originally constructed (fig. 10.107).

Both Joel Shapiro and Miriam Schapiro may be used to indicate one of the differences between eighties and sixties arts: the use of a wide variety of media and techniques. Some of the media are new, requiring new techniques, and very often a single format might display a wide diversity of media. For example, where acrylic painting dominated the pictorial arts in the 1960s, we now often see used conté crayon, pastels, oil paint sticks and pens, paper and cloth collage,

▲ **10 · 106**
Susan Rothenberg, *Reflections*, 1981. Oil on canvas, 3 ft 8 in × 3 ft 4 in (1.12 × 1.02 m).
The Postconceptual work of this artist has run the gamut from simple, heavily pigmented canvases of horses to expressionistic and abstract seascapes, such as this.
Private collection. (Photograph courtesy of the Greenberg Gallery, St. Louis, MO.)

▶ **10 · 107**
Joel Shapiro, *Untitled*, 1980–81. Bronze, 4 ft 4⅞ in × 5 ft 4 in × 3 ft 9½ in (1.34 × 1.63 × 1.16 m).
From his Process art beginnings Shapiro turned to a more objective approach. These large stick figures in active poses illustrate a perceptible craving in the 1980s for a more easily grasped content and a return to figurative art generally.
Collection of the Whitney Museum of American Art, New York.

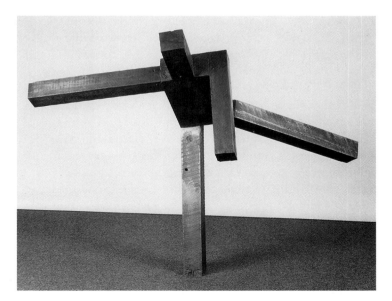

powdered metallics, oils, and acrylics – sometimes many combinations of these appear in the same work of art. This juxtaposition of media is mirrored by a combining of techniques, particularly in the realm of printmaking: lithography, silk-screen, etching, and engraving are often employed in the same image. Some of these "combo-techniques" are descended from history, of course, but not as great a variety of techniques were put together in the past for lack of scientific development.

The new art of social comment

Although it was difficult to predict the exact form much of the newer art of representation would take, by the late 1980s one direction was becoming clearer. Much of it reflects the momentous social and political changes that have taken place in the last decade. The arts have reacted dramatically to those changes. Many of the artists born in the last forty years tend to reject not only the works of their predecessors, but also all the philosophical beliefs that accompanied them. Their work responds to what they feel are the disinformation and lies fed to them by all forms of communication from earlier modern art to films, television, newsprint, and so on. They question not only both the originality of art and what is presented as authentic, but also the concept of originality as a worthwhile goal; they must therefore question their own individuality. They react to the violence being shown – sexual, political, social, and environmental – on our film and television screens. Much of what they see in these forms of information seems, like advertising, to be largely untruthful, or at least to convey a partial and deeply conservative view of the world. Yet their sources are often found in these media, which they then parody or satirize, often by laying bare the structures through which our entertainment and information are disseminated.

Another side to the art of these Postmoderns is found in those who are willing to try almost anything to succeed in their careers, promoting their art, and becoming engaged in the expanded art market of the 1980s. Their artworks seem less important to them than the profit they may gain from them. This is indicative of a culture which saw ruthless company takeovers and mergers, the rise of junk bonds and insider dealing among investors, banks, savings and loan institutions, and a general increase in materialism among otherwise ordinary people in the 1980s. The decade promoted the message that it was all right to seek your own aggrandizement, and art reflected this attitude. A common stance among such artists was to say they were actually satirizing these trends. However, much of the enthusiasm for exploring new directions, the idealism and high philosophical positions that accompanied the arts in the early post-World War II period appears to have been lost. The point of view displayed in this new art of social comment is more morose and cynical than at any time since the Great Depression.

Reality is also in question again! What is real, the film or television portrayals of "ordinary" people in their beautiful apartments and designer clothes, or those found in tenements, or "really everyday" working women or men? Are the handsomely staged street scenes of Hollywood as real as those decaying inner-city streets all over America?

These conditions and the questions they have raised have been responsible for the work of such artists as Sherrie Levine, Cindy Sherman, Robert Longo, and others. As can be seen from our citing of two women together, the new art of social comment has been strongly influenced by the feminist movement. Women have long been relatively neglected in the arts; historically, it has been a male-dominated discipline, as with other aspects of life. Women are working to change that situation, not only in society generally, but in the arts, too.

ART OF THE 1980s INTO THE 1990s

Neo-Expressionism

So far, the longest-lasting and seemingly strongest movement of the new figurative approach to art during the 1980s has been that of the *Neo-Expressionists*. There was such a widespread desire among the general populace for a return to figurative art, and for a more personalized expression, that it seemed for a time in the early eighties that these artists were being deliberately forced on the public for commercial purposes. In hindsight, however, it has become evident that Neo-Expressionism had deeper roots and the values it expressed were those genuinely being sought by a new generation of artists. One method conceived to satisfy the growing appetite for recognizable images and an art with newly meaningful content was a return to monumentally dramatic figures with broad gestures, painted in broad brushstrokes. Chief among European Neo-Expressionists are the Italians Enzo Cucchi (fig. 10.108) and Sandro Chia (see fig. 7.39), who had their first exhibits in New York in 1981. In 1982 they were followed by such Germans as Rainer Fetting and Anselm Kiefer (see fig. 8.16). The common denominator of style, of course, was a reawakening of the emotional fervor of early twentieth-century Expressionism, but often updated with modern techniques and themes which had for many years fallen into disfavor. Late Renaissance Mannerism; the weaker phases of de Chirico's classicizing decadence; the more representational styles of Picasso – all were sources for Neo-Expressionists and others working in other Postmodern veins. We should not leave the Neo-Expressionists without mentioning the audacious use of crockery, photographs, metal, straw, and other unusual materials in their paintings. By and large, these Neo-Expressionists were rejecting what the mainstream avant-garde

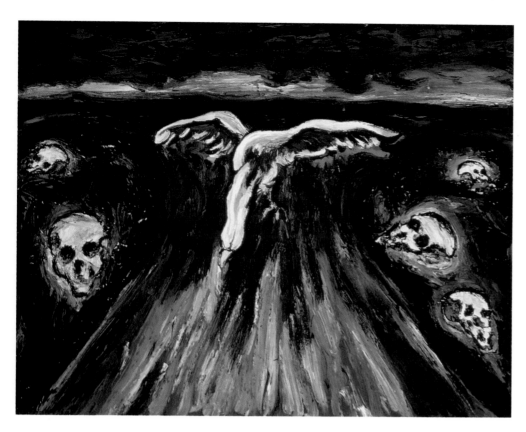

◀ **10 · 108**
Enzo Cucchi, *Paesaggio Barbaro*, 1983. Oil on canvas, 4 ft 3 in × 5 ft 2¾ in (1.30 × 1.59 m).
The Italian Neo-Expressionist Enzo Cucchi paints heavily pigmented canvases contrasting living creatures with symbols of death, abandonment, and decay.
Collection of Angela Westwater, New York. (Photograph courtesy of the Sperone Westwater Gallery, New York.)

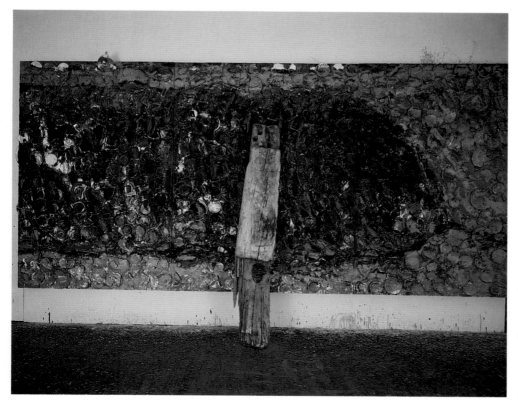

◀ **10 · 109**
Julian Schnabel, *Affection for Surfing*, 1983. Oil, plates, wood, and bondo on wood, 108 × 228 × 24 in (274.3 × 579.1 × 61 cm).
Julian Schnabel, one of the Neo-Expressionists of the early 1980s, uses size and bulky collage to symbolize the discarded materials of a dying civilization.
Courtesy of the Pace Gallery, New York.

establishment (for an establishment it had become) had dictated as "acceptable" subjects for art in the modern age.

One of the first Americans to paint in a Neo-Expressionist manner was Texas-born Julian Schnabel (fig. 10.109). Though he is a commentator on modern life, many of Schnabel's themes are gleaned from the Old and New Testaments. A notable feature of his work is the use of unusual materials, ranging from canvases made of velvet to broken bits of ceramic adhered to the picture plane. Another American Neo-Expressionist is the multimedia virtuoso Robert Longo, whose early works drew attention for their satirical view of the yuppie generation and its implicit violence. His large-scale graphite, charcoal, and sometimes ink drawings feature well-dressed "Wall Street" types either in hand-to-hand combat or madly active poses (fig. 10.110). More recently Longo has become quieter and more abstract in manner.

Cindy Sherman, a photographer working in a Neo-Expressionist idiom, has become well known for her self-portraits. These show her dressed in all kinds of costumes, modern and historical, and serve as metaphysical scrutinies of her own persona and reminders that all photographic reality is in some way a staged fable. They are also commentaries on the visual clichés which the motion picture film industry, in particular, uses to promote stereotypes of women. In the later 1980s, Sherman's work became more abstract; her images were sometimes very grotesque and sinister, and were possibly meant to undermine the belief that women are easy victims (fig. 10.111).

Neo-Abstraction

At the same time as the Neo-Expressionists were making themselves known in the 1980s, and other young

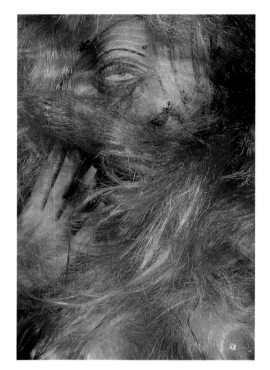

▲ **10·111**
Cindy Sherman, *Untitled*, 1989. Color photograph, 7 ft 6 in × 5 ft (2.29 × 1.52 m).
Sherman, like other Postmodernist artists, focuses her creative energies on many of the environmental and social problems of our times. She deals, in particular, with the various trite ways in which women are viewed by society and through the various visual media. Her photographs generally take the form of theatrical self-portraits which parody female stereotypes. Recent images, as found here, are often more abstract and sometimes grotesque.
Courtesy of Metro Pictures, New York.

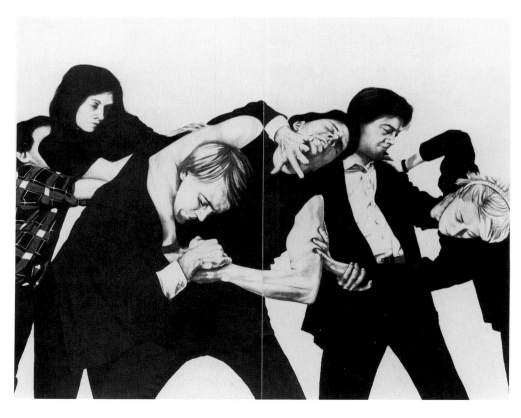

◄ **10·110**
Robert Longo, *Untitled (White Riot Series)*, 1982. Charcoal, graphite, and ink on paper, 8 × 10 ft (2.44 × 3.05 m).
The Neo-Expressionist Robert Longo is a gifted artist in many media. Here we have one of a series of satirical drawings from the 1980s in which he makes explicit the social and commercial rivalry of the yuppie generation.
Courtesy of Metro Pictures, New York.

artists were trying to find new ways to produce recognizable form and content, others were reacting against these trends. By the mid eighties some younger artists were creating more abstract and near-abstract works in both hard-edged and organic manners. Even Neo-Expressionists like Julian Schnabel and Robert Longo have shown this tendency in the late eighties. None of these artists is exactly alike, so again Neo-Abstraction must be seen as a loose affiliation made up of many individuals with distinct styles.

A noticeable trend in the late eighties and early nineties has been the tendency of certain artists to borrow from the work of others. This tendency has appeared in all forms of Postmodernist work, and *Neo-Abstraction* is no exception. In appropriating the work of others, Neo-Abstract artists have usually modified or transformed the original by changing the scale, media, or colors to show the older work in a new frame of reference and, as a result, with a new meaning. Sometimes the meanings are satirical or scathing, or are intended as comments on the decadence of eighties society. Their styles range from the near abstract/nonobjective to semiabstract, as in earlier modern art.

Examples may be found in the work of Sherrie Levine, who made her name by adapting photographs and paintings of well-known masters. The paintings were usually executed in watercolor or gouache and inspired by illustrated art books. By changing the scale to match the illustrations, rather than duplicating the size and media of the original, she asserted her own personality, while showing a respect for the master from whom she borrowed. Later Levine made her own originals, consisting of new abstractions, which are essentially an amalgamation of all the stripe painters from Hard-Edge to Minimalist art.

Other artists, like Nancy Graves, appropriate images from non-art sources. She is often inspired by the natural world, and scientific exhibits, which she turns into sculptural forms (see fig. 9.37). Best

described as biomorphic abstraction, her work has an organic quality, reminiscent of insect life. This is perhaps due to the iridescent colors which she hand-paints on to the metal, plaster and wood of her sculptures. The finished effect is quite beautiful, and we would probably never suspect that the assemblages are made up of found objects from nature and industry – the detritus of our decaying factories and environment – if we were not told.

Lynda Benglis was trained as a painter, but began to be fascinated by sculpture in the early 1970s, when she was considered a Process artist. She developed a method of adding beautiful colors to different plastics in their molten state. After allowing the plastics to flow freely on to the floor, she shaped them into large insectlike creatures, which were then usually mounted on a wall. She has also created mock videos and advertisements of herself, aiming to satirize normally hackneyed representations of women in these media and in society. In recent work, Benglis has turned to shaping knots, bows, and more insectlike, pleated sculptures in shiny metal (fig. 10.112).

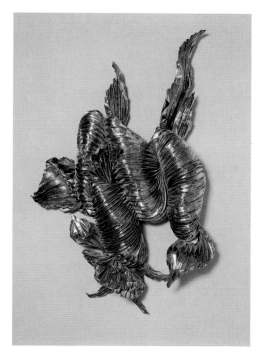

◀ 10 · 112
Lynda Benglis, *Passat*, 1990. Aluminum, 78 × 52 × 27 in (198.1 × 132.1 × 68.6 cm).
This artist began as a painter, then moved over to Process art using heated, free-flowing plastics which were shaped before the material had set. Recently she has switched to working in shiny metals, forming knots, bows, and insectlike pleated sculptures.
Paula Cooper Gallery, New York. (Photograph by Douglas Parker.) © Lynda Benglis/DACS, London/ VAGA, New York 1994.

▶ **10 · 113**

Bryan Hunt, *Prodigal Son*, 1985. Cast bronze, 54¾ × 25½ × 25½ in (139.1 × 64.8 × 64.8 cm).

This Neo-Abstract sculptor, though he has recently turned to painting, has produced effective work in three dimensions. Adopting the form of amorphous natural or manmade objects, they often have a tenuous, flowing quality reminiscent of Giacometti's work (see fig. 10.59).

Blum Helman Gallery, New York.

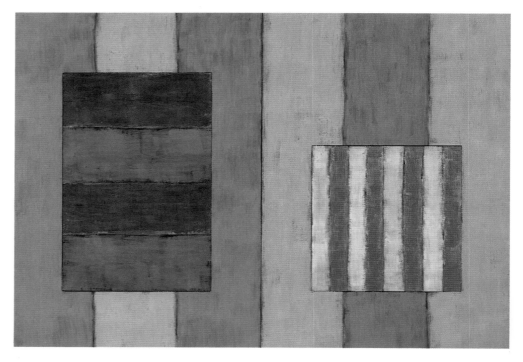

Another example of Neo-Abstraction is found in the art of Bryan Hunt, who began working as a sculptor in the 1960s. He was particularly influenced by sculpture from the Cycladic Islands, the work of previous sculptors, architecture, and the work of Joel Shapiro. His method was to start with drawings, basing small forms on them, but gradually adding parts to the sculptural work as he progressed until they might become quite large. Materials consisted of plaster, steel, and wood, and sometimes drawings. Earlier pieces, inspired by airships and natural forms, have an airy quality that shows a deeply responsive sensitivity; he is often able to capture the essence of the most intangible, changing forms of nature, such as waterfalls and lakes (fig. 10.113). In the late 1980s Hunt adopted a more abstract linear style, employing wire as a kind of armature and integral part of the finished form; while in early 1990 he began to paint near-abstract images that look like rock formations.

Finally, in concluding our survey of the Neo-Abstract style, we will look at two painters who represent the opposite poles of geometric and biomorphic abstraction. The Irish-American Sean Scully (fig. 10.114) paints mostly in vertical and horizontal stripes, which are related to the work of geometric abstractionists, as well as to that of the Hard-Edge Post-Abstract-Expressionists Kenneth Noland and Frank Stella.

▶ **10 · 114**

Sean Scully, *A Bedroom in Venice*, 1988. Oil on canvas, 8 × 10 ft (2.44 × 3.05 m).

This Neo-Abstract painter works in a manner reminiscent of early twentieth-century geometric abstraction, as well as Hard-Edge Post-Abstract-Expressionist painters like Kenneth Noland.

The Museum of Modern Art, New York. Fractional gift of Agnes Gund.

Bill Jensen takes an organic approach that is more obviously expressive of nature. He dislikes being called an abstract artist, even though this label seems most conveniently to fit his work. Many of Jensen's forms seem to speak of an underlying tumult of nature, as though we are witnessing an earthquake taking place (fig. 10.115).

This brings us to the conclusion of our survey of modern art. There are very many, very good artists working today, more than we could ever hope to cover, or do full justice to. But in the authors' estimations, no truly major figures have emerged, as they did in the late nineteenth and earlier twentieth centuries. Perhaps the "natural selection" of a few more decades is needed to reveal the most durable artists and styles of the late modern era. One thing is clear about the art of our time: the unparalleled diversity of techniques and media employed. The sheer quantity of work being produced raises questions about whether much of today's art will in the future be dismissed as trivial. Finally, what will become of all those works of art produced this century, which are currently piling up in the vaults of our institutions? Museums and galleries cannot hope to hold more than a limited number. In fact, even galleries come and go, matching the fate of many they promote as artists each year. Such questions will only be answered, if at all, in the years ahead.

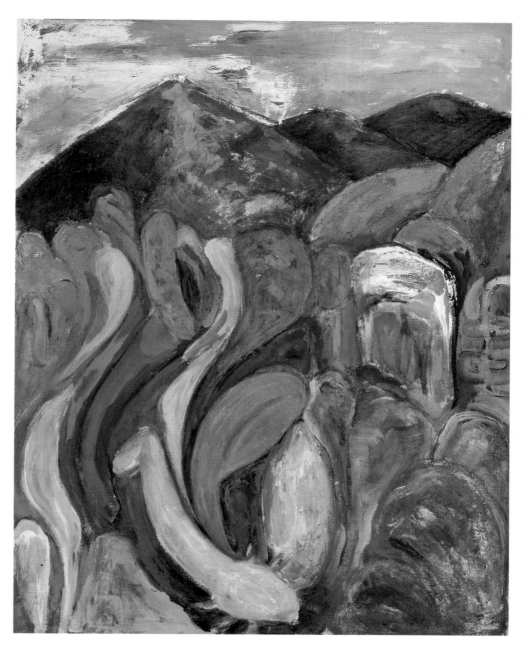

▲ 10·115
Bill Jensen, *Study of "Paradise Lost"*, 1987–88. Gouache and egg tempera, 43 × 33 in (109.2 × 83.8 cm).
Though he is a Neo-Abstractionist, Jensen's style is organic compared to the geometries of Sean Scully.

Collection of Elliot K. Wolk. (Photograph courtesy of the Washburn Galley, New York.)

Chronological Outline of Western Art

PREHISTORIC ART (c.35,000–3000 B.C.)

35,000 B.C.	**Upper Paleolithic**: Old Stone Age. Stone tool industries.
28,000	Art beginnings, cave painting; fertility goddesses.
10,000	**Mesolithic**: Middle Stone Age, Middle East. End of Ice Age.
6000	**Neolithic**: New Stone Age, Middle East.
3000	Settled agricultural communities; polished stone tools.

ANCIENT ART (c.4000 B.C.–A.D.146)

4000 B.C.	**Egyptian Art**: Old Kingdom.
3000	**Sumerian Art**: Iraq.
2800	**Aegean Art**: Isle of Crete: Minoan I & II.
2300	**Akkadian Art**: Syria and Iraq.
2100	**Egyptian Art**: Middle Kingdom.
1800	**Aegean Art**: Greece: Mycenaean Age. Isle of Crete: Minoan III.
1700	**Babylonian Art**: Syria and Iraq.
1600	**Egyptian Art**: New Empire.
1500	**Neolithic**: Ends in Europe.
1100	**Aegean Art**: Turkey: Homeric Age.
	Etruscan Art: Italy.
1000	**Egypt**: Decadence
900	**Assyrian Art**: Middle East.
750	**Greek Art**: Greece and south Italy: Archaic Age.
	Etruscan Art: north Italy.
600	**Neo-Babylonian Art**: Middle East.
550	**Achaemenid Persian Art**: Middle East.
470	**Greek Art**: Greece: Classical Age.
330	**Greek Art**: Egypt: Ptolemaic Age.
320	**Greek Art**: Greece and Middle East: Hellenistic Age.
280	**Roman Art**: Rome a republic, Italy.
140	**Graeco-Roman Art**: Greece to Middle East.
30 B.C.–A.D.146	**Imperial Roman Art**: Italy, parts of Europe and Middle East.

EARLY AND MEDIEVAL ART (c.200–1300 A.D.)

500 B.C.–A.D. 400	**Migratory Period Art**: Art of the Celts, Germans, Slavs, Scandinavians in Europe.
100 A.D.	**Late Imperial Roman Art** and **Early Christian Art**: Italy and Europe.
330	**Early Byzantine Art**: Middle East.
	Coptic Christian Art: Egypt.
	Early Christian Art: west Europe; decline of Rome.
550	**Islamic Art**: Middle East and North Africa.
	Moorish Art: south Spain.
760	**Carolingian Art**: France, Germany, and north Italy.
800	**Developed Byzantine Art**: Middle East, Greece, Russia, and parts of Italy (Venice, Ravenna, Rome, and Sicily).
950	**Ottonian Art**: mostly in Germany.
1000	**Romanesque Art**: France, England, north Spain, Italy, and Germany.
1150	**Gothic Art**: France, Italy, Spain, Germany, and England.

RENAISSANCE ART (c. 1300–1600)

1300	**Proto-Renaissance**: Italy: Duccio, Giotto, Pisano.
1400	**Early Renaissance**: Italy: Donatello, Francesca, Fra Angelico, Fra Filippo Lippi, da Vinci, Masaccio.
	Early Northern Renaissance (modified by vestiges of Medievalism): Netherlands: van Eyck, van der Goes, van der Weyden; France: Limbourg brothers, Fouquet; Germany: Lochner, Moser, Witz, Pacher, Schongauer.
1500	**High Renaissance**: Italy: Giorgione, Michelangelo, Raphael, Tintoretto, Titian.
	High Renaissance in Western Europe (affected by Italy): Netherlands: Bosch, Breughel; Germany: Dürer, Grünewald; France: Master of Moulins; Spain: El Greco.
1520	**Mannerism and Early Baroque**: Italy: Bernini, Caravaggio.

BAROQUE ART (c. 1600–1700)

1600	**Baroque Art in Europe**: The Netherlands (Belgium; Holland): Rubens, van Dyck; Hals, Rembrandt; France: Poussin, Claude; Spain: Ribera, Velazquez.
	Early Colonial Art: Americas.

ROCOCO ART (c. 1700–1780)

1700	**Rococo**: Primarily French, but spreads to other European countries: France: Boucher, Chardin, Fragonard, Watteau; Italy: Canaletto, Guardi, Tiepolo; England: Gainsborough, Hogarth, Reynolds.
	Colonial Art and Early Federal Art in US: Copley, Stuart, West.

NINETEENTH-CENTURY ART*

* From here on, listed artists are painters unless otherwise indicated in parentheses.

c. 1780	**Neoclassicism**: France: David, Ingres; Italy: Canova (sculpture).
1820	**Romanticism**: France: Barye (sculpture), Delacroix,
1826	Joseph N. Niépce (first permanent camera image), Géricault,
1835	Daguerre (photographic process); Spain: Goya; England: Fox Talbot (photographic process), Turner; United States: Ryder.
1850	**Realism and Naturalism**: France: Daumier, Courbet, Manet, Rejlander (photography); England: Constable; United States: Brady (photography), Eakins, Homer, O'Sullivan (photography).
1870	**Impressionism**: France: Monet, Pissarro, Renoir, Degas, Rodin (sculpture); England: Sisley; United States: Hassam, Muybridge (photography), Twachtman; Italy: Medardo-Rosso (sculpture).
1880	**Post-Impressionism**: France: Cézanne, Gauguin, Seurat, Toulouse-Lautrec; Holland: van Gogh.
	Symbolism: France: Bonnard.

TWENTIETH-CENTURY ART

1900 **Post-Impressionist Sculpture**: France: Maillol; United States: Lachaise; Germany: Lehmbruck, Marcks, Kolbe.

1902–07 Steichen and Stieglitz found **291 Gallery** to advance photography and avant-garde art.
Expressionism: Picasso† (Blue, Rose, and Negro periods).
French Expressionism: Les Fauves ("Wild Beasts"): Dufy, Matisse, Modigliani (Italy); Rouault, Utrillo, Vlaminck.
Later French Expressionism (1930): Soutine, Buffet, Balthus.
German Expressionism: Die Brücke (The Bridge): Kirchner, Kokoschka, Munch (Norway); Nolde, Schmidt-Rotluff;
Der Blaue Reiter (The Blue Rider):
Jawlensky, Kandinsky, Kuehn (photography), Macke, Marc;
Die Neue Sachlichkeit (The New Objectivity): Dix, Grosz, Heckel, Sander (photography).
Independent German Expressionism: Beckmann, Kokoschka.
American Expressionism: Avery, Baskin, Broderson, Levine, Shahn, Weber.
Mexican Expressionism: Orozco; Siqueiros.
Expressionist Sculpture: England: Epstein; Italy: Marini; United States: Zorach.

† Artists frequently change their styles, and so some names may appear under more than one category of style. Most notable in this respect was Pablo Picasso.

ABSTRACT ART (early phase)

1906 **Cubism**: France: Braque, Léger; Spain: Gris, Picasso; United States: Coburn, Strand (photography).
Futurism: Italy: Balla, Boccioni (painting and sculpture), Bragaglia (photography), Carra, Severini; France: Duchamp (influenced by for short time).

1910–50 **Developed Abstract and Nonobjective Art**: Germany: Albers, Kandinsky; Hungary: Moholy-Nagy; Russia: **Constructivism**: Larionov, Malevich, Tatlin; France: Delaunay; England: Nicholson; Holland: **De Stijl**: Mondrian, Rietveld, van Doesburg, van Tongerloo; United States: Coburn (photography), Davis, Demuth, Dove, Feininger, Hartley, Knaths, Marin, O'Keeffe, Pereira, Rothko, Stieglitz (photography), Steichen (photography), Strand (photography).
Abstract Sculpture: France: Archipenko (Russia), Arp, Brancusi (Romania); England: Epstein, Passmore; United States: de Rivera, Nevelson, Noguchi, Gabo, Pevsner (Russia).

Artists are listed under the country where they did their major works; countries of origin are given in brackets.

FANTASY IN ART

c. 1910 **Individual Fantasists**: France: Chagall (Russia), Henri Rousseau (Primitive Art); Italy: de Chirico; Switzerland/Germany: Klee.

1913 **Armory Show, New York**: Helps introduce avant-garde art to United States.

1914 **Dada**: France: Arp, Duchamp, Picabia, Tzara; Germany: Ernst, Schwitters; United States: Man Ray (photography).

1924 **Surrealism**: France: Cartier-Bresson (photography), Delvaux, Masson; Belgium: Magritte; England: Bacon; Germany: Ernst; United States: Dali (Spain) (Surrealist cinemas with Luis Buñel), Man Ray (photography).

1925 **Surrealist Sculpture**: France: Arp; Spain: Gonzalez, Picasso; Switzerland: Giacometti.
Surreal Abstraction: France: Picasso; Spain: Miró; Mexico: Tamayo; United States: Baziotes, de Kooning (Holland), Gorky (Armenia), Hofmann (Germany).

TRADITIONAL REALISM IN THE UNITED STATES

1930–40 **Regionalism**: Adams (photography), Benton, Burchfield, Cunningham (photography), Sloan, Weston (photography), Wood, Wyeth (independent realist).

ART FORMS OF THE LATE 1930s, 1940s, AND 1950s

c. 1945

Abstract Expressionism:
The Forerunners (most from abroad): Albers, de Kooning, Gorky, Hofmann, Matta, Mirò, Mondrian, Tobey (United States).
The Abstract-Expressionist Movement (mostly in the United States):
Action Painting: Frankenthaler, Kline, Pollock, White (photography); **Color Field Group**: Callahan (photography), Motherwell, Reinhardt, Rothko, Still, Tworkov; France: Manessier, Mathieu, Soulages; Portugal: Vieira da Silva; Holland: Appel, de Stael; Japan: Okada; Spain: Tapies.
Surreal-Abstract and Abstract-Expressionist Sculpture: England: Chadwick, Hepworth, Moore; United States: Bontecou, Calder, Lipchitz (Lithuania), Lassaw (Egypt), Lipton, Nakian, Noguchi, Roszak, David Smith; France: Richier.

ART FORMS OF THE LATE 1950s, 1960s, AND 1970s

c. 1955

Post–painterly Abstraction:
Hard-Edge Painters: Ron Davis, Kelly, Newman, Noland, Poons, Stella. **Minimalist Painters**: Olitsky, Reinhardt, Yves Klein (France).
Neo-Dada and Pop Art (includes assemblages and Happenings or Performance Art):
Neo-Dada (mostly United States): Johns, Rauschenberg; **Pop Art**: Chamberlain, Frank (Ireland – photography), Marisol Escobar (Venezuela), Indiana, Kienholz, Lichtenstein, Nevelson, Oldenburg, Samaris (Greece), Segal, Warhol, Wesselmann, Winogrand (photography); France: César, Dubuffet.
Op Art: France: Vasarely; United States: Anuskiewicz, Ortmann, Stanczak, Agam (Israel); England: Riley, Denny.
Kinetics and Light: France: M. Duchamp (1920s); United States: Wolfert (color organ, 1930–63); Bury (Poland), Chryssa and Samaris (Greece), Flavin, Lippold (England), Rickey, Tinguely (Switzerland), Soto (Venezuela), Castro-Cid (Chile), Le Parc (Argentina), Takis (Greece); Germany: Hess.
Minimalist/Primary-Structurist Sculpture or ABC Art: United States: Bell, Caro (England), di Suvero, di Witt, Judd, Katzen, Kipp, Meadmore, Morris, David Smith, Tony Smith (England), Snelson; England: King, Paolozzi; Switzerland: Bill.

POSTMODERNISM

c. 1965–80

New Realism: United States: Close, de Andre (sculpture), Estes, Gallo (sculpture), Hanson (sculpture), Katz, Lindner, Pearlstein, Ramos.
Environmental Art (includes Earthworks, Siteworks, Floorworks and Scatterworks) (Earliest examples by Marcel Duchamp (France) and Kurt Schwitters (Germany) in 1920s to 1930s): United States: Christo, Heizer, Morris, Oldenburg, Samaris, Smithson.
Process and Conceptual Art: Germany: Beuys; United States: Kosuth, Robert Morris, Nam June Paik (Korea) (video assemblage).

POST-MINIMALIST AND CONCEPTUALIST REACTIONS

c. 1975

New Content/Figurative Art: United States: Philip Guston predicts new style in mid 1960s; Rothenberg, M. Schapiro, Sultan, J. Shapiro.
New Art of Social Comment: United States: Levine, Longo, Sherman (photography).

ART OF THE 1980s INTO THE 1990s

1980 into 1990s

Neo-Expressionism: Italy: Cucchi, Chia; Germany: Baselitz, Fetting, Kiefer; United States: Fischl, Longo, Rothenberg, Schnabel, Sherman (photography).
Neo-Abstraction: United States: Graves, Jensen, Levine, Scully (Ireland).

Glossary

abstract, abstraction
A term given to the visual effects that derive their appearance from natural objects but which have been simplified and/or rearranged to satisfy artists' needs for organization or expression. Abstraction is a process of varying degrees of change – from near naturalism through semiabstraction to pure abstraction. Sometimes any resemblance of the final product to the original object(s) depicted is difficult to detect.

abstract art
The term given to one of the major forms of nonrepresentational and semi-representational art of the twentieth century. It began with Cubism in the second decade of the twentieth century and reached a peak about the middle of the century.

Abstract Expressionism
An American style of painting that developed in the late 1940s. It had two branches, one called "Action painting" and the other "Color Field painting." Both were characterized by a nonrepresentational style that stressed psychological or emotional meaning.

abstract texture
A texture derived from the appearance of an actual surface but altered by the artist to satisfy the demands of the artwork.

academic
A term applied to any kind of art that stresses the use of accepted rules for technique and form organization. It represents the exact opposite of the creative approach, which results in a vital, individualistic style of expression.

accent
Any stress or emphasis given to elements of a composition that makes them attract more attention than other features that surround or are close to them. Accent can be created by a brighter color, darker tone, greater size, or any other means by which a difference is expressed (see *dominance*).

achromatic
Relating to differences of light and dark; the absence of color.

Action painting
An Abstract-Expressionist style that involves dripping, spraying, and brushing techniques in the application of pigment to the painting surface. Beaded lines, roughly textured surfaces, and interwoven shards of color were meant to carry the emotional message to the spectator without reference to anything in the objective world.

actual shape
A clearly defined or positive area (as opposed to an implied shape).

actual texture
A surface that can be experienced through the sense of touch (as opposed to a surface visually simulated by the artist).

addition
A sculptural term that means building up, assembling, or putting on material.

additive color
Color created by superimposing light rays. Adding (superimposing) the three physical primaries (lights) – red, blue, and green – will produce white. The secondaries are magenta, yellow, and cyan.

aesthetic, aesthetics
Relating to the artistic or the "beautiful"; traditionally a branch of philosophy, but now a compound of the philosophy, psychology, and sociology of art. As such, aesthetics is no longer solely confined to determining what is beautiful in art, but attempts to discover the origins of sensitivity to art forms and the relationships of art to other phases of culture (such as science, industry, morality, philosophy, and religion). Frequently used in this book to mean concern with artistic qualities of form, as opposed to descriptive form or mere recording of facts in visual form. (See *objective*.)

allover pattern
Refers to the repetition of designed units in a readily recognizable systematic organization covering the entire surface.

amorphous shape
A shape without clarity or definition; formless, indistinct, and of uncertain dimension.

analogous colors
Colors that are closely related in hue(s). They are usually adjacent to each other on the color wheel.

approximate symmetry
The use of similar imagery on either side of a central axis. Each side of the artwork may be very close in appearance, but they are varied to prevent visual monotony.

art
The formal expression of a conceived image or imagined conception in terms of a given medium (Sheldon Cheney).

artificial texture
A texture made by humans, as opposed to one produced in nature.

assemblage
A technique which brings together individual items of rather bulky three-dimensional nature that are displayed *in situ* (in its original position) rather than being limited to a wall.

asymmetry
Having unlike, or noncorresponding appearances – without symmetry. An example: a two-dimensional colorwork which, without any necessarily visible or implied axis, displays an uneven distribution of parts throughout the composition.

atectonic
A sculptural term meaning open in structure, as opposed to massive (or tectonic), and often with extended appendages.

atmospheric (aerial) perspective
The illusion of deep space produced in graphic works by lightening values, softening details and textures, reducing value contrasts, and neutralizing colors in objects as they recede.

balance
A sense of equilibrium achieved through implied weight, attention, or attraction, by manipulating the visual elements within an artwork, in order to accomplish unity.

Bauhaus
Originally a German institute of design that flourished between the two world wars. The Bauhaus attracted many leading experimental artists in both two- and three-dimensional fields.

biomorphic shape
Irregular shape that resembles the naturally developed curves found in live organisms.

calligraphy
Elegant, decorative writing. Lines used in artworks that possess the qualities found in this kind of writing may be called "calligraphic." They are generally flowing and rhythmical.

casting
A sculptural technique in which liquid materials are shaped by being poured into a mold.

cast shadow
The dark area that occurs on a surface as a result of something being placed between that surface and a light source.

chiaroscuro
1. Distribution of light and dark in a picture.
2. A technique of representation that blends light and shade gradually to create the illusion of three-dimensional objects in space or atmosphere.

chroma
1. The purity of color or its freedom from white, black, or gray. 2. The intensity of hue.

chromatic
Pertaining to the presence of color.

classical
Art forms that are characterized by a rational, controlled, clear, and intellectual approach. The term derives from the ancient art of Greece in the fourth and fifth centuries B.C. The term "classical" has an even more general connotation, meaning an example or model of first rank or highest class in any kind of form, literary, artistic, natural, or otherwise. Classicism is the

application of, or adherence to, the principles of Greek culture by such later cultural systems as the Roman and Renaissance civilizations, and the art of the Neoclassical movement in the early nineteenth century.

closed-value composition
Values are limited by the edges or boundaries of shapes.

collage
A pictorial technique in which the artist creates the image, or a portion of it, by adhering real materials that possess actual textures to the picture-plane surface, often combining them with painted or drawn passages.

color
The visual response to the wavelengths of light, identified as red, green, blue, etc.

Color Field painting
Another branch of Abstract Expressionism in which the artists filled extremely large canvases with bright color meant to involve the viewer psychologically. They were more restrained in handling than the Action group and created unified shapes, fields, and/or symbols of the artists' personal feelings. The fields of color were flat in technique and bonded or integral to the surface.

color tetrad
Four colors equally spaced on the color wheel that include a primary and its complement and a complementary pair of intermediates. This has also come to mean any organization of color forming a rectangle which could include a double split-complement.

color tonality
An orderly planning, in terms of selection and arrangement, of color schemes or color combinations; involves relatedness of hue, value, and intensity.

color triad
Three colors spaced an equal distance apart on the color wheel that form an equilateral triangle. The twelve-color wheel has a primary triad, a secondary triad, and two intermediate triads.

complementary colors
Two colors directly opposite each other on the color wheel. A primary color is complementary to a secondary color that is a mixture of the two remaining primaries.

composition
An arrangement and/or structure of all the elements which achieves a unified whole. Often used interchangeably with the term *design*.

concept
1. A comprehensive idea or generalization. 2. An idea that brings diverse elements into a basic relationship.

Conceptual art
Although called art, Conceptual art is anti-aesthetic or anti-artistic, usually denying the use of art materials and form in preference to conveying a message or analyzing an idea through photography, words and "found" objects of human construction. At the extreme, all that is needed is an idea or concept. It first appeared in the 1960s.

conceptual perception
Creative vision that derives from the imagination.

content
The expression, essential meaning, significance, or aesthetic value of a work of art. Content refers to the sensory, subjective, psychological, or emotional properties we feel in a work of art, as opposed to our perception of its descriptive aspects alone.

contour
In art, the line that defines the outermost limits of an object or a drawn or painted shape. It is sometimes considered to be synonymous with "outline"; as such, it indicates an edge that also may be defined by the extremities of values, textures, or colors.

craftsmanship
Aptitude, skill, or manual dexterity in the use of tools and materials.

cross-contour
A line that crosses and defines the surface undulations between, or up to, the outermost edges of shapes or objects.

Cubism
The name given to the painting style invented by Pablo Picasso and Georges Braque between 1906 and 1914. Cubists used multiple views of objects to create the effect of their three-dimensionality, while acknowledging the two-dimensional surface of the picture plane. The beginning of abstract art, it is a semi-abstract style that continued the strong trend away from representational art, initiated primarily by Cézanne in the late 1800s.

curvilinear
Stressing the use of curved lines; as opposed to "rectilinear," which stresses straight lines.

Dada
A nihilistic, anti-art, anti-everything movement resulting from the social, political, and psychological dislocations of World War I. The movement, which literally means "hobbyhorse," is important historically as a generating force for Surrealism. The Dada movement began in Zurich, Switzerland, in 1916.

decorative
Ornamenting or enriching but, more importantly in art, emphasizing the two-dimensional nature of an artwork or any of its elements. Decorative art stresses the essential flatness of a surface.

descriptive (art)
A manner or attitude based upon adherence to visual appearances.

design
A framework or scheme of construction on which artists base the nature of their total work. In a broader sense, design may be considered synonymous with the term "form".

De Stijl
A Dutch form of art featuring primary colors within a balanced structure of lines and rectangles. It was a style meant to perfectly express the higher mystical unity between

humankind and the universe. Translated as "the Style," it was the form of abstraction developed by Piet Mondrian and Theo van Doesburg about 1914–17.

dominance
The principle of visual organization that suggests certain elements should assume more importance than others in the same composition or design. Some features are emphasized and others are subordinated.

elements of art
Line, shape, value, texture and color. These are the basic ingredients that the artist uses separately or in combination to produce artistic imagery. Their use produces the visual language of art.

expression
1. The manifestation through artistic form of a thought, emotion, or quality of meaning. 2. In art, expression is synonymous with the word "content."

Expressionism
A form of art in which there is a desire to express what is felt rather than perceived or reasoned. Expressionistic form is defined by an obvious exaggeration of natural objects for the purpose of emphasizing an emotion, mood, or concept. It can be better understood as a more vehement kind of Romanticism. The term is best applied to a movement in art of the early twentieth century, encompassing the Fauves and German groups, although it can be used to describe all art of this character.

Fantastic art
Not a particular style or movement, but a term used to describe the departure from accepted appearances or relationships for the sake of psychological expression in the arts. Fantasy may exist within any art style, but is usually thought of in connection with unencumbered flights of pictorial imagery, freely interpreted or invented.

Fauves (Fauvism)
A name (meaning "wild beasts") for an art movement that began in Paris, France, about 1905. It was expressionistic art in a general sense, but more decorative, orderly, and charming than German Expressionism.

form
1. The arbitrary organization or inventive arrangement of all the visual elements according to the principles that will develop unity in the artwork. 2. The total appearance or organization.

four-dimensional space
A highly imaginative treatment of forms that gives a sense of intervals of time or motion.

fractional representation
A device used by various cultures (notably the Egyptians), in which several spatial aspects of the same subject are combined in the same image.

Futurism
A sub-movement within the overall framework of abstraction adopted by many twentieth-century artists. The imagery of Futurist artists was based on an interest in time, motion, and rhythm, which they felt were manifested in the machinery and human activities of modern times and their extension into the future.

genre
Subject matter that concerns everyday life, domestic scenes, family relationships, etc.

geometric shape
A shape that obeys the laws of geometry. Geometric shapes are usually simple, such as triangles, rectangles, and circles.

Gestalt, Gestalt psychology
A German word for "form," defined as an organized whole in experience. The *Gestalt* psychologists, about 1912, advanced the theory which explains psychological phenomena by their relationships to total forms rather than their parts.

glyptic
1. The quality of an art material like stone, wood, or metal that can be carved or engraved. 2. Referring to an art form that retains the tactile, color, and tensile quality of the material from which it was created. 3. The quality of hardness, solidity, or resistance found in carved or engraved materials.

Golden Mean/Golden Section
1. Golden Mean – "perfect" harmonious proportions that avoid extremes; the moderation between extremes. 2. Golden Section – a traditional proportional system for visual harmony expressed when a line or area is divided into two so that the smaller part is to the larger as the larger is to the whole. The ratio developed is 1:1.6180 . . . or, roughly, 8:13.

graphic art
1. Two-dimensional art forms such as drawing, painting, making prints, etc. 2. The two-dimensional use of the elements. 3. May also refer to the techniques of printing as used in newspapers, books, magazines, etc.

harmony
The quality of relating the visual elements of a composition. Harmony is achieved by repetition of characteristics that are the same or similar. These cohesive factors create pleasing interaction.

hatching
Repeated strokes of an art tool producing clustered lines (usually parallel) that create values. In "cross"-hatching similar lines pass over the hatched lines, following a different direction and usually resulting in darker values.

high-key color
Any color which has a value level of middle gray or lighter.

highlight
The portion of an object that, from the observer's position, receives the greatest amount of direct light.

hue
Designates the common name of a color and indicates its position in the spectrum or on the color wheel. Hue is determined by the specific wavelength of the color in a ray of light.

illusionism
The imitation of visual reality created on the flat surface of the picture plane by the use of perspective, light-and-dark shading, etc.

illustration(al)
An art practice, usually commercial in character, that stresses anecdotes or story situations and stresses subject more than form.

image
1. A mentally envisioned thing or plan given concrete appearance through the vehicle of an art medium. 2. A likeness or portrait.

implied shape
A shape suggested or created by the psychological connection of dots, lines, areas, or their edges, creating the visual appearance of a shape that does not physically exist. (See *Gestalt*.)

Impressionism
A movement of the late nineteenth century primarily connected with such painters as Claude Monet and Camille Pissarro. A form of realistic painting based on the way in which changing aspects of light affect human vision, it challenged older modes of such representation.

infinite space
A concept in which the picture frame acts as a window through which objects can be seen receding endlessly.

intensity
The saturation, strength, or purity of a color. A vivid color is of high intensity; a dull color, of low intensity.

intermediate color
A color produced by the mixture of a primary color and a secondary color.

interpenetration
The movement of planes, objects, or shapes through each other, which locks them together within a specific area of space.

intuitive space
The illusion of space that the artist creates by *instinctively* manipulating certain space-producing devices, including overlapping, transparency, interpenetration, inclined planes, disproportionate scale, fractional representation, and the inherent spatial properties of the art elements.

invented texture
A created texture whose only source is in the imagination of the artist. It generally produces a decorative pattern and should not be confused with an abstract texture.

isometric projection (perspective)
A mechanical drawing system in which a three-dimensional object is presented two-dimensionally; starting with the nearest vertical edge, the horizontal edges of the object are drawn at a thirty-degree angle and all verticals are projected perpendicularly from a horizontal base.

kinetic art
Art that involves an element of random or mechanical movement.

line
The path of a moving point, that is, a mark made by a tool or instrument as it is drawn across a surface. A line is usually made visible by the fact that it contrasts in value with the surface on which it is drawn.

linear perspective (geometric)
A system used to develop three-dimensional images on a two-dimensional surface; it develops the optical phenomenon of diminishing size by treating edges as converging parallel lines. They extend to a vanishing point or points on the horizon (eye-level) and recede from the viewer. (See *perspective*.)

local (objective) color
The color as seen in the objective world (green grass, blue sky, red barn, etc.).

local value
The relative light or dark of a surface, seen in the objective world, that is independent of any effect created by the degree of light falling on it.

low-key color
Any color which has a value level of middle gray or darker.

manipulation
The sculptural technique which refers to the shaping of pliable materials by hands or tools.

mass
1. In graphic art, a shape that appears to stand out three-dimensionally from the space surrounding it, or that creates the illusion of a solid body of material. 2. In the plastic arts, the physical bulk of a solid body of material. (See *plastic*.)

medium, media
The material(s) and tool(s) used by the artist to create the visual elements perceived by the viewer.

mobile
A three-dimensional, moving sculpture.

modeling
Another term (see *manipulation*) which refers to the shaping of a pliable material.

modern art, modernism
The term "modern art" is applied to almost all progressive or avant-garde phases of art from the time of the Impressionists in the late 1880s to the growth of Postmodernism in the 1960s. Modernism is usually associated with the nonrepresentational, formally organized kinds of modern art, as opposed to its organic and/or fantastic branches.

moments of force
Direction and degree of energy implied by the art elements in specific compositional situations; amounts of visual thrust produced by such matters as dimension, placement and accent.

monochromatic (color)
Having only one color; the complete range of value of one color from white to black.

motif
A designed unit or pattern that is repeated often enough in the total composition to make it a significant or dominant feature. Motif is similar to theme or melody in a musical composition.

naturalism
The approach to art which is essentially a description of things as they are experienced visually. Pure naturalism would contain no personal interpretation introduced by the artist, but is a physical impossibility.

natural texture
Textures that are created as a result of nature's processes.

negative area(s)
The unoccupied or empty space left after the positive elements have been created by the artist. However, when these areas have boundaries, they

also function as design shapes in the total structure.

Neo-Abstraction
Within the broad church of Postmodern art there exists a hard core of artists who have chosen to remain within the abstract manner. Most of them are influenced by the rich color work of such artists as Frank Stella or Al Held.

Neoclassicism
A style, initiated in the late 1700s in France, which centered upon a reintroduction of Classical Greek and Roman forms of art, as then understood. It became the basis for the "approved" or official art of the French government until about the middle of the nineteenth century. The main exponents were Jacques-Louis David and Jean-Auguste-Dominique Ingres.

Neo-Expressionism
Dating from the early 1980s, this style reaffirmed the psychic emotionalism of early twentieth-century Expressionism. It became perhaps the most distinctive direction in Postmodernism.

neutralized color
A color that has been grayed or reduced in intensity by being mixed with any of the neutrals or with a complementary color.

neutral
1. The inclusion of all color wavelengths will produce white and the absence of any wavelengths will be perceived as black. With neutrals, no single color is noticed – only a sense of light and dark or the range from white through gray to black. 2. A color altered by the addition of its complement so that the original sensation of hue is lost or grayed.

nonobjective (art)
A type of art that is entirely imaginative and not derived from anything visually perceived by the artist. The elements, their organization, and their treatment by the artist are entirely personalized and, consequently, not associated by the observer with any previously experienced natural objects.

nonrepresentational
A term used to define a range of work encompassing non-recognizable imagery that varies from pure abstraction (non-recognizable but derived from a recognizable object) to nonobjective (not a product of the abstraction process, but deriving from the artist's mind).

objective (art)
That which is based, as near as possible, on physical actuality or optical perception. Such art tends to appear natural or real.

oblique projection (perspective)
A mechanical drawing system in which a three-dimensional object is presented two-dimensionally: the front and back sides of the object are parallel to the horizontal base; and the other planes are drawn as parallels coming off the front plane at a forty-five degree angle.

open-value composition
In such a work, values cross over shape boundaries into adjoining areas.

optical perception
A way of seeing in which the mind has no other function than the natural one of providing the visual sensation of object recognition.

organic unity
A condition in which the components of an artwork, that is, subject, form, and content, are so vital and interdependent that it may be likened to a living organism. A work having organic unity is not guaranteed to have "greatness" or unusual merit.

orthographic drawing
Graphic representation of two-dimensional views of an object, showing a plan, vertical elevations, and/or a section.

paint quality
Refers to the way in which paint can enrich a surface through textural interest. Interest is created by the ingenuity in handling paint for its intrinsic character.

papier collé
A visual and tactile technique in which scraps of paper with various textures are pasted to the picture surface to enrich or embellish areas. In addition to the actual texture of the paper, the print on tickets, newspapers, etc., can function as visual richness or decorative pattern in the same way as an artist's invented texture.

patina
1. A natural film, usually greenish, that results from oxidation of bronze or other metallic material. 2. Colored pigments, chemicals, and so on, applied to a sculptural surface.

pattern
1. Any artistic design (sometimes serving as a model for imitation). 2. Any composition with a repeated element and/or design; most often these are varied, and produce interconnections and obvious directional movements.

Performance art
This type of art engages an audience in live-action participation in mixed-media performances of painting, music, theatrics, kinetics and the like – "happenings." It stemmed from Dada and came into being with Pop art in the mid to late 1950s. Being ephemeral, Performance art is often recorded by photographers and cinema-makers.

perspective
Any graphic system used to create the illusion of three-dimensional images and/or spatial relationships on a two-dimensional surface. There are several types of perspective: atmospheric, linear, and projection systems.

photogravure
The process of printing a photographic image from an etched plate.

Pictorialism
A branch of photography dating from the early nineteenth century. Pictorialist photographers were opposed to the dreary predictability of Realist, or straight, photography and to the academic, artificial Pictorialism of Rejlander. They believed in the possibility of a personal expression of order and beauty in which science and art would combine in photographic imagery. Many Pictorialists turned to manipulating focus and film development in a misguided attempt to arrive at this result.

picture frame
The outermost limits or boundary of the picture plane.

picture plane
The actual flat surface on which the artist executes a pictorial image. In some cases the picture plane acts merely as a transparent plane of reference to establish the illusion of forms existing in a three-dimensional space.

pigments
Color substances which give their color property to another material by being mixed with it or covering it. Pigments, usually insoluble, are added to liquid vehicles to produce paint or ink. Colored substances dissolved in liquids, which give their coloring effects by being absorbed or staining, are referred to as dyes.

planar (shape)
Having to do with planes.

plane
1. An area that is essentially two-dimensional, having height and width. 2. A flat or level surface. 3. A two-dimensional surface which extends in a three-dimensional spatial direction.

plastic (art)
1. Refers to the use of the elements to create the illusion of the third dimension on a two-dimensional surface. 2. Three-dimensional art forms such as architecture, sculpture, ceramics, etc.

Pop art
The name given to the form of art which uses, often satirically, the mundane products of mass popular culture, such as magazine, newspaper, billboard, and television advertising; comic strips and books; supermarket shelves, and so on, as its subject matter. It derived from certain early modern art forms and ideas, especially from Marcel Duchamp's "ready-made" and "found" objects of the 1920s through 1950s. It began to take shape in England in the late 1950s and spread quickly during the 1960s in the United States, where it was most widely accepted.

positive (shape, line, etc.)
The state in the artwork in which the art elements (shape, line, etc.), or their combination, produce the subject – nonrepresentational or recognizable objects. (See *negative areas*.)

Post-Impressionism
The name applied to a few artists at the end of the nineteenth century who sought to restore formal organization, decorative unity, and expressive meaning to art. The most important were Paul Cézanne, Georges Seurat, Paul Gauguin, and Vincent van Gogh. These artists believed that the qualities cited above had been lost in contemporary art, particularly by the Impressionists. Post-Impressionism began the strong divergence from representational art which was to occupy such a strong place in twentieth-century abstract art.

Postmodernism
It began to seem in the 1970s that the dominant styles of art – Minimalism and Conceptualism – no longer fitted a world struggling with such rising social problems as drugs, crime, divorce, and commercial greed. As a result, a plurality of styles developed as a reaction to these worsening circumstances. Other Postmodernists, however,

more forcefully expressed a desire to do away with art which seemed to have no meaningful content, and began to turn back to figurative art and the establishment of meaning. Still other forms of Postmodernism extend modern art in new ways by appropriating earlier styles, with minor or major modifications, and pastiching them. Due to the sheer variety of sources and styles in Postmodernism, it has been difficult to categorize such artists with the same ease as those of earlier styles or movements.

primary color
A fundamental color that cannot be separated into any other colors. When primaries are mixed, they can produce all the remaining colors.

Primitive art
The art of a people with a tribal social order or an early (though complex) stage of culture. The art of such people is often characterized by a heightened emphasis on form and a mysterious or vehement expressive content. Modern primitive art, like that of Henri Rousseau in France and Grandma Moses in the United States, is mostly the work of untrained or slightly trained artists. This kind of recent primitive art shows a naïveté of form and expression closely related to the untrained, but often sensitive imagery of folk art.

proportion/scale
Comparison of the art elements, in terms of their properties of size, quantity, and degree of emphasis. Proportion can be expressed in terms of a definite ratio, such as "twice as big," or be more loosely indicated in such expressions as "darker than," "more neutralized," or "more important than." Scale is established when proportional relationships of size are created relative to a gauge or specific unit of measure.

radial
Refers to compositions that have the major images or design parts emanating from a central point or location.

realism, Realism (art movement)
A style of art that retains the basic impression of visual actuality without going to extremes of detail. In addition, realism attempts to relate and interpret the universal meanings that lie beneath surface appearances. As a movement, it relates to painters like Honoré Daumier in France and Winslow Homer in the United States in the 1850s.

Realist (or straight) photography
The branch of photography opposed to the "false" imagery of the Pictorialists. They believed primarily in the honest use of available materials and technology to provide a photographic image, as opposed to the blurry, altered images of the Pictorialists, which amounted to a misguided attempt to "enhance" content.

rectilinear shape
A shape whose boundaries usually consist entirely of straight lines.

relief sculpture
An artwork, graphic in concept, but sculptural in application, which makes use of relatively shallow depth to establish images. The projection may range from very limited – "low relief" – to more exaggerated – "high relief." Relief sculpture is meant to be viewed frontally, not in the round.

repetition
The use of the same visual effect a number of times in the same composition. Repetition may produce the dominance of one visual idea, a feeling of harmonious relationship, an obviously planned pattern, or a rhythmic movement.

representation(al) art
A type of art in which the subject is presented through the visual art elements so that the observer is reminded of actual objects. (See *naturalism* and *realism*.)

rhythm
A continuance, a flow, or a sense of movement achieved by the repetition of regulated visual units; the use of measured accents.

Romanticism
In the visual arts, the romantic spirit is characterized by an experimental point of view and extols spontaneity of expression, intuitive imagination, and the picturesque rather than a carefully organized, rational approach. Romanticism, a movement of nineteenth-century artists, such as Delacroix, Géricault, Turner, and others, is characterized by just such an approach to form. (See *classical*.)

scale
See *proportion*.

sculpture
The expressive shaping of three-dimensional materials. "Man's expression to man through three-dimensional form" (Jules Struppeck, *The Creation of Sculpture*, 1952).

secondary color
A color produced by a mixture of two primary colors.

shadow, shade, shading
The darker value on the surface of an object that gives the illusion that a portion of it is turned away from the source of light.

shallow space
The illusion of limited depth. In the case of shallow space, the imagery moves only a slight distance back from the picture plane.

shape
An area that stands out from the space next to or around it because of a defined or implied boundary, or because of differences of value, color, or texture.

silhouette
The area between or bounded by the contours, or edges, of an object; the total shape.

simulated texture
The copying, or imitation, of object surfaces.

simultaneity
In art the use of separate views, representing different points in time and space, that are brought together and sometimes superimposed to create one integrated image.

simultaneous contrast
When two different color tones come into direct contact, the contrast intensifies the difference between them.

space
The distance between points or images.

spectrum
The band of individual colors that results when a beam of white light is broken into its component wavelengths, identifiable as hues.

split-complement(s)
A color and the two colors on either side of its complement.

style
The specific artistic character and dominant form trends noted during periods of history and recent art movements. Style may also refer to artists' expressive use of media to give their works individual character.

subject
1. In a descriptive approach to art, subject refers to the persons or things represented, as well as the artist's experiences, that serve as inspiration. 2. In abstract or nonobjective forms of art, subject refers merely to the visual signs employed by the artist. In this case, the subject has little to do with anything experienced in the natural environment.

subjective (art, shape, color, etc.)
1. That which is derived from the mind and reflects an individual's viewpoint or bias. 2. Art that is subjective tends to be inventive or creative.

substitution
In sculpture, replacing one material or medium with another. (See *casting*.)

subtraction
A sculptural term meaning to carve or cut away materials.

subtractive color
The sensation of color that is produced when wavelengths of light are reflected back to the viewer after all other wavelengths have been subtracted and/or absorbed.

Surrealism
Influenced by Freudian psychology, this style of artistic expression emphasizes fantasy. Surrealist subjects are usually experiences revealed by the subconscious mind through the use of automatic techniques. Originally a literary movement and an outgrowth of Dadaism, Surrealism was established by a literary manifesto in 1924.

symbol
The representation of a quality or situation through the use of another object, emblem, or sign. Here are some examples: the owl represents wisdom; the flag represents country – freedom or oppression – and the color yellow represents cowardice.

Symbolism
A literary movement that spread to painting in the 1880s. Symbolists tried to grapple with the notion of subjective ideas, stating that the senses are inseparable from human emotions and that people and objects are, therefore, merely symbols of a deeper existence beyond the everyday. It was not a style as such, and merely set a goal for artists to reach in a number of ways. The painters Odilon Redon and Pierre Bonnard, among others, are associated with the movement, and Paul Gauguin is considered a father figure.

symmetry
The exact duplication of appearances in mirror-like repetition on either side of a (usually imaginary) straight-lined central axis.

tactile
Pertaining to the sense of touch.

technique
The manner and skill with which artists employ their tools and materials to achieve a predetermined expressive effect. The ways of using media can have an effect on the aesthetic quality of an artist's total concept.

tectonic
Relating to the quality of simple massiveness; lacking any significant extrusions or intrusions.

tenebrism
A style of painting that exaggerates or emphasizes the effects of chiaroscuro. Large amounts of dark value are placed close to smaller areas of highly contrasting lights (and vice versa) in order to concentrate attention on important features.

tension
The manifested energies and forces of the art elements as they pull or push in affecting balance or counterbalance.

tertiary color
Color resulting from the mixture of two secondary colors, characterized by the neutralization of intensity and hue. On the color wheel tertiary colors are positioned inside the outermost ring of colors.

texture
The surface character of a material that can be experienced through touch or the illusion of touch. Texture is produced by natural forces or through an artist's manipulation of the art elements.

three-dimensional
To possess, or to create the illusion of possessing, the dimension of depth in addition to the dimensions of height and width.

tone
1. The value or color character of a surface, determined by the quantity of light reflected from it. The amount of light reflected can be determined by the character of the medium that has been applied to the surface. 2. Color variety due to slight changes within the same hue.

transparency
A visual quality in which a distant image or element can be seen through a nearer one.

trompe l'oeil
Literally, a "trick of the eye"; a technique that copies nature with such exactitude that the subject depicted can be mistaken for a natural form.

two-dimensional
To possess the dimensions of height and width, especially when considering the flat surface, or picture plane.

unity
The result of bringing the elements of art into appropriate ratio between harmony and variety to give a sense of oneness.

value
1. The relative degree of light or dark. 2. The characteristic of color determined by light or dark, or the quantity of light reflected by the color.

value pattern
The organization and total effect of the relationships of light and dark; with the resulting control of the spectator's eye movement there is a unifying effect throughout the composition (the term can be applied to decorative or plastic space).

variety
Differences achieved by opposing, contrasting, changing, elaborating, or diversifying elements in a composition to add individuality and interest; the counterweight of harmony in a work of art.

void
1. Areas lacking positive substances and consisting of negative space. 2. A spatial area within an object that penetrates and passes through it.

volume
1. A measurable area of defined or occupied space.

Bibliography

AGOSTON, GEORGE A., *Color Theory and its Application in Art and Design*. Berlin, Heidelberg, New York: Springer Verlag, 1987.

ALBERS, JOSEF, *Interaction of Color*. New Haven, Conn.: Yale University Press, 1963.

ANDERSON, DONALD M., *Elements of Design*. New York: Holt, Rinehart & Winston, 1961.

ARMSTRONG, TOM, *200 Years of American Sculpture*, catalog for Whitney Museum of American Art. Boston, Mass.: The Godine Press, 1976.

ARNASON, H. H., *History of Modern Art*. Englewood Cliffs, N.J.: Prentice-Hall, 1986.

ARNHEIM, RUDOLPH, *Art and Visual Perception*. Berkeley, Calif.: University of California Press, 1966.

BABCOCK, GREGORY, *The New Art*. New York: E. P. Dutton, 1966.

BATES, KENNETH F., *Basic Design: Principle and Practice*. New York: Funk & Wagnalls, 1975.

BEAM, P. C., *Language of Art*. New York: John Wiley & Sons, 1958.

BETHERS, RAY, *Composition in Pictures*. New York: Pitman Corporation, 1956.

BETTI, CLAUDIA AND SELE, TEEL, *A Contemporary Approach: Drawing*. New York: Holt, Rinehart & Winston, 1980.

BEVLIN, MARJORIE E., *Design Through Discovery*. New York: Holt, Rinehart & Winston, 1980.

BIRREN, FABER, *Creative Color*. New York: Van Nostrand Reinhold, 1961.

———, *Principles of Color*. New York: Van Nostrand Reinhold, 1969.

———, *Color Perception in Art*. New York: Van Nostrand Reinhold, 1976.

BLOCK, JONATHAN, *ET AL.*, *Understanding Three Dimensions*. Englewood Cliffs, N.J.: Prentice-Hall, 1987.

BLOOMER, CAROLYN M., *Principles of Visual Perception*. New York: Van Nostrand Reinhold, 1976.

BRO, L. V., *Drawing: A Studio Guide*. New York: W. W. Norton, 1978.

BURNHAM, JACK, *Beyond Modern Sculpture*. New York: George Braziller, 1968.

CANADAY, JOHN, *What is Art?*. New York: Alfred Knopf, 1980.

CAPERS, ROBERTA M. AND MADDOX, J., *Images and Imagination: An Introduction to Art*. New York: John Wiley & Sons, 1965.

CARPENTER, JAMES M., *Visual Art: An Introduction*. New York: Harcourt Brace Jovanovich, 1982.

CHAET, BERNHARD, *The Art of Drawing*. New York: Holt, Rinehart & Winston, 1970.

CHEATHAN, FRANK R.; CHEATHAN, JANE HART; OWENS, SHERYL HATER, *Design Concepts and Applications*. Englewood Cliffs, N.J.: Prentice-Hall, 1983.

CHEVREUL, M. E., *The Principles of Harmony and Contrasts of Colors and Applications to the Arts*. New York: Van Nostrand Reinhold, 1981.

CHILVERS, IAN; OSBORNE, HAROLD; AND FARR, DENNIS, *The Oxford Dictionary of Art*. New York: Oxford University Press, 1988.

CLEAVER, DALE G., *Art: An Introduction*. New York: Harcourt Brace Jovanovich, 1972.

COGOLI, JOHN E., *Photo-Offset Fundamentals*. Bloomington, Ill.: McKnight & McKnight, 1967.

COLEMAN, RONALD, *Sculpture: A Handbook for Students*. Dubuque, Iowa: Wm. C. Brown, 1990.

COLLIER, GRAHAM, *Form, Space and Vision*. Englewood Cliffs, N.J.: Prentice-Hall, 1972.

COMPTON, MICHAEL, *Pop Art*. London: Hamlyn, 1970.

CRAWFORD, WILLIAM, *The Keepers of the Light: A History and Working Guide to Early Photographic Processes*. New York: Dobbs Ferry, 1979.

DANTZIC, CYNTHIA MARIS, *Design Dimensions*. Englewood Cliffs, N.J.: Prentice-Hall, 1990.

DAVIS, PHIL, *Photography*. Dubuque, Iowa: Wm. C. Brown, 1990.

DIAMOND, DAVID G., *Art Terms*. Boston, Mass.: A Bulfinch Press Book; Little, Brown, 1992.

EDWARDS, BETTY, *Drawing on the Right Side of the Brain*. Los Angeles: Tarcher, 1979.

ELSEN, ALBERT E., *Origins of Modern Sculpture*. New York: George Braziller, 1974.

FAULKNER, RAY; SMAGULA, HOWARD; ZIEGFELD, EDWIN, *Today: An Introduction to the Visual Arts*. New York: Holt, Rinehart & Winston, 1987.

GARDNER, HELEN, revised by de la Croix, Horst and Tancy, Richard G., *Art through the Ages*. New York: Harcourt Brace Jovanovich, 1980.

GILBERT, RITA AND McCARTER, WILLIAM, *Living with Art*. New York: Alfred Knopf, 1988.

GOLDSTEIN, NATHAN, *The Art of Responsive Drawing*. Englewood Cliffs, N.J.: Prentice-Hall, 1977.

HARLAN, CALVIN, *Vision and Invention: A Course in Art Fundamentals*. Englewood Cliffs, N.J.: Prentice-Hall, 1970.

HELLER, JULES, *Printmaking Today*. New York: Holt, Rinehart & Winston, 1972.

HELLER, NANCY, *Women Artists: An Illustrated History*. New York: Abbeyville Press, 1981.

HIBBARD, HOWARD, *The Metropolitan Museum of Art*. New York: Harper & Row, 1980.

HUNTER, SAMUEL, *American Art of the 20th Century*. New York: Harry N. Abrams, 1972.

ITTEN, JOHANNES, *The Art of Color*. New York: Van Nostrand Reinhold, 1970.

———, *Design and Form*. New York: Van Nostrand Reinhold, 1975.

JANIS, HARRIET AND BLESH, RUDI, *Collage: Personalities, Concepts, Techniques*. Philadelphia, Pa.: Chilton, 1962.

KEPES, GYORGY, *Language of Vision*. Chicago: Paul Theobald, 1951.

KNOBLER, NATHAN, *The Visual Dialogue*. New York: Holt, Rinehart & Winston, 1980.

KUEPPERS, HARALD, *The Basic Law of Color Theory*. New York: Barron's Educational Series, 1982.

———, *Color Atlas*. New York: Barron's Educational Series, 1982.

KUH, KATHERINE, *Art Has Many Faces*. New York: Harper & Row, 1957.

LAUER, DAVID, *Design Basics*. New York: Holt, Rinehart & Winston, 1989.

LERNER, ABRAM, *ET AL*. *The Hirshhorn Museum and Sculpture Garden*. New York: Harry N. Abrams, 1974.

LONGMAN, LESTER, *History and Appreciation of Art*. Dubuque, Iowa: Wm. C. Brown, 1949.

LOWRY, BATES, *Visual Experience: An Introduction to Art*. New York: Harry N. Abrams, 1961.

LUCIE-SMITH, EDWARD, *Late Modern: The Visual Arts Since 1945*. New Praeger, 1969.

———, *The Thames and Hudson Dictionary of Art Terms*. New York: Thames and Hudson, 1984.

MACAULAY, DAVID, *The Way Things Work*. Boston, Mass.: Miffen, 1988.

MENDELOWITZ, DANIEL M., *A Guide to Drawing*. New York: Holt, Rinehart & Winston, 1976.

MOHOLY-NAGY, L., *Vision in Motion* (5th edn.) Chicago: Paul Theobald, 1956.

MYERS, JACK FREDRICK, *The Language of Visual Art*. Orlando, Fla., . New York: Holt, Rinehart & Winston, 1989.

NELSON, ROY P., *Design of Advertising*. Dubuque, Iowa: Wm. C. Brown, 1967.

PREBLE, DUANE, *We Create, Art Creates Us*. New York: Harper & Row, 1976.

———, *Art Forms*. New York: Harper & Row, 1985.

PROCTOR, RICHARD M., *The Principles of Pattern*. New York: Van Nostrand Reinhold, 1969.

RICHARDSON, JOHN ADKINS, *ET AL.*, *Basic Design*. Englewood Cliffs, N.J.: Prentice-Hall, 1984.

RUSSELL, STELLA PANDELL, *Art in the World*. Orlando, Fla.: Holt, Rinehart & Winston, 1989.

SAFF, DONALD AND SACILOTTO, DELI, *Printmaking*. New York: Holt, Rinehart & Winston, 1978.

SARGENT, WALTER, *The Enjoyment of Color*. New York: Dover Publications, 1964.

SCHLEMMER, RICHARD M., *Handbook of Advertising Production*. Englewood Cliffs, N.J.: Prentice-Hall, 1966.

SIMMONS, SEYMOUR, III, AND WINER, MARC S. A., *Drawing: The Creative Process*. Englewood Cliffs, N.J.: Prentice-Hall, 1977.

SPARKE, PENNY; HODGES, FELICE; DENT, EMMA; STONE, ANNE, *Design Source Book*. Secaucus, N.J.: Chartwell, 1982.

STRUPPECK, JULES, *The Creation of Sculpture*. New York: Henry Holt, 1952.

VERITY, ENID, *Color Observed*. New York: Van Nostrand Reinhold, 1980.

WEISS, HILLARY, *The American Bandanna*. San Francisco, Calif.: Chronicle, 1990.

WILLIAMS, RICHARD L., Series Editor, *Life Library of Photography*. New York: Time-Life, 1971.

WINGLER, M., HANS, *The Bauhaus*. Cambridge, Mass.: First M.I.T. Press Paperback, 1986.

WONG, WUCIUS, *Principles of Three-dimensional Design*. New York: Van Nostrand Reinhold, 1977.

YENAWINE, PHILIP, *How to Look at Modern Art*. New York: Harry N. Abrams, 1991.

ZELANSKI, PAUL, *ET AL.*, *Shaping Space*. New York: Holt, Rinehart & Winston, 1987.

Index

Media Index